WITHDRAWN

Power and reputation at the court of Louis XIII

MANCHESTER
1824

Manchester University Press

STUDIES IN EARLY MODERN
EUROPEAN HISTORY

This series aims to publish
challenging and innovative research in all areas
of early modern continental history.
The editors are committed to encouraging work
that engages with current historiographical
debates, adopts an interdisciplinary
approach, or makes an original contribution
to our understanding of the period.

SERIES EDITORS
Joseph Bergin, William G. Naphy, Penny Roberts and Paolo Rossi

Already published in the series

Sodomy in early modern Europe
ed. Tom Betteridge

The Malleus Maleficarum *and the construction of witchcraft*
Hans Peter Broedel

Latin books and the Eastern Orthodox clerical elite in Kiev, 1632–1780
Liudmila V. Charipova

Fathers, pastors and kings:
visions of episcopacy in seventeenth-century France
Alison Forrestal

Popular science and public opinion in eighteenth-century France
Michael R. Lynn

Religion and superstition in Reformation Europe
eds Helen Parish and William G. Naphy

Religious choice in the Dutch Republic: the reformation of
Arnoldus Buchelus (1565–1641)
Judith Pollman

Witchcraft narratives in Germany: Rothenburg, 1561–1652
Alison Rowlands

Authority and society in Nantes during the French Wars of Religion, 1559–98
Elizabeth C. Tingle

The great favourite:
the Duke of Lerma and the court and government of Philip III of Spain, 1598–1621
Patrick Williams

Power and reputation at the court of Louis XIII

The career of Charles d'Albert, duc de Luynes (1578–1621)

SHARON KETTERING

Manchester University Press

Manchester and New York

distributed exclusively in the USA by Palgrave

Published by Manchester University Press
Oxford Road, Manchester M13 9NR, UK
and Room 400, 175 Fifth Avenue, New York, NY 10010, USA
www.manchesteruniversitypress.co.uk

Distributed exclusively in the USA by
Palgrave, 175 Fifth Avenue, New York,
NY 10010, USA

Distributed exclusively in Canada by
UBC Press, University of British Columbia, 2029 West Mall,
Vancouver, BC, Canada V6T 1Z2

British Library Cataloguing-in-Publication Data
A catalogue record for this book is available from the British Library

Library of Congress Cataloging-in-Publication Data applied for

ISBN 978 0 7190 7786 9 hardback

First published 2008

17 16 15 14 13 12 11 10 09 08   10 9 8 7 6 5 4 3 2 1

Typeset in Perpetua with Albertus display
by Koinonia, Manchester
Printed in Great Britain
by Antony Rowe Ltd, Chippenham, Wiltshire

For everyone who made this book possible

Contents

Illustrations

Abbreviations

A.A.E.	Archives des Affaires Etrangères, Paris
A.C.	Archives communales
A.D.	Archives départementales
A.N.	Archives Nationales, Paris
A.N., M.C.	Archives Nationales, Minutier Central
B. Arsenal	Bibliothèque de l'Arsenal, Paris
B. Avignon	Bibliothèque municipale d'Avignon
B.I.F.	Bibliothèque de l'Institut de France, Paris
B. Inguimbertine	Bibliothèque Inguimbertine, Carpentras
B. Méjanes	Bibliothèque Méjanes, Aix-en-Provence
B.N.	Bibliothèque nationale de France, Paris
B.N., Ms fr.	Bibliothèque nationale, Manuscrits français
B.N., CC Colbert	Bibliothèque nationale, Cinq Cents de Colbert
DBF	*Dictionnaire de biographie française*, eds. R. d'Amat et al.
Fr Hist	*French History* (journal)
Fr Hist Stud	*French Historical Studies* (journal)
Rev hist	*Revue historique* (journal)

Acknowledgements

I would like to thank Joe Bergin, Orest Ranum, and John Salmon for reading all or parts of the manuscript, and making useful suggestions on how to revise it. Any errors that remain are my own. I owe special thanks to Joe Bergin for his assistance in researching the career of Luynes (pronounced Lou-een), especially the loan of microfilm from the Archives des Affaires Etrangères in Paris. I am indebted to Bonita Favin and Beatrice Carasso of Montgomery College Interlibrary Loan for their help in obtaining books, and to the university libraries who lent them. I am also indebted for their help to the staffs of the Library of Congress and the Folger Library of Washington, D.C., and to the microfilm and photographic reproduction divisions of the Bibliothèque nationale de France and the Archives Nationales in Paris. I would like to thank J.H. Elliott and L.W.B. Brockliss for inviting me to attend a 1996 conference on favorites at Magdalen College, Oxford. The papers presented there helped to focus my initial research on key issues. Finally, I would like to thank my husband for listening to endless discussions of court patronage and politics. The dance leitmotiv running through these pages aptly describes the nature of court politics.

Acknowledgements

Introduction:
Luynes and the historians

Charles d'Albert, duc de Luynes, a favorite of Louis XIII, died of scarlet fever
at about three o'clock on the afternoon of 15 December 1621 at the château
of Longuetille near Condom in southwestern France. This was the headquarters of the royal army besieging the little Protestant town of Monheurt several
leagues away.[1] As constable or commander-in-chief of the army, Luynes had
been blamed when the siege of Montauban had to be lifted in the previous
month, although he had not been the field commander. Anonymous pamphlets
accusing him of incompetence and cowardice had circulated throughout Paris
at this time, and more than 100 pamphlets attacking him had appeared between
1620 and 1622.[2] In fact, there was a flood of political pamphlets on all topics
during Louis XIII's reign, about 3,300 titles in all.[3] Their devastating impact
on Luynes's reputation is the subject of this book, which is a revisionist study
seeking to rehabilitate his reputation and improve his historical image. Luynes
was a shrewd politician who controlled the distribution of royal patronage at
court, so this book is also about the impact of his patronage power on court
politics. Richelieu, who succeeded Luynes as a minister favorite, learned much
from him, although he never admitted it.

François Du Val, marquis de Fontenay-Mareuil, thought Luynes had little
intelligence or ability. Unpopular royal favorites were often ridiculed and criticized by their contemporaries. Fontenay-Mareuil wrote in his memoirs, "...
this great and powerful man found himself abandoned and despised during
his illness and afterward. During the two days he lay dying, no one wanted
to remain in his bedchamber, although the doors were always open so anyone
could enter as if he were the least important of men. When they transported
his body to be buried at his duchy of Luynes, instead of priests praying for him,
I saw servants playing cards on his coffin while waiting for their horses to be
fed."[4] This famous anecdote, demonstrating the fickleness of fortune, delighted
contemporaries.

Fontenay-Mareuil, however, did not accompany Luynes's coffin on its journey northward to the Loire valley – no one from the court did – so he could not himself have seen servants playing cards on its lid. Had this story been repeated to him by an eye-witness or was it apocryphal? An epidemic of scarlet fever was raging in the army at the time, causing numerous deaths. No one wanted to be near Luynes for fear of catching this highly contagious disease, which Fontenay-Mareuil did not mention in his memoirs either. The king's doctors had forbidden him to enter Luynes's rooms when the severity of his illness became apparent, which Fontenay-Mareuil also failed to mention. He noted only that the king had stopped going to see Luynes when he became seriously ill, and added that the king did not show sorrow or unhappiness at the news of his death. Instead, he rode out at once for Damazan, and did not accompany the coffin on its journey northward. François de Bassompierre, another courtier who disliked Luynes, noted the king's hasty departure and surmised, wrongly, that Luynes was out of favor.[5]

A stony-faced Louis XIII saddled up and rode out upon hearing of his favorite's death because he did not wish to show grief in public. He had refused to show emotion in public from an early age.[6] Héroard, his doctor, mentioned his great distress at Luynes's sudden illness and death, giving that as the reason he departed so suddenly for Damazan on 15 December. He did not stay long, riding to Casteljaloux on 17 December, Bazas on 18 December, Pruignat on 20 December, and Bordeaux on 21 December where he stopped with a stomach ailment and stayed to celebrate Christmas.[7] Flight is not the response of an uncaring individual.

Relying on ambassadorial dispatches, historian Berthold Zeller noted that boatmen taking Luynes's embalmed body by river to Bordeaux had carelessly knocked it about and damaged it, then had trouble finding somewhere to shelter it for the night.[8] An eye-witness, the comte de Souvigny, an army lieutenant general who was on the Bordeaux docks when the body arrived, noted that it was in a simple coffin without funerary trappings, surrounded only by servants and baggage without an entourage of priests or anyone of rank accompanying it, a significant social slight.[9] The coffin rested in the Bordeaux church of the Chartreux overnight, and then went by river to Blaye where it was put on a cart traveling north to the Loire. It was taken upriver by boat to Amboise to rest in a funerary chapel, and then transported to Tours for a funeral service in the lovely gothic cathedral of Saint Gatien.

On 11 January 1622, Luynes's coffin arrived at the river quai beneath the medieval fortified bridge on the street leading to the cathedral. Members of the city's religious orders carrying white candles met the coffin, and escorted it to Saint Gatien. The government newspaper, the *Mercure françois*, reported that thirty men on horseback rode first in the funeral cortege, followed by five pages on horses draped in black, then members of the city's six religious orders on foot carrying white candles, a Swiss guard on horseback dressed in mourning, a dozen Swiss guards on foot in mourning with their halberds pointed down, and ten of Luynes's household gentlemen in mourning on foot in five ranks of two carrying white candles. The coffin came next, draped in black velvet with a white satin cross on its top, resting on a bier drawn by six horses, followed by four of Luynes's household officials on foot in mourning, and finally by one hundred men on horseback. The coffin was met at the church door by the cathedral canons, and placed in the choir for an all-night vigil.

The funeral service the next day was attended by the governor of Tours, Gilles de Souvré, his two sons, and members of the municipal government and presidial court of Tours. Souvré, the king's governor, had helped to launch Luynes's career, but he had not liked Luynes, and he was present only in an official not in a personal capacity. The king had stayed in the southwest for Christmas, so no other courtiers were present. Afterward, the coffin was taken to Luynes's nearby château for burial.[10] An impressive public funeral had been held for him in Tours where his duchy was, and his passing had been marked with the proper respect if not with lavish display.

Relying upon the dispatches of the papal nuncios and the Florentine and Venetian ambassadors, historians Louis Batiffol and Berthold Zeller emphasized the casual treatment of Luynes's coffin on its journey northward, and ignored the funeral procession after it arrived. Zeller noted that the cathedral canons had refused to receive the body, and had only agreed after the king had angrily insisted, which is dubious because the king was not there. In contrast, the *Mercure françois* reported that the canons had waited respectfully at the church door to greet the coffin, and then had held an all night vigil for it. Batiffol noted that numerous witnesses had seen servants playing cards on Luynes's coffin.[11] In fact, only one witness, Fontenay-Mareuil, had reported the card-playing incident, which he could not have seen himself because he was not there. Batiffol and Zeller did not describe the funeral procession because it had not been mentioned in their sources, the dispatches of the Italian ambassadors, who had not been there either. The Florentine ambassadors and papal nuncios were friends of the Queen Mother, Marie de Médicis, and delighted in repeating court gossip ridiculing Luynes. She loathed Luynes, whom she blamed for the violent deaths of her favorites, Concini and his wife, and for her own exile from the court. She considered him a dangerous enemy, an attitude which the ambassadors shared, and their dispatches always criticized him.

Cardinal Richelieu, a client of the Queen Mother, wrote a fantastic account of Luynes's death. He reported that when the favorite was dying, he rose from his sickbed to burn papers locked in a casket, which were magic charms and treaties with the Protestants. The charms had been acquired from magicians who had given him herbs to put in the king's shoes and powder to put in his clothes. (Richelieu insisted that an Italian magician had been strangled on Luynes's orders.) The treaties were supposedly the result of numerous secret trips that Luynes had made to see the Protestant leader, the duc de Rohan, although in reality he had gone only once and not in secret. In a conversation with his old friend Contades, Luynes was supposed to have avowed that he sought to reach an agreement with the Protestants in order to safeguard his future in case he lost favor.[12] Malice and spite characterized the accounts of Fontenay-Mareuil and the ambassadors, but Richelieu's account demonstrated rancor and a deep-seated animosity.

Unpopular favorites seldom left behind their own accounts of their years in power, and are usually known only through their detractors.[13] Traditionally, favorites have suffered from a bad press, which was the case with Luynes as these accounts of his burial demonstrate. Favorites were never viewed objectively by contemporaries who envied and resented their success. What was written about them depended upon when the writer was at court, if he was writing immediately after events or years later, whether he was a rival or a client, what his loyalties were, and whether he was dependent upon patronage or not. Historians relying upon hostile contemporary sources have dismissed Luynes as an inept mediocrity. Their sources have included the memoirs of envious courtiers such as Fontenay-Mareuil and Bassompierre who wrote their accounts years later; political enemies such as Richelieu who deliberately maligned Luynes; anonymous satirical pamphlets; hostile ambassadorial reports repeating dubious court gossip; and biased contemporary histories.[14] Was Luynes really the timid, indecisive bungler that historians have claimed he was?

Contemporary historians wrote biased accounts because they needed patronage. Without financial means of their own, they needed the support of patrons to write, usually in the form of pensions or employment in great households. Their need to please a patron and their continuing need for patronage determined what they wrote.[15] The king, his family, favorites, and ministers distributed extensive patronage, so historians needing financial assistance filled their work with propaganda glorifying the monarchy in order to secure and keep their patronage.[16]

Luynes's political enemies, particularly Richelieu and his successor Mazarin, were the patrons of contemporary historians, and gave royal pensions to those who portrayed them and their policies in a favorable light.[17] Richelieu employed a number of historian-clients to write polemical defenses of him and his ministry. They used documents supplied by him, submitted their work to him for correction and approval, and were rewarded financially.[18] The portrayal of Luynes as a timid, inept bungler originated in the anti-Luynes pamphlets commissioned by the Queen Mother that Richelieu incorporated into his memoirs. These distortions and inaccuracies were repeated by Richelieu's historian-clients and historians who relied upon his memoirs such as Gabriel Hanotaux whose work influenced that of Louis Batiffol. A contemporary propaganda campaign, therefore, became the basis of the traditional historical interpretation of Luynes's career.

Richelieu despised Luynes whom he savaged in his memoirs in a devastating character assassination that significantly influenced later historiography.[19] He described Luynes as weak, cowardly, deceitful, and disloyal. He insisted that Luynes had duped the king into favoring him, and manipulated the king by surrounding him with his own relatives and friends who kept everyone else away. Arrogant and ambitious, Luynes had begun to act as if he were king, and because he was low-born without civility, he was often high-handed and rude. His family was Italian, so he had the attitudes of a foreigner, which was why he was tyrannical and authoritarian. Richelieu accused Luynes of greedy self-interest in advancing a horde of dependents, although he would advance an even larger horde himself, and he insisted that Luynes had persuaded the king to murder Concini, alienated the king from his mother, and treated her harshly by exiling her from the court, although he himself would later exile her from France.[20] The Cardinal ended his diatribe on the favorite's deficiencies with the comment that his death "seemed to be a God-sent deliverance from evil."[21]

In power for only five years when he died, Luynes was overshadowed by the two larger-than-life individuals between whom he was sandwiched, his predecessor as a royal favorite, the widely despised Concini to whom he was often compared, and the brilliant but vindictive Richelieu who ruthlessly crushed his enemies, and worked hard to destroy Luynes's reputation both before and after his death. Because there is little direct evidence, historians have been forced to rely upon circumstantial evidence in analyzing Luynes's motives and actions. There are almost no documents in Luynes's own words giving his version of events because most of his family papers were destroyed by fire in 1649 and 1944.[22] His letters tended to be short, polite, and formulaic without much substance, and there are almost no administrative documents expressing his views because being a favorite was an unofficial if influential position. Although he became a minister eight months before he died, Luynes tended to remain in the shadows. He said little in public to avoid arousing the king's jealousy, and committed nothing to paper in order not to leave a prejudicial paper trail. This evidential problem, and the widely accepted negative assessments by well known historians such as Louis Batiffol and Gabriel Hanotaux, have made Richelieu's attack influential to this day.[23]

The Cardinal's animosity and the bias in histories based upon his memoirs justify another look at Luynes. The traditional historical interpretation needs revision. A more critical reading of contemporary printed sources such as pamphlets, the Paris newspaper the *Mercure françois*, the journal of the king's doctor, and courtiers' memoirs provide new insight into his actions, while archival sources provide new information about his origins, family, and friends. This book has emphasized French sources as being more objective and reliable than the Italian and Spanish ambassadorial correspondence upon which many historians have relied. An extensive secondary literature published during the twentieth century has been of inestimable value. The new secondary literature alone justifies another look at Luynes. What follows is a more positive assessment of his career as a favorite, and long-overdue recognition of his contributions to Louis XIII's government.

Luynes had a caring father-son relationship with the young king, whom he guided to the best of his ability and helped learn how to govern. His understanding reassurance became the model for Richelieu's later relationship with Louis XIII. Luynes became in turn a personal, a political, and then a minister favorite, and he influenced decision-making through private conversations with the king, serving in general as a moderating influence. He regularly attended council meetings, voted with a group of conservative council members, favored negotiation and compromise, and mediated between opposing factions on the council. Acting as the king's spokesman, messenger, and go-between, he supervised the distribution of royal patronage, which he used to secure the cooperation of the court nobility. Luynes was ambitious, greedy, and sycophantic as most courtiers were, and he was defensive about his unpopularity, but his faults have been exaggerated. Overall, his good qualities outweighed his bad, and he made significant contributions to the early years of Louis XIII's government.

Luynes became one of the most powerful men in France. Accumulating a large fortune, he became a duke and peer, constable or commander-in-chief of the army, and acting keeper of the seals. He created a large noble clientele that included an informal group of his own political advisers, and he launched a vigorous multi-media propaganda campaign against the pamphleteers' attacks on him. He established an independent power base in the important border province of Picardy, which he expanded to include Normandy, the Ile-de-France, and Paris, and his power base was instrumental in helping him to suppress the Queen Mother's revolt against the new regime. He advocated a non-interventionist foreign policy until the problem of Protestant disobedience could be solved, and he accompanied the king on his 1621 campaign against the Protestants. He was not cowardly, vacillating, or inept, whatever his enemies may have claimed.

This book provides another look at Luynes untainted by the malice of Richelieu. Demonstrating the bias in contemporary sources, it sifts through numerous distortions and half-truths to set the record straight by asking, what kind of a man was he? How greedy and ambitious was he? What type of influence did he have, and how did he use it? How much of what has been written about him is true, and how much is false? What follows, therefore, is as much about Luynes's detractors, and what they had to say about him, as it is about the favorite himself, and for this reason throws light upon a dark, unpleasant corner of Richelieu's personality that is often ignored by historians.

Notes

1 Eugène Halphen, ed., *Journal inédit d'Arnauld d'Andilly 1621* (Paris, 1891), pp. 102, 104.

2 *Recueil des pièces les plus curieuses qui ont esté faites pendant le règne du Connestable M. de Luynes* (Paris, 1628), *Requeste présentée au Roy Pluton par Conchino Conchini* (1620), p. 73; *Le Comtadin Provençal* (1620), pp. 83–4; *La Chronique des Favoris* (1622), p. 465; *Plaintes de l'espée de M. le Connestable* (1621), pp. 149–50; *L'Horoscope du Connestable* (1621), pp. 152–3; *Le Passe Par-Tout des Favoris* (1620), p. 156.

3 Hélène Duccini, *Faire Voir, Faire Croire* (Paris, 2003), pp. 10–14.

4 Fontenay-Mareuil, François Du Val, marquis de, *Mémoires du Messire Du Val*, ed. Louis Monmerqué, 2 vols. (Paris, 1826), I, 525. "... cest homme sy grand et sy puissant se trouva neanmoins tellement abandonné et mesprisé, tant dans sa maladie qu'après sa mort, que pendant deux jours qu'il fust à l'agonie, à peine y avoit-il un de ses gens qui voulust demeurer dans sa chambre, les portes en estant tousjours ouvertes, et y entrant qui vouloit, comme sy c'eust esté le moindre des hommes; et quand on porta son corps pour estre enterré, je crois, à sa duché de Luynes, au lieu de prestres qui priassent pour luy, j'y vis de ses valets jouer au piquet sur son cercueil, pendant qu'ils faisoient repaistre leurs chevaux."

5 Ibid.; Bassompierre, François de, *Journal de ma vie. Mémoires du maréchal de Bassompierre*, ed. Edouard de Chanterac, 4 vols. (Paris, 1870–77), II, 174, 395.

6 A. Lloyd Moote, *Louis XIII. The Just* (Berkeley, 1989), pp. 139–46; Madeleine Foisil, *L'Enfant Louis XIII* (Paris, 1996), pp. 85–6, 112.

7 Jean Héroard, *Journal*, ed. Madeleine Foisil, 2 vols. (Paris, 1989), II, 2797–9; *Journal d'Arnauld 1621*, p. 104.

8 Berthold Zeller, *Le Connêtable de Luynes* (Paris, 1879), p. 271.

9 Baron Ludovic de Contenson, ed., *Mémoires du comte de Souvigny*, 3 vols. (Paris, 1906–9), I, 81.

10 *Mercure françois*, 25 vols. (Paris, 1605–44), VII (1621), 930–1; Jean-Antoine Pithon-Curt, *Histoire de la noblesse du Comté Venaissin*, 4 vols. (Paris, 1743–50), IV, 173; Henri Griffet, *Histoire du règne de Louis XIII*, 3 vols. (Paris, 1758), I, 326; Héroard, *Journal*, II, 2802–3.

11 Zeller, *Le Connêtable de Luynes*, p. 271; Louis Batiffol, "Louis XIII et le duc de Luynes," *Rev hist* 102 (1909), 270–1; *Mercure françois*, VII (1621), 930–1.

12 Charles, comte Horric de Beaucaire, ed., *Mémoires du Cardinal de Richelieu*, 10 vols. (Paris, 1907–13), III, 175–7; *Recueil, Remonstrance à Théophile* (1620), p. 122; *La Sybille françoise* (1620), p. 281; B.N., imprimés Lb 36, *La Magie des Favoris* (1619).

13 J.H. Elliott and L.W.B. Brockliss, *The World of the Favourite* (New Haven, 1999), p. 304, n. 4.

14 Madeleine Bertaud, "Louis XIII vu par quelques mémorialistes," *La Cour au miroir des mémorialistes, 1530–1682*, ed. Noémi Hepp (Paris, 1991), pp. 77–88.

15 Mario Biagioli, *Galileo Courtier* (Chicago, 1993), pp. 1–101, 112–20; F.E. Sutcliffe, *Guez de Balzac et son temps* (Paris, 1959), pp. 17–42.

16 Orest Ranum, *Artisans of Glory* (Chapel Hill, 1980), pp. 148–96; Roland Mousnier, ed., *Richelieu et la culture* (Paris, 1987), pp. 124–37; Joseph Klaits, *Printed Propaganda under Louis XIV* (Princeton, 1976), pp. 3–34; Peter Burke, *The Fabrication of Louis XIV* (New Haven, 1992), pp. 23, 25, 76, 153, 185; Joseph Bergin and Laurence Brockliss, eds., *Richelieu and His Age* (Oxford, 1992), pp. 202–35.

17 Ranum, *Artisans of Glory*, pp. 103–68; Mousnier, *Richelieu et la culture*, pp. 69–137; William Church, *Richelieu and Reason of State* (Princeton, 1972), pp. 82–101, 461–504.

18 Robert Knecht, *Richelieu* (London, 1990), p. 177; Orest Ranum, "Richelieu, l'histoire et les

historiographes," *Richelieu et la culture*, pp. 125–37; Françoise Hildesheimer, *Richelieu* (Paris, 2004), pp. 498–526.

19   Denis-Louis-Martial Avenel, ed., *Lettres, instructions diplomatiques et papiers d'état du Cardinal de Richelieu*, 8 vols. (Paris, 1853–77), VII, 473, n. 2; Victor Tapié, *France in the Age of Louis XIII and Richelieu*, trans. D. McN. Lockie (Cambridge, 1974), p. 94; Eusèbe Pavie, *La Guerre entre Louis XIII et Marie de Médicis* (Angers, 1899), p. 621; Batiffol, "Louis XIII et le duc de Luynes," *Rev_hist* 103 (1910), 50; Joseph Bergin, *The Rise of Richelieu* (New Haven, 1991), p. 164.

20   Beaucaire, *Mémoires de Richelieu*, I, 304–7, III, 164–97.

21   Ibid., III, 197.

22   *Frondeurs* in 1649 burned to the ground Luynes's country house of Lésigny-en-Brie south of Paris, destroying its contents including family papers. Retreating Germans set fire to most of the remaining family papers in the courtyard of the château of Luynes in 1944. On the evening of 24 August 1944, a group of *maquisards* (resistance fighters) ambushed a retreating German troop convoy near Maillé, the village below the château. Regarding the village as a terrorist base, German troops the next day massacred 124 of its 627 inhabitants, using machine guns, grenades, and bayonets, and set fire to the buildings. The stone château itself was not put to the torch, but family property and furniture were piled in the courtyard and burned. Robert Gildea, *Marianne in Chains* (New York, 2002), pp. 314–15, 384–5.

23   Louis Batiffol, "Louis XIII et le duc de Luynes," *Rev hist* 102 (1909), 241–64; 103 (1910), 33–62, 248–79; idem, *Le Roi Louis XIII à vingt ans* (Paris, 1910), pp. 478–573; Gabriel Hanotaux and the duc de La Force, *Histoire du Cardinal de Richelieu*, 6 vols. (Paris, 1893–1947), II, part 2, 209.

1

A falconer from the Comtat

Richelieu wrote in his memoirs that Luynes's grandfather had been a canon of the cathedral of Marseille, and that his grandmother had been the canon's house-keeper. Since her family name was Albert, the implication was that her son, Luynes's father, had been illegitimate and low-born. According to Richelieu, the family had been forced to move to Tarascon after Luynes's mother had stabbed a butcher to death in his shop for insulting her when he tried to collect the money that she owed him.[1] Anti-Luynes pamphlets declared that the favorite's father had been of humble birth, penniless, and illiterate, and that he had been foreign-born, a Protestant, a soldier of fortune, and an adventurer. None of this was true. Richelieu and the pamphleteers had fabricated it all to destroy Luynes's reputation and favor with the king.

The Albert family had been governors of the Rhône fortress town of Pont-Saint-Esprit for nearly two centuries when Luynes was born. Located on the river's western bank, the town anchored the only bridge to cross the Rhône between Vienne and Avignon. Thomas Platter, a Swiss visitor, noted that his boat had sailed with the speed of an arrow under the stone-paved bridge of eighteen arches, which was twelve hundred paces long with fortified towers at either end and in the middle.[2] Still in use today, its narrow arches have been replaced by a single wide span. These narrow arches were dangerous because they could hole or capsize a boat that got too close to their pilings. Henri III and his court were traveling down the Rhône from Lyon to Avignon in November 1574, when the boat carrying the household officials of the king's sister capsized at Pont-Saint-Esprit, drowning everyone. The town's governor, Honoré d'Albert de Luynes, the favorite's father, received a letter of thanks from the Queen Mother, Catherine de Médicis, for aiding the royal party.[3]

Charles d'Albert de Luynes was the sixth generation of a sword noble family that had emigrated from Florence into the upper Rhône valley in the late fourteenth century. They had owned fiefs in the valley for nearly two centuries when he was born. His great-great-great-grandfather, Thomas Alberti, had been the *viguier* or royal judge of Pont-Saint-Esprit in 1415, and the youngest of his three sons became the town's governor. He established the family tradition of serving as its governor, and was named to the Order of *Saint Michel* for his services to the crown.[4] Luynes's grandfather, Léon, an infantry captain who was killed in the Italian wars, changed the family name to d'Albert, and married Jeanne de Ségur of Marseille in 1535 for a dowry of 10,000 livres and the Provençal fief of Luynes. His only son, Honoré, was born five years later. He styled himself the sieur de Luynes, although he was only coseigneur or part owner of this fief, and he, too, served the crown as an infantry captain.[5]

Honoré d'Albert de Luynes, the favorite's father, had begun his military career at the age of thirteen when he joined the French army that invaded and occupied Corsica in 1553.[6] He styled himself "capitaine de Luynes" after he became captain of an infantry company in the regiment of Sarlabous in 1565.[7] Four years later he was named a knight in the Order of Saint Michel, probably through the patronage of Henri de Montmorency-Damville, governor of Languedoc, who wrote the duc d'Anjou a letter on 12 September 1570 praising his services to the crown.[8] Honoré purged the Pont-Saint-Esprit garrison of Protestant soldiers after Damville had named him its commander the previous February. He was appointed governor of Pont-Saint-Esprit in 1573, and again in 1576, because he was a staunch Catholic, and the king wanted this important military fortification in the upper Rhône valley safely in Catholic hands. Damville also named him colonel of the Languedoc provincial militia and a provincial artillery officer for annual salaries of about 300 livres each, and governor of the fortress town of Beaucaire in the lower Rhône valley. The king named him governor of Beaucaire again in 1580. Honoré had been serving the crown faithfully for nearly forty years when he died in 1592.[9]

In March 1573, he had married Anne de Rodulf, daughter of the seigneur de Limans, an Italian noble family who had settled at Mornas in the late fifteenth century.[10] Her dowry included 3,000 livres, a pension of 400 livres a year, joint ownership of the fief of Mornas, and property in the village of Mornas to which her husband added a house and lands that he purchased. The family home was in Mornas.[11] A fortified medieval château still clings to the cliff above this village, which stands on the eastern side of the Rhône thirteen kilometers north of Orange.[12] Mornas was a fief in the Comtat Venaissin, which was a papal principality governed by a vice-legate with Avignon as its capital. The Comtadins considered themselves French, but they were papal subjects and in customs and speech more Italian than French.[13]

When and where Luynes was born is controversial. He concealed his family's Florentine origins because his enemies insisted on comparing him to the despised Florentine favorite Concini.[14] Luynes declared that his paternal kin were Languedocian French, ignoring the fact that his family home was at

Figure 1 The Rhône River Valley.

Mornas in the Comtat Venaissin. Genealogical documents produced to support his candidacy for membership in the Order of *Saint Esprit* declared that the Albert family had come from Languedoc, and that the Provençal branch of the family included families of the feudal nobility.[15] Although Richelieu's disdainful comments about his dubious birth have been widely accepted, Luynes came from a solidly respectable family of the Midi sword nobility.[16] The Albert de Luynes were members of the *noblesse seconde* of the upper Rhône valley. They were not doubtful or obscure provincial nobles.[17]

The traditional date of Luynes's birth is 5 August 1578, and most historians agree he was born sometime during that year. There is less agreement about where he was born. Some sources give his birthplace as Mornas in the Comtat Venaissin, making him Comtadin by birth and a papal subject.[18] Other sources give Pont-Saint-Esprit as his birthplace, making him Languedocian and French by birth.[19] Existing documents do not allow certainty about when and where he was born.[20] The absence of his name in local baptismal records may be explained by the tradition that he was baptized in the Paris abbey of Saint Denis in 1592, which would have been his naming baptism, not his birth baptism.[21] There are no records confirming this date either, and such a belated baptism must be regarded with caution because postponement until adolescence was unusual, although delay among the nobility was common. Lacking evidence to the contrary, Luynes's traditional date and place of birth of 5 August 1578 at Mornas in the Comtat Venaissin have been accepted here.

In fact, there is some circumstantial evidence that Mornas was his birthplace. Luynes's father was the governor of Pont-Saint-Esprit, and the family home was thirteen kilometers south across the bridge in Mornas. Luynes's mother, Anne, died there six years later while her uncle was the town's governor.[22] It seems likely that she would have remained in the family home for her confinement in August 1578 because her husband could easily have ridden across the bridge to see her, and there was popular unrest in Pont-Saint-Esprit at the time.[23] It seems unlikely he would have allowed a heavily pregnant wife whose first child had died in infancy the year before to remain in Pont-Saint-Esprit when a popular revolt was brewing. On the other hand, if Luynes was born in the spring of 1578 or in the previous year, he could have been born in Pont-Saint-Esprit when Anne was living there with her husband before the troubles began.

The court career of Luynes's father

Honoré d'Albert de Luynes was not a soldier of fortune who sold his services to the highest bidder, although he has often been described in this way.[24] He was a devout Catholic royalist who fought for a legitimate Catholic monarchy during the religious wars. Ambitious and seeking advancement, he went to court in the autumn of 1573, hoping to profit from a recent marriage connection to Joseph de Boniface, sieur de La Molle, a favorite of the duc d'Alençon and master of his wardrobe.[25] The timing of his trip, however, proved disastrous. In March 1574, a few months after his arrival, La Molle was implicated in a treasonous conspiracy against Charles IX led by the duc d'Alençon, the king's youngest brother, and Honoré was also implicated. The conspirators, who had been meeting openly in Alençon's court apartments, included Henri de Navarre; La Molle; the prince de Condé; the comte de Coconas who was Alençon's guard captain; Guillaume de Montmorency-Thoré and Charles de Montmorency-Méru, the younger brothers of Henri de Montmorency-Damville, who had remained in the south in his government of Languedoc; and Henri de La Tour, vicomte de Turenne, their nephew. In an ambitious gamble, Honoré began to attend these meetings with La Molle, thereby attaching himself to Alençon's fortunes.

Alençon and Navarre had planned to escape the king and his court by fleeing to Sedan where they would be met by 300 horsemen under Turenne's command. La Molle was put in charge of their escape, but he bungled it, and news of their plans reached the Queen Mother. She told the king, and he immediately put the two princes under heavy guard and ordered the arrest of La Molle, Coconas, and about fifty supporters. La Molle and Coconas were beheaded in April.[26] Honoré had left Paris as soon as the conspiracy was discovered, and Coconas implicated him by saying that he had gone to the meetings in Alençon's apartments, and then had gone south to prepare the princes' retreat into Languedoc where they would be under Damville's protection.[27] As a result, the *Parlement* of Paris on 21 May 1574 ordered the arrest of twenty-one men including the capitaine de Luynes, who was named for carrying treasonous letters from the duc d'Alençon to Damville. Honoré, however, was already safe in the south under Damville's protection.[28]

The new king, Henri III, considered Honoré unreliable as a former conspirator and Damville's client, so he gave his government of Pont-Saint-Esprit to another Comtat gentleman, capitaine Pierre d'Anselme, sieur de Joucas.[29] A ray of sunlight penetrated the darkness, however, because the fortunes of Alençon had improved. Henri III had married, but he never had any children. So, his younger brother became the heir presumptive and received the title of duc d'Anjou. With the additional income, Anjou was able to quadruple the size of his household, so Honoré rode north in the autumn of 1575, hoping to benefit from this change in the duke's fortunes.[30]

The new duc d'Anjou had already proven himself loyal to those who were loyal to him. His household list of 5 August 1576 contains the names of six participants in the La Molle-Coconas conspiracy.[31] Honoré had received a place as an ordinary chamberlain in February 1576, but he must have given it up soon afterward because his name does not appear on the August list.[32] His annual salary as a royal governor was 1,500 livres, but his salary as a household chamberlain would have been only 600 livres, and he needed the extra money for his growing family.[33] Besides, life in the Midi was cheaper than at court, and household service was a career better suited to a bachelor than to the head of a large family. So, Honoré gave up his place after convincing Henri III that Pont-Saint-Esprit was too important to be left in Damville's hands. He offered to seize it for the king if he could become its governor, and the king gave him permission. Not surprisingly, Damville severed their ties when he heard about this.[34]

For political reasons, the king had named Damville governor of Pont-Saint-Esprit in May 1576, and he had arrived in August to enlarge the town's defenses, putting his Protestant younger brother, Montmorency-Thoré, a former conspirator, in command of the garrison. Thoré was joined by Protestant captains from the nearby Protestant army, and Honoré used their presence to persuade the king that Thoré intended to deliver the town into Protestant hands. He offered to install as its garrison a company of 200 Catholic foot soldiers that he would recruit himself in the Comtat, and he promised to arrest Thoré and his friends.[35] In return, he asked to become the town's governor. His victory in a duel may have convinced the king of his ability to do as he promised. Henri III authorized this duel, which was allegedly held during the summer of 1576 in an open field near Vincennes. Honoré had challenged an officer in the Scots royal guards for making insulting remarks about his role as a conspirator and then killed him, thereby earning the court's respect for his courage and prowess, if not the king's favor or trust.[36] François Billaçois is skeptical about the occurrence of this duel, and suggests that it was a later embellishment of the favorite's background. It was first mentioned in a pro-Luynes pamphlet in 1619, and then repeated as fact in the Parisian newspaper, the *Mercure françois*.[37]

Returning to Pont-Saint-Esprit as commander of a newly recruited Catholic garrison, Honoré announced to the town that Thoré had been plotting against the king, and arrested him and his friends. They did not remain long in captivity, however, escaping a day or so later by a postern gate opening onto the Rhône. The news reached Paris on 20 December 1576 that Honoré had seized Pont-Saint-Esprit for the king, which Henri de Navarre announced in a letter to the Protestant nobility and towns of Guyenne.[38] A furious Damville threatened to retake Pont-Saint-Esprit by force, but Alençon, now the duc d'Anjou, asked him not to do so, and Damville heeded his request, if reluctantly.[39] The king named Honoré governor of Pont-Saint-Esprit in March 1577, much to Damville's disgust.[40]

The cost of maintaining the Catholic garrison made Honoré unpopular.[41] The king ordered a treasury official at Montpellier to advance 8,000 livres for the garrison's support.[42] He also wrote Honoré a letter in June 1577, forbidding him to confiscate salt in transit on the Rhône to pay his garrison, which he had been doing.[43] Honoré wrote Catherine de Médicis in September asking for more money.[44] Finally, in the summer of 1578, he levied a sales tax of three per cent on all goods entering the gates of Pont-Saint-Esprit in order to pay his troops. In response, an angry mob drove him out of town and ransacked his lodgings![45] He got off lightly. The tax demands of Damville's favorite, Pierre de Baudéan, sieur de Parabère, governor of Beaucaire, were so onerous that in September he was murdered as he came out of church, and his head, encircled by a crown of straw, was displayed on the ramparts of the château![46]

The king now ordered that the garrison of Pont-Saint-Esprit should be reduced to 60 soldiers commanded by the sieur de Glandais at a monthly expense of 800 livres paid from the royal treasury.[47] This reduction in the town's garrison and the removal of Honoré as governor were meant to pacify Pont-Saint-Esprit. To placate Honoré, the king gave him 15,000 livres, a royal pension of 4,000 livres, and the government of Beaucaire,[48] which brought a salary of 1,500 livres.[49]

Meanwhile, during the winter of 1580–81, the duc d'Anjou had raised an army to relieve Cambrai in Flanders.[50] Honoré rode into his camp in July at the head of a company of Midi recruits.[51] By September, the duke had left Flanders and was heading for the Channel.[52] Honoré would have been back in Beaucaire by October 1581.[53] His willingness to fight for the duke proclaimed to the world that he was a client of Anjou, who wrote him several personal letters.[54] Honoré's loyalty to the heir presumptive, who was impatiently waiting for the king to die, meant that he would never gain the trust or favor of Henri III, but it also meant that his government of Beaucaire was safe through the protection of Anjou, who might one day be king.[55]

The duke's premature death ended that hope, and Honoré's court career as well. The first catastrophe occurred on 7 May 1584 when Honoré's wife died at Mornas, probably of complications from the birth of her youngest daughter, having had eight children in eight years. Her first son François had been born in 1577, but had died in infancy, so Charles became her oldest son. She left behind seven children under the age of eight, three sons, Charles born in 1578, Honoré in 1581, and Léon in 1582, and four daughters, Marie born in 1579, Antoinette in 1580, Louise in 1583, and Anne in 1584.[56] The second catastrophe occurred on 10 June 1584, when Anjou died at Château-Thierry of chronic disseminated tuberculosis.[57] Honoré was in Mornas at the time, and the duke's death left him without a protector at court, which was dangerous because of Damville's enmity and Henri III's distrust. The king became increasingly paranoid as he aged. As governor of Languedoc, Damville had the authority to dismiss fortress governors, and he promptly removed Honoré as governor of Beaucaire. The king did not intervene.

All was not lost, however. The new heir presumptive was the king's cousin, Henri de Navarre, later Henri IV, whom Honoré knew personally because they had been conspirators together. Henri was a Protestant, however, and he was unlikely to forget that Honoré had levied a Catholic garrison and driven the Protestants from Pont-Saint-Esprit.[58] He never favored or trusted Honoré, who was neither a fellow Protestant nor a comrade-in-arms, although he has been described as both.[59]

Honoré went to court six months after his wife's death to seek the protection and support of a new patron. Evidently, he was unsuccessful because he lost the government of Beaucaire sometime in 1585. That December he received a royal order sending him back to the Midi to deliver letters of instruction to all postmasters along the way, presumably a face-saving way of getting rid of him because he never returned to court while Henri III was alive, and he never obtained another royal government. He came home to Mornas, aged forty-six, and remained there for the rest of his life. His campaigning days were over along with his dreams of a court career. He bequeathed his ambitions and dreams to his eldest son.[60]

As compensation for his lost government of Beaucaire, the king gave Honoré a cash gift of 30,000 livres drawn on the salt-tax revenues of Pont-Saint-Esprit, an annual royal pension of 2,000 livres, and the privilege of using the Rhône and its banks toll-free. A few years later, the papal vice-legate named him governor of the town of Bollène in the Comtat Venaissin.[61] Honoré was returning home to Mornas in February 1592, after escorting his eldest son to the Christmas court to join the royal pages when, aged fifty-two, he died suddenly at Melun near Paris and was buried there.[62] His 13-year-old son now became the head of a large family of six younger brothers and sisters for whom he had to provide.

The family fortune

Contemporaries joked that a hare could quickly jump across the Albert family lands – an exaggeration, but Honoré's difficulties in paying the Pont-Saint-Esprit garrison indicate that he was not a wealthy man. Contemporary historian Charles Bernard noted that the Albert family home near Mornas was unimpressive, and appeared to be of "a very mediocre nobility" to the court visiting after the 1622 campaign, while a pamphleteer sneered at Luynes's "poor shack of a house at Mornas."[63] The family income was described by another contemporary as modest.[64]

Honoré owned four coseigneuries, Luynes, Mornas, Cadenet, and Brantes. He had inherited Luynes from his mother, and Mornas was part of his wife's dowry, while he bought the other two. The countryside around Luynes south of Aix-en-Provence is pretty. A tree-shaded stream, the Luyne, for which the place is named, wanders into the Arc river, which is bordered by fields of wheat, vineyards, and groves of olive and almond trees flowering white in the spring sunshine. There was no village then, just a few small country houses.[65]

A range of white limestone cliffs rises at Bollène and runs along the Rhône south behind Mornas to Orange. Honoré owned a fief near Mornas, then a walled village of narrow streets built into a cliff. The twelfth-century château of Mornas, already a ruin when Honoré lived there, stood then as it does now at the edge of a promontory overlooking the village with a sheer drop on three sides. It has a splendid view of the Rhône, which is visible for miles in all directions, a silver snake curling off into the distance. In May, red poppies are everywhere, and the air is full of wood smoke.

Honoré bought the coseigneury of Cadenet on an island in the Rhône south of Mornas for 750 *florins* or about 4,500 *livres* in 1572.[66] At the same time, he bought the coseigneury of Brantes, a farm between Mornas and Piolenc, for 517 florins or about 3,100 livres from the widow of André d'Ardaillon, a councillor in the Parlement of Aix. A small fief because most of the island was owned by the bishops of Carpentras, Cadenet included a *clos*, which was a piece of cultivated land surrounded by a wall, as well as a garden and some woods, but no house. Brantes was a somewhat larger fief along the river bank, and Honoré had enlarged it by purchasing eleven adjoining parcels of land. The total price of eight of the parcels was 447 florins or about 2,700 livres; no price was given for two parcels; and land was exchanged for one.[67] Brantes had good farmland, a house, a garden with orange trees, a barn, a mill, a walled vineyard, groves of olive and almond trees, pasture land, and some woods.

Honoré also bought a house with a garden and stables south of Mornas on the road to Orange for 2,170 florins or about 13,100 livres, and a dozen assorted small pieces of farmland around Mornas including a vineyard, duck pond, orchards, and meadowland for 1,742 florins or about 10,500 livres. For 3,300 florins or about 20,000 livres, he bought a large farm with a house and garden, a vineyard, orchards, and pastureland at Frigolet, now La Figoule, on the river bank at the edge of the woods next to his father-in-law's property. Finally, he bought more pastureland for 194 florins or about 1,200 livres.[68] The total value of the purchased property was 9,120 florins or about 55,000 livres, most of which had come from the crown.

All four of his fiefs were farms worked by tenants, and three, Mornas, Cadenet, and Brantes, were papal fiefs.[69] He was only part owner of these small fiefs. Richelieu contemptuously remarked about the size of the Albert family lands that "they (Honoré and his wife) acquired there (at Mornas) a little house from President (sic) d'Ardaillon of Aix-en-Provence ... a small, wretched farm named Brantes that sat on rock and was planted in vines, and a half-washed away island in the Rhône called Cadenet." Richelieu added that these lands could not have provided an income of more than 1,200 livres a year.[70] It is difficult to estimate Honoré's income or fortune without knowing his acreage or what it produced, but Richelieu was probably correct in estimating that his landed income was somewhere between 1,000 and 2,000 livres a year. He had other sources of revenue, however, that Richelieu overlooked.

Most of his income came from the crown. In 1570, Honoré had only the revenues from his coseigneury of Luynes, and whatever he made soldiering, usually about 100 livres a month as captain of an infantry company.[71] In 1572, he added a salary of 1,500 livres as governor of Beaucaire, and the next year he traded Beaucaire for the government of Pont-Saint-Esprit, which he held for four years, probably for about the same salary. With his marriage in 1573, he added an annual pension of 400 livres, the revenues from the coseigneury of Mornas, and 3,000 livres in cash, most of which he probably spent during his months at court in 1574. He was granted an annual royal pension of 4,000 livres in 1579, and another pension of 2,000 livres in 1587, and when added to his wife's dowry, he was receiving 6,400 livres a year in pensions by the late 1580s, which was half his income.[72] He used the king's cash gift of 15,000 livres in 1579 to buy the fiefs of Cadenet and Brantes, and the farmland at Frigolet and Mornas. His royal pension in 1587, and another cash gift from the king of 30,000 livres, compensated for losing his salary as governor of Beaucaire, which was replaced when he became papal governor of Bollène in 1589. With 4,000 livres a year from the sale of salt, Honoré's annual income at his death would have been 13,000 to 14,000 livres, which was considerably above average for a sixteenth-century provincial noble.

In addition, Honoré secured money from salt transactions. A municipal memorandum to the king in the late 1580s complained that he had obtained a contract to sell 2,000 *muids* of salt to the warehouse at Pont-Saint-Esprit without bidding for it. The price of salt fluctuated, but in 1586 a *muid* was worth about 240 livres. The usual commission was 5 percent, so he would have made at least 12,000 livres on this sale.[73] Salt sales increased his income by 4,000 livres a year from 1588 to 1591, and he was almost certainly involved in other similar transactions.[74] Selling salt was a quick way to obtain cash.

Honoré had prospered financially from his court career. Provincial nobles went to court seeking the wealth and offices distributed there, and courtiers were widely regarded as greedy and ambitious for this reason. Permeated by duplicity and deceit, the court was a maze of rivalries, intrigues, and conflicts with pitfalls everywhere for the unsuspecting or careless. A misstep could result in permanent exile from the court, which had been Honoré's fate.[75]

Honoré d'Albert de Luynes was not low-born, illegitimate, or impoverished. He had a landed fortune of more than 55,000 livres, and he came from a sword noble family. He owned four fiefs, and his great-grandfather had also been a governor of Pont-Saint-Esprit and a knight of Saint Michel. With an old family name but no title or fortune, Honoré had entered the army at the age of thirteen and worked his way up through the ranks to become captain of an infantry company. He had acquired the patronage of the governor of Languedoc to become governor of the Rhône fortress towns of Pont-Saint-Esprit and Beaucaire, while the royal salaries, pensions, and cash gifts he had earned had significantly increased his income.

It was a long way geographically and socially from Mornas in the Comtat Venaissin to the royal court. The death of Luynes's father soon after his arrival must have made the transition even more difficult for a lonely thirteen-year-old. The family's income shrank to less than 2,000 livres a year after his father's death, a worrying problem for a boy who had to pay his own expenses and provide for six brothers and sisters. There were no paternal kin to help because his father had been an only child who had married late in life. Luynes had gone to court to join the royal pages, a traditional way for provincial nobles to begin an army career, and this is probably what his father had intended for him. After his father's death, however, with limited financial resources, he remained a page longer than usual and then entered household service.

A royal page

It was customary for sixteenth-century nobles to send their sons at age six or seven to serve as pages in great noble households to learn military skills and good manners. The higher a noble's rank and position, the more pages he had.[76] The comte Du Lude was a well-known courtier, and so when Luynes's father came to court in 1585, he may have asked him for a place as a household page for his seven-year-old son. Richelieu reported that Luynes had served as a page in the household of the comte Du Lude.[77] More likely, however, Luynes had remained at home. His father was a widower who never remarried and lived permanently at Mornas after 1585, and probably preferred having his eldest son with him for company. Luynes's close relationship with his two younger brothers, Honoré, sieur de Cadenet, and Léon, sieur de Brantes, makes it unlikely that he was constantly away from home when they were growing up. They had learned falconry in Provence before they went to court, and he had probably taught them. They may have hawked together in the Rhône marshes near Mornas.[78]

Luynes's handwritten letters as an adult are scrawled in a clumsy, child-like script with phonetic spelling, no punctuation, words divided in two, and endless run-on sentences. He received little formal education, and his quasi-literacy suggests that his father never employed a tutor.[79] Sixteenth-century provincial nobles were notorious for their reluctance to incur the expense of hiring tutors.[80] Du Lude in the late 1580s was a bachelor without sons or younger brothers, so he would not have employed a tutor either.[81] In fact, the only certainty about Luynes's early life is that he went to court to join the royal pages sometime during Christmas 1591.

Luynes had obtained a place as a page through Du Lude's patronage. The 6-year-old François de Daillon had been an ordinary gentleman in the household of the duc d'Anjou in August 1576, when Luynes's father had secured a place as an ordinary chamberlain.[82] As a household member, the 11-year-old François would have accompanied Anjou on his campaign to the Low Countries in 1581, and he may have met Luynes's father then. Honoré had served with his father, the old comte Du Lude, at the siege of La Rochelle in 1573, and probably during the campaigns of 1569 as well.[83] The personal ties between nobles who had served together in the army often extended to their sons.[84] Honoré could also have met François during visits to court in 1582, 1583, and 1585, since they were both members of Anjou's entourage. It is quite likely, therefore, that Luynes's father had made the young comte Du Lude's acquaintance sometime during the 1580s.

A few years later, Du Lude used his friendship with one of Henri IV's favorites, Roger de Saint Lary, sieur de Bellegarde, to secure Luynes a place in the royal pages.[85] As a drinking and gambling buddy of the king, Bellegarde could easily have requested a place for him, and probably did so because he was named as a godparent at Luynes's supposed baptismal ceremony in the church of Saint Denis in 1592.[86] In any event, Henri IV may have felt obliged to give Luynes a place in the royal pages because of his father's long years of service to the crown.[87]

Royal pages served in the king's bedchamber and in the stables, hunt, kennels, and *fauconnerie*, the falcon or hawk house. Luynes's father lacked the influence to secure him an appointment as a bedchamber page or the money to pay his expenses, so he almost certainly joined the less prestigious stable pages whose expenses were paid by the king.[88] The stable pages accompanied the king on horseback whenever he went riding, hunting, or to war; participated with him in jousts, tournaments, and royal entries; rode beside his carriage as part of his armed retinue when he traveled; lit his path with torches when he went to chapel; walked behind him on official occasions; and followed his coffin after his death. They numbered nineteen in 1487 during Charles VIII's reign; forty-five in 1585 during Henri III's reign; and seventy-two by Louis XIV's reign. Good-looking pages were chosen to enhance the king's grandeur.[89] Luynes's portraits show a handsome man with black curly hair, an elegant goatee and mustaches, and large dark eyes. He was tall and slender as a young man. His brothers were also handsome, and the flourishing mustachios of his brother Cadenet set a style known as "cadenettes."[90]

1650.

CHARLES, MARQVIS D'ALBERT,
Duc de Luines, Pair Connestable, et Grand Faulconnier
de France Gouuerneur et Lieutenant General pour le Roy Picardie.
Moncornet excu.

Figure 2 Portrait of Charles, marquis d'Albert, duc de Luines [Luynes], by Moncornet.

The *Grande Ecurie* or great stables located north of the Tuileries housed the saddle horses used for war, hunting, and parade. The *Petite Ecurie* or small stables located west of the Place du Carrousel housed the carriage horses and coaches, sedan chairs, and other types of royal conveyances. In January 1589,

Henri III had named Roger de Saint Lary, sieur de Bellegarde, to the newly created office of *Grand Ecuyer* or grand master of horse, and he became known as Monsieur le Grand. Bellegarde's appointment was confirmed by Henri IV, and he held this office more or less continuously until 1639. Henri IV also increased the number of stable pages to sixty, and Luynes probably secured one of these new places.

The *Petite Ecurie* or small stables was headed by the *Premier Ecuyer* or Monsieur le Premier, who was Charles du Plessis de Liancourt from 1579 to 1620, and his son Roger from 1620 to 1625. The two stable heads were always quarreling over authority and precedence. Noble pages were attached to both stables, wore the same livery, and went to school at the king's expense. Great stable pages walked behind the king on his right, and small stable pages walked behind him on his left, which was less prestigious.[91] Luynes probably belonged to the small stables because of his later friendship with Charles de Liancourt.[92]

Stable pages usually came from families of the provincial sword nobility, and were thirteen or fourteen years old when they arrived at the stable school to begin their military education. They remained for three to five years before joining the army.[93] Luynes came when he was thirteen, but he remained for eight years before entering household service. Equitation, dressage, trick-riding, and mounted gymnastics were taught at the school. The boys lived together in dormitories, slept several to a room, and ate in a common dining hall. They attended class in the morning and practiced military and equitation exercises in the afternoon. They had to be physically fit, learn discipline, and master the martial arts including the use of the lance, pike, sword, musket, and rapier.[94] They also learned good manners, but not much else, which helps to explain Luynes's rudimentary written French as an adult. Louis Batiffol attributes his semi-literacy to a disorganized, undisciplined, even "unstable" mind.[95] A more likely explanation is the inadequate noble education of the period. The English ambassador was surprised that Luynes did not know where Bohemia was, which Batiffol cited as an example of his "mediocre" intelligence.[96] Such ignorance was not unusual; most court nobles at the time would not have known where Bohemia was. Victor Tapié believes that Luynes's lack of intelligence has been exaggerated.[97]

As a royal page, Luynes would have lost his Midi accent and country bumpkin ways, and learned the language, manners, and mores of the court. He may have also decided that he did not wish to pursue a military career. The majority of the family's income had disappeared at his father's death, and the small landed income remaining was needed to support his brothers and sisters. He lacked the capital to purchase an army office, and household service did not require a capital investment. He may have also decided that finding a patron to advance himself and his family would be easier at court than in the army, and having spent eight years in the royal stables, he may have preferred life at court to campaigning in distant provinces. Louis Batiffol attributed his dislike of campaigning to his "timidity" and "cowardice."[98] It is more likely that Luynes did not enter the army because he did not have the money to purchase a commission.

A household gentleman

The château of Le Lude stands on the south bank of the Loir river, a tributary of the Loire. The fourteenth-century square stone château, which has great round towers at the corners and smaller round supporting towers on each wall, is a huge hulking mass of stone that is impressive from the river. The Daillon Du Lude were *grands* or great court nobles. They claimed fourteenth- and could document fifteenth-century origins.[99] Henri IV visited Le Lude in 1598 because its owner, 28-year-old François de Daillon, was a friend whose sense of humor and skill at repartee he enjoyed. Du Lude, like Bellegarde, spent evenings with the king gambling at cards, throwing dice, drinking, and chasing women.[100] As a stable page, Luynes probably accompanied the king to Le Lude, and used the visit to renew his acquaintanceship with the comte Du Lude because he joined the latter's household as an ordinary gentleman the next year. Luynes was twenty years old at this time, good-looking and charming. The comte's household numbered about ninety including ten noble gentlemen who served as his entourage, and Luynes became one of them.[101]

André de Contades joined Du Lude's household at about the same time. Newly ennobled from Narbonne, he had come to court to serve as a gentleman in the small stables of the king's household when Luynes was serving there as a stable page. Nearly the same age from the Midi, they became good friends and joined Du Lude's household together where they served as ordinary gentlemen. A trusted member of the comte's household, Contades was rewarded with the fief of La Roche-Thibault in Jarzé in April 1604. He received a salary of 300 livres a year as an ordinary gentleman and the comte's silver plate at his death, a legacy only given to trusted retainers.

In April 1618, Du Lude was named governor and Contades under-governor of the king's 10-year-old brother, Gaston, duc d'Orléans, through the patronage of Luynes, now the favorite. Du Lude also became first gentleman of Gaston's bedchamber and superintendent of his household. Both Du Lude and Contades were described by contemporaries as devoted to Luynes, who was able to repay their friendship with these appointments, and at the same time place reliable eyes and ears in the household of the king's brother. By this time,

Du Lude was a prematurely aging man in poor health incapable of fulfilling his duties, which he delegated to his oldest son, Timéolon, and to Contades who was described as an uneducated man with crude manners. Aged forty-nine, Du Lude died at Tours of scarlet fever in September 1619. Ironically, the same disease killed Luynes three years later. The king had visited Du Lude at his château in the month before he died, probably at Luynes's suggestion.[102]

As an ordinary gentleman in Du Lude's household, Luynes would have received room and board, plus firewood, candles, clothing, medical care, and a salary of 300 livres a year. A year after joining the household, he secured a place in it as a page for his youngest brother Brantes, who was promoted to an ordinary gentleman four years later. The duties of a gentleman included acting as a companion to the household head, accompanying him when he went riding and hunting, dining with him, seeing him to bed, waiting upon him when he was ill or depressed, reading to him, amusing him, and helping to entertain his guests. Gentlemen accompanied their masters on public occasions since it was prestigious to appear with a large entourage.[103] In great households, the chamberlains, stewards, gentlemen-attendants, ladies-in-waiting, and the gentlemen and pages of the stables, hunt, and fauconnerie were nobles, who composed 20–30 percent of the membership of a great household. Nobles were even more numerous in royal households.[104]

Household members suffered physical and emotional discomfort from standing long hours on their feet and living in cramped, unpleasant quarters. They endured frequent travel, a lack of privacy and personal freedom, and long separations from their families, and it was often difficult for them to marry and establish families of their own. There was a rigid social hierarchy within great households, and although nobles were higher in rank than non-nobles, they were often treated with the same condescension. Their living quarters were separate from those of the family, and they had to fetch and carry on demand; cheerfully accept complaints and criticisms; ignore being made the object of pranks and jokes; and endure the indignity and humiliation of trying to please a capricious master or mistress who might be arrogant, disagreeable, or unkind. Nobles were the companions, not the equals, of their masters and mistresses. They waited on them just as non-noble domestic servants did, and they, too, had to perform disagreeable household tasks. For this reason, nobles came to regard household service as debasing to their rank. Although service to someone higher in rank was still considered honorable, the everyday reality was servility and subservience, so nobles increasingly avoided household service.[105]

The formative years of Luynes's life were spent in household service. What influence did this experience have on his character? He became someone who could charm and please, and he was able to manipulate others in this way. Even Richelieu acknowledged his charm, although he emphasized his guile and deceit in exercising it.[106] Luynes used his affability to mask his thoughts, and he was more apt to conciliate and pacify than to confront or challenge. He had acquired a staunch Catholicism at home, and he was paternal by nature with a strong sense of family duty. Having experienced loneliness, he sympathized with others who were lonely. He had learned to be flexible and adaptable, and he was almost certainly skilled at household politics. He lacked administrative or military experience, however, because he had never held a high household office or gone to war, and he did not have a family tradition of administrative service. Nonetheless, Luynes was ambitious and intelligent. He had received a military education; he had been promoted several times in household service; and he had been put in charge of two departments in the fauconnerie. Although he was only seven years older than Richelieu, their early lives had been very different because Richelieu was able to acquire the education and administrative experience that Luynes lacked.[107] Service in a great court household was good training for a personal favorite, but not for a political or minister favorite, which Luynes became.

A royal falconer

When André de Contades received a fief in 1604 as a reward for his service to the comte Du Lude, Luynes probably received a reward, too. Almost certainly at his own request, a minor position was found for him in the king's household, and he left Du Lude's household in 1606 to become a gentleman in the royal fauconnerie, which was a promotion with a higher salary. At this time, Henri IV's falcon or hawk house had 97 members.[108] Richelieu in his memoirs insisted that the king also gave Luynes an annual pension of 400 écus (1,200 livres) to pay his living expenses, later increased to 1,200 écus (3,600 livres), which would have been ample since 2,000 livres a year provided for a modest lifestyle at court.[109] Whether Luynes received such a pension or not, which is dubious, he could afford by 1608 to bring his brothers to court to live with him, and he had Cadenet assist him in the fauconnerie.[110]

How did Luynes secure this place? Again, the comte Du Lude seems to have secured it for him, and may even have spoken to Henri IV on his behalf. Du Lude enjoyed the king's favor to the extent that in 1609 his eldest son, Timoléon, was named an *enfant d'honneur* or playmate of the dauphin Louis, who was nearly the same age.[111] Du Lude may also have asked Bellegarde to speak to Henri IV on Luynes's behalf. Bellegarde was one of the more elegant, refined, and charming of the king's inner circle of friends. A favorite of Henri III, Bellegarde had been present at his deathbed with Epernon and Henri de Navarre, the heir apparent, and he quickly rallied to the new king's support to become one of his favorites. Named first gentleman of the king's bedchamber and *Grand Ecuyer*, he may have asked the king for a place in the royal fauconnerie for Luynes, having already requested a place for him as a royal page. In fact, he probably did so because he was made a duke in September 1619 through Luynes's patronage.[112]

Richelieu attributed Luynes's advancement to another courtier. He wrote in his memoirs that Luynes owed his place as a royal falconer to the patronage of Guillaume Fouquet, sieur de La Varenne (1560–1616).[113] La Varenne, a commoner, had begun his career in the household of the king's sister, and then had joined Henri IV's household in 1583. Ennobled by the king on the battlefield of Fontaine-Françoise for handing him a gun at a critical moment, La Varenne became a royal favorite and was often employed on confidential missions requiring discretion such as carrying messages to the king's mistresses. Accompanying Henri incognito whenever he went carousing in the evenings, La Varenne acquired the reputation of finding women for him. The king rewarded him with several minor household positions and the titles of marquis de La Varenne, baron de Sainte Suzanne, and a knight in the order of Saint Michel; the offices of postal controller general, lieutenant-general of Anjou, councillor of state, and governor of the cities of Angers and La Flèche; and a pension, four abbeys, a priory, and lands in Anjou.[114]

Du Lude may have asked La Varenne to help him find Luynes a place in the king's household because La Flèche, where La Varenne was born and of which he became governor, was only twenty kilometers from Le Lude, so they were neighbors. La Varenne was newly ennobled, however, and despite being a royal favorite, he was socially far beneath Du Lude and Bellegarde, who were great feudal nobles. It seems more likely that Du Lude would have asked Bellegarde for help, especially since he had done so in the past.

Richelieu probably suggested that Luynes owed his advancement to La Varenne in order to tarnish his reputation by association. La Varenne was of humble birth with a reputation for pimping, and by association so was Luynes. Richelieu always insisted that Luynes was a low-born Provençal servant who had advanced himself by catering to a boy's whims and manipulating him. With a strong whiff of scandal clinging to him, La Varenne's patronage better suited Richelieu's portrayal of Luynes as a conniving arriviste than the patronage of either Bellegarde or Du Lude, who were great court nobles. Historians have tended to accept Richelieu's account of Luynes's lowly origins,[115] meager fortune,[116] and advancement through La Varenne's patronage,[117] but these were falsehoods meant to discredit him.

Joseph Bergin has noted that Richelieu's family origins, in fact, were similar to Luynes's, since the du Plessis family had been quite undistinguished before the early sixteenth century. They were modest in rank and fortune, and had only acquired the fief of Richelieu in 1488. Luynes's family had owned fiefs for a century before they did. Richelieu had also begun his court career in household service as grand almoner in Anne of Austria's household before becoming intendant of the Queen Mother's household.[118] Successful court careers often began with service in royal households.[119] Richelieu's disparaging comments about Luynes's origins, therefore, appear duplicitous when viewed against his own similar background. A master of the slur and innuendo, Richelieu was skilled at making damaging remarks about others based on a mixture of half-truths, implications, and exaggerations, and he even fabricated untruths when these suited his purpose.

Pamphlets sponsored by the Queen Mother lampooned Luynes as a domestic servant and a bird keeper. Richelieu remarked disdainfully that all Luynes had ever done was train hunting birds and find birds for the king to hunt, thus encouraging him in childish pastimes. Richelieu and the pamphleteers insisted that Luynes had begun his service as a page in Du Lude's household, a lesser position than that of gentleman which he had actually held, or even that he had begun as a non-noble valet. Luynes's years as a royal stable page indicating noble birth and military training were ignored.[120] The anti-Luynes pamphleteers portrayed him as another Haran, the elderly ex-soldier of common birth who was the royal kennel master. The king visited him often at the kennels where they cooked and ate omelettes together, and gave him a gift of 500 écus (1,500 livres) to show his favor.[121] Haran lacked the rank, training, and experience to hold high office, and by implication so did Luynes.

Luynes is first mentioned on 28 November 1611 in the journal of the king's doctor, Héroard, who recorded that the half-asleep king had cried out, "Oh, how beautiful it is! How beautiful it is, the lure, the lure. Luynes, Luynes." Héroard, who spelled his name "Loines," noted laconically, "He is the gentleman in charge of his merlins."[122] Luynes took care of the king's favorite hunting birds, the small falcons known as merlins. A lure was an object of leather and feathers attached to a long cord, used by falconers to recall their birds. Lures were often quite beautiful, and Luynes must have helped the king to make a particularly handsome one. The lonely 10-year-old was overwhelmed by the pressures of his new position.[123] An excellent rider, he loved hunting, which became the great passion of his life, and allowed him to escape the gawking crowds of courtiers in the Louvre and his coldly critical mother into the fields and forests around Paris. The sunshine, fresh air, and wind on his face as he galloped through the countryside must have been exhilarating and liberating, and Luynes was a part of these happy times. Hunting not only offered the king an escape from the court and the duties of kingship, but also provided him with an inner circle of friends who went hunting with him.[124] He had first hunted at the age of three, and he began hawking at six, becoming accomplished at this sport, which fascinated him. By 1611, he was hunting with his dogs and falcons outside Paris at least once a week, sometimes as often as four times, and by 1615, he was hunting regularly on Mondays, Wednesdays, and Saturdays.[125]

Charles d'Arcussia, the author of a well-known book on falconry, described a day spent hawking with the king at Saint Denis. The hunting party had not ridden far when someone spied a crested lark. Luynes brought up two merlins named Demoiselle and Sparrow Tiercelet, and handed them to the king. By this time, the crested lark had flown away. When the merlins were released, they followed in swift pursuit and killed it. Two other merlins, Fousque and Baron, were brought up. The king took Fousque on his wrist, and the party rode on looking for more birds. A flock of skylarks rose into the air, and the merlins were released to follow them out of sight, soon returning with those they had killed to the king who was very pleased.[126]

Luynes taught hard-to-train magpies and hawks, whose talons had been removed so they could not kill, to swoop down and seize little song birds and pigeons, who were unable to fly away because they had no tail feathers. The magpies and hawks would then bring back these little birds alive to the king, who was enchanted with this cruel game, which could be played endlessly in his private apartments or in the palace corridors and galleries.[127] When Richelieu remarked that Luynes's favor came from his ability to train birds, he probably had this game in mind. He was implying that Luynes had trained the king in the same way.[128] Falconry was already an arcane sport at this time, and Luynes became a royal favorite because he could teach its finer points to a boy fascinated by it.[129]

Luynes specialized in the greater flights of hunting birds, that is, falcons flown from the lure. The royal hawk house was divided into greater and lesser flights of birds, *hauts* and *bas vols*. Charles d'Arcussia, who had visited the fauconnerie in 1615, noted that Luynes assisted by his brother Cadenet and ten other men was in charge of the *vol pour milan*, a greater flight featuring the small black hawks known as kites or *milans*, male and female gyrfalcons, sakers or great falcons, buzzards, and black fishing eagles among the most difficult birds to train and fly. Luynes was also in charge of the *vol pour émerillon*, the small falcons known as merlins, the king's favorite hunting birds.[130]

Falcons were long-winged with black eyes and notched beaks. They were flown from the lure on open land where they could rise swiftly to hover over their prey, then swoop down with lethal precision like an arrow to the target. Hawks belonged to the lesser flight of hunting birds. Shorter in the wing with yellow eyes and curved beaks, they were flown from the fist and were adept at chasing their prey over wooded ground. Falcons were released to circle above game flushed by dogs from cover or water. They also pursued their quarry in the air until they could strike from above. Crow hunting when the prey was seized in the air was one of the most spectacular flights in falconry. Falcons were flown in the air against jaybirds, magpies, wild hawks, herons, and buzzards. In game hunting, the prey was lifted from the woods and fields by hawks flown from the fist against fur (hares and rabbits) and feather (pheasants, quail, partridges, ducks, and wild geese). Merlins and sparrow hawks were flown against song birds and pigeons.[131]

Luynes saw even more of the king after he was put in charge of the *oiseaux du cabinet* sometime during 1611. The king had started a personal collection of hunting birds, mostly the smaller falcons, because he liked to keep some of them in his rooms, and Luynes was put in charge of these birds.[132] How did he receive such a coveted appointment? Nicolas de Vitry, who had recently replaced his father as a captain in the royal guards, and his friend La Curée, who commanded the light horse company in the royal guards, decided that they could gain greater favor by suggesting to the king that he appoint someone to look after his personal collection of hunting birds. This person would be known as the king's *maître du cabinet des oiseaux*, and Vitry had in mind the sieur de La Coudrelle, a member of the royal light horse company. La Coudrelle often went hawking with the king who liked him. So, Vitry and La Curée proposed La Coudrelle to the king for this new position. From the king's reaction, they thought they had been successful and did not keep the appointment a secret, which was a mistake. Gilles de Souvré, the king's governor, heard about it and sought this position for his eldest son, Jean, marquis de Courtenvaux, whom the king liked. Souvré asked Concini, the Queen Mother's favorite, to help him secure the new position for his son.

Concini, however, did not intend for either La Coudrelle or Courtenvaux to have this appointment, which he wanted for one of his own clients. Concini chose Luynes for it because he knew falconry; the king liked him; and Concini considered him "un fort bon homme," who would recognize his obligation to him by helping to increase his influence over the king. This suggests that Luynes was not yet a client, but that he had made himself agreeable to the Queen Mother's favorite, who expected that his appointment would make him a client. It must have helped Luynes in securing Concini's favor that his family was Italian in origin; his personal circumstances were modest; and he was twenty-three years older than the king. At Concini's request, Souvré reluctantly suggested to the king that Luynes be appointed instead. The king was delighted because he preferred Luynes who got the appointment, and Fontenay-Mareuil commented that everyone involved in the affair was astonished and chagrined when Luynes later became a royal favorite.[133]

The occupation of falconer reveals something about Luynes's character. A medieval guide to hawking noted that a falconer had to be patient, good-tempered, shrewd, and inventive with keen eyesight, sharp hearing, a strong voice, and a habit of sleeping lightly in order to hear his birds at night if they became agitated.[134] Catching, taming, and training wild birds of prey took both patience and intelligence, while caring for them took reliability and gentleness. Much time and energy were spent in keeping the birds alive and in a good condition to fly. They needed a daily ration of fresh meat, their droppings inspected for illness, their feathers and talons groomed, and their hawk house kept clean, warm, and dry. They had to be carefully watched because they were subject to numerous diseases and parasites, and died quickly if they became ill. They were difficult to obtain and expensive to replace, so it was wise to keep them as strong and well-fed as possible.[135] Arcussia devoted a large part of his book on falconry to the diseases his birds developed and his remedies for curing them.[136] Because it took skill and perseverance to capture and train these birds, Luynes necessarily had to be patient, calm, and intelligent.

Able to understand his birds and empathize with their reactions, he also had to be gentle, kind, and caring. Sixteenth-century French society did not value these qualities in noblemen, who were expected to be warriors and men of action.[137] Luynes's father fitted the contemporary noble ideal of martial valor better than he did. Exhibiting feminine traits of gentleness and empathy was considered unmanly and weak, making Luynes vulnerable to ridicule and charges of timidity and cowardice.

An anti-Luynes pamphleteer remarked that the favorite's sword had complained it was rusty because it was never used, abandoned in a corner and "unhappy like women who fall under the yoke of impotent husbands." Another pamphleteer declared that the favorite's death demonstrated his cowardice because he had died in bed, not on the battlefield, while still another asserted that Luynes was "the most timid poltroon (coward) ever to come from Provence."[138] Richelieu remarked that Luynes had never gotten within cannon range of the besieged city of Montauban.[139] Luynes's surgeon supposedly told his wife that she should not worry he might be killed during the 1621 campaign because he was always with the favorite, meaning that he was behind the lines far from the fighting. Luynes was said, falsely, to have only visited the front once during a two-hour truce.[140] The surgeon's anecdote appeared in the memoirs of the duc de La Force, commander of the besieged city of Montauban, which suggests that it was court gossip whispered behind the favorite's back with much sniggering.[141] Of doubtful veracity, it has been given too much credence by historians.[142] Character traits of empathy and kindness made Luynes a royal favorite, and did not demonstrate his cowardice or stupidity, whatever his enemies may have claimed.

Most members of the fauconnerie were commoners by birth. There were about ninety-five members in 1640, and only twenty-seven or one-quarter were noble. They included the heads of the nine different *vols* or flights, their assistants, and four pages.[143] The membership had been much the same in 1585 and 1615.[144] The percentage of nobles was even less in the royal kennels and hunt (*vénerie*), which had 55 nobles among approximately 265 members in 1640 or about 20 percent.[145] Noble gentlemen of the fauconnerie like those of the stables and hunt came from the provincial sword nobility, and wore royal livery as servants did. Great nobles who held the higher offices in the king's household did not wear livery.[146] The provincial origins of royal falconers and their performance in livery of menial tasks added a taint of baseness to their rank similar to that acquired in household service, which was another reason why Richelieu was able to declare that Luynes was a lowly domestic servant.

Luynes, in fact, came from a Midi noble family who had soldiered for the crown for nearly two hundred years. He was not low-born, foreign, Protestant, or an obscure provincial noble. His French Catholic family belonged to the *noblesse seconde* of the Rhône river valley with branches in Languedoc, Dauphiné, Provence, and the Comtat Venaissin. His father had owned four fiefs, enjoyed a comfortable income, was known at court, and had fought for a Catholic monarchy for almost forty years. Luynes was no more an upstart or a parvenu than Richelieu was. He was badly educated as most nobles were, but this did not make him muddle-headed or stupid. He had received a military education, and he was in charge of two departments in the royal fauconnerie with fifteen to twenty men under his supervision. He had spent most of his adult life at court, having served eight years as a page in the royal stables and seven years as an ordinary gentleman in a courtier's household before joining the king's household as a falconer. He had obtained these positions through the patronage of Du Lude and Bellegarde, who were great court nobles, and he probably would have lived out his days as a minor member of the king's household if he had not attracted the attention of a lonely boy fascinated by falconry. The fatherless young king became fond of this kind supportive older man who shared his love of birds. Luynes's caring concern for the king indicates the intelligence, patience, and empathy that made him a royal favorite, not the cowardice, ignorance, or baseness described by his enemies.

Notes

1   Charles, comte Horric de Beaucaire, ed. *Mémoires du Cardinal de Richelieu*, 10 vols. (Paris, 1907–31), I, 304, 306.

2   *Félix et Thomas Platter à Montpellier* (Montpellier, 1892, Marseille, 1971), pp. 180–1.

3   Catherine de Médicis, *Lettres*, eds. Hector de La Ferrière and Gustave Baguenault de Puchesse. 11 vols. (Paris, 1880–95), V, 105, X, 378; Gustave Brunet et al., eds., *Mémoires-journaux de Pierre de l'Estoile*, 11 vols. (Paris, 1875–83), I, 33.

4   B.N., Cabinet des Titres, Dossiers bleus 8, fols. 1–2, 7, 115–17; B. Inguimbertine, ms. 1847, fols. 190v–2; Jean-Antoine Pithon-Curt, *Histoire de la noblesse du Comté Venaissin*, 4 vols. (Paris, 1743–50), IV, 147–53; A.C., Pont-Saint-Esprit, CC 3, fol. 16; CC 7, fols. 1–71; FF4; Marcel Gouron, *Inventaire archives communales Pont-Saint-Esprit* (Nimes, 1947), pp. 161–2, 199; François Bluche, *Les Honneurs de la cour* (Paris, 1957), 2 vols., I, non-paginated.

5 B.N., Dossiers bleus 8, fol. 114; B. Inguimbertine, ms. 1847, fols. 190–190v; Pithon-Curt, *Noblesse*, IV, 151, 156–7, 159–161; René de Borricand, *Nobiliaire de Provence*, 3 vols. (Aix, 1974–79), II, 1135–6; Edouard Baratier et al., *Atlas historique* (Paris, 1969), p. 111.

6 Pithon-Curt, *Noblesse*, IV, 162; B.N., Dossiers bleus 8, fol. 113.

7 Ibid., fols. 28, 113, royal letters dated 27 July 1565; B. Inguimbertine, ms. 1147, fol 188v; Pithon-Curt, *Noblesse*, IV, 162.

8 B.N., Dossiers bleus 8, fols. 29, 113v, royal brevet of 1 December 1569; Pithon-Curt, *Noblesse*, IV, 162; Catherine de Médicis, *Lettres*, X, 263–4.

9 B.N., Dossiers bleus 8, fols. 113–14v; Baluze 214, fols. 88, 90; B. Inguimbertine, ms. 1847, fols. 188v–9v; A.C., Pont-Saint-Esprit, BB 1, fols. 310–11, 314–16, 334 (1572–74); CC 57 (1571–74), 58 (1577); GG 1 (12 January 1578); *Inventaire Pont-Saint-Esprit*, pp. 16–18, 175, 208; Charles Achard, *Dictionnaire de la Provence et du Comtat Venaissin*, 4 vols. (Marseille 1786–87, Geneva, 1971), I, 459–461; A.C. Beaucaire, BB 12, 13, 14; EE 26; *Inventaire archives communales, Beaucaire, série BB* (Nîmes, 1867), pp. 4–7; James Wood, *The King's Army* (Cambridge, 1996), p. 77; Marcel Gouron, *Histoire de la ville du Pont-Saint-Esprit* (Nîmes, 1934), pp. 93–4.

10 B.N., Dossiers bleus 8, fols. 33, 112v; ms. fr. 2748, fol. 127; Baluze 214, fols. 70–3; B. Inguimbertine, ms. 1847, fols. 187v–8, copies of their marriage contract.

11 Pithon-Curt, *Noblesse*, III, 106–9, IV, 161–2, 168; Borricand, *Nobiliaire*, II, 1040; B. Avignon, ms. 1786, fols. 40–40v, 50–50v; B.N., Baluze 214, fols. 71–71v; B. Inguimbertine, ms. 1847, fol. 26.

12 Robert Bailly, *Dictionnaire des communes: Vaucluse* (Avignon, 1985), pp. 292–4; idem, *Les Châteaux historiques vauclusiens* (Avignon, 1979), pp. 89–92.

13 Edouard Baratier, ed., *Histoire de la Provence* (Toulouse, 1969), p. 229; René Mouliérac-Lamoreux, *Le Comtat Venaissin pontifical* (Avignon, 1977), pp. 396–8.

14 *Recueil des pièces les plus curieuses qui ont esté faites pendant le règne du Connestable M. de Luynes* (Paris, 1628), *Le Comtadin Provençal*, p. 111; Beaucaire, *Mémoires de Richelieu*, III, 189.

15 B.N., Dossiers bleus 8, fols. 112–17; B. Inguimbertine, ms. 1847, fols. 187–192v. Genealogies can be found in B.N., Dupuy 511, fol. 51, 662, fols. 36–54; Clairambault 1148, fols. 41, 48; Baluze 214, fols. 62–9; Nouveau d'Hozier 5, fol. 35v-36; Duchesne 58, fol. 58; B.I.F, Collection Godefroy 519, fols. 288–90; B, Arsenal, ms. 5260, fol. 74.

16 Berthold Zeller, *Louis XIII, Marie de Médicis* (Paris, 1898), pp. 27–8; Elizabeth Marvick, *Louis XIII* (New Haven, 1986), p. 134; Jean Mariéjol, *Henri IV et Louis XIII* in *Histoire de France*, ed. Ernst Lavisse, 9 vols. (Paris, 1911), VI–2, 195; Louis Vaunois, *Vie de Louis XIII*, 2d edn (Paris, 1944), p. 141; Pierre Chevallier, *Louis XIII* (Paris, 1979), p. 154; Michel Carmona, *Marie de Médicis* (Paris, 1981), p. 322; François Bluche, ed., *Dictionnaire du Grand Siècle* (Paris, 1990), p. 922; A. Lloyd Moote, *Louis XIII* (Berkeley, 1989), p. 80.

17 J.H.M. Salmon, "A Second Look at the *noblesse seconde*," *Fr Hist Stud* 25 (2002), 575–93.

18 B.N., Dupuy 92, fol. 113; Clairambault 1132, *Le Comtadin Provençal*, p. 3; Gédéon Tallemant des Réaux, *Historiettes*, ed. Antoine Adam, 2 vols. (Paris, 1960–61), I, 157; Pithon-Curt, *Noblesse*, IV, 170; Achard, *Dictionnaire*, I, 462; François-Alexandre Aubert de La Chesnaye-Desbois, *Dictionnaire de la noblesse*, 19 vols. (Paris, 1863–76), I, 232.

19 B.N., Dossiers bleus 8, fols. 1v-2; Jean-François Michaud, *Biographie universelle*, 45 vols. (Paris, 1854, Graz, 1986), XXV, 524; Casimir Barjavel, *Dictionnaire historique du départment de Vaucluse*, 2 vols. (Carpentras, 1841), I, 28; Gouron, *Histoire du Pont-Saint-Esprit*, p. 95; Auguste Aubert, *Les Vauclusiens*, 2 vols. (Avignon 1890–92), I, 4.

20 Private communication from Michel Hayez, director of the Archives départementales of the Vaucluse at Avignon. A.C. Mornas, GG 1, 1577–78; A.C., Pont-Saint-Esprit, GG 1, 1 January 1571 to 27 April 1578, baptismal registers; GG 2, 15 December 1588 to 30 January 1592.

21 B.N., Dossiers bleus 8, fol. 57; Pithon-Curt, *Noblesse*, IV, 170; Baptiste Legrain, *Décade commençant l'histoire du Roy Louis XIII* (Paris, 1618), p. 269.

22 Pithon-Curt, *Noblesse*, III, 106–7, 109; IV, 167.

23 Gouron, *Histoire du Pont-Saint-Esprit*, pp. 95–6.

24 Zeller, *Louis XIII: Marie de Médicis*, p. 27; Marvick, *Louis XIII*, p. 134; Moote, *Louis XIII*, p. 80; Mariéjol, *Henri IV et Louis XIII*, p. 195.

25 Pithon-Curt, *Noblesse*, IV, 168, 389–98; Mack Holt, *The Duke of Anjou and the Politique Struggle during the War of Religion* (Cambridge, 1986), p. 215; Marin Le Roy, sieur de Gomberville, ed., *Les Mémoires de Monsieur le duc de Nevers*, 2 vols. (Paris, 1665), I, 370.

26 Holt, *The Duke of Anjou*, pp. 29–44; Gomberville, *Les Mémoires de Nevers*, I, 354–64.

27 Ibid., I, 355.

28 Pithon-Curt, *Noblesse*, IV, 163–4; Théodore Agrippa d'Aubigné, *Histoire universelle*, ed. A. de Ruble, 10 vols. (Paris, 1886–1909, Geneva, 1987), VI, 198–202; Gomberville, *Les Mémoires de Nevers*, I, 73.

29 B.N., Dossiers bleus 8, fol. 114; A.C., Beaucaire, BB 14; *Inventaire Beaucaire*, p. 5; Gouron, *Histoire du Pont-Saint-Esprit*, p. 94; Claude de Vic and Joseph Vaissete, *Histoire générale de Languedoc*, 15 vols. (Toulouse, 1872–92), XI, 660.

30 Pithon-Curt, *Noblesse*, IV, 164–5; A.C., Pont-Saint-Esprit, CC 57; *Inventaire Pont-Saint-Esprit*, p. 175; A.C., Beaucaire, BB 14; *Inventaire Beaucaire*, p. 5; Gouron, *Histoire du Pont-Saint-Esprit*, p. 94; Mack Holt, "Patterns of *Clientèle*: The Household of François, Duke of Anjou," *Fr Hist Stud*, 13 (1984), 305–22; idem, *The Duke of Anjou*, pp. 56–8, 67, 218.

31 Gomberville, *Les Mémoires de Nevers*, I, 73, 577–8, 588.

32 B.N., Dossiers bleus 8, fol. 114; B. Inguimbertine, ms. 1847, fol. 190; Pithon-Curt, *Noblesse*, IV, 164–5.

33 Gomberville, *Les Mémoires de Nevers*, I, 598.

34 Agrippa d'Aubigné, *Histoire universelle*, VI, 208.

35 Ibid., VI, 117–18; Gouron, *Histoire du Pont-Saint-Esprit*, p. 95; Vic and Vaissete, *Histoire de Languedoc*, XI, 625 and n.3, 626.

36 B.N., Dossiers bleus 8, fol. 113; B. Inguimbertine, ms. 1847, fols. 188–188v; Pithon-Curt, *Noblesse*, IV, 165; Michaud, *Biographie universelle*, XXV, 524, n.1.

37 François Billaçois, *Le Duel dans la société française* (Paris, 1986), p. 380, n.56; *Mercure françois*, VI (1619), 191; B.N., imprimés Lb 36, *Le Tourment de l'envie courtisane* (1619).

38 Gouron, *Histoire du Pont-Saint-Esprit*, p. 95; Catherine de Médicis, *Lettres*, X, 419; Berger de Xivrey and Joseph Gaudet, eds., *Recueil des lettres missives de Henri IV*, 9 vols. (Paris, 1843–76), I, 115, 21 December 1576; Vic and Vaissete, *Histoire de Languedoc*, XI, 625–6, n.2.

39 Ibid., XI, 626, n.2; B.N., Ms. fr. 3420, fol. 20, 20 December 1576.

40 B.N., Dossiers bleus 8, fol. 9; B. Inguimbertine, Ms. 1847, fol. 190; Pithon-Curt, *Noblesse*, IV, 166–7; Gouron, *Histoire du Pont-Saint-Esprit*, p. 96; La Chesnaye-Desbois, *Dictionnaire de la noblesse*, I, 231; Henri III, roi de France, *Lettres*, ed. Michel François, 4 vols. (Paris, 1959–84), III, 179, March 1577.

41 A.C., Pont-Saint-Esprit, CC 58; *Inventaire sommaire de Pont-Saint-Esprit*, p. 175.

42 B.N., Pièces originales 21, fol. 138.

43 Henri III, *Lettres*, III, 290–1.

44 B.N., Cinq Cents de Colbert 9, fol. 31.

45 Gouron, *Histoire du Pont-Saint-Esprit*, p. 96; A.C., Beaucaire, BB 13; *Inventaire Beaucaire*, p. 5.

46 A.C., Beaucaire, BB 14; *Inventaire Beaucaire*, p. 5; Catherine de Médicis, *Lettres*, VI, 400; Pierre Chevallier, *Henri III* (Paris, 1985), p. 471; Vic and Vaissete, *Histoire de Languedoc*, XI, 660.

47 Catherine de Médicis, *Lettres*, VI, 29, n. 3, 20 June 1578, 105–6, 5 November 1578.

48 B.N., Dossiers bleus 8, fol. 113v; Pithon-Curt, *Noblesse*, IV, 167; Gouron, *Histoire du Pont-Saint-Esprit*, pp. 96, n.4, 97, n.1; Achard, *Dictionnaire de la Provence*, I, 461.

49 Jacqueline Boucher, *Société et mentalités autour de Henri III*, 4 vols. (Lille and Paris, 1981), I, 403; B.N., Ms. fr. 26166, fol. 1746; A.C., Beaucaire, BB 16; *Inventaire Beaucaire*, p. 16.

50 Holt, *The Duke of Anjou*, p. 152.

51 B.N., Dossiers bleus 8, fol. 99; Tallemant des Réaux, *Historiettes*, I, 157, n. 4; Pithon-Curt, *Noblesse*, IV, 167.

52 Holt, *The Duke of Anjou*, pp. 155–6, 158.

53 Gouron, *Histoire du Pont-Saint-Esprit*, p. 96. Honoré's nephew was captain of a regiment levied in Provence and the Dauphiné in August 1578 for Anjou's expedition to the Netherlands.

54 Louis Batiffol, *Le Roi Louis XIII à vingt ans* (Paris, 1910), p. 480, n. 1; Michaud, *Biographie universelle*, XXV, 524, n. 1. Batiffol and Michaud consulted these letters, written in 1582 and 1583, in the family archives, which no longer exist.

55 B.N., Dupuy 937, fol. 93v, an unhelpful, undated letter from Henri III in response to a letter from Honoré asking how he might serve the king.

56 Pithon-Curt, *Noblesse*, IV, 168–9.

57 Holt, *The Duke of Anjou*, pp. 208–9.

58 A.C., Beaucaire, BB 16; Agrippa d'Aubigné, *Histoire universelle*, VI, 119; Batiffol, *Le Roi Louis XIII*, p. 480, n. 1; Michaud, *Biographie universelle*, XXV, 524, n. 1.

59 Victor Cousin, "Le Duc et connêtable de Luynes," *Journal des Savants* (May 1861), 266, n. 1; Zeller, *Marie de Médicis*, p. 27.

60 Pithon-Curt, *Noblesse*, IV, 167; Achard, *Dictionnaire*, I, 461.

61 Gouron, *Histoire du Pont-Saint-Esprit*, p. 108; La Chesnaye-Desbois, *Dictionnaire de la noblesse*, I, 231.

62 B.N., Dossiers bleus 8, fols. 112–112v; B. Inguimbertine, ms. 1847, fol. 187v; Pithon-Curt, *Noblesse*, IV, 168. His will was dated February 6, 1592.

63 Moote, *Louis XIII*, p. 80; Charles Bernard, *Histoire des guerres de Louis XIII* (Paris, 1636), pp. 242–3; *Recueil, Les Psaumes des Courtisans* (1622), p. 399.

64 B.N., Dupuy 93, fol. 113; 662, fol. 36v.

65 B.N., Dossiers bleus 8, fols. 112–112v. Luynes is now a commuting suburb of Aix and Marseille, and the site of a modern prison built in 1990.

66 A florin was a Florentine coin in gold and silver, which in late sixteenth-century Marseille was worth 121 sous or between 6 and 7 livres. Its value fluctuated. Wolfgang Kaiser, *Marseille au temps des troubles*, trans. Florence Chaix (Paris, 1992), p. 356.

67 B. Avignon, ms. 1786, fols. 38–42.

68 Ibid., fols. 34–42, 50–8, 60–4; 2098, fols. 50–50v; Pithon-Curt, *Noblesse*, IV, 161–2.

69 Bailly, *Dictionnaire des communes*, pp. 292–3.

70 Beaucaire, *Mémoires de Richelieu*, I, 305. "Ils y acquirent une petite maison du président d'Ardaillon, d'Aix-en-Provence … une métairie chétive, nommée Brantes, assise sur une roche, où il fit planter une vigne, et une île que le Rhône a quasi toute mangé, appelée Cadenet …". This description was repeated by Zeller, *Louis XIII, Marie de Médicis*, p. 28; Vaunois, *Louis XIII*, p. 141; Chevallier, *Louis XIII*, p. 154; Marvick, *Louis XIII*, p. 134; Mariéjol, *Henri IV et Louis XIII*, p. 195; Gabriel Hanotaux and the duc de la Force, *Histoire du Cardinal de Richelieu*, 6 vols. (Paris, 1893–1947), vol. II, part 1, 107.

71 Wood, *The King's Army*, pp. 88, 244–5, 275–81; Roger Doucet, *Les Institutions de la France au XVIe siècle*, 2 vols. (Paris, 1948), II, 165–6, 625, 638; Jonathan Dewald, *Pont-St-Pierre, 1398–1789* (Berkeley, 1987), p. 179.

72 Ibid., p. 181; B.N., Mélanges Colbert 324, 325; T.J.A. Le Goff, "Essai sur les pensions royales," *Etat, marine et société*, eds. Martine Acerra et al. (Paris, 1995), pp. 252–81.

73 A.C., Pont-Saint-Esprit, C 46; *Inventaire sommaire de Pont-Saint-Esprit*, p. 169; Gouron, *Histoire du Pont-Saint-Esprit*, pp. 107, n.1, 108.

74 Henri III, *Lettres*, III, 290–1; Gouron, *Histoire du Pont-Saint-Esprit*, pp. 104–8.

75 Xavier Le Person, *"Practiques" et "Practiqueurs:" La vie politique à la fin du règne de Henri III* (Geneva, 2002).

76 Audiger, *La Maison reglée* (Paris, 1692), in Alfred Franklin, *La Vie privée d'autrefois. La Vie de Paris sous Louis XIV* (Paris, 1898), p. 29; Maximin Deloche, *La Maison du Cardinal de Richelieu* (Paris, 1912), pp. 321, 329; Mark Motley, *Becoming a French Aristocrat* (Princeton, 1990), pp. 20–1, n. 1, 66.

77 Beaucaire, *Mémoires de Richelieu*, I, 305.

78 *La Fauconnerie de Charles d'Arcussia de Capre, seigneur d'Esparron, de Pallières et du Revest, en Provence,*

divisée en trois livres (Aix-en-Provence, 1598). The edition used here is Charles d'Arcussia, *La Fauconnerie ... divisée en dix parties* (Rouen, 1643), p. 166.

79 B.N., Ms. fr. 3795, fol. 100; Clairambault 374, fol. 290; Cinq Cents de Colbert 97, fols. 100, 102; Moote, *Louis XIII*, p. 104; Batiffol, *Le Roi Louis XIII*, p. 489.

80 Boucher, *Société et mentalités*, II, 633–7; Roland Mousnier, *The Institutions of France*, 2 vols., *Society and the State*, trans. Brian Pearce (Chicago, 1979), I, 166.

81 Père Anselme de Sainte Marie, *Histoire généalogique et chronologique de la Maison royale*, 3rd edn, 9 vols. (Paris, 1723–33, New York, 1967), VIII, 191–2, IV, 334.

82 Gomberville, *Les Mémoires de Nevers*, I, 586.

83 Wood, *The King's Army*, pp. 24–7, 254; DBF, IX, 1500; Michaud, *Biographie universelle*, XXV, 524, 442; Catherine de Médicis, *Lettres*, X, 263–4; Pithon-Curt, *Noblesse*, IV, 162.

84 Nicolas Le Roux, *La Faveur du Roi* (Paris, 2001), p. 128.

85 Tallemant des Réaux, *Historiettes*, I, 157.

86 B.N., Dossiers bleus 8, fol. 57; Legrain, *Décade du Roy Louis XIII*, p. 269; Pithon-Curt, *Noblesse*, IV, 170.

87 David Buisseret, *Henri IV* (London, 1984), pp. 28, 105; Louis Batiffol, "Louis XIII et le duc de Luynes," *Rev hist* 102 (1909), 242, n. 3.

88 Tallemant des Réaux, *Historiettes*, I, 157.

89 Jean Du Tillet, *Recueil des Roys de France* (Paris, 1618), p. 430; Edouard Barthélemy, *Les Grands Ecuyers et la Grande Ecurie* (Paris, 1867), pp. 19–20; Hubert Willems and Jean-Yves Conan, *Liste alphabétique des pages de la Grande Ecurie* (Dison-Verviers, 1962), pp. 15–17; Marcel Marion, *Dictionnaire des institutions de la France aux XVIIe et XVIIIe siècles* (Paris, 1968), p. 413; François Bluche, *Les Pages de la Grande Ecurie*, 3 vols. (Paris, 1967), I, introduction; Motley, *Becoming a French Aristocrat*, pp. 178–9; Jeroen Duindam, *Vienna and Versailles* (Cambridge, 2003), p. 57.

90 Tallemant des Réaux, *Historiettes*, I, 157; Edouard Fournier, ed., *Variétés historiques et littéraires*, 10 vols. (Paris, 1855–63), III, 269, "Pasquil de la Cour;" Batiffol, "Louis XIII et le duc de Luynes," *Rev hist* 102 (1909), 244; idem, *Le Roi Louis XIII*, pp. 481–2.

91 Daniel Reytier and Daniel Roche, eds., *Les Ecuries royales du XVIe au XVIIIe siècle* (Versailles, 1998), pp. 61–5; Henri Lemoine, "Les Ecuries du Roi," *Revue de l'histoire de Versailles* 35 (1933), 152–83; Olivier Chaline, "The Valois and Bourbon Courts," *The Princely Courts of Europe*, ed. John Adamson (London, 1999), p. 70; Willems, *Liste des pages de la Grande Ecurie*, p. 16; Bluche, *Dictionnaire*, pp. 521–2; Barthélemy, *Les Grands Ecuyers*, p. 30; Boucher, *Société et mentalités*, I, 209; Sophie Laverny, *Les Domestiques commensaux du Roi au XVIIe siècle* (Paris, 2002), pp. 51–2.

92 Gaston de Carné, *Les Pages des Ecuries du Roy* (Paris, 1886), p. 107; Hubert Willems and Jean-Yves Conan, *Liste alphabétique des pages de la Petite Ecurie* (Dison-Verviers, 1966), p. 11; Le Roux, *La Faveur du Roi*, p. 30. The *Premier Ecuyer* supervised the *fauconnerie* where Luynes obtained an office. The names of stable pages were not recorded before 1643.

93 Bluche, *Les Pages de la Grande Ecurie*, I, introduction; Motley, *Becoming a French Aristocrat*, pp. 173–5; Willems, *Liste des pages de la Grande Ecurie*, p. 15; Laverny, *Les Domestiques*, pp. 162, 219, 310, 314.

94 Carné, *Les Pages des Ecuries*, pp. 99–162; Marcel Dugué MacCarthy, *La Cavalerie française* (Paris, 1985), pp. 93–136; Barthélemy, *Les Grands Ecuyers*, pp. 89–90; Reytier, *Les Ecuries royales*, pp. 75–81, 171–5; Willems, *Liste des pages de la Petite Ecurie*, pp. 12–4; Bluche, *Les Pages de la Grande Ecurie*, I, introduction.

95 Batiffol, "Louis XIII et le duc de Luynes," *Rev hist* 102 (1909) 250; idem, *Le Roi Louis XIII*, p. 489.

96 Ibid., pp. 488–9; Sidney Lee, ed., *The Autobiography of Edward, Lord Herbert of Cherbury* (London, 1906), p. 105.

97 Victor-Lucien Tapié, *La Politique étrangère de la France et le début de la Guerre de Trente Ans (1616–1621)* (Paris, 1934), p. 232 and n. 2.

98 Batiffol, *Le Roi Louis XIII*, p. 490.

99   Anselme, *Histoire généalogique*, VIII, 189–92; Michaud, *Biographie universelle*, XXV, 442–3; Philippe Calbo and Michel Bouttier, *Un château* (Poitiers, 1987), pp. 7–40; Jean-Pierre Labatut, *Les Ducs et pairs de France au XVIIe siècle* (Paris, 1972), pp. 93, 99.

100 Tallemant des Réaux, *Historiettes*, I, 77; Bassompierre, François de, *Journal de ma vie. Mémoires du maréchal de Bassompierre*, ed. Edouard de Chanterac. 4 vols. (Paris, 1870–77), I, 72–4.

101 A.D., Maine-et-Loire, E 2189, "Livre des gages (1616–19)," fols. 1–69; B. N., Dupuy 92, fol. 113; *Recueil, Le Comtadin Provençal*, p. 84; François Paule de Clermont, marquis de Montglat, *Mémoires*, ed. Petitot, 2nd ser., vol. 49 (Paris, 1825), p. 24; Calbo and Bouttier, *Un château*, pp. 38, 45–7.

102 Achille Halphen, ed., *Journal d'Arnauld d'Andilly 1614–1620* (Paris, 1857), pp. 368–71, 444, 450; Jean Héroard, *Journal*, ed. Madeleine Foisil, 2 vols. (Paris, 1989), II, 2633–4; Etienne Algay de Martignac, *Mémoires de Gaston, duc d'Orléans*, ed. Petitot, 2nd ser., vol. 31 (Paris, 1824), pp. 11–12, 45–6; Georges Dethan, *LaVie de Gaston d'Orléans* (Paris, 1992), pp. 369–72; Jacques Bois d'Annemets, *Mémoires d'un favory du duc d'Orléans*, *Archives curieuses de l'histoire de France*, eds. F. Danjou and M.L. Cimber, 2nd ser., vol. 2 (Paris, 1838), pp. 263–344, esp. 267–9; Bassompierre, *Journal*, II, 136, 144, 146; Calbo and Bouttier, *Un château*, p. 45; Tallemant des Réaux, *Historiettes*, I, 768, n. 4; Beaucaire, *Mémoires de Richelieu*, II, 382; Jean Charay, ed., *Vie du maréchal Jean-Baptiste d'Ornano* (Grenoble, 1971), p. 61 and n.48.

103 A.D. Maine-et-Loire, E 2189, fol. 1; Franklin, *La Vie privée*, pp. 29–30; Claude Fleury, *Le Devoir des maîtres et des domestiques* (Paris, 1688), pp. 87–90, 93, 152–62, 175–7.

104 Katia Béguin, *Les Princes de Condé* (Paris, 1999), pp. 208–9; Holt, "Patterns of *Clientèle*," 309–11; S. Amanda Eurich, *The Economics of Power* (Kirksville, MO, 1994), p. 108; Laverny, *Les Domestiques*, pp. 310–16; Deloche, *La Maison du Cardinal Richelieu*, pp. 53–4; A.D. Maine-et-Loire, E 2189, fols. 1–69.

105 Wendy Gibson, *Women in Seventeenth-Century France* (New York, 1989), pp. 97–100; André Burguière et al., *A History of the Family*, 2 vols, *The Impact of Modernity*, II, trans. Sarah Hanbury Tenison et al. (Cambridge, MA, 1996), 42; Sharon Kettering, "The Household Service of Early Modern French Noblewomen," *Fr Hist Stud* 20 (1997), 78–82; Jean-Pierre Gutton, *Domestiques et serviteurs dans la France de l'Ancien Régime* (Paris, 1980), pp. 52–3, 65–6; Philippe Ariès, "Le Service domestique: permanence et variations," *XVIIe siècle* 129 (1980), 415–20.

106 Beaucaire, *Mémoires de Richelieu*, II, 26, 199; III, 185, 188, 190.

107 Joseph Bergin, *The Rise of Richelieu* (New Haven, 1991), pp. 50–115.

108 A.D. Maine-et-Loire, E 2189, fol. 1. Luynes's position had an annual salary of 300 livres in 1585, and about 700 livres in 1639. Eugène Griselle, *Ecurie, vénerie, fauconnerie et louveterie du Roi Louis XIII* (Paris, 1912), pp. 28–9; A.N., KK 145, non-paginated; Philippe Salvadori, *La Chasse sous l'Ancien Régime* (Paris, 1996), p. 195.

109 Beaucaire, *Mémoires de Richelieu*, I, 307; Henri Griffet, *Histoire du règne de Louis XIII*, 3 vols. (Paris, 1758), I, 95; Jacqueline Boucher, *La Cour de Henri III* (La Guerche-en-Bretagne, 1986), p. 84.

110 A.D. Maine-et-Loire, E 2189, fol. 1; Arcussia, *La Fauconnerie*, p. 265.

111 Eugène Griselle, *Etat de la maison du roi Louis XIII* (Paris, 1912), p. 48.

112 Tallemant des Réaux, *Historiettes*, I, 24–30; Anselme, *Histoire généalogique*, IV, 295, 303, 306; Jean-Pierre Babelon, *Henri IV* (Paris, 1982), pp. 290, 432, 511–f14, 632, 634, 636–7, 856–61; Buisseret, *Henry IV*, pp. 79, 86, 92, 104–5, 160; Boucher, *Société et mentalités*, I, 161, 209–10, 262; Le Roux, *La Faveur du Roi*, pp. 151–2, 173–4, 421–7, 687–9, 699, 704–5, 711–12; Barthélemy, *Les Grands Ecuyers*, pp. 159–61.

113 Buisseret, *Henry IV*, p. 105; Beaucaire, *Mémoires de Richelieu*, I, 143 and n.1; *Recueil, Méditations de l'hermite Valérien* (1621), pp. 321, 332.

114 Tallemant des Réaux, *Historiettes*, I, 48, 717, 725–6; Anselme, *Histoire généalogique*, I, 471; La Chesnaye-Desbois, *Dictionnaire de la noblesse*, VIII, 493–4; Raymond Ritter, *Catherine de Bourbon*, 2 vols. (Paris, 1985), I, 342, 445; II, 149, 226, 308, 389, 404, 409, 493; Buisseret, *Henry IV*, pp. 58, 90; Babelon, *Henri IV*, pp. 634, 663–5, 698, 701, 759, 858, 861; Eusèbe Pavie, *La Guerre entre Louis XIII et Marie de Médicis* (Angers, 1899), p. 30, n. 1.

115 Beaucaire, *Mémoires de Richelieu*, I, 304, 306; François Eudes Mézeray, *Histoire de la mère et du fils*, 2 vols. (Amsterdam, 1731), I, 282–3; Tallemant des Réaux *Historiettes*, I, 157; Zeller, *Louis XIII, Marie de Médicis*, pp. 27–8; Chevallier, *Louis XIII*, p. 154; Marvick, *Louis XIII*, p. 134; Victor Cousin, *Madame Chevreuse* (Paris, 1856), p. 9; Moote, *Louis XIII*, p. 80; Carmona, *Marie de Médicis*, p. 322; Bluche, *Grand Dictionnaire*, p. 922; Mariéjol, *Henri IV et Louis XIII*, p. 195.

116 Beaucaire, *Mémoires de Richelieu*, I, 305–6. Richelieu's description has been repeated by Zeller, *Louis XIII, Marie de Médicis*, p. 28; Vaunois, *Louis XIII*, p. 141; Chevallier, *Louis XIII*, p. 154; Marvick, *Louis XIII*, p. 134; Mariéjol, *Henri IV et Louis XIII*, p. 195.

117 Zeller, *Louis XIII, Marie de Médicis*, p. 28; Vaunois, *Louis XIII*, p. 140; Hanotaux, *Histoire du Cardinal de Richelieu*, vol. II, part 1, 107.

118 Bergin, *The Rise of Richelieu*, pp. 14, 159, 188; Ruth Kleinman, *Anne of Austria* (Columbus, 1985), pp. 61–2; Elizabeth Marvick, *The Young Richelieu* (Chicago, 1983), pp. 169, 172–4.

119 Chaline, "The Valois and Bourbon Courts," pp. 72–3; Laverny, *Les Domestiques*, pp. 309–16, 333.

120 Beaucaire, *Mémoires de Richelieu*, I, 307, II, 192.

121 Héroard, *Journal*, I, 2236, 2242–3, 2251, 2272, 2299, 2305; François Du Val, marquis de Fontenay-Mareuil, *Mémoires du Messire Du Val*, ed. Louis Monmerqué, 2 vols. (Paris, 1826), I, 340.

122 Héroard, *Journal*, II, 1975.

123 Moote, *Louis XIII*, pp. 39–60.

124 Salvadori, *La Chasse*, pp. 215, 148–62.

125 Héroard, *Journal*, II, 1891–1983, 1910, 1955; Madeleine Foisil, *L'Enfant Louis XIII* (Paris, 1996), pp. 80–5; Arcussia, *La Fauconnerie*, p. 168.

126 Ibid., p. 167.

127 Ibid., p. 171; Jean-Charles Chenu, *La Fauconnerie ancienne et moderne* (Paris, 1862), pp. 20–1; Lee, *Autobiography of Cherbury*, p. 104; Tallemant des Réaux, *Historiettes*, I, 157.

128 Beaucaire, *Mémoires de Richelieu*, II, 192.

129 Richard Grassby, "The Decline of Falconry in Early Modern England," *Past and Present* 157 (1997), 57–62.

130 Arcussia, *La Fauconnerie*, p. 165; Chenu, *La Fauconnerie*, p. 13. In 1609, the *fauconnerie* was composed of 9 *vols*, one kite, two river used to hunt ducks, two crow, two magpie, and two field used to hunt game. Salvadori, *La Chasse*, p. 195.

131 Bluche, *Dictionnaire*, p. 577; William Russell, *Falconry. A Handbook for Hunters* (New York, 1940), pp. 18–19, 21, 25, 93–129; Laverny, *Les Domestiques*, pp. 40–1; Grassby, "The Decline of Falconry," 37–8; Frank Beebe, *A Falconry Manual* (Blaine, WA, 1984), pp. 41–6, 168–92; idem, *Hawks, Falcons and Falconry* (Seattle, WA, 1976), pp. 13–20; Edward Michell, *The Art and Practice of Hawking* (London, 1900), pp. 9–39, 101–49; Salvadori, *La Chasse*, pp. 37–66.

132 Ibid., p. 195; Fontenay-Mareuil, *Mémoires*, I, 137–9.

133 Ibid.

134 John Cummins, *The Hound and the Hawk* (New York, 1988), p. 220.

135 Russell, *Falconry*, pp. 33–91, 130–45; Beebe, *A Falconry Manual*, pp. 129–67; idem, *Hawks, Falcons and Falconry*, pp. 219–73; Michell, *The Art and Practice of Hawking*, pp. 225–43; Georgine Brereton and Janet Ferrier, *Le Ménagier de Paris* (Oxford, 1981), pp. 147–69.

136 Arcussia, *La Fauconnerie*, pp. 61–296.

137 J. Dewald, *Aristocratic Experience and the Origins of Modern Culture* (Berkeley, 1993), pp. 45–68; John Lynn, *Giant of the Grand Siècle* (Cambridge, 1997), pp. 248–59; F.E. Sutcliffe, *Guez de Balzac* (Paris, 1959), pp. 113–63; Stuart Carroll, *Noble Power during the French Wars of Religion* (Cambridge, 1998), pp. 116–59; Kristen Neuschel, *Word of Honor* (Cornell, 1989), pp. 38–69.

138 *Recueil, Le Comtadin Provençal*, pp. 83–4, *Requeste présentée au Roy Pluton par Conchino Conchini*, p. 73; *L'Horoscope du Connestable*, pp. 152–3; *Plaintes de l'espée de M. le Connestable*, pp. 149–50, *Le Passe Par-Tout des Favoris*, p. 156, *Méditations de l'hermite Valérien*, pp. 331–2; Beaucaire, *Mémoires de Richelieu*, II, 175; III, 183, 185, 189.

139 Ibid., III, 167.
140 *Recueil, La Chronique des Favoris*, p. 465, *L'Ombre du duc de Mayenne*, p. 379.
141 Jacques, duc de La Force, *Mémoires du duc de La Force*, ed. Marquis de La Grange, 4 vols. (Paris, 1842), IV, 205.
142 Batiffol, *Le Roi Louis XIII*, pp. 483, 488–9l; idem, "Louis XIII et le duc de Luynes," *Rev hist* 102 (1909), 245; Marvick, *Louis XIII*, pp. 134–8; Chevallier, *Louis XIII*, pp. 154–9.
143 Griselle, *Ecurie*, pp. 28–32.
144 A. N., KK 145, non-paginated; Arcussia, *La Fauconnerie*, p. 165.
145 Griselle, *Ecurie*, pp. 20–8.
146 Charles Loyseau, *Cinq livres du droict des offices*, 2nd edn (Paris, 1613), pp. 405–6, 417–20; Laverny, *Les Domestiques*, pp. 40–41, 162, 309–16; Roland Mousnier, *The Institutions of France*, 2 vols., *Organs of State and Society*, trans. Arthur Goldhammer (Chicago, 1984), II, 121; Jean-François Solnon, *La Cour de France* (Paris, 1987), pp. 136–48; Jacqueline Boucher, "L'Evolution de la maison du Roi," *XVIIe siècle* 34 (1982), 363–8; idem, *Société et mentalités*, I, 160–1.

2

The king's favorite

The royal ballet "The Deliverance of Renaud" was first performed in the grand salon of the Louvre on 29 January 1617. This long, narrow room, sixty-four yards long and sixteen yards wide, had several tiers of seats in galleries on three sides so the spectators could look down on the dancing, although they soon moved down to the floor to see it better. The stage was at one end of the room, and a dais where the royal family sat under a canopy was at the other. There was no admission fee, so anyone who could get in could see the performance. Besides court nobles, the audience included ordinary Parisians with their wives and children, students, servants, and anyone well-dressed enough to slip past the guards at the door, who were selling places surreptitiously, anyway. The news that the king was dancing always attracted a large crowd, who began packing into the hall in the early morning to get a place for the evening's performance. It was known as a royal ballet when the king danced.

The dance floor lay between the dais and the stage. Two fifteen-foot runways connected the dance floor to the stage hidden behind a painted curtain, which was dropped to the floor and pulled aside when the performance began. The room was lit by a thousand candles in silver candelabra, and the bejeweled costumes were sewn with gold and silver thread so that they sparkled in the candlelight. The flickering light added a shimmering magical quality to the production. The ballet began when torch-bearing pages made an entrance in procession to take up their positions along the walls. So much light was both rare and expensive at night. Beginning late in the evening, royal ballets lasted three to four hours, and were repeated once or twice during the next few days. The performances took place in the Paris town hall, the Arsenal of the duc de Sully, which had its own theater, and the ballrooms and grand salons of the noble mansions in the city. Performances could be seen by several thousand people.[1]

Renaud was the hero of a popular epic, *Jerusalem Delivered*, by the sixteenth-century Italian poet Tasso. A Christian knight of great renown, Renaud had

Figure 3 "Cinquième Entrée de Six Monstres d'Armide" [Fifth Entry of Armide's Six Monsters] in the ballet, "La Délivrance de Renaud" (1617).

languished for a long time in a dreaming state in the gardens of the enchantress Armide far from the crusader armies fighting to free Jerusalem. Sixty-four vocalists, twenty-eight viol players, and fourteen lutists were hidden in fake groves of trees on either side of the stage, and began to play as the curtain fell to the floor. It revealed a mountain full of caves in which thirteen demons were huddled, keeping watch over the bewitched Renaud asleep on a bed of grass below. Luynes danced Renaud.

The demons came down from their caves along the runways to perform a fast dance, then vanished back into their caves. The demons of fire, water, and air made the first *entrée* or entrance. The king danced the role of the fire demon with a headpiece of flames, and his legitimized half-brother Vendôme, danced the water demon with a stand-up collar of bulrushes, while a royal favorite, Montpouillan, danced the air demon with wings on his back. Several more entrances introduced the demons of hunting, tomfoolery, insanity, vanity, gambling, greed, vulgarity, frivolity, war, and Moors. They had identifying detail on their costumes such as a boar's head and hunting horn, a jester's head and bells, and a gaming board with dice cups. After they had disappeared, two knights came on stage dressed as Roman soldiers. They wore plumed metal helmets and breastplates, and carried shields and swords. They danced to a martial tune and started to follow the demons from the stage when suddenly the set changed, and the mountain pivoted to reveal behind it the enchanted garden of Armide with a fountain spouting water surrounded by flowers and bushes. Armide appeared and tried to dissuade the knights from disturbing Renaud's sleep. She was danced by Marais, a professional male dancer and choreographer. Men danced all the roles in court ballets, while ladies of the royal family and their attendants danced in their own special ballets.

Refusing to listen, the knights used magic wands to dry up the fountains, and Armide called up six monsters to drive them away, two owls, two dogs, and two monkeys, who wore masks, wings, paws, and tails, and performed a bizarre dance. The knights routed the monsters, and gave Renaud a magic crystal in which he saw himself asleep, dreaming away his life. Aghast and ashamed, he awoke from his enchantment and followed his rescuers from the stage. Armide rushed back to find her fountains dried up, her garden devastated, and Renaud gone. Furious, she conjured up six shelled monsters, two lobsters, two turtles, and two snails, to pursue Renaud and his rescuers. They mocked her by dropping their shells to become grotesque creatures, with the heads of elderly women wearing old-fashioned headdresses, and the bodies of men wearing boots and spurs. They performed a ludicrous leaping, whirling dance around Armide, parodying her frustrated anger, and then carried away the weeping, powerless enchantress.

There was another set change: there were four in "Renaud." A grove of trees on carts was wheeled in. Christian knights from the army of Godefroy de Bouillon were standing within the grove and singing in praise of their command-er-in-chief danced by Louis XIII. Sixteen knights came forward to speak to an old hermit with a long, white beard who informed them of Renaud's rescue. After they left the stage, the trees were rolled away to reveal Godefroy de Bouillon's camp in Palestine. In a tent of gold cloth, the crusader knights sat in three rows with Louis XIII as the crusader king sitting at the top. The knights and Godefroy danced the final grand ballet expressing their joy at Renaud's rescue, thus ending a hugely successful performance.[2]

The king as a teenager enjoyed dancing in ballets, and the noble dancers in "Renaud" were his favorites, friends, and household officials. It was a great honor to be chosen to dance in a royal ballet and a good way to secure favor. The length and complexity of the *grands ballets du Roy* made them expensive, so only one or two were produced a year, usually in late January or in February during Carnival. Malherbe noted that a ballet presented in January 1614 had cost more than 10,000 écus (30,000 livres). Another fifteen to twenty shorter court ballets with fewer dancers were staged during the rest of the year in the royal family's Louvre apartments and the city's mansions.[3]

The king himself chose "The Deliverance of Renaud" to serve as a political message, and Renaud who represented him was danced by his favorite Luynes. Renaud was held captive by Armide representing Concini, the Queen Mother's favorite, and Louis XIII danced Godefroy de Bouillon, who was himself ruling alone after having defeated Armide-Concini. Louis also danced the fire demon to symbolize purging his kingdom by fire of impurities such as Concini. "Renaud" was a political allegory meant for the court nobility who detested Concini as much as the king did, and it foreshadowed Concini's murder three months later.[4] It condemned the usurpation of the king's authority by the Queen Mother and her favorite, and announced his intention to rule alone with the help of his favorite Luynes. This chapter discusses the nature of the king's relationship with Luynes as demonstrated by their staging of royal ballets.

The duties of a favorite

Luynes was first mentioned in the journal of the king's doctor in November 1611 as the royal falconer in charge of the king's favorite hunting birds. After he was put in charge of the king's personal collection of hunting birds, Luynes began to see the king more often, and he had become a royal favorite by 1614. No one had a monopoly on royal favor, however. The king often had several favorites at once, and Montpouillan, Courtenvaux, La Rochefoucauld, La Rocheguyon, La Coudrelle, La Curée, Termes, Vitry, and the young Liancourt were among his favorites from 1614 to 1617. Most had danced in his ballets.[5] They remained favorites after Luynes became the favorite-in-chief in 1615, and he developed personal ties to some of them including Bassompierre, La Rocheguyon, and Liancourt. But he sent from court those who became rivals for his position as favorite-in-chief such as Vitry and La Curée.

A favorite was the trusted companion and confidant of a king, and Luynes had been a personal favorite since 1614. He amused and reassured Louis XIII, shared his life in public and private, acted as his friend, and participated in activities they both enjoyed. He began to use their personal relationship for political purposes only after he helped to organize Concini's murder in 1617. Then he became a political favorite, and regularly attended council meetings, giving the king political advice. He became a minister favorite in 1621 after acquiring the offices of constable and keeper of the seals, which made him a minister. He never became a first minister, however, because he never dominated the decision-making process.[6]

Luynes's personal relationship with the king was based on their shared interests and activities, and on his ability to make the king feel appreciated, valued, and understood. He saw the king daily, and they shared a love of riding, hawking, hunting, and dancing in court ballets at which they both excelled. The king went hawking in the afternoon two or three times a week. Luynes always accompanied him, and usually went with him when he went hunting with his dogs. Luynes's rooms in the Louvre were on the floor above those of the king, who came upstairs to see him at least once a day, usually at dinnertime or before bedtime for a chat. Discussing the day's events led naturally to Luynes's offering advice, and in this way he began to have political influence. The king dined with him in his rooms at least once a week, and visited him often at the royal château of Amboise after he became its governor, and later at Luynes's own château of Lésigny-en-Brie near Fontainebleau. Luynes always attended the king's *levers* and *couchers*, ceremonies when he arose and went to bed. When the king became seriously ill in October 1616, Luynes sat by his bedside until he went to sleep, then slept on a couple of mattresses on the floor next door. Occasionally, Luynes arranged banquets and parties for the king, for instance, on Twelfth Night, and these were always held in his own rooms.[7]

Court ballets were a shared enthusiasm. Luynes regularly staged royal ballets in which he and the king danced together, and they watched and commented critically on other ballets. On 12 January 1614, the 13-year-old king danced in a short ballet, while on 23 and 26 January and on 3 February, he watched three ballets. He danced in a ballet in the grand salon of the Louvre on 27 November 1616, and before the performance put on his comic costume of baggy trousers in Luynes's rooms where he dined with the other dancers. There were only five rehearsals for this short ballet, and its performance was followed by a ball.[8] There were thirteen rehearsals after dinner in the rooms of Luynes and the king for the ballet of "Renaud" from 23 December until its presentation on 29 January 1617, and the king dined with Luynes before this performance, too. There were eleven evening rehearsals for the ballet of "Roland" from 11 February until its performance on 22 February 1618. There were twenty-seven evening rehearsals for the ballet "Tancrède" in Luynes's rooms from 6 January until its presentation on 12 February 1619.

On 17 February 1619, five days after the performance of "Tancrède," the queen and her ladies danced in the "Ballet of Psyche," performed in the great hall of the Hôtel de Bourbon using the same sets. This ballet received a lengthy write-up in the *Mercure français*.[9] The king watched the queen dance in one of her ballets in Luynes's apartments on 26 January 1620, and he watched two ballets presented there by the city of Paris on 29 and 30 January. He attended a performance of the "Ballet of the Drunkards" on 18 February staged by the prince de Condé in the grand salon of the Louvre, and on 27 September a short ballet performed in the grand salon of the Château Trompette at Bordeaux where he had gone on campaign.

Only two royal ballets were performed in 1621. There were fifteen rehearsals for "Apollo" in Luynes's rooms from 25 January until its performance on 18 February, and there were eight rehearsals for the ballet of "The Sun" in Luynes's apartments from 19 February until its performance on 2 March.[10] No ballets were staged after this because the king and Luynes went on military campaign in the southwest, where Luynes died of scarlet fever on 15 December 1621.

Dancing in ballets was fun and entertaining, and Luynes organized these events to keep the king amused. Athletic by nature, the king excelled at dancing as a teenager, and ballets did not require him to speak, a great advantage because he had a bad stutter. Dancing the lead role made him the center of the court's admiring attention, and he received praise for something he knew that he did well, allowing him to outshine his mother and forget the awkwardness and humiliation that he had felt as a teenager ignored by her and her friends, which Luynes was quick to recognize and exploit. He was clever enough to realize that starring in court ballets was good for the king's ego, increased his self-confidence, and helped to alleviate his deep-seated anxieties. So, ballets became a regular winter activity. The time spent on rehearsals increased Luynes's access to the king and influence over him. One of Luynes's primary duties as a favorite was to keep the king happy and amused, which he never forgot. Fontenay-Mareuil observed this when he remarked that "Monsieur de Luynes thought of nothing but going hunting and dancing in ballets."[11] These were activities that the king enjoyed.

Luynes's rooms in the Louvre became a refuge for the king, a place where he felt happy and relaxed, and most of their ballet rehearsals, banquets, plays, and parties were held there. A pamphlet in defense of the favorite argued that the king was isolated in "His Majesty," and needed a place where he could be among trusted friends in order to have a personal life. The king lived his life in public. He needed somewhere private and quiet to escape the constant pressure of daily affairs, and he needed someone faithful and caring in whom he could confide and who would reassure him. Unobtrusive servants often played this role.[12] Luynes was such a person, and by 1616 he was always at the king's side, giving him comfort and support.

The king's father had died in 1610, and he had a poor relationship with his mother, whom Richelieu described as cold. She was not maternal, and she was sharply critical of the king's behavior, openly preferring her younger son Gaston who was next in line for the throne, followed by his cousin Condé. Both Gaston and Condé later intrigued against the king. The Queen Mother did not like the king's friends, especially Luynes and his brothers. Although the king had reached his majority in 1614 at the age of thirteen, she insisted that he was not yet ready to rule. She had enjoyed being regent, so she insisted that he was still too young and inexperienced to rule alone, encouraged by Concini whom the king hated and despised, but whom his mother needed and trusted. She and Concini pushed the king aside and excluded him from affairs of state. As a teenage boy, he naturally resented his mother's control, but in addition, she was taking his rightful place and listening to her hated favorite, not to him. He felt deprived, neglected, and humiliated.[13]

Luynes was a sympathetic older man who took the king's side against his mother and her favorite. Orphaned at thirteen, Luynes knew from personal experience how lonely the king must have felt. As a gentleman-attendant in a great household, he had learned the art of pleasing, and as a falconer, he had to be calm, patient, and caring. Luynes was described by his contemporaries as courteous, kind, and affable, someone who seldom lost his temper and was always charming and deferential. James Howell, a contemporary English observer, described him as a man of "mild comportment, humble, and debonair to all suitors." A. Lloyd Moote has noted the self-deprecating quality of his letters.[14] The king began to regard Luynes as a family member, perhaps an uncle or an older brother, while Luynes's brothers became his stepbrothers or cousins. They, too, were charming, good-looking, and fashionably dressed, and they went hawking and hunting with the king, attended his *levers* and *couchers*, entertained him at meals, and danced in his ballets. They became ordinary gentlemen of the king's bedchamber on 18 September 1614 at a salary of 1,500 livres each. Ordinary gentleman performed personal errands for the king and often came from the provincial *noblesse seconde*.[15] The king may even have regarded Luynes as a substitute father, and Luynes, who was twenty-three years older, almost certainly regarded him as a son.

Luynes was thirty-six years old in 1614, middle-aged by the standards of the day, but he and his brothers Cadenet and Brantes, who were thirty-three and thirty-two years old respectively, were still younger than most of the other members of the king's entourage. Louis's doctor, Héroard, was over sixty; his governor, Souvré, was over seventy; and his tutors, Nicolas Lefevre and David Rivault de Fleurance, were in their late sixties and early forties.[16] His mother and her favorites were in their forties, while many of her ministers were older. To the teenage king, they must have seemed ancient. On the other hand, Luynes and his brothers were in their thirties, and probably seemed younger because of their athleticism, gaiety, elegance, and charm. Always laughing and fun to be around, Luynes and his brothers shared the interests and activities of the king, who enjoyed their company and preferred them to his own family. After the king married, Luynes installed his sister as the queen's mistress of robes, and his young charming wife became superintendent of her household and a favorite, strengthening the surrogate family feeling, especially after the Queen Mother had left court. Richelieu, Déagent, and the duc de Rohan noted that Luynes had surrounded the king with his relatives and clients in order to influence and control him, but they failed to recognize that in so doing, he had also provided the king with a much needed surrogate family and a younger, more amusing entourage.[17]

Court ballets

Luynes was an important innovator and an enthusiastic patron of the dramatic court ballet. These were not ballets in the modern sense, but more like masques, which were also popular at this time. Masques were a series of short, loosely coordinated, allegorical dramatic sketches in which the performers wore masks. Court ballets in contrast were multimedia performances that combined dance, opera, drama, poetry, and pantomime. Dramatic court ballets had a unified, coherent plot recounting a heroic story taken from classical mythology or medieval romances. The action unfolded through verse recitations, libretti read by the audience, sung narratives accompanied by instrumental and choral music, mimed scenes, and multiple entrances in various styles of dancing. Luynes used dramatic court ballets as political propaganda to convince the nobility and Parisian elite of his valuable services to the king, especially the removal of the tyrant Concini, the allegorical theme of many of his ballets.[18]

The Queen Mother, Marie de Médicis, loved court ballets and understood their propaganda value. The Medici were famous for staging spectacular pageants to influence elite opinion, and Marie herself was skilled at political propaganda.[19] She staged the "Ballet of Minerva," which was performed on 19 and 22 March 1615 with the king sitting in the audience. The grand salon of the Louvre was lit by 1,200 candles and decorated with Doric columns and Turkish carpets on the floor. The Queen Mother had commissioned this ballet to commemorate the marriage of her daughter Elizabeth to Philip IV of Spain. Elizabeth danced the role of Minerva, the goddess of wisdom and peace, and came on stage in a chariot drawn by two cupids, followed by her ladies-in-waiting dressed as amazons. The ballet's theme was the victory of Minerva in capturing the king of Spain, but it was also a political allegory meant to celebrate the regency of Marie de Médicis, who was often represented as Minerva in paintings and medals. The ballet praised the Queen Mother for restoring France to its rightful place of power and influence in Europe.[20] The young king, who had recently attained his majority but was not yet allowed to rule, must have sat seething at this effusive praise of his mother's regency. "Renaud" became his response to the "Ballet of Minerva." He and Luynes commissioned it, chose its story, danced in it, and sought to repeat its success in later ballets.

Luynes has often been held responsible for the execution of Estienne Durand, one of the authors of "Minerva." Durand had been writing ballet libretti for years, and was the recipient of an annual pension from the Queen Mother as her client and the poet-in-residence of her household. He was introduced to the king by Luynes when they were staging "Renaud," and he received 2,000 livres for writing this ballet. After the Queen Mother was exiled from court in May 1617, Durand wrote and published a pamphlet comparing the king to the Roman emperor Nero, who had murdered his mother. For this act of folly, Durand was arrested and imprisoned in the Bastille in May 1618. Tried for treason before the *Grand Conseil* on 16 July 1618, he was found guilty, condemned to death, and executed that afternoon. He was broken on the wheel in the Place de Grève, and his body was burned with copies of his pamphlet, the ashes scattered to the winds.

Richelieu declared in his memoirs that Luynes was responsible for Durand's death.[21] It was probably the king, however, who had insisted upon his execution because Durand, whom he knew personally, had publicly denounced him as a matricide and a tyrant. Durand was tried before the *Grand Conseil* because it was swifter and more reliable than the Parlement of Paris, and the sentence, harsh for someone of his standing, was carried out immediately, although it was customary to wait a day to allow the condemned to prepare himself. His execution caused a scandal at court.[22] A week earlier, on 9 July 1618, a new royal law intended to stop the wild pamphleteering of recent years had established stringent prohibitions against printing and distributing seditious books and pamphlets, and Durand's execution under this new law was meant to be exemplary.[23]

Luynes usually exiled his enemies from court; he did not execute them. The poet Théophile de Viau had circulated verses satirizing him in 1619. Viau was sent from court, but allowed to return ten months later, and became Luynes's client when he published a poem declaring that Durand had deserved his fate. In January 1621, a gentleman who had commissioned pamphlets attacking Luynes was found guilty of sedition and imprisoned in the Bastille for life but not executed.[24] Cooptation, exile, and imprisonment were more Luynes's style than unpopular executions. It was almost certainly the king who had insisted upon Durand's death, and Luynes supported his decision to retain favor. The publication of anti-Luynes pamphlets did not begin until 1620, so their suppression was not a motive for the 1618 law or Durand's execution.

On 22 February 1618, the king and Luynes staged and danced together in the ballet, "The Fury of Roland." The story, chosen by Luynes, was taken from the epic poetry of Ariosto, and he danced the lead role of Astolphe, who sought to heal the bedeviled Roland danced by the young Roger de Liancourt. Roland represented France, whose well-being and tranquility had been endangered by the hellish Fury Concini. The king danced the role of a great hunter who helped Astolphe to slay the Fury. The ballet emphasized Luynes's growing political influence and his self-proclaimed goal of achieving peace and prosperity for France. Lacking the dramatic tension of "Renaud," however, it was less successful.[25]

For this reason, Luynes and the king decided to return to *Jerusalem Delivered* for the subject of their next royal ballet. Luynes chose the story, enlisted the same dancers, selected the composers and set designers, and supervised the ballet's staging and production. The music, dancing, costumes, and scenery were superb, and the set changes were accomplished in darkness, a novelty. The impressive technical effects, however, were the real achievement because nothing like them had ever been seen before. The ballet of "Tancrède in the Enchanted Forest" was first performed in the grand salon of the Louvre on 12 February 1619 to celebrate the marriage of the king's sister Christine to the duke of Savoy. The grand salon had to be widened because there were 137 dancers, the largest number ever seen, and a bigger stage had to be built.

A new stage curtain costing 1,100 livres was painted with a scene portraying the siege of Jerusalem, and when it dropped to the floor, it revealed a forest of trees on moveable carts. In front of this forest stood the magician Ismen, sent by the beleaguered king of Jerusalem, to enchant the forest in order to defend it against the approaching crusaders. Ismen drew a magic circle, and sketched cabalistic signs with his wand, while saying spells and charms to call up forest spirits, who danced and sang for him. They were followed by monsters and demons dancing with frenzied steps.

Woodcutters and soldiers now entered the forest, sent by Godefroy de Bouillon, commander of the crusader army, to cut wood for his siege machines and scaling ladders, but they were driven away by the monsters and demons. Three Christian knights came in search of Tancrède, who was danced by Luynes in a white satin costume embroidered in gold and silver. Historically, Tancrède had commanded the army that had captured Jerusalem during the first crusade. Luynes and the knights danced together, swords in hand, battling the armed monsters and demons. Their victory was signaled by the enchanted forest suddenly bursting into flames, an effect achieved by pots around the stage containing charcoal set alight by alcohol-soaked rags. This was the first time that fire had been used on stage, and it caused an uproar in the audience.

Just as suddenly, the stage went dark, and in the darkness the defeated monsters and demons could be heard roaring, screaming, and howling, the sound slowly fading away as they disappeared. That had never been done before either, and the noise frightened some members of the audience into crying out. When candles and torches were brought in, the painted backdrop of the sky parted to reveal twenty-eight angels singing in praise of Tancrède. They descended in a cloud to the stage where they sang and danced in honor of Godefroy, who was danced by Louis XIII. Then the cloud bearing them rose again into the sky, and the stage went dark. When it became light again, the audience saw sixteen knight-conquerors of Palestine sitting in an amphitheater. They sang in praise of Godefroy and Tancrède, and danced in the final ballet. "Tancrède" was an immediate, enormous success, and Luynes deserved much of the credit.[26]

The fight of Tancrède and his knights against demons and monsters represented the efforts of Luynes and the king to end the unrest troubling France, which had been provoked by the Queen Mother and her favorite Concini. "Tancrède" was a reworking of the Concini theme, and a political allegory meant to convince the court that Luynes was a valuable royal adviser who had helped the king to get rid of Concini and restore peace and prosperity to France. The ballet's dedication to Luynes stated that he was a peacemaker who desired "the protection of the state and the restoration of order, that he was a wise and good advisor of the young king ... and that he sought to make the ship of France sail in a calm sea of profound peace." Scipion Gramont, who wrote the dedication, declared that "It is you, Monseigneur, who by your valor have courageously swept away the monsters of war and sedition that civil disorder has brought up from Hell to impede the just plans of Louis the Just."[27] "Tancrède," like "Renaud," was political propaganda meant to influence public opinion in Luynes's favor, and the government newspaper, the *Mercure françois*, published a synopsis of "Tancrède," significantly increasing the size of its audience.[28]

The royal ballets produced by Luynes after "Tancrède" were less successful.

Their plots were confused and vague, and they lacked the marvelous stage effects. They had too many stultifying verse recitations, and their political message obscured the action. They lacked the originality, flair, and fantasy of "Renaud" and "Tancrède." Beginning an hour after midnight on 18 February 1621, the "Ballet of Apollo" lasted nearly four hours, and was repeated on February 21 with Luynes dancing the lead role of Apollo, the Sun God. Resplendent in a golden costume, he came on stage to announce that he was Apollo, the god of poetry and music who had rid the earth of theft and illness, and killed the mighty python Concini strangling France. Luynes predicted the birth of a dauphin, and enthusiastically sang his own praises, surrounded by a crowd of dancing, singing muses and sirens who praised him, too. This self-glorification gave the ballet a heavy leaden feeling, and it was not a success.[29]

A month later on 2 March 1621, the "Ballet of the Sun" was performed in the grand salon of the Louvre, beginning after midnight and lasting for three hours. The curtain fell on a stage black as night, and the audience could hear ghouls, demons, and chimeras (fire-breathing monsters in Greek mythology) moaning, howling, and belching fire in the darkness. They were driven away by the coming of dawn as the sun, danced by Louis XIII, appeared on the now brightly lit stage in a gleaming chariot covered with gold and ivory. Apollo, danced by Luynes, remained lurking behind in the dark, overwhelmed by the king's brilliance. This ballet had the same problems as "Apollo," a weak story line, too many suffocating recitations praising the hero, and a heavy-handed political message overshadowing everything else. Lacking dramatic interest, neither ballet was a success.[30]

After Luynes's death, the dramatic court ballet declined swiftly in popularity to be replaced by the masquerade or burlesque ballet featuring comic dancing. Episodic without a unified plot, the masquerade ballet emphasized farce and satire rather than allegory, and consisted of humorous, bizarre characters in comic, grotesque costumes who made a series of entrances. The dancing was acrobatic and expressive, meant to entertain not tell a story, and there was no political message. Masquerade ballets continued to be popular until the last decades of Louis XIV's reign.[31]

Richelieu attempted a revival of the dramatic court ballet. He was responsible for the production of five ballets between 1635 and 1642, including the "Ballet of the Four Christian Monarchies" (1635), expressing French political aspirations; the "Ballet of the Navy" (1635), reflecting his desire to build a French fleet rivaling those of the Dutch and English; the "Ballet of Happiness" (1639), celebrating the birth of the dauphin; the "Ballet of the Success of French Arms" (1641), praising French military victories; and "Europe" (1642), a statement of national political strategy portraying a Europe dominated by the Bourbons. The king appreciated these themes, and may have suggested their production. Richelieu's ballets were stately and impressive, but their didactic political propaganda repelled spectators who found them as pompous and dull as their titles. His ballets were less creative, less entertaining, and thus less successful than those of Luynes on which they had been modeled.[32]

Luynes's staging of court ballets demonstrated that he had imagination and dramatic flair, and that he understood the uses of political propaganda. He recognized that ballets could be used to praise the monarchy and enhance his own public image. He knew that the court was a stage on which he and the king had to display their power and magnificence in order to awe, impress, and intimidate the great nobility, whose cooperation they needed to govern successfully. This was the goal of "Renaud" and "Tancrède," which were deliberately staged as breathtaking spectacles.

Dancing in royal ballets was prestigious because the participants appeared before the whole court in beautiful costumes, dancing beside the king and his family in a public demonstration of their favor and status. The prince de Condé staged one of his own ballets on 22 February 1615, featuring twelve entrances by twelve judges from the Parlement of Paris. No courtiers besides the prince danced in this ballet, causing the Queen Mother to jeer at the performance and say how ugly and graceless it was without *gens de qualité* as dancers. The court echoed her remarks, speculating that the prince lacked the money to stage a more impressive ballet. Luynes secured parts for himself and nine dependents in the king's and queen's ballets of 1617–19. They numbered one quarter of the forty-one dancers, and their selection was a public demonstration of Luynes's influence and favor. They included his brother, brother-in-law, wife, sister-in-law, niece, cousin's wife, two clients' wives, and an inamorata.[33]

Luynes was a complex man, far more enigmatic and complicated than most of his contemporaries realized. His easygoing charm masked another side of his personality and allowed his enemies to underestimate him. Luynes was an intelligent, ambitious realist who had spent his life at court and knew how it operated. He understood human nature and how to manipulate people, and he was shrewd enough to provide the personal and family support that the king needed. The ballets they produced together illustrated the nature of their relationship. Luynes supplied the ideas and planned the productions, and the king approved his plans, making any changes that he thought necessary. In their two most successful ballets, Louis danced the crusader king who commanded a Christian army, while Luynes danced the courageous knights who fought for him. Luynes danced the secondary role; he was Apollo to the king's sun. He had considerable influence over the emotionally dependent teenager, but Concini's fate was always a reminder of how far he could go; his influence was not limitless. Mentioned time and again in court ballets, Concini's death was a reminder of what could happen if Luynes forgot where real power lay and outshone the king. He could suggest, but he could not insist, and he could not oppose what the king really wanted to do. He had to defer to his wishes. The king had a taste for power and knew his own mind. He was jealous of his authority, and he would not tolerate its usurpation in public, although he was willing to accept advice in private. He meant to rule, and he would never again allow himself to be pushed aside. The balance of power in their relationship was in the king's favor, which Luynes never forgot.

The favorite-in-chief

By the autumn of 1614, the king was spending most of his time with Luynes and his brothers. Gilles de Souvré complained to the Queen Mother that they were interfering with the king's performance of his duties such as entertaining foreign ambassadors . He demanded that Luynes be excluded from the king's presence, and on 29 October 1614, the king's doctor Héroard noted in his journal that Souvré had stopped Luynes from entering the king's rooms to attend a *lever*.[34] Two decades earlier, Souvré, governor of Tours, had refused 100,000 livres from the duc de Mayenne to deliver the city to the Catholic Holy League. As a reward, Henri IV had named him governor of the Touraine, elevated his fief of Courtenvaux to a marquisat, and named him the dauphin's governor, first gentleman of his bedchamber, and a marshal of France. Souvré died in 1626 at the age of eighty-four. He and his sons were the only courtiers to attend Luynes's funeral.[35]

Souvré was ambitious for his older son, Courtenvaux, a childhood friend whom the king liked. Regarding Luynes as a rival, Souvré sought to have him excluded from the king's presence. When Louis discovered that Souvré was responsible for Luynes's absence, he angrily told his mother that he could no longer stand to have Souvré around him and wanted him replaced. Concini, however, spoke to the Queen Mother on Luynes's behalf. Having launched his career three years earlier, he still hoped that Luynes might become his client, and he may even have tried to buy his loyalty with gifts and favors, having already offered another royal favorite, Montpouillan, a pension of 16,000 livres for his support.[36] Luynes's friend, Jacques de Beziade, sieur de Sauveterre, a trusted bedchamber servant of the Queen Mother, convinced her that Luynes was a modest, unassuming nobody whom she could easily manage, so she rescinded the order banishing him from the king's presence, a decision she would later regret.[37]

Luynes became the favorite-in-chief when he accompanied the king on his journey south to marry the Spanish Infanta, Anne of Austria. The royal party left Paris toward the end of September 1615, and arrived in Bordeaux on 7

October. The king sent Luynes to Bayonne on 9 November with a letter for Anne in which he described Luynes as "one of my most trusted friends." A week later he met her at Bordeaux where they were married on 25 November. The king's letter to Anne with its flattering description of his favorite was published in the *Mercure françois*, which noted that Luynes was "someone for whom the king has a special affection."[38] Luynes's mission to Anne and his mention in the newspaper accounts were significant marks of royal favor indicating that he had become the favorite-in-chief.

The king heaped gifts on Luynes to show his affection. On 1 March 1615, he named Luynes governor of the château of Amboise, an office valued at 300,000 livres. Luynes's brother Cadenet was named lieutenant general or second-in-command of Amboise, and his brother Brantes joined a royal guard company. The king thanked the Queen Mother for allowing him to make these gifts, but it was Concini who had arranged for Luynes to receive Amboise, hoping to use him to offset the influence of Souvré and his son. When Luynes tried to thank the Queen Mother, she told him to thank the king. She still did not like or trust him and never would. In August 1615, the king rode south for the first time to visit Amboise. He would make this trip often in 1616.[39]

The king showered favors on Luynes during the next two years. On 1 March 1615, Luynes was named an ordinary gentleman of the king's bedchamber with a salary of 2,000 livres a year, and on 14 June with the king's financial help, he bought the office of captain of the Tuileries for a salary of about 2,500 livres a year. On 14 November the king named him a councillor of state with a salary of 4,000 livres, an office allowing him to attend meetings of the royal council and enter the Parlement of Paris. On 12 December, Luynes became first ordinary gentleman of the king's bedchamber, an office created especially for him. On 6 May 1616, the king gave him a cash gift of 100,000 livres, which he used on 30 October to buy the household office of grand falconer with a salary of 4,200 livres for the sum of 45,000 écus (135,000 livres). During November 1616, Luynes bought the office of captain-governor of the Louvre giving him rooms in the palace. Most members of the king's household had to spend the night in Paris apartments or town houses because the Louvre was too small to accommodate them all, but now Luynes could remain in the Louvre overnight. On 27 November, Héroard mentioned for the first time that the king had climbed the staircase to visit Luynes.[40] From then on, Luynes was always at the king's side.[41]

Concini and the Queen Mother had not been consulted when Luynes was made grand falconer or captain-governor of the Louvre, and they became apprehensive about his growing favor, realizing that they had misjudged him. He now appeared to them to be an ambitious intriguer. They tried to separate him from the king in the autumn of 1616, but he was too firmly entrenched to be dislodged. Instead, the Queen Mother angrily dismissed Sauveterre from her household for deceiving her.[42]

Luynes was ambitious, and his relationship with the king was based on self-interest. He wanted the brilliant court career that had eluded his father, and the key to such a career was royal favor. His concern for the king, however, was not entirely selfish. Unlike members of the royal family, Luynes was wholly dependent on the king for his position and fortune, and he knew that the king's happiness was necessary to his own success and longevity as a royal favorite. For this reason, he provided the king with a safe haven in his own rooms, discussed the day's events with him, gave him advice and support, and made an insecure teenager feel greater confidence in himself. He supported the king against his mother and her friends, and would later reluctantly support his decision to execute Concini. Luynes wanted what was best for the king, who knew it and trusted him for this reason.

The nature of their relationship was revealed in a conversation that Bassompierre had with Luynes in November 1621. Warning him that the king had been grumbling about him behind his back, Bassompierre told Luynes that he should try harder to stay in favor, and take care to be humble, grateful, and submissive in the king's presence. Luynes thanked Bassompierre for his concern and advice, and for taking the trouble to speak to him as a nephew, and said that he would reply as an uncle. He said that he knew the king to the depths of his soul, and that as well as knowing how to acquire favor, he knew how to keep it. He said that the king's complaints were meaningless and did not threaten the affection they shared. Bassompierre commented that Luynes was like all favorites who thought their good fortune was eternal, and only realized their impending disgrace when it was too late to prevent it.[43] Luynes died the next month, so the validity of his observation was never tested. Bassompierre was jealous of Luynes, who stood in the way of his becoming the favorite-in-chief. Knowing this, Luynes did not trust him, and probably considered his advice presumptuous.

Luynes was genuinely fond of the king. The king remarked to the Venetian ambassador on 24 December 1621, a week after Luynes's death, that "I loved him despite his faults because he loved me."[44] Louis wrote to the prince de Condé, "I cannot bear the loss that has just come to me through the death of my cousin, the constable."[45] The king had written to his mother in 1619, "I can only love someone who loves me more."[46] Héroard had written in his journal on 3 January 1615 that Luynes had shown a marked concern for the king's safety and happiness when they were out hawking, and noted that the king loved him.[47] Luynes's genuine care and compassion was responsible for the king's growing attachment to him.[48] He even encouraged the king to form a loving relationship with his neglected wife, although she might become a rival. One evening in January 1619, at about eleven o'clock at night when the king was preparing once again to sleep alone, Luynes took him firmly by the arm and led him, despite his protests, to the queen's bedchamber and shut the door on him.[49] Luynes safeguarded his own interests, however, by placing his wife and sister in the most important offices in the young queen's household.

The proximity of their sleeping arrangements in the Louvre, their constant companionship, the king's daily visits, their frequent ballet rehearsals in the evenings, the king's coldness toward his wife, and his obvious infatuation with Luynes have led modern observers to ask if their relationship was sexual. It was evident that the king had a strong, even a neurotic dependency on Luynes that increased over time and reproduced his mother's obsession with Léonora Galigai.[50] In both cases, the dependency may have been a reaction to being constantly surrounded by fawning, obsequious courtiers, and in the king's case to having close family members whom he disliked and distrusted including his own mother. Luynes made the king feel appreciated, understood, and loved, an addictive feeling for anyone, but especially for someone who was deeply insecure. They shared a genuine bond of affection, but there is no evidence that their relationship was sexual.

Most historians including Louis Batiffol, Gabriel Hanotaux, Pierre Chevallier, Louis Vaunois, A. Lloyd Moote, Elizabeth Marvick, Madeleine Foisil, Françoise Hildesheimer, Berthold Zeller, and Victor Cousin do not believe that the king and Luynes had a homosexual affair.[51] The exception is Jean Claude Pascal, who has argued in favor of such a relationship without offering any evidence for it. Pascal admits that Luynes "liked women," but argues that since Luynes was ambitious, he acquiesced in the king's pressure to turn their relationship into something other than that of "older brother-younger brother." Pascal asserts that Louis had homosexual tendencies, an opinion based on the king's behavior after Luynes's death, and argues that the king must also have had a homosexual relationship with Luynes, who tolerated him for the sake of his career.[52] Pascal offers no evidence for this assertion beyond a syllogistic argument based on supposition and conjecture.

There is strong circumstantial evidence, however, that Luynes had a father-son relationship with the king. There was a difference of twenty-three years in their ages. Luynes had first attracted the king's favor when he was a child of ten before puberty and immediately after his father had died. Luynes became a royal favorite in 1614 when the king was thirteen, and the publicly acknowledged favorite-in-chief a year later. As a fatherless boy young for his age and slow to mature, Louis XIII behaved like a child when he was with Luynes, for example, amusing himself by making up comic verses about members of his entourage, in Luynes's case his big nose.[53] He once dreamed that Luynes was dressed up like a Swiss guard playing a fife, while his wife was dressed the same and playing a drum.[54] Héroard noted that one Sunday afternoon the king ate four or five éclairs that Luynes had bought for him in a Paris pastry shop.[55] The king ate in the kitchens one evening, probably at Luynes's suggestion because he was giving a dessert party in his rooms for some friends, and the king did not want to attend.[56] The king needed a father, and Luynes assumed this role from long practice.

During his serious illness in October 1616, the king had slept in the bed of a servant, while Luynes had slept on several mattresses on the floor next door. The feverish king had amused himself by playing on Luynes's bed for a couple of hours, but then had returned to his own room to sleep in the bed of a servant, an incident often cited as evidence of his homosexuality.[57] Louis Vaunois has satisfactorily refuted this suggestion by comparing the inaccurate nineteenth-century edited entries on the incident in Héroard's journal with the very different language of the original manuscript. Madeleine Foisil has agreed with Vaunois in her recent transcription of Héroard.[58] Their father-son relationship persisted until Luynes's death, and even when the king was older, he continued to depend heavily on Luynes's advice and support.

The king's desire to be cared for and comforted like a child conflicted with his desire to be a man and rule independently. This is a common emotional conflict of teenagers, the clash between the desire to assert themselves as adults, and the inability to do so because of their immaturity. The king's deep-seated insecurities, and his problems with his mother and her favorite, intensified this conflict. Luynes walked a narrow line between advising and guiding the young king on the one hand, and offering him unconditional support on the other. It took intelligence, maturity, and sensitivity to handle an insecure teenager successfully, and the paternal Luynes was able to do so because he had already parented six younger brothers and sisters.

Richelieu and Déagent, who were both hostile to Luynes, never suggested that there was anything improper in his relationship with the king. Contemporary memoirs, pamphlets, correspondence, and histories never hinted at a homosexual relationship, and they accused Luynes of everything else including using magic and sorcery to bewitch the king, a common enough accusation.[59] The king did not have a homosexual relationship with any of his other male favorites at this time. Historical evidence of homosexuality includes police reports, trial records, letters, journals, and memoirs, to which may be added the less reliable evidence of rumors, gossip, and speculation.[60] There was no evidence of any kind in Luynes's case.

Tallemant des Réaux, who often repeated court gossip, remarked that before 1622 the king had had nine favorites including Luynes. He neither stated nor implied that they were anything other than favorites, and he did not describe the king's feelings for Luynes as a "violent love," which was how he described Louis's feelings for François Barradat, a favorite his own age a few years later.[61] Given their age difference, Luynes would undoubtedly have been accused of seducing the king and exploiting him sexually if there had been any basis for such an accusation. There were numerous court rumors during the early 1640s about the king and Cinq Mars, a much younger favorite, but there were never any rumors about Luynes. Historians have projected these rumors backward in time, but there were no homosexual rumors about Luynes during his lifetime.

There is no evidence that Luynes liked boys. He had at least one documented love affair with a young woman at court. It was reported that the sieur de Chazan had been named Gaston d'Orléans's appointments secretary because he had helped Luynes in his trysts with "La Clinchamp." Mademoiselle Claude de Mailly de Clinchamps was named one of the queen's maids of honor in 1618, and danced in her ballet of that year, probably through Luynes's patronage. She left the household in 1619 to marry Jean-Baptiste de Monchy, marquis de Montcarvel, and the next year was named mistress of robes or *dame d'atour* of the king's youngest sister, Henriette Marie, an office she lost after Luynes's death.[62]

In September 1617, Luynes had married the pretty 17-year-old Marie de Rohan whom he did not neglect, and they had three children in three years. Madame de Motteville reported in her memoirs that Marie was on very good terms with her husband, and Richelieu noted that Luynes was very much in love with his wife.[63] Marie de Rohan was neither reticent nor shy. If she had been dissatisfied with Luynes, or if he had been having a liaison with the king, everyone at court would have known about it. She never breathed a word about anything of the sort.[64]

Marie fell in love with Claude de Lorraine, duc de Chevreuse, and had an affair with him during the summer and fall of 1621 when Luynes was away with the king on campaign in the southwest. On 20 April 1622, four months after Luynes's death, she married Chevreuse.[65] Marie was a slender vivacious blonde of twenty, and Chevreuse was a dashingly attractive military man from one of the best families in France. He had a reputation for gallantry and making feminine conquests, and Marie found him irresistible. Their affair, however, does not discredit her marriage with Luynes, which seems to have been satisfactory. Married noblewomen often had affairs after they had born an heir as she did in December 1620, especially if their husbands were complaisant or absent as Luynes was, because they did not marry for love. Affairs were an amusing way of passing the time, and Marie became legendary for her affairs.[66] If she had had anything unpleasant to say about her husband or his relationship with the king, she would probably have said it in the summer of 1621, but she did not.

Marie de Rohan became a member of a surrogate family that Luynes created for the king. He placed his relatives in key household offices to act as surrogate family members replacing the king's own unsatisfactory family relationships. They included his two brothers, father-in-law, brother-in-law, wife, sister, two nieces, four cousins, and a cousin's wife, and they helped him to influence and manage the king. Luynes placed eighteen male relatives and clients in key offices in the king's household where they were highly visible and saw the king often.[67] He placed nine more in key offices in the household of the king's brother, Gaston d'Orléans,[68] and another fourteen in key offices in the young queen's household. His wife became her household superintendent and first lady of honor in December 1618, while his sister Antoinette du Vernet became her mistress of robes. They held the highest offices in the queen's household and joined her inner circle of friends, acting as the distaff side of this surrogate family.[69] Within five years, Luynes placed a total of forty-one kin and clients in the households of the king, his brother, and the queen. They gave him a power base at court, and helped to reinforce his father-son relationship with the king.

Luynes and the king shared the same Jesuit confessor, Père Arnoux.[70] They were both devout Catholics, and some historians believe that they were too devout to have had a homosexual affair. Others believe that the king was too cold and repressed by nature, and that any tendencies he had in that direction were latent.[71] Pierre Chevallier has noted that one explanation for Luynes's strong emotional hold over the king may have been physical attraction, but another may have been the emotional need created by the king's feelings of abandonment at his father's death and his mother's rejection.[72] A. Lloyd Moote has noted that it is impossible to say with absolute certainty whether or not the king was sexually involved with Luynes. It is possible that the infatuated teenager had a latent sexual interest in Luynes, who tolerated his feelings in order to stay in favor.[73] The strong circumstantial evidence for a father-son relationship, however, and the lack of evidence for an active homosexual affair makes its existence doubtful.

Notes
1 Marie-Françoise Christout, "The Court Ballet in France, 1615–1641," *Dance Perspectives* 20 (1964), 5–7; idem, *Le Ballet occidental* (Paris, 1995), p. 21.
2 Margaret McMcGowan, *L'Art du ballet de cour en France, 1581–1643* (Paris, 1963), pp. 101–15; Henry Prunières, *Le Ballet de cour en France* (Paris, 1914, New York, 1970), pp. 115–19, 153; Paul LaCroix, *Ballets et mascarades de cour de Henri III à Louis XIV*, 6 vols. (Geneva, 1868), II, 97–135; Marie-Françoise Christout, *Le Ballet de cour au XVIIe siècle* (Geneva, 1987), pp. 156–9, 167–9; idem, "The Court Ballet," 8–9; idem, *Le Ballet occidental*, pp. 18–20.
3 François Malherbe, *Oeuvres*, ed. Ludovic Lalanne, 5 vols (Paris, 1862–9), ed. Antoine Adam. (Paris, 1971), III, 378; McGowan, *L'Art du ballet*, pp. 279–86.
4 Ibid., pp. 108–13.
5 Ibid., pp. 105 n.27, 118 n.9; Eugène Griselle, *Etat de la maison du Roi Louis XIII* (Paris, 1912), pp. 10–11, 126; Jean-Pierre Labatut, *Les Ducs et pairs de France au XVIIe siècle* (Paris, 1972), passim; DBF, fasc. 111, 1011–14; Père Anselme, *Histoire généalogique et chronologique de la*

Maison royale, 3rd edn, 9 vols. (Paris, 1722–23, New York, 1967), IV, 414, 428–9, 472–3; Jean Héroard, *Journal*, ed. Madeleine Foisil, 2 vols. (Paris, 1989), II, 2174, 2241.

6 Nicolas Le Roux, *La Faveur du Roi* (Paris, 2001), p. 39; J.H. Elliott and W.L.B. Brockliss, *The World of the Favourite* (New Haven, 1999), pp. 1–10, 71–2, 279–309; Arlette Jouanna, "Faveur et Favoris," *Henri III et son temps*, ed. Robert Sauzet (Paris, 1992), pp. 155–65; A. Lloyd Moote, "Richelieu as Chief Minister," *Richelieu and His Age*, eds. Joseph Bergin and Laurence Brockliss (Oxford, 1992), pp. 16–17; Jeroen Duindam, *Vienna and Versailles* (Cambridge, 2003), pp. 245–53.

7 Héroard, *Journal*, II, 2173–798.

8 Ibid., II, 2173–83; Pierre Chevallier, *Louis XIII* (Paris, 1979), pp. 123–30; Achille Halphen, ed., *Journal inédit d'Arnauld d'Andilly 1614–1620* (Paris, 1857), p. 243.

9 Ibid., pp. 399–400; Héroard, *Journal*, II, 2439; McGowan, *L'Art du ballet*, p. 119, n.13; *Mercure françois*, 25 vols. (Paris, 1605–44), V (1619), 104–8; B.N., imprimés Lb 36, *Discours du ballet de la reine, tiré de la fable de Psyché* (1619).

10 Héroard, *Journal*, II, 2660–755.

11 François Du Val, marquis de Fontenay-Mareuil, *Mémoires du Messire Du Val*, ed. Louis Monmerqué, 2 vols. (Paris, 1826), II, 461.

12 B.N., imprimés, Lb 36, *Seconde partie et responce à la Chronique des Favoris* (1622), pp. 3–4; Duindam, *Vienna and Versailles*, pp. 234–5.

13 Charles, comte Horric de Beaucaire, *Mémoires du Cardinal de Richelieu*, 10 vols. (Paris, 1907–13), I, 126; A. Lloyd Moote, *Louis XIII* (Berkeley, 1989), pp. 39–96; Elizabeth Marvick, *Louis XIII* (New Haven, 1986), pp. 120–200; Chevallier, *Louis XIII*, pp. 103–72; Michel Carmona, *Marie de Médicis* (Paris, 1981), pp. 315–44.

14 B.N., imprimés Lb 36, *Discours en forme d'apologie envoyée à Monseigneur le duc Despernon* (1619), p. 11; *La Conjuration de Conchine* (1618), pp. 291–2; *Apologie pour Monseigneur de Luynes* (1619), p. 13; *Le Tourment de l'envie courtisane* (1619), p. 12; *Lettre de Cléophon à Polémandre* (1618), p. 12; James Howell, *Lustra Ludovici* (London, 1646), p. 38, cited by Marvick, *Louis XIII*, p. 137; Moote, *Louis XIII*, p. 104; Baptiste Legrain, *Décade commençant le règne de Louis XIII* (Paris, 1619), p. 429; Louis Batiffol, "Louis XIII et le duc de Luynes," *Rev hist*, 102 (1909), 244; idem, *Le Roi Louis XIII à vingt ans* (Paris, 1910), pp. 481–2.

15 B.N., Pièces originales 21, fol. 139; Edouard Fournier, ed., *Variétés historiques et littéraires* 4 vols. (Paris, 1655–63), III, 269, "Pasquil à la cour"; Gédéon Tallemant des Réaux, *Historiettes*, Antoine Adam, 2 vols. (Paris, 1960–61), I, 157–8; Charles d'Arcussia, *La Fauconnerie* (Rouen, 1643), p. 165; Berthold Zeller, *Louis XIII. Marie de Médicis, chef du conseil* (Paris, 1898), p. 25; Sophie de Laverny, *Les Domestiques commensaux du roi de France au XVIIe siècle* (Paris, 2002), p. 226.

16 Madeleine Foisil, *L'Enfant Louis XIII* (Paris, 1996), p. 210.

17 Beaucaire, *Mémoires de Richelieu*, III, 185–6; Guichard Déagent, *Mémoires de Monsieur Déagent envoyez à Monsieur le Cardinal de Richelieu* (Grenoble, 1668), p. 135; Henri, duc de Rohan, *Mémoires*, eds. Michaud and Poujoulat, 2nd ser., vol. 5 (Paris, 1837), p. 512.

18 Marie-Françoise Christout, *Histoire du ballet* (Paris, 1975), pp. 15–16; idem, *Le Ballet occidental*, pp. 17–21; Prunières, *Le Ballet de cour*, p. 156; Peter Burke, *The Fabrication of Louis XIV* (New Haven, 1992), pp. 17, 45; Moote, *Louis XIII*, pp. 267–8.

19 Sara Mamone, *Paris et Florence, deux capitals du spectacle pour une reine, Marie de Medicis* (Paris, 1990), passim.

20 McGowan, *L'Art du ballet*, pp. 85–99; Prunières, *Le Ballet de cour*, pp. 114–15; Deborah Marrow, *The Art Patronage of Maria de' Medici* (Ann Arbor, 1982), pp. 14, 58.

21 Beaucaire, *Mémoires de Richelieu*, II, 294–5.

22 McGowan, *L'Art du ballet*, pp. 87, 103, 113–15; Prunières, *Le Ballet de cour*, p. 119; Frédéric Lachèvre, *Estienne Durand* (Paris, 1905); idem, *Méditations de E.D.* (Paris, 1906), x–xi, xlvi, 250, 253; Déagent, *Mémoires*, p. 116; *Journal d'Arnauld 1614–1620*, pp. 374–5.

23 B.N., Ms. fr. 22061, fols. 241–52; Henri Martin, *Livre, pouvoirs et société à Paris au XVIIe siècle*, 2 vols. (Paris, 1969), I, 197–274; Jeffrey Sawyer, *Printed Poison* (Berkeley, 1990), pp. 137–43.

24 Antoine Adam, *Théophile de Viau* (Paris, 1954), pp. 157–63, 180–1, 355–424; Christian Jouhaud, *Les Pouvoirs de la littérature* (Paris, 2000), pp. 43–50; *Mercure françois* VI (1620), 263–4; Eugène and Jules Halphen, eds., *Journal inédit d'Arnauld d'Andilly 1620* (Paris, 1888–1909), pp. 15–16.
25 LaCroix, *Ballets et mascarades*, II, 149–60; McGowan, *L'Art du ballet*, p. 176.
26 Ibid., pp. 117–31; LaCroix, *Ballets et mascarades*, II, 161–98; Prunières, *Le Ballet de cour*, pp. 119–21, 155; Christout, "The Court Ballet," 9–10; B.N., imprimés Lb 36, *Relation du grand ballet du Roi, dansé en la salle du Louvre, le 12 février, sur l'aventure de Tancrède en la forêt enchantée* (1619).
27 McGowan, *L'Art du ballet*, p. 119, n.13; Tallemant des Réaux, *Historiettes*, I, 741, II, 1034, 1036. "C'est vous, Monseigneur (de Luynes), qui, par vostre valeur, avez courageusement debellé les monstres des guerres et seditions que la discorde civile avoit faict venir de l'enfer pour empescher les justes desseins de Louys le Juste ... comme vous avez dans le vostre de bons desirs, pour la conservation de l'Etat, duquel vous emportez à bon droict le juste titre de restaurateur. Que si pour assister la jeunesse du Roy de bons et sages conseils, pour former son esprit aux vértus royales, pour sacrifier vos particuliers interests au salut le public, pour faire nager le vaisseau de la France dans le calme d'une profonde paix ..." LaCroix, *Ballets et mascarades*, II, 163–4.
28 *Mercure françois*, V (1619), 88–104.
29 McGowan, *L'Art du ballet*, p. 180; LaCroix, *Ballets et mascarades*, II, 271–3; Prunières, *Le Ballet de cour*, p. 122.
30 Ibid., pp. 122–3; McGowan, *L'Art du ballet*, pp. 182–3.
31 Christout, "The Court Ballet," pp. 8–10, 15; idem, *Histoire du ballet*, pp. 14–16; idem, *Le Ballet occidental*, pp. 18–21.
32 McGowan, *L'Art du ballet*, pp. 176–8, 184–90; Christout, "The Court Ballet," 12; Eric Caldicott, "Richelieu and the Arts," *Richelieu and His Age*, pp. 233–4; H. Gaston Hall, "Europe, allégorie théatrale de propagande politique," *L'Age d'or du mécénat*, eds. Roland Mousnier and Jean Mesnard (Paris, 1985), pp. 319–27; Georges Couton, *Richelieu et le théâtre* (Lyon, 1986), pp. 55–61.
33 Fontenay-Mareuil, *Mémoires*, I, 266–7; Malherbe, *Oeuvres*, III, 486–8. The dancers were Luynes's brother Brantes, his brother-in-law the comte de Rochefort, his wife Marie, his sister-in-law the comtesse de Rochefort, his niece Anne du Roure de Combalet, his cousin's wife the marquise de Montlaur, his two clients' wives the marquises de Mauny and Courtenvaux, and his inamorata Claude de Mailly de Clinchamps. Héroard, *Journal*, II, 2439, 2521, 2595–6; *Journal d'Arnauld 1614–1620*, pp. 399–400; LaCroix, *Ballets et mascarades*, II, 97–160, 139–45; McGowan, *L'Art du ballet*, pp. 105, n.7, 118, n. 9.
34 Héroard, *Journal*, I, 2243.
35 Le Roux, *La Faveur du Roi*, pp. 262, 428–9, 715–16; Anselme, *Histoire généalogique*, VII, 397–401; Griselle, *Etat de la maison du Roi*, p. 10.
36 Florentin Du Ruau, *Propos dorés sur le glorieux règne* (Paris, 1618), p. 30, cited by Marvick, *Louis XIII*, p. 179, n.27; Nicolas Pasquier, *Lettres* (Paris, 1623), p. 556; Jacques, duc de La Force, *Mémoires du duc de La Force, et de deux fils, les marquis de Montpouillan et de Castelnaut*, ed. Marquis de La Grange. 4 vols. (Paris, 1843), IV, p. 23.
37 Héroard, *Journal*, II, 2243; Fontenay-Mareuil, *Mémoires*, I, 268–70, 325–7; Griselle, *Etat de la maison du Roi*, pp. 74, 190; Marvick, *Louis XIII*, p. 162.
38 Héroard, *Journal*, II, 2317–9, 2327–9; Fontenay-Mareuil, *Mémoires*, I, 317–19, 341; *Mercure françois*, IV (1616), 331; Carmona, *Marie de Médicis*, pp. 290–6; Moote, *Louis XIII*, pp. 81–5; Ruth Kleinman, *Anne of Austria* (Columbus, 1985), pp. 23–5.
39 *Journal d'Arnauld 1614–1620*, p. 59; Héroard, *Journal*, II, 2341–2432; François Annibal d'Estrées, *Mémoires*, ed. Petitot, 2nd ser. vol. 16 (Paris, 1822), pp. 284–5; B.N., Dupuy 92, fol. 113; Dossiers bleus 8, fols. 61, 99; Lalanne, *Oeuvres de Malherbe*, III, 417; Beaucaire, *Mémoires de Richelieu*, I, 417.
40 Héroard, *Journal*, II, 2423; B.N., Dossiers bleus 8, fols. 61, 99; Pièces originales 21, fols.

87–8; Dupuy 92, fol. 113; *Journal d'Arnauld 1614–1620*, pp. xx, 56–7, 59, 222; Jean-Antoine Pithon-Curt, *Histoire de la noblesse du Comté-Venaissin*, 4 vols. (Paris, 1743–50), IV, 170; Anselme, *Histoire généalogique*, VI, 230–1; Richard Bonney, *The King's Debts* (Oxford, 1981), p. 91, ns.2,3; Louis Batiffol, "Le Coup d'état du 24 avril 1617," *Rev hist* 97 (1908), 49; idem, *Le Louvre sous Henri IV et Louis XIII* (Paris, 1930), p. 49; idem, "Louis XIII et le duc de Luynes," *Rev hist* 102 (1909) 248, n. 9; Jonathan Dewald, *Pont-St-Pierre 1398–1789* (Berkeley, 1987), p. 181; Eugène Griselle, *Ecurie, vénerie, fauconnerie et louveterie du Roi Louis XIII* (Paris, 1912), p. 28.

41 Beaucaire, *Mémoires de Richelieu*, II, 171; *Relation exacte de tout de qui s'est passé à la mort du mareschal d'Ancre*, eds. Michaud and Poujoulat (Paris, 1837), p. 455; François de Paule de Clermont, marquis de Montglat, *Mémoires*, ed. Petitot. 2nd ser. vol. 49. (Paris, 1825), pp. 24–5; Paul Phélypeaux de Pontchartrain, *Mémoires concernant les affaires de France sous la régence de Marie de Médicis*, eds. Michaud and Poujoulat, 2nd ser., vol. 5 (Paris, 1837), p. 386.

42 Fontenay-Mareuil, *Mémoires*, I, 338–40; Griselle, *Etat de la maison du Roi*, pp. 74, 190.

43 François de Bassompierre, *Journal de ma vie. Mémoires du maréchal de Bassompierre*, ed. Edouard Chanterac, 4 vols. (Paris, 1870–77), II, 386–7.

44 Berthold Zeller, *Le Connêtable de Luynes* (Paris, 1879), p. 268.

45 Eugène Griselle, ed., *Lettres à la main de Louis XIII*, 2 vols. (Paris, 1914), I, 259.

46 Batiffol, "Louis XIII et le duc de Luynes," *Rev hist* 102 (1909), 246; B.N., Cinq Cents de Colbert 98, fol. 150.

47 Héroard, *Journal*, II, 2259.

48 Chevallier, *Louis XIII*, p. 439; Moote, *Louis XIII*, pp. 80, 148.

49 Héroard, *Journal*, II, 2591; *Journal d'Arnauld 1614–1620*, p. 379; Armand Baschet, *Le Roi chez la Reine* (Paris, 1866), pp. 311–90; Kleinman, *Anne of Austria*, pp. 28–44.

50 Louis Batiffol, *La Vie intime d'une reine de France au XVII siècle* (Paris, 1906), pp. 322–403.

51 Batiffol, "Louis XIII et le duc de Luynes," *Rev hist* 102 (1909), 243–4; idem, *Le Roi Louis XIII à vingt ans*, pp. 480–1; Louis Vaunois, *Vie de Louis XIII* (Paris, 1944), pp. 219–22; Chevallier, *Louis XIII*, pp. 437–55; Foisil, *L'Enfant Louis XIII*, p. 223; Moote, *Louis XIII*, pp. 148–9; Marvick, *Louis XIII*, p. 223; Gabriel Hanotaux and the duc de La Force, *Histoire du Cardinal de Richelieu*, 6 vols. (Paris, 1893–1947), II, part 1, 103–9; Zeller, *Le Connêtable de Luynes*, pp. 7–8; Victor Cousin, "Le Duc et connêtable de Luynes," *Journal des Savants* (May 1861), 266–7; Françoise Hildesheimer, *Richelieu* (Paris, 2004), pp. 82, 421.

52 Jean Claude Pascal, *L'Amant du Roi* (Monaco, 1991), pp. 140–3, 375–87.

53 Héroard, *Journal*, II, 2189, 10 March 1614, 2253, 8 December 1614; Malherbe, *Oeuvres*, I, 250; Batiffol, "Louis XIII et le duc de Luynes," *Rev hist* 102 (1909) 244.

54 Héroard, *Journal*, II, 2247, 6 November 1614.

55 Ibid., 2256, 21 December 1614.

55 Héroard, *Journal*, II, 2247, 6 November 1614

56 Ibid., II, 2512–3, 10 January 1618.

57 Ibid., II, 2414–5, 4 and 5 November 1616; 2417, 7 November 1616.

58 Vaunois, *Louis XIII*, pp. 563–7; Chevallier, *Louis XIII*, pp. 437–41; Héroard, *Journal*, II, 2415, 2692.

59 Beaucaire, *Mémoires de Richelieu*, III, 175–7; *Recueil des pièces les plus curieuses qui ont esté faites pendant le règne du Connestable M. de Luynes* (Paris, 1628), *La Remonstrance à Théophile* (1620), p. 122; *La Sybille françoise* (1620), p. 281; B.N., imprimés Lb 36, *La Magie des Favoris* (1619).

60 Robert Oresko, "Homosexuality and the Court Elites of Early Modern France," *The Pursuit of Sodomy*, eds., Kent Gerard and Gert Hekma (New York, 1989), pp. 105–28.

61 Tallemant des Réaux, *Historiettes*, I, 335–48, 1016, n. 6; Moote, *Louis XIII*, pp. 165–6, 285–9; Chevallier, *Louis XIII*, pp. 441–52.

62 Etienne Algay de Martignac, *Mémoires de Gaston, duc d'Orléans*, ed. Petitot, 2nd ser., vol. 31 (Paris, 1824), p. 45; Griselle, *Etat de la maison du Roi*, pp. 83, 93; Anselme, *Histoire généalogique*, VII, 557, 637.

63 Françoise de Bertaut de Motteville, *Mémoires pour servir à l'histoire d'Anne d'Autriche*, ed.

Petitot, 2nd ser., vol. 36 (Paris, 1824), p. 338; Beaucaire, *Mémoires de Richelieu*, III, 103; Louis Batiffol, *La Duchesse de Chevreuse* (Paris, 1913), p. 13.

64   Moote, *Louis XIII*, pp. 148–9.

65   Bassompierre, *Mémoires*, II, 387; Batiffol, *La Duchesse de Chevreuse*, pp. 25–33.

66   Wendy Gibson, *Women in Seventeenth-Century France* (New York, 1989), pp. 62–9, 196–208; Kleinman, *Anne of Austria*, pp. 62–3; Batiffol, *La Duchesse de Chevreuse*, pp. 49–54, 91–137, passim; Chevallier, *Louis XIII*, pp. 411–25; DBF, vol. 8, 1111–13.

67   Griselle, *Etat de la maison du Roi*, p. 3; idem, *Ecurie, vénerie, fauconnerie*, p. 28; Anselme, *Histoire généalogique*, IV, 61–4, 272–4, VI, 230–1; *Journal d'Arnauld 1614–1620*, pp. 376, 418–9; Eugène Halphen, ed., *Journal inédit d'Arnauld d'Andilly 1621* (Paris, 1892), p. 13. For a fuller account, see the author's "Household Appointments and Dismissals at the Court of Louis XIII," *French History*, 21 (2007), 269–88.

68   *Mémoires de Gaston, duc d'Orléans*, pp. 11–12, 45–6; Jean Charay, ed., *Vie du maréchal de Jean-Baptiste d'Ornano* (Grenoble, 1971), p. 63; idem, *Vie du maréchal Alphonse d'Ornano* (Aubenas, 1975), p. 192; Eugène Griselle, *Maisons de la Grande Mademoiselle et de Gaston d'Orléans* (Paris, 1912), p. 8.

69   Griselle, *Etat de la maison du Roi*, pp. 89–90, 93, 103, 327–8; *Journal d'Arnauld 1614–1620*, p. 390; Batiffol, *La Duchesse de Chevreuse*, pp. 13–14; Kleinman, *Anne of Austria*, pp. 38, 48–9, 54–6, 61; Eugène Halphen, ed., *Journal inédit d'Arnauld d'Andilly 1622* (Paris, 1898), pp. 16–17.

70   Griselle, *Etat de la maison du Roi*, p. 3; Moote, *Louis XIII*, pp. 103, 110, 122.

71   Vaunois, *Louis XIII*, p. 221; Chevallier, *Louis XIII*, pp. 181, 453.

72   Ibid., pp. 411, 439, 441.

73   Moote, *Louis XIII*, p. 148.

3

Concini's murder

The *Mercure françois* reported that Concini was killed while resisting arrest for treason. He was killed in the courtyard of the Louvre at about ten o'clock on the morning of Monday 24 April 1617 by Nicolas de l'Hôpital, marquis de Vitry, a captain in the royal bodyguards. Concini, the maréchal d'Ancre, was the favorite of the Queen Mother, who was still acting as if she were regent for the young king, although he had come of age three years earlier. The newspaper account quoted the brash, unpopular Concini as saying, "I'll bite off the fingers of anyone who opposes me!" According to this account, the king had told Vitry "to arrest Concini, and to take some men with him in case he resisted, in short, to arrest him alive or dead."[1]

Concini was usually accompanied by an entourage of fifty to one hundred men because he feared assassination or kidnapping. His entourage included ten noble gentlemen, plus twelve guards wearing his yellow and orange livery, and a number of servants, making it difficult and dangerous to arrest him. Vitry asked his brother Du Hallier, his brother-in-law the baron de Persan, his cousin Du Fay, some gentlemen friends, and reliable members of his guard company to help him make the arrest.[2] He decided to arrest Concini in the long passageway between the entry door and the courtyard of the Louvre. He told his men to close the great door of the Louvre behind Concini when he entered that morning, cutting him off from most of his entourage. Concini was reading a letter that had just been handed to him, so he did not notice their absence. Walking toward him, Vitry met him on the drawbridge leading to the courtyard and said, "I arrest you in the name of the king." Concini, surprised, backed up a few paces until he was against the bridge railing and said, "Who, me?" Vitry's men then shot him in the head, heart, and stomach, and he died instantly, falling on his right side against the railing without saying another word. Vitry's men stabbed him several times, and dumped his body in a nearby guardroom after stripping it of its valuables including a large diamond ring, a scarf, the diamond cross he wore around his neck, and his black velvet cloak.[3]

His body, wrapped in a linen sheet, was buried that night in a plain wooden coffin under the paving stones of the church of Saint Germain de l'Auxerrois. The next day the Paris mob disinterred the body, dragged it across the Pont-Neuf where they hung it by its heels and mutilated it, then dragged it through the streets of Paris shouting, "Long live the king!" Finally, they burned it before Concini's house on the rue Tournon, and threw the ashes and bones into the river.[4]

In a letter to the provincial governors published in the Paris newspaper, the *Mercure françois*, and then separately as a pamphlet in twelve editions including a German translation, the king declared that Concini and his wife used their influence over his mother to usurp royal authority and start a civil war. Their ambition had become a threat to the crown and the king, who ordered Concini's arrest, and when Concini had resisted arrest, his guard captain had shot him dead. This letter emphasized the king's personal involvement in the coup against Concini,[5] and since the *Mercure françois* was a government mouthpiece, Concini had been officially killed for resisting arrest.[6]

Concini's wife, Léonora Galigai, the childhood friend of the Queen Mother and mistress of her wardrobe, was arrested on the same day as an accomplice in her husband's treason. Accused of practicing magic and sorcery, she was tried in June before the Parlement of Paris, found guilty, and decapitated on the evening of 8 July in the Place de Grève before a large crowd. Her body was burned and the ashes thrown to the winds.[7] The Queen Mother was exiled to the château of Blois. She left the Louvre on the afternoon of 3 May after saying good-bye to the young king who was dressed all in white.[8] He had refused to yield to her tearful entreaties to remain at court, making it clear that her political dominance was over and that he intended to rule by himself. Luynes was not mentioned in this account in the *Mercure françois*.

The basic facts of Concini's murder have never been in dispute, but the respective roles of Vitry, the king, and Luynes have been debated ever since. Did Vitry and his men kill Concini in the heat of the moment or did he resist arrest? Did Luynes persuade a reluctant young king to agree to Concini's death if he resisted arrest, and did the king understand what would happen when he agreed? Was Concini murdered or was he executed? Most historians have believed that Concini was killed on the king's orders, so he was executed, which is what Concini's wife and the Italian ambassadors believed.[9] But who was responsible for these orders?

Who killed Concini?

The memoirs of twelve contemporaries provide the most detailed accounts of the murder, and contain significant differences. Seven memoirs were first-hand accounts by individuals with a personal knowledge of events including Montpouillan, Chaulnes, Richelieu, Déagent, Pontchartrain, Arnauld d'Andilly, and Brienne.[10] Montpouillan, Chaulnes, and Déagent were actual conspirators but not eyewitnesses to the murder. There were five second-hand accounts by individuals who had no personal knowledge of events, and four of them, Bassompierre, d'Estrées, Rohan, and Fontenay-Mareuil, had not even been in Paris at the time. The fifth, Montglat, was probably at court, but he did not belong to the king's inner circle.[11] All twelve accounts declared that Louis XIII had ordered Concini's arrest. The question has always been whether or not the king also ordered Concini's death if he resisted arrest. The brief, official account in the *Mercure françois* stated that the king had told Vitry to arrest Concini "alive or dead," but what did this phrase mean? It is ambiguous, and the newspaper account does not elaborate. The *Mercure françois* was only published once a year in book form, and its accounts were often terse because of space limitations, which encouraged ambiguity.[12]

The *Relation exacte de tout ce qui s'est passé à la mort du mareschal d'Ancre* is the most extensive account of the murder, although there is a question about the author's identity. From internal evidence, he was probably Luynes's brother Cadenet, later the duc de Chaulnes, and his account must reflect to some extent Luynes's own view of the murder.[13] The *Relation exacte* was at first attributed to the Marillac brothers, but the author may also have been Marsillac, comte and later duc de La Rochefoucauld, a member of the king's inner circle whose account Chaulnes may have heavily edited.[14] Chaulnes reported that when Vitry told Concini he was under arrest, he took a step backward and bumped into the bridge railing, appearing to put his hand on the hilt of his sword. Vitry had then grabbed Concini's sword arm and signaled to his men to seize him. Five of them had surrounded Concini, and several shots had rung out. No one knew who had fired the first shot, but all five would later claim to have done so. Concini fell and Vitry shouted, "Long live the king," kicking the body flat on to the ground.[15] Concini was killed for appearing to resist arrest, which agrees with the newspaper account.

According to the Chaulnes account, the king, Luynes, and the other conspirators had decided that Concini should be arrested, and Luynes had asked Vitry if he would make the arrest, using as an intermediary his friend Du Buisson, the royal falconer in charge of the *vol de la rivière*, because Vitry knew him.[16] Buisson's father had been a member of the household of Vitry's father. Vitry agreed to arrest Concini if the king ordered it, and the next day he went to see Louis to have his orders verified. Nothing was said directly in this interview about what Vitry should do if Concini resisted arrest. Chaulnes made it clear that Vitry and the king were the decision-makers, not Luynes, who dithered in apprehension.

There are several other versions of how Concini died. Déagent and Pont-chartrain reported that members of Concini's entourage looked as if they were putting their hands on their sword hilts, which provoked Vitry's men to fire.[17] Montglat stated that Vitry ordered his men to fire because Concini was trying to defend himself.[18] Arnauld d'Andilly said that after telling Concini he was under arrest, Vitry had stabbed him with a sword so hard that he was thrown back against the railing, and four of his men had then shot him.[19] Brienne declared that Vitry had denied he fired first, and said that when he had told Concini he was under arrest, several shots had rung out unexpectedly, knocking Concini to the ground and killing him. So, Vitry's men had killed him on their own initiative.[20] Exactly what happened will probably never be known.

In short, there was no agreement on who had fired the first shot, whether Vitry had done so, whether he had ordered his men to fire, or whether a killing frenzy had broken out spontaneously among them, and there was no agreement on whether the shots had been fired because Concini had tried to defend himself, or because someone among his remaining men had appeared to do so. It is clear that any attempt Concini may have made at self-defense was slight, and that he was killed for appearing to resist arrest rather than for actually doing so. In fact, he was probably killed without provocation in a summary-style execution. His death must have had Vitry's prior approval because his men had acted immediately without hesitation or fear of the consequences.

Vitry had the temperament to kill in the heat of the moment. He had a reputation for being angry, ambitious, and violent. Brienne described him as "having a nature boiling (with emotion), the desire to advance himself being so overpowering that nothing appeared impossible to him, nor too contemptible in order to succeed."[21] Cardinal de Retz remarked that Vitry had little sense, and was daring to the point of recklessness.[22] He had already fought in several duels.[23] His portrait shows a short, stout man in black armor with thick white hair and mustaches, the florid face, fat jowls, and big nose of a heavy eater and drinker. He has an angry stubborn look, and his conduct to those around him was habitually rude and ugly. After becoming governor of Provence, he had quarreled constantly with local officials, and in a rage had attacked and beaten Richelieu's personal representative, the archbishop of Bordeaux, with his walking stick. Violent tempers and lack of self-restraint were common among the nobility, but Vitry's excesses had become a political liability. He was recalled in September 1637, sent to the Bastille, and only released after Richelieu's death.[24]

Why did Vitry and his men feel so confident about doing murder? Why did they have no qualms about killing the Queen Mother's favorite? Evidently, they must have already had the king's consent to Concini's murder or thought they had. They would not have been so quick to kill him otherwise. The account of Jean de Caumont, marquis de Montpouillan, is similar to that in the *Mercure françois* except he reported that the king had explicitly agreed to Concini's death if he resisted arrest. Montpouillan said that when Luynes told Vitry he was to arrest Concini on the king's orders, Vitry had insisted on verification of these orders because he did not want the king to deny all knowledge of them later, making him solely responsible for the murder. During the interview, Vitry had asked what he should do if Concini resisted arrest, and the king, Luynes, and his brothers did not answer. Finally, Montpouillan told Vitry to kill him. Vitry then asked the king directly if that was his order, and the king said yes.[25] Since Luynes still had said nothing, he had tacitly endorsed the king's order.

Montpouillan's memoirs were written by his brother, the marquis de Castelnaut, after his death from a head wound received during the siege of Tonneins in 1621. The memoirs were based on what he had told his brother about the murder, but Castelnaut tended to exaggerate his brother's importance, so the memoirs are not entirely reliable. In his interview with the king, for example, Montpouillan was supposed to have told Vitry to kill Concini because Luynes lacked the courage to do so. According to Castelnaut, a jealous Luynes had destroyed Montpouillan's favor with the king by insisting that he was untrustworthy as a Protestant. Montpouillan had left court permanently in August 1618 to join the Huguenot armies fighting in the southwest where he died four years later.[26] Louis Batiffol said that Déagent, not Montpouillan, had told Vitry to kill Concini if he resisted arrest, but he cited Montpouillan's memoirs as his source for this. As a soldier, Montpouillan would have been more likely to have given this order than Déagent, who was a financial official. Castelnaut reported several occasions on which Montpouillan had offered to kill Concini because Luynes and his brothers had refused to do so.[27] Batiffol probably thought that Montpouillan's role had been exaggerated by his brother, and that since Déagent had played a more important role in the conspiracy, he had given the order to Vitry to kill Concini. Déagent in his memoirs said that he was one of a group of conspirators who had told the king Concini must be killed, but that he had suggested the judicial process be used for this purpose.[28]

Brienne in his memoirs stated that the king had embraced Vitry and assured him of his protection, but he had only ordered him to arrest Concini, not kill him. With Luynes's support, Vitry had then asked the king what he should do if Concini resisted arrest, which allowed the king to fall into the trap set for him of agreeing to Concini's death if he resisted arrest.[29] In Brienne's account, Vitry had secured the king's agreement to Concini's death with Luynes's tacit support. Richelieu reported that Vitry and Luynes had discussed the murder beforehand, and then had secured the king's agreement to their plans. Jean-Baptiste Matthieu, who later wrote a history of Louis XIII, endorsed Richelieu's view by declaring that there had been a plot between Vitry and Luynes to kill Concini.[30] He gave no details of this plot, however, and there is no other confirmation of its existence.

It was widely believed that the king had not known Concini was to be killed, and that he had not agreed to his death. Brienne and Fontenay-Mareuil stated that the king had been tricked into agreeing to Concini's death.[31] Richelieu endorsed this view.[32] Maréchal d'Estrées remarked that it was often said in later years that the king had not understood that Concini was to be killed.[33] The essential question has always been whether or not the king fully understood what he was ordering. Elizabeth Marvick believed that the murder was committed with his full knowledge and consent.[34] A. Lloyd Moote, however, thought that the king did not explicitly order Concini's death, and that he may not have understood the probable consequences of his implicit agreement.[35]

In the king's version, Vitry and Luynes were responsible for Concini's death. In Richelieu's version, Luynes alone was responsible for Concini's murder. Richelieu declared that Luynes had poisoned the king's mind against Concini, and convinced him that Concini must die. Luynes had planned the murder, convinced Vitry to do it, and persuaded a reluctant young king to agree. Motivated by ambition, greed, envy, and fear, Luynes had wanted to acquire Concini's power and fortune, but he was afraid that Concini would discover what he was planning and kill him first. So, he had plotted with Vitry to strike quickly and unexpectedly. Concini was killed on the king's orders, but Luynes was responsible for these orders and for Concini's death.[36] Richelieu wrote, "The king, who had been displeased with the maréchal d'Ancre for a long time, decided to arrest and imprison him. Luynes, who believed that he could be safe only if he died ... made a case for killing him, to which the king did not want to agree, but felt obliged to ignore his own wishes in the matter."[37]

Six of the twelve contemporary accounts, the memoirs of Déagent, d'Estrées, Montglat, Rohan, Fontenay-Mareuil, and Bassompierre, echoed Richelieu's version of Luynes's role in the murder repeated by the anti-Luynes pamphleteers. This version appeared in the seventeenth-century histories of Scipion Dupleix, François Mézeray, Vittorio Siri, and Jean-Baptiste Matthieu.[38] Through Mézeray, this version was incorporated into the eighteenth-century histories of Michel LeVassor, Henri Philippe de Limiers, Gabriel Daniel, Henri Griffet, and Madame d'Arconville, and came to influence twentieth-century historians Louis Batiffol and Gabriel Hanotaux.[39] Which of them is closer to what actually happened, the official version, the king's version, or Richelieu's version?

Historical accounts of the murder

There are a considerable number of discrepancies and inconsistencies in the twelve accounts of the murder.[40] The most reliable repeat the official version in the *Mercure françois* and do not hold Luynes responsible for the murder. Seven first-hand accounts were written by individuals with a personal knowledge of events, and five of these follow the *Mercure françois* version. Only the first-hand accounts by Richelieu and Déagent accuse Luynes of the murder, and they both had a personal grudge against him.

Richelieu had been appointed secretary of state for foreign affairs in November 1616 through Concini's patronage, but the king soon developed a strong dislike of him because of his imperious manner. Attempting to lessen his antipathy, Richelieu had made overtures to his favorite, offering to keep Luynes informed of events in the Queen Mother's camp, but Luynes did not take him up on this offer, and Richelieu had no idea that a conspiracy was in progress. After the murder, Déagent and Luynes tried to lessen the king's aversion to Richelieu, but he lost his office, anyway, and was forced to retire in June 1617 to his abbey of Coussay in Anjou, then in November to his bishopric of Luçon, and five months later to the papal enclave at Avignon. Luynes recalled him a year and a half later, but Richelieu always blamed him for destroying his first ministerial career.[41] Luynes had the power and position that Richelieu wanted.

Through Concini's patronage, Guichard Déagent was appointed deputy to the financial superintendent. Then he joined the conspirators, and was rewarded by being named a financial intendant and a member of the royal council. Losing favor, he was sent in disgrace to Grenoble in 1619 to become chief justice of its *Chambre des Comptes* or financial high court. He blamed his disgrace on the jealousy of Luynes, whom he said had felt threatened by his growing influence over the king. Déagent returned to court after Luynes's death, but Richelieu sent him to the Bastille in 1624 for policy differences. Released five years later, he returned to Grenoble where he died in 1645. At Richelieu's request, he wrote his memoirs shortly before his death and dedicated them to the Cardinal. They were published in 1668 by a grandson. Déagent praised Richelieu and blamed Luynes and Vitry for Concini's death. His memoirs are not always reliable, however, as he admitted on the first page, because he had burned his papers when he left Paris, so he had to rely on his not entirely unbiased memory in writing them.[42]

The other five first-hand accounts echo the official version in the *Mercure françois*. The authors of two, Montpouillan and Chaulnes, were court nobles and conspirators belonging to the king's inner circle. The other three, Pontchartrain, Brienne, and Arnauld d'Andilly, were high government officials outside this circle. The memoirs of secretary of state Paul Phélypeaux, sieur de Pontchartrain, were written shortly before his death in 1621. Covering the years from 1610 to 1620, they seldom mentioned Richelieu. Pontchartrain supported the new regime because he had been dismissed from office by the Queen Mother and Concini in 1616, and then restored a year later by the king after Concini's murder.[43] Henri de Loménie de Brienne wrote his memoirs sometime between his retirement in 1643 and his death in 1666. He had entered with his father into joint tenure as a secretary of state in 1615, and exercised this office for the next three decades. Neither he nor his father had much influence, and a reoccurring theme in his memoirs was hostility toward Richelieu and his clients.[44] Robert Arnauld d'Andilly wrote his memoirs in the 1660s. He had begun his career in 1615 as the deputy of an uncle who was a financial intendant. He did not receive his uncle's office at his death, although he had been promised it by Luynes, who did secure him the office of deputy to the superintendent of finance. Richelieu later secured him the office of intendant of Gaston d'Orléans's household, but he lost this office in a scandal and had to retire to his estates. Arnauld d'Andilly returned to political life in 1634 through Richelieu's patronage, and served the crown for two more decades. He died in 1674 at the age of eighty-five.[45]

The account of Concini's death in the *Mercure français* was written before 1620. Pontchartrain's memoirs were written between 1620 and 1621, and the accounts of Chaulnes and Montpouillan were written in the early 1620s. Their accounts were the least influenced by Richelieu, who had not yet come to power, and are the most favorable to Luynes for this reason. The accounts by Brienne and Arnauld followed the official version in the *Mercure français*, and were more objective than the other seven accounts, which were written years later and tainted by Richelieu's views. The first-hand accounts by Montpouillan, Chaulnes, Pontchartrain, Brienne, and Arnauld d'Andilly are the most reliable, and they do not hold Luynes responsible for the murder.[46]

The second-hand accounts by Fontenay-Mareuil, Bassompierre, Rohan, Estrées, and Montglat followed Richelieu's version of events, and blamed Luynes for the murder, insisting that he had persuaded a reluctant young king to agree to Concini's death.[47] Written much later and based on second-hand information, these accounts reflected their authors'dislike of Luynes and eagerness to please Richelieu. Fontenay-Mareuil, Bassompierre, and Rohan were not even in Paris when the murder was committed. They were serving with the army in Champagne.[48]

Henri, duc de Rohan, was an ardent supporter of the Queen Mother, and he despised Luynes as much as the favorite detested him. Rohan insisted that Luynes had poisoned the king's mind against his mother's favorite. According to him, Luynes had been influenced by the group of "dishonorable" men who were his friends, and he had convinced the king to murder Concini. Rohan wrote his memoirs sometime between 1629 when he went into Italian exile, and his death in 1638.[49]

Bassompierre was dining with Rohan in Champagne when they received the news of Concini's murder. Bassompierre had been a supporter of the Queen Mother, but he had switched his loyalty to the king after Concini's death, and had cultivated Luynes to become his client. He had led a royal army against the Queen Mother in 1620. Luynes sent him to Spain in 1621 to negotiate the treaty ending the Valteline affair, and Bassompierre reported in his memoirs that the abbé Ruccellai had told him that Luynes was sending him away from court because the king had grown too fond of him. Bassompierre's comment was that "he [Luynes] was like a man who feared to be cuckolded every time someone flirted with his wife." The abbé advised Bassompierre to accept the ambassadorial assignment and return to court. Bassompierre came back to court in June 1621, and fought at the siege of Montauban that autumn. Jealous of Luynes, he showed no sorrow at his death, returning to the Queen Mother's party for which Richelieu sent him to the Bastille in 1631. He wrote his memoirs in prison, and was only released after Richelieu's death.[50]

Fontenay-Mareuil had been a childhood playmate of Louis XIII. Forced by the king to sell his office of captain of the Louvre to Luynes, he bought an office of camp master in the Piedmont regiment through Concini's patronage and reluctantly left court, blaming Luynes for his exile. He was serving with Bassompierre in the royal army in Champagne when Concini was killed. Fontenay-Mareuil loathed Luynes, and his memoirs written during the 1650s are consistently hostile to him.[51]

In April 1617, Marshal d'Estrées was residing in his government of Laon. He customarily wrote only about what he knew, so he had little to say about Concini's murder because he had not been in Paris at the time. The first edition of his memoirs ended in 1617, and the second in 1624. The marshal had been the Queen Mother's client and Concini's friend, and he enjoyed the patronage of Richelieu whom he served as a diplomat. His memoirs were written at Richelieu's request and are filled with effusive praise of the Cardinal.[52] He had almost nothing to say about Luynes.

The marquis de Montglat may have been at court in April 1617, but he was not a member of the king's inner circle. He obtained his information from his grandmother, the king's governess now retired and living behind the Louvre, and his mother, the Queen Mother's choice for governess of her daughters who knew Richelieu well. Covering the years from 1635 to 1685, Montglat's memoirs had little to say about the years before 1635, and what they did say was unfavorable to Luynes.[53]

Another important contemporary source was the daily journal of the king's doctor, Jean Héroard, who did not record any details of the murder in his entry

for 24 April 1617, just a one-sentence notation that Concini had been killed on
the Louvre drawbridge between ten and eleven o'clock that morning.[54] Elizabeth Marvick has noted that beginning in March 1617, Héroard's daily entries
showed signs of extensive editing and recopying, and became increasingly
minimal and unrevealing in content.[55] There was a large blank space left after
the notation on Concini's death, which Héroard may have meant to fill in later
but never did.[56] Since he recorded the minutiae of the king's daily existence,
the reason why he omitted an account of Concini's murder remains a mystery.
Héroard may not have wanted to implicate the king in the murder, and his mute
journal may testify to the king's direct participation in Concini's death.

The best scholarly accounts of the murder are those by Louis Batiffol,
Hélène Duccini, and Elizabeth Marvick. Batiffol's account has been the most
influential. He believed that the king had implicitly agreed to the murder because
he did not countermand the order to Vitry to kill Concini, and he believed that
Déagent was the driving force in the conspiracy, noting that Luynes and his
brothers were silent during the king's interview with Vitry. Batiffol considered
Luynes too indecisive and cowardly to have planned and executed a successful
political murder. In his opinion, Luynes had needed the support of his brothers,
Déagent, Marcillac, Tronson, and Vitry in order to act. Batiffol's negative assessment of Luynes shows the influence of Richelieu's memoirs.[57]

Hélène Duccini has followed Batiffol's interpretation, although she views
the question as being whether the king ordered Concini's murder, making it
premeditated, or whether Concini was killed for resisting arrest, making it an
execution. She comments that Luynes was not violent by nature, but that he
was pressured by those around him into persuading the king that Concini had
to be killed.[58] Elizabeth Marvick notes that the finger of blame has often been
pointed at Luynes, but that his role was secondary to that of the king, who was
the driving force in the conspiracy.[59] Batiffol and Duccini agree that Luynes was
not primarily responsible for the murder, although they have a more negative
view of his character than Marvick. What was Luynes's role in the conspiracy?

The anatomy of a conspiracy

An incident on 12 November 1616 demonstrates why Louis XIII despised his
mother's favorite. Concini arrived at the Louvre that morning accompanied by
an entourage of about a hundred men, a noisy crowd. He entered the grand
gallery running along the Seine to find the king and three companions standing
at a window overlooking the river. Usually accompanied by only a few retainers,
the king would often appear alone and forgotten. Concini stopped at a window
but did not speak, and he allowed his entourage to remove their hats to him as

if he were king. No one doffed his hat to Louis, who left the gallery in a seething fury without saying a word.[60] He had been snubbed and humiliated again in public by his mother's favorite. There had been many such incidents, and a contemporary described Concini's behavior as "reckless" and "insolent."[61]

A month earlier, Concini had asked the king to compensate him for the pillaging of his Paris mansion by a mob, telling the king that because of the attack "he had lost much" in the royal service, an effrontery coming from a foreigner who had made a fortune from the crown. Louis turned away from him in silence, but Concini familiarly persisted, declaring that the king had not answered his question. The king turned back to him and said enigmatically, "Didn't you hear what I said?" The king, of course, had said nothing, but his body language had been eloquent. When he learned that Concini had received the outrageous sum of 150,000 écus (450,000 livres) in compensation from the finance minister who was his client, the king remarked bitterly that there was never any money in the treasury when he wanted 30 livres, but that "they" had easily found 450,000 livres for Concini. Arnauld d'Andilly estimated that Concini's actual loss was 150,000 livres.[62]

A few months earlier, the king had been refused 2,000 écus (6,000 livres) to cover his expenses. Concini accompanied by a large entourage had gone over to him and offered to give him the money by speaking to one of his clients in the treasury. His presumption and his arrogant display of power infuriated the king, who remarked sarcastically that a certain foreigner, always accompanied by a large crowd and penniless when he had first come to France, had said that he should come to him whenever he needed money.[63] Money was power, and the king had neither. Stony-faced as usual, he repressed his fury and resentment, which may have made him ill in October 1616.[64]

Concini's wife, Léonora, was also overly familiar with the king, making him feel young and powerless. The king was romping with his dogs under her palace windows when she sent down word that she had a migraine, and that he was making too much noise, implying that he should go play somewhere else. The king sarcastically remarked that if her rooms were too noisy, Paris was big enough that she could easily find rooms elsewhere, that is, outside the palace.[65]

Concini's power was based on his own and his wife's relationship with the Queen Mother. As a husband and wife team of royal favorites, they had amassed a fortune because Léonora controlled the distribution of royal patronage and approved the annual list of pensions and gifts. She and her husband had elevated bribe-taking into an art form. Named first gentleman of the king's bedchamber, Concini bought the marquisat of Ancre, while Léonora became the Queen Mother's mistress of robes. They were both influential members of her private advisory group on political affairs. As a councillor of state and a marshal,

Concini attended meetings of the royal council. He sat on the council of finance and had clients in the ministry of finance. He maintained a large clientele in Picardy where he created a provincial power base that included the fortresses of Amiens, Montdidier, Péronne, and Roye, all heavily fortified to the dismay of the local nobility. He was in turn lieutenant general of Picardy and Normandy, and he had wanted to be governor. He became interested in politics after the noble revolt of 1614, and he had become the Queen Mother's trusted political adviser by 1616, although his authoritarian attitude frightened the great nobility. Widely regarded as crass, greedy, and ambitious, Concini enjoyed displaying his wealth and power, and his brash, arrogant manner offended the court nobility who loathed him. Regarding him an upstart foreigner, they resented his control over royal patronage.[66] His downfall was inevitable by 1617.

The openly contemptuous attitude of Concini and his wife toward the young king reflected that of the Queen Mother, who did not realize that he was growing up. She treated the sixteen-year-old as if he were a rather stupid child. She enjoyed the exercise of power and wanted to continue acting as regent with Concini's advice and support, so she ignored the king and pushed him aside. There were rumors in Paris during the autumn of 1616 that she had showed little concern for the king and excluded him from affairs of state. She discouraged him from attending council meetings over which she presided, telling her ministers not to talk to him, and she encouraged him to pursue frivolous activities such as drilling his soldiers, building forts, and going hunting with Luynes and his brothers. The king was greatly upset in February 1617 when his mother cancelled a planned morale-building tour of the army in Champagne, and sent him instead on a tour of the Ile-de-France, which had little military significance at the time.[67] Louis had a stronger personality than either his mother or Concini realized, and he deeply resented his exclusion from power.

The conspiracy to get rid of Concini began on 27 November 1616 when the king climbed the stairs in the Louvre to visit Luynes in his rooms above for the first time. Their discussions on what to do about Concini began then, and continued during the ballet rehearsals for "Renaud" in December and January. The wildly successful performance on 29 January convinced them that the court would welcome Concini's removal from power and the end of the Queen Mother's dominance. Luynes suggested ways of getting rid of Concini in the feverish planning that followed during February and March, and he assembled a small group of conspirators who helped in deciding what to do. They included his brothers and his first cousin Modène; Déagent, a financial intendant; Tronson, a royal secretary; Marcillac, a gentleman of Condé's household now in the Queen Mother's service; Du Buisson, the head of a fauconnerie department; and Chevallier, the first president of the Paris Cour des Aides, a financial high court. They were joined by the king, Montpouillan his young favorite, Vitry a guard captain, Vitry's brother Du Hallier, and Persan, Vitry's brother-in-law.[68]

The conspirators quickly reached the conclusion that killing Concini was the only way to get rid of him permanently. At first, Luynes suggested that the Queen Mother should send her favorites home to Florence with all the wealth that they had acquired in France as an inducement to speed their departure. Luynes spoke to an old acquaintance, Christophe Vital de Lestang, bishop of Carcassonne, a former master of the royal chapel now at court as a deputy from the Estates of Languedoc, and asked him if he would advise the Queen Mother to send her favorites away, and the bishop, who knew nothing of the conspiracy, agreed. Luynes in gratitude would later nominate him for membership in the Order of Saint Esprit, although the pamphleteers insisted that he was never rewarded. Lestang spoke to the Queen Mother about the delegation's affairs, and during the conversation, he tactfully suggested that she might consider sending her unpopular favorites from court. The Queen Mother spoke to Léonora, who was willing to leave and began to pack immediately, but Concini with his usual bravado refused to go. He had levied an army to fight the rebellious nobles at Soissons, and he did not want to leave France.[69]

Luynes then suggested that the king should tell his mother that her political dominance was over, that he intended to rule alone, and that he commanded her to send her favorites away. Because the king was of age and had been crowned, he had the authority to do this, but he did not have the power. After discussing this idea, the conspirators decided that the Queen Mother would refuse and tell Concini, who would realize what they were planning and strike first.[70] The king would be imprisoned; Luynes would be killed; and the others would be imprisoned or exiled. The conspirators decided that sending Concini to Italy would never be a permanent solution, anyway, because of his ambition. He would almost certainly return to France, and try to restore the Queen Mother to power. Another solution had to be found.

The conspirators next urged the king to leave Paris for a safe refuge where he could gather the troops to oppose Concini. Luynes suggested his château of Amboise in the Loire valley where the king could issue a plea to the French nobility to join him, and levy an army with which to confront his mother and her favorite. Because Concini had placed his own men among the royal bodyguards, Luynes suggested that the king leave court escorted by only a few trusted servants and loyal members of the Paris city guard. Luynes would send the light horse company garrisoned at Amboise under the command of his brother Brantes to meet the king on the road from Paris.[71] This plan was discarded, however, because the king could be kidnapped on the road by Concini's men, and it was uncertain how many nobles would actually respond to his plea for assistance, especially if the Queen Mother countermanded it.

Luynes and the conspirators now suggested that the king leave Paris for Champagne to take command of the royal army there, since it was already in existence and did not have to be levied.[72] Luynes suggested that the king consider joining the rebellious nobles at Soissons, who were protesting Concini's influence over royal policy, and that he lead their army, or their troops combined with the royal army, against his mother and her favorite. Cardinal Guise had already been in correspondence with Luynes about such an alliance, and the Cardinal's brothers, the ducs de Guise and Chevreuse, had joined the rebels at Soissons.[73] Bassompierre reported that one of Luynes's men came to his Paris lodgings in February 1617 to tell him that the Queen Mother wanted to send Luynes away from court, and that Luynes had advised the king to leave Paris to escape her control. The message was a warning, and Bassompierre went to see the Queen Mother to tell her so that evening. He advised her to allow the king to rule, and to send her favorites away from court, but she did not heed him.[74]

The conspirators rejected the plan of having the king leave Paris to join the army in Champagne because there was no reason to think that he would be any safer there from kidnapping and imprisonment than at court, and if he used the royal army to take back his throne, there would be civil war. Concini had already levied a sizeable force to use against the rebel nobles.[75] He could use these troops against the king, especially if the king had allied himself with the rebels, and if the Queen Mother had ordered the royal army in Champagne to support Concini. The outcome of a military confrontation between the 16-year-old king and the 42-year-old Concini was uncertain. If Concini won, he would imprison the king and revitalize the spluttering noble revolt, turning it into a civil war between the king and his mother.

Besides, the Queen Mother could use the king's departure from Paris as an excuse to put her favorite son Gaston on the throne. Luynes had already warned the king that his mother preferred his brother.[76] Younger and more malleable, Gaston would allow her political dominance to continue. The king could be imprisoned or killed, which was not a groundless fear because both his predecessors, Henri III and Henri IV, had been murdered. Since his father's experience had made it clear that whoever controlled Paris ruled France, the conspirators decided that the king's absence from Paris would endanger his throne, and that it was politically too risky for him to leave the capital.

The suggestion was now made that Concini and his wife should be arrested and tried for treason by the Parlement of Paris. Déagent probably made this suggestion because he was certain that there would be enough incriminating evidence among their papers to convict them both of treason.[77] The king liked the idea of using the judicial system to eliminate Concini and letting the high court take the responsibility for executing him. He decided to have Concini arrested at his Paris house and put on trial before the Parlement, which despised him and would condemn him. Once Concini was imprisoned in the Bastille, the king would explain to his mother that her favorite's ambition had made him so dangerous that his arrest was necessary. Considering her probable reaction, the king decided to send her to a royal château outside Paris for awhile, allowing him to get a firm grip on the affairs of state. He also decided to recall his father's old ministers, especially those whom his mother and Concini had removed from office. So, he summoned Du Vair, Brûlart de Sillery, Jeannin, Villeroy, Puysieux, Pontchartrain, Brienne, Gesvres, Sceaux, and Châteauneuf to form a new government.[78]

Because the king liked this idea, Luynes agreed to it, but he pointed out its flaws. Bringing Concini to trial would take time, allowing the Queen Mother to gather her forces and act. She could intervene in the judicial process to have Concini released, or she could make certain that he was not convicted, which meant that the conspirators would not control the trial's outcome.[79] Six months earlier, the rebel nobles had discussed ways of getting rid of Concini, including seizing him and putting him on trial before the Parlement of Paris, but they had discarded this idea because of the slowness of the judicial process and the likelihood of the Queen Mother's revenge. They next considered taking Concini to a distant city under their control and putting him on trial there, knowing that they would have to leave Paris immediately after the kidnapping to escape the Queen Mother's vengeance. Finally, they decided that killing Concini would be the easiest and safest solution. Nothing was done, however, because their leader, the prince de Condé, was arrested the next month, and the rebels left court for Soissons.[80]

The conspirators knew that time was not on their side. The conspiracy had been in progress for three months, and sooner or later the Queen Mother and her favorite would discover what was going on. Mangot, Keeper of the Seals and one of Concini's clients, had nearly discovered the conspiracy in March. By then, Brûlart de Sillery, Villeroy, and Jeannin had learned about it, and Villeroy had told the duc de Bouillon, a leader of the Huguenot party. Luynes had been in touch with the rebel nobles at Soissons, so they knew about it. When Vitry joined the conspiracy, he began to recruit men to help him arrest Concini, so more people heard about it, and Concini's spies were everywhere. The conspirators were not discovered, however, because Concini himself was away from court at the time, and he was so unpopular that no one told the Queen Mother, hoping that the conspirators would succeed. When Concini returned to court in mid-March, the king insisted on his immediate arrest.[81]

The logic of the conspirators' planning had led them inevitably to the conclusion that if Concini resisted arrest, which he probably would, then he would have to be killed. They had by now recognized that death was the only permanent way of getting rid of him, and that being killed while resisting arrest would give his death the quasi-legal appearance of executing a traitor. The problem was to find someone who would do it. The conspirators asked whether Luynes or his brothers would do it, since using a new favorite to get rid of an old was a classic tactic, but Luynes refused for them all. They next asked the lieutenant civil of the Paris *prévôté* court, Henri de Mesmes, who said that he would arrest Concini because that was his job, but that he would not kill him for resisting arrest because that was not his job.[82]

Vitry was asked next, probably at the king's suggestion because he knew him well. Luynes asked Vitry if he would arrest Concini, and he agreed after he had been promised the king's protection and gratitude once the deed was done. Concini's death for resisting arrest was compatible with Vitry's duties as a guard captain because he would be enforcing the king's orders and protecting his life. The only remaining question was where to arrest Concini. The king said that he did not want the arrest to occur in his mother's apartments or in his own rooms in the palace, so Concini had to be arrested outside the Louvre, which suggests that the king knew the arrest would be violent. Concini was arrested and killed a few weeks later at the entrance to the Louvre.[83]

Contemporary accounts, including those by actual conspirators, stated that Luynes was apprehensive about killing Concini.[84] His uneasiness was attributed to character flaws of timidity, cowardice, fear, and indecisiveness. If Luynes had been as fearful and vacillating as his enemies claimed, he would never have played an organizing role in the conspiracy. He hesitated because he did not think Concini's murder would be in his own best interests as the new favorite. The murder set a bad precedent with potentially damaging effects. There was no easy way to stop being a favorite because they did not usually retire or resign, and Luynes feared that one day Concini's fate would be his own. He had a father-son relationship with the king, but he was nearly forty, and the king was sixteen and growing up fast. The king had already made it clear that he intended to rule alone. Inevitably, one day he would no longer need or want Luynes's advice. What would happen to him then? If the king agreed to Concini's murder as a way of getting rid of him, he might deal with Luynes the same way. Murdering an unwanted favorite set a bad precedent, and there were already Henri III's murders in 1588 of his favorite, the duc de Guise, and his brother, the Cardinal de Guise. If Luynes lost the king's favor and the great nobles detested him as much as they despised Concini, would that be his fate? Luynes knew that being held responsible for Concini's murder would increase his unpopularity, and make securing the acceptance and support of the court nobility more difficult. It would also make a rapprochement with the Queen Mother nearly impossible, and he needed her tacit acceptance to survive. Luynes had good reason to worry about the effects of Concini's murder, a more plausible explanation for his hesitation than cowardice.

The king had none of these worries. To him, Concini's death meant liberation, freedom, the end of his mother's dominance, and the opportunity to rule alone. The king loathed Concini for having repeatedly humiliated him in public. Luynes did not despise Concini, although a competitive rivalry existed between them. Luynes was an older man known for his kindness, sympathy, and charm. It was widely known that he did not have the temperament of a killer, and that he had refused to arrest Concini or allow his brothers to do so. Luynes had benefited from Concini's patronage, and they were about the same age, both being favorites of Italian origin who were unpopular at court.[85] Luynes may not have liked Concini, but he did not detest him in the way that the king did.

Luynes did not have to persuade a reluctant young king to agree to Concini's death because the king had never opposed it. If anyone was reluctant, it was Luynes. Concini was killed with the king's full knowledge and consent because, like the other conspirators, he knew that Concini would probably resist arrest. Concini's foolhardiness made that almost a certainty. The king did not countermand Montpouillan's order to Vitry to kill him. He did not instruct Vitry to arrest but not kill him, and he showed no remorse at Concini's death. Instead, he was jubilant.

The news of Concini's death was brought to the king by Jean-Baptiste d'Ornano, a distant cousin of Luynes. Ornano had not been present during the planning stages, but he knew all about the conspiracy, and he made sure that he was in the Louvre when the murder occurred.[86] Ornano hugged the king, and hoisted him to the window so that he could be seen in the courtyard below. The king cried, "Many thanks to you all. At this moment I am king!" Arnauld d'Andilly reported that Louis appeared at the window with a sword in his hand, shouting, "Courage, my friends. Now I am king." Return shouts of "Long live the King!" could be heard from below. A huge crowd of nobles came and went all afternoon, congratulating the king. At Luynes's suggestion, he was playing billiards, so there was room for them all to see him and crowd around him informally. Montpouillan reported that the king was "joyous" when he heard the news of Concini's death. The *Mercure françois* reported that when Vitry told the king that he had not arrested Concini alive, the king had received him with a "joyous" face and hugged him.[87]

The king did not denounce Vitry's action, but instead rewarded him by making him a marshal. He gave him 200,000 livres from Concini's fortune as reimbursement for his office of guard captain, which was given to his brother Du Hallier, who also received 60,000 livres worth of Léonora's jewelry. Vitry was named governor of Berry, and his brother-in-law, Henri de Vaudétar, baron de Persan, and his brother, Jean de Vaudétar, sieur de Bournonville, were named lieutenants of the Bastille of which Luynes was the titular captain-governor. They were dismissed from office a year later for intriguing with the Queen

Mother's agents, and replaced by Luynes's brother Brantes and his brother-in-law Du Vernet. Vitry was so angry at this that he left court, much to the satisfaction of Luynes who distrusted and feared him as a rival for the king's favor.[88]

Luynes was apprehensive about Concini's murder, but he recognized its necessity and tacitly endorsed it by his silence. He supported the king in his decision to kill Concini, just as he had supported him in his decision to execute Estienne Durand, because his support was the basis of their relationship. Luynes was shrewd enough to know when he could and could not disagree with the king. He played a leading role in the conspiracy, providing ideas on what to do, gathering together a group of conspirators, and convincing Vitry to make the arrest, but the king himself made the final decisions on when and where to arrest Concini. The king was the moving force in the conspiracy, not Luynes. Chaulnes said that Luynes was apprehensive about killing Concini, which is probably all we will ever know about his attitude toward the murder.[89]

As a pious and devout Christian, the king felt guilty about his role in murdering Concini: "His Most Christian Majesty" did not kill people. The king refused to consider himself another Henri III, who had watched from behind a tapestry while his guards had killed the duc de Guise and then had gone through the corpse's pockets. Louis XIII went daily to mass, and he felt the need to justify his participation in Concini's murder, a need that grew over time as the emotions of the moment dimmed and the logic of events was forgotten. A government propaganda campaign launched immediately after the murder sought to turn Concini into a monster who deserved to be killed, and Louis into the hero who had killed him, justifying the sobriquet of "Louis the Just."[90] The problem was that the king did not believe his own propaganda.

Concini and his wife were attacked in seventy-six pamphlets published within the next year. Concini was depicted as a dragon and a python destroying France, and the king as a dragon and a python slayer, which became a theme of royal ballets. Concini was dehumanized as a leech, toad, scorpion, monkey, and chameleon, and his wife was denounced as a sorceress, heretic, and atheist. The pamphleteers declared that she and her husband were demons who would burn forever in hell. The king was glorified as Solomon, Hercules, Jupiter, Perseus, and a Roman emperor dispensing justice. He was a Christian king chosen by God and inspired by Him to rule wisely, so he had slain the monster Concini.[91]

Three works by the historian Pierre Matthieu published in 1617 formed the basis of the propaganda campaign against Concini . The first, *La Magicienne étrangère*, was a dramatic tragedy presented in June listing the charges against Léonora in her trial for sorcery. She was thereafter called "the foreign magician" in the pamphlets attacking her. A few months later, Matthieu published *Histoire d'Aelius Séjanus*, and a pamphlet entitled, *La Vie et mort misérable de Séjanus*, depicting Concini as Sejanus, the evil favorite of the emperor Tiberius, and there-after Concini was called Sejanus in the pamphlets attacking him. In November, Matthieu published a biography of Concini entitled *La Conjuration de Conchine*, creating the "black legend" of his evil character and deeds, which appeared unchanged in the histories of d'Autreville in 1617, Boitel de Gaubertin and Legrain in 1618, Gaspard in 1623, and Loisel in 1626. Pierre Matthieu's work was incorporated into Scipion Dupleix's history of Louis XIII's reign, and into the history of Louis XIII by his son Jean-Baptiste Matthieu. The "black legend" of Concini thus came to dominate the historical literature.[92] Luynes's reputation would suffer the same fate, and his "black legend" would become the standard historical interpretation.

By the time Richelieu wrote his memoirs, the version that the king had not known Concini was to be killed had been widely accepted. Richelieu incorporated this version into his memoirs because it would have been unwise not to have done so, and because he wanted to destroy Luynes's reputation. Although this version had blamed both Vitry and Luynes for the murder, Richelieu now made Luynes solely responsible. In a long diatribe on Luynes's bad advice to the king, Richelieu wrote, "And, therefore, this was hasty advice, unfair and evil, unworthy of the king's majesty and virtue; he [the king] took no part in this action [the murder] because he simply ordered that they arrest the prisoner and not harm him; even if he put his hand to his sword, they were only to wound him."[93] As a long-dead royal favorite, Luynes made the perfect scapegoat because he could not refute the accusations of his culpability, while favorites were the traditional scapegoats for royal flaws and mistakes. Richelieu portrayed Luynes as a conniving, duplicitous murderer with the king's permission, and together they shifted the blame for the murder onto Luynes where it has remained ever since.

The aftermath of the murder

The conspirators knew that they had to act quickly because the Queen Mother was as much of a threat to them as Concini, and that they had to eliminate her favorite Léonora Galigai because they assumed that both women would seek revenge for Concini's murder. The king could not allow his mother to be killed, so nine days after the murder she was exiled to the Loire château of Blois under guard for an indefinite stay. Lacking the protection of royal mother-hood, Léonora was arrested, tried for treason and sorcery, condemned, and executed two months later. Richelieu blamed Luynes's cowardice, duplicity, vindictiveness, and greed for the fate of both women. The king, however, had decided before Concini's murder to exile his mother to a royal château outside Paris, and he held firmly to his decision afterward.[94] He sent Ornano to tell his mother that the royal council had decided to send her to Blois. When she strenuously objected, Luynes went to see her, and she finally agreed to go, probably because he persuaded her that she could return to court sooner if she cooperated.[95] The king refused to see her until the day she left, insisting that she stay in her rooms in the Louvre under guard with no visitors except family members, and she was no longer allowed to participate in affairs of state.[96]

On 3 May at two o'clock in the afternoon, the king arrived at the door to her rooms accompanied by his brother Gaston, Luynes, his brothers Cadenet and Brantes, Bassompierre, and a few others, but not Vitry or Du Hallier who had participated in the actual murder. His mother emerged with a long face. When the king went to her and kissed her, she burst into tears, but he refused to be swayed or answer her tearful entreaties. Cold and distant, he made a short prepared speech, then turned and left. When Luynes took his leave of the Queen Mother, she pleaded with him, and he looked as if he was going to answer her until the king called his name several times. Then he turned and followed the king from the room. Louis watched his mother leave the Louvre from the balcony of his wife's apartments, showing no distress at her departure, and then he went hunting in the forest of Vincennes.[97]

In his memoirs, Richelieu accused Luynes of turning the king against his mother, making him envious of her power, and convincing him to exile her.[98] Richelieu's condemnation of Luynes for her exile was repeated by Rohan, Fontenay-Mareuil, Mézeray, and the anti-Luynes pamphleteers.[99] This accusation has been rejected by most historians, who believe that Luynes supported the king's decision to exile his mother, but did not inspire him to make it because the king himself had wanted to get rid of her.[100] Basic incompatibility and conflicting interests had caused their estrangement, not Luynes's interference. Luynes, in fact, served as a lightning rod to deflect criticism from the king for exiling his mother.

Historians have tended to accept Richelieu's assertion that Luynes was responsible for the death of Léonora Galigai, although this accusation is also groundless.[101] Richelieu wrote that "neither her sex nor her rank could save her from the fury of those who wanted her fortune." Rohan and Fontenay-Mareuil agreed. By "those," Richelieu meant Luynes and Vitry whom he declared were motivated by greed and vindictiveness in seeking her death. In order for the crown to confiscate her property, Léonora had to be condemned because Concini had put most of their fortune in her name. Only then could the king give her property to Luynes.[102] This does not mean, however, that Luynes contrived her death. Anti-Luynes pamphlets written by the Queen Mother's supporters declared that Luynes had killed Concini in order to replace him;

that he had intimidated the Parlement judges into condemning Léonora so he could have her property; and that he had engineered the Queen Mother's exile to Blois so he could control her son. Richelieu incorporated these accusations into his memoirs, and in this way they entered the historical literature.[103]

Most contemporary accounts did not hold Luynes responsible for Léonora's death.[104] Déagent stated that the king had already decided before her husband's murder that she should be tried for treason with her execution as the certain outcome.[105] The king held to this decision because he despised Léonora as much as her husband. Hélène Duccini has noted that Léonora's trial was part of the propaganda campaign to justify her husband's murder. Léonora had to be legally tried and executed because Concini had not been; her execution justified her husband's execution for treason. Richard Bonney has noted that her trial was simultaneously the posthumous trial of Concini's regime.[106]

The king sent Vitry to arrest Léonora and ask for her jewelry.[107] Then he signed the order for her trial and sent it to the Parlement of Paris.[108] He left Paris to stay at Saint-Germain-en-Laye during her trial, and he went hunting on the day the verdict was announced. That evening he went to bed at 8:00 PM, the time she was to be executed, although Héroard noted that he did not actually go to sleep until 3:30 AM because he was worried about the outcome.[109] He may have been afraid that she would be reprieved or rescued, or that the Paris mob would protest her execution, but her death did not upset him, and he showed no remorse.

The conspirators regarded Léonora as a threat because of her influence, and assumed that her fury at her husband's murder would make her persuade the Queen Mother to seek revenge. They did not consider her exile a solution because she might return. The Queen Mother abandoned Léonora, however, and did not intercede for her with the king. Any intercession on her part would have been useless, and might have worsened her own situation.[110] Léonora's death followed inevitably and necessarily from her husband's murder without any need by Luynes to interfere. A. Lloyd Moore and Elizabeth Marvick have agreed that it was the king's decision to execute her, not Luynes's.[111]

Richelieu in his memoirs declared that Luynes had persuaded a reluctant king to agree to Concini's murder, and then had convinced him to exile his mother and execute Léonora. This version appeared in most of the histories and memoirs written after Richelieu came to power and soon dominated the historical literature. The official version of Concini's murder published in the *Mercure François*, however, is closer to what actually happened. The king ordered Vitry to arrest Concini for treason, and either explicitly or implicitly told him to kill Concini if he resisted arrest. Death was the only solution to the problem of how to get rid of Concini permanently, and the king needed to do this if he was going to rule alone, which he desperately wanted to do. So, Concini was killed with the king's full knowledge and consent. In other words, he was executed. Afterward, the king sent his mother to Blois, and ordered the trial and execution of her favorite Léonora. Luynes's agreement and support was the price of royal favor. Luynes knew, however, that the king had not gotten rid of Concini to replace him with another all powerful favorite, and that he would have to tread carefully in future. Luynes's fear of sharing Concini's fate haunted him for the rest of his life.

Notes

1 *Mercure françois*, 25 vols. (Paris, 1605–4f4), IV (1617), 194, 196. The king told Vitry "… de se saisir du Mareschal d'Ancre, et de se faire assister en cas de resistance; bref de l'arrester vif ou mort."

2 Ibid., 196; Nicolas Pasquier, *Lettres* (Paris, 1623), pp. 553–4; Jean Héroard, *Journal*, ed. Madeleine Foisil, 2 vols. (Paris, 1989), II, 2419; Achille Halphen, ed., *Journal d'Arnauld d'Andilly 1614–1620* (Paris, 1857), p. 281; Hélène Duccini, *Concini* (Paris, 1991), pp. 294–5.

3 *Mercure françois*, IV (1617), 197–8; *Relation exacte de tout de qui s'est passé à la mort du mareschal d'Ancre*, eds. Michaud and Poujoulat, 2d ser., vol. 5 (Paris, 1837), pp. 457–8; *Journal d'Arnauld 1614–1620*, pp. 280–1.

4 Ibid., 205–6, 217–18; Duccini, *Concini*, pp. 322–36; Orest Ranum, "The French Ritual of Tyrannicide," *The Sixteenth Century Journal*, 11 (1980), 63–82.

5 *Mercure françois*, IV (1617), 201–3; Duccini, *Concini*, pp. 348–9; Louis Batiffol, "Le Coup d'état du 24 avril 1617," *Rev his* 97 (1908), 272, n. 5; Jeffrey Sawyer, *Printed Poison* (Berkeley, 1990), pp. 128–9.

6 Claude Belland et al., eds., *Histoire générale de la presse française*, 5 vols. (Paris, 1969–76), I, 78–9.

7 *Mercure françois*, IV (1617), 220, 225–30; *Relation exacte*, p. 459; Duccini, *Concini*, pp. 362–89.

8 *Mercure françois*, IV (1617), 215–16.

9 A. Lloyd Moote, *Louis XIII* (Berkeley, 1989), p. 94; *Assassinat du Maréchal d'Ancre* (Paris, 1853), p. 29; R. de Crèvecoeur, *Un document nouveau sur la succession des Concini* (Paris, 1891), p. 2.

10 Jean de Caumont, marquis de Montpouillan, *Mémoires*, vol. 4, *Mémoires de Jacques Nompar de Caumont, duc de La Force*, ed. Marquis de la Grange, 4 vols. (Paris, 1843); *Relation exacte*; Charles, comte Horric de Beaucaire, ed., *Mémoires du Cardinal de Richelieu*, 10 vols. (Paris, 1907–13); Guichard Déagent, sieur de Saint Martin (Marcellin), *Mémoires de Monsieur Déagent envoyez à Monsieur le Cardinal* (Grenoble, 1668); Paul Phélypeaux de Pontchartrain, *Mémoires concernant les affaires de France sous la régence de Marie de Médicis*, eds. Michaud and Poujoulat, 2nd ser., vol. 5 (Paris, 1837); Halphen, *Journal d'Arnauld 1614–1620*; Henri de Loménie de Brienne, *Mémoires du comte de Brienne*, eds. Michaud and Pouloulat, 3rd ser., vol. 3 (Paris, 1838).

11 François de Bassompierre, *Journal de ma vie. Mémoires du maréchal de Bassompierre*, ed. Edouard de Chanterac. 4 vols. (Paris, 1870–77); François Annibal d'Estrées, *Mémoires*, ed. Petitot, 2nd ser., vol. 16 (Paris, 1822); Henri de Rohan, *Mémoires du duc de Rohan*, eds. Michaud and Poujoulat, 2nd ser., vol. 5 (Paris, 1837); François Du Val, marquis de Fontenay-Mareuil, *Mémoires du Messire Du Val*, ed. Louis Monmerqué, 2 vols. (Paris, 1826); François Paule de Clermont, marquis de Montglat, *Mémoires*. ed. Petitot, 2nd ser., vol. 49 (Paris, 1825).

12 Belland, *Histoire générale de la presse*, I, 78–9; Emile Bourgeois et al., *Les sources de l'histoire de France*, 8 vols. (Paris, 1924), vol. III, part 4, 25.

13 Batiffol, "Le Coup d'état," *Rev hist* 95 (107), 292, n.1; Moote, *Louis XIII*, pp. 321–2, n. 29; Elizabeth Marvick, *Louis XIII* (New Haven, 1986), pp. 196–7.

14 Duccini, *Concini*, pp. 258, 304, 400; idem, *Faire Voir, Faire Croire* (Paris, 2003), p. 319, n. 1.

15 *Relation exacte*, p. 457.

16 Ibid., pp. 452–7; Marvick, *Louis XIII*, p. 197; Charles d'Arcussia, *La Fauconnerie* ... *divisée en dix parties* (Rouen, 1643), p. 165; Eugène Griselle, *Ecurie, vénerie, fauconnerie et louveterie du Roi Louis XIII* (Paris, 1912), pp. 30–1.

17 Déagent, *Mémoires*, pp. 64–5; Pontchartrain, *Mémoires*, p. 387.

18 Montglat, *Mémoires*, p. 26.

19 *Journal d'Arnauld 1614–1620*, p. 281.

20 Brienne, *Mémoires*, p. 12.

21 Ibid., "... le baron de Vitry, capitaine des gardes du corps ... car, outre qu'il avoit un naturel plus bouillans, l'envie de s'élever le dominoit de telle manière, que rien de lui paroissoit impossible, ni à méprise pour y réussir."

22 Henri de Gondi, Cardinal de Retz, *Mémoires du Cardinal de Retz*, eds. Michaud and Poujoulat, 3rd ser., vol. 1 (Paris, 1837), p. 28.

23 *Journal d'Arnauld 1614–1620*, p. 129; Duccini, *Concini*, p. 290.

24 Sharon Kettering, *Judicial Politics and Urban Revolt in Seventeenth-Century France* (Princeton, 1978), pp. 118–28.

25 Montpouillan, *Mémoires*, p. 33. "Le Roi entend qu'on le tue ... Sire, me le commandez-vous? ... Oui, je vous le commande."

26 Ibid., pp. 4, 8–10, 22, 31–3, 39–64; *Journal d'Arnauld 1614–1620*, p. 377.

27 Montpouillan, *Mémoires*, pp. 23–9; Marvick, *Louis XIII*, pp. 196–7.

28 Batiffol, "Le Coup d'état," *Rev hist* 97 (1908), 62; Déagent, *Mémoires*, pp. 44–5.

29 Brienne, *Mémoires*, p. 12.

30 Beaucaire, *Mémoires de Richelieu*, II, 178–9; Jean-Baptiste Matthieu, *Histoire de Louis XIII, roy de France et de Navarre*, in Pierre Matthieu, *Histoire de France du règne du roy Henri IV*, 2 vols. (Paris, 1631), II, 70; Joseph-François Michaud, ed., *Biographie universelle*, 45 vols. (Paris, 1854, Graz, 1986), XXVII, 287; XLIII, 681.

31 Brienne, *Mémoires*, p. 12; Fontenay-Mareuil, *Mémoires*, I, 374, 376.

32 Beaucaire, *Mémoires de Richelieu*, II, 171–81.

33 Maréchal d'Estrées, *Mémoires*, p. 322.

34 Marvick, *Louis XIII*, pp. 185–200.

35 Moote, *Louis XIII*, pp. 321–2, n.29.

36 Beaucaire, *Mémoires de Richelieu*, II, 156, 171, 173, 176–9.

37 Ibid., II, 177–8. "Le Roi, dès longtemps mécontent du maréchal d'Ancre, se résolut sur toutes ces choses de le faire arrêter prisonnier. Luynes, qui ne croit pas pouvoir trouver sûreté que dans sa mort ... fait instance de le faire tuer, à quoi le Roi ne voulut point consentir, qu'en cas qu'il se mit en devoir de résister à ses volontés."

38 Scipion Dupleix, *Histoire de Louis le Juste* (Paris, 1637), pp. 97–8; François Eudes de Mézeray, *Histoire de la mère et du fils*, 2 vols. (Amsterdam, 1731), II, 169–219; idem, *Les Mémoires de la Reyne Marie de Médicis* (Paris, 1666); idem, *Histoire de la régence de la reine Marie de Médicis* (The Hague, 1743); Vittorio Siri, *Anecdotes du ministère de Richelieu*, 2 vols. (Amsterdam, 1717), I, 36–42.

39 Michel Le Vassor, *The History of the Reign of Lewis III*, 3 vols. (London, 1700), III, 375–533; Henri Philippe de Limiers, *Abrégé chronologique de l'histoire de France*, 4 vols. (Amsterdam, 1740), IV, 50–132; Gabriel Daniel, *Histoire de France*, 17 vols. (Paris, 1756), XIII, 175–331; Henri Griffet, *Histoire du règne de Louis XIII*, 3 vols. (Paris, 1758), I, 94–331; Madame d'Arconville, *Vie de Marie de Médicis*, 3 vols. (Paris, 1778), II, 339–42. Michel Le Vassor depended heavily upon the *Relation exacte* by Chaulnes, first published by Pierre Dupuy in *Histoire des plus illustres favoris anciens et modernes* (Paris, 1660), pp. 517–624; Batiffol, "Le Coup d'état," *Rev hist* (1907), 292–308, 97 (1908), 27–77, 266–86; idem, *Le Roi Louis XIII à vingt ans* (Paris, 1910), pp. 1–93, 478–573; Gabriel Hanotaux and the duc de La Force, *Histoire du Cardinal de Richelieu*, 6 vols. (Paris, 1893–1947), vol. II, part 1, 185–99, vol. II, part 2, 203–17; Robert Lavollée, "La Mort de Conchine," *Le Correspondant*, 237 (1909), 320–41, 531–62.

40 Duccini, *Faire Voir*, pp. 319–24; Marvick, *Louis XIII*, pp. 185–200.

41 *Relation exacte*, p. 453; Beaucaire, *Mémoires de Richelieu*, II, 198; Joseph Bergin, *The Rise of*

Richelieu (New Haven, 1991), pp. 140–73; Moote, *Louis XIII*, pp. 89–92, 101–2; Batiffol, "Le Coup d'état," *Rev hist* 97 (1908), 65–6.

42 Déagent, *Mémoires*, pp. 1–3, 48, 51–6, 101–2; DBF, X, 406–7; Michaud, *Biographie universelle*, X, 238; Batiffol, "Le Coup d'état," *Rev hist* 97 (1908), 50–4, 62.

43 Pontchartrain, *Mémoires*, pp. 295–6; Michaud, *Biographie universelle*, XXXIV, 74; Duccini, *Concini*, pp. 310, 348; Charles Frostin, "La Famille ministérielle des Phélypeaux," *Annales de Bretagne*, 86 (1979), 117–40; Sophie de Laverny, *Les Domestiques commensaux du roi de France au XVIIe siècle* (Paris, 2002), p. 149.

44 Brienne, *Mémoires*, pp. 277–86; Michaud, *Biographie universelle*, XXV, 56–8; Orest Ranum, *Richelieu and the Councillors of Louis XIII* (Oxford, 1963), pp. 29–30, 69–71.

45 *Journal d'Arnauld 1614–1620*, pp. i–xxxi; *Mémoires de Messire Robert Arnauld d'Andilly*, ed. Petitot, 2nd ser., vols. 33–4, 2 vols. (Paris, 1824), I, 372–91; Duccini, *Concini*, p. 348; Alexander Sedgwick, *The Travails of Conscience. The Arnauld Family* (Cambridge, MA, 1998), pp. 92–123; DBF, III, 878–883.

46 A letter at this time by Nicolas Pasquier repeated the version in the *Mercure françois*. Pasquier, *Les Lettres*, pp. 548–62.

47 Fontenay-Mareuil, *Mémoires*, I, 363–4, 376, 381; Bassompierre, *Mémoires*, II, 122–3; Rohan, *Mémoires*, pp. 512–13; Maréchal d'Estrées, *Mémoires*, pp. 325–7; Montglat, *Mémoires*, pp. 24–7.

48 Fontenay-Mareuil, *Mémoires*, I, 372–3; Bassompierre, *Mémoires*, II, 113–14, 122–3; Rohan, *Mémoires*, p. 512.

49 Ibid., pp. 487–91, 511–12; Duccini, *Concini*, p. 348; J.A. Clarke, *Huguenot Warrior. Henri de Rohan* (The Hague, 1966); Solange and Pierre Deyon, *Henri de Rohan* (Paris, 2000).

50 Bassompierre, *Mémoires*, I, 122, II, 224–5; DBF, V, 762; Père Anselme de Sainte Marie, *Histoire généaloqique et chronologique de la Maison Royale de France*, 3rd ed., 9 vols. (Paris, 1726–33, New York, 1967), VII, 464–8; Paul Bondois, *Le Maréchal de Bassompierre* (Paris, 1925).

51 Fontenay-Mareuil, *Mémoires*, I, 3–10, 341, 363–4, 373; DBF, XIV, 354–5; Eugène Griselle, *Etat de la maison du Roi Louis XIII* (Paris, 1912), p. 49.

52 Maréchal d'Estrées, *Mémoires*, pp. 170–3, 324; Bergin, *Rise of Richelieu*, p. 140; Anselme, *Histoire généalogique*, VII, 470.

53 Montglat, *Mémoires*, 3–12, 24–7; Griselle, *Etat de la maison du Roi*, pp. 55, 81, 83; Emile Magne, *La Vie quotidienne au temps de Louis XIII* (Paris, 1942), pp. 144–52; Héroard, *Journal*, I, 79–86; Vincent Pitts, *La Grande Mademoiselle and the Court of France* (Baltimore, 2000), pp. 6, 14, 27; Jean-Pierre Labatut, *Les Ducs et pairs de France au XVIIe siècle* (Paris, 1972), pp. 372–3.

54 Héroard, *Journal*, II, 2458.

55 Marvick, *Louis XIII*, p. 194.

56 Ibid., p. 204; Héroard, *Journal*, II, 316–17.

57 Batiffol, "Le Coup d'état," *Rev hist* 97 (1908), 60–3, 64, n. 1.

58 Duccini, *Concini*, pp. 277, 292; idem, *Faire Voir*, p. 321.

59 Marvick, *Louis XIII*, pp. 196–8.

60 Héroard, *Journal*, II, 2419; Pontchartrain, *Mémoires*, pp. 386–7; B.N., imprimés Lb 36, *Seconde partie et responce à la Chronique des Favoris* (1622), p. 23.

61 Gédéon Tallemant des Réaux, *Historiettes*, ed. Antoine Adam, 2 vols. (Paris, 1960–1), I, 77; Batiffol, "Le Coup d'état," *Rev hist* 97 (1908), 33–6; Moote, *Louis XIII*, pp. 90–2.

62 *Journal d'Arnauld 1614–1620*, pp. 205, 221–2; Richard Bonney, *The King's Debts* (Oxford, 1981), p. 89, n. 6. Léonora said her husband's compensation had only been 300,000 livres, not 450,000. Fernand Hayem, *Le Maréchal d'Ancre et Léonora Galigai* (Paris, 1910), p. 283.

63 Pontchartrain, *Mémoires*, p. 383.

64 Héroard, *Journal*, II, 2400–15; Maréchal d'Estrées, *Mémoires*, p. 322; *Journal d'Arnauld 1614–1620*, p. 224; Marvick, *Louis XIII*, pp. 176–80; Batiffol, "Le Coup d'état," *Rev hist* 97 (1908), 36; Michel Carmona, *Marie de Médicis* (Paris, 1981), pp. 325–8.

65 Montglat, *Mémoires*, p. 25.

66 Jean-François Dubost, "Between Mignons and Principal Ministers: Concini, 1610–1617," *The World of the Favourite*, eds. J.H. Elliott and L.W.B. Brockliss (New Haven, 1999), pp. 71–8; Duccini, *Concini*, pp. 73–103, 109–10, 433–40; Bonney, *The King's Debts*, pp. 77–8, 85–95; Carmona, *Marie de Médicis*, pp. 225–8.

67 Montglat, *Mémoires*, pp. 24–5; Pontchartrain, *Mémoires*, pp. 378, 383, 388; Carmona, *Marie de Médicis*, p. 321.

68 Pontchartrain, *Mémoires*, p. 339; Beaucaire, *Mémoires de Richelieu*, I, 333, n.2, II, 172, ns. 2, 3; *Relation exacte*, pp. 452–3, 455; Fontenay-Mareuil, *Mémoires*, I, 363–4, 382–3; Déagent, *Mémoires*, pp. 60–1; Rohan, *Mémoires*, p. 512.

69 Déagent, *Mémoires*, pp. 41–2; Joseph Bergin, *The Making of the French Episcopate* (New Haven, 1996), p. 641; B.N., imprimés Lb36, *Seconde partie et responce*, p. 13; Anselme, *Histoire généalogique*, IX, 133.

70 Déagent, *Mémoires*, p. 44.

71 Ibid., pp. 49–50, 67–8; *Relation exacte*, pp. 451–2; Montpouillan, *Mémoires*, pp. 26–7.

72 Ibid.

73 Maréchal d'Estrées, *Mémoires*, pp. 325–6; Duccini, *Concini*, pp. 234, 239–40.

74 Bassompierre, *Mémoires*, II, 112–4.

75 Fontenay-Mareuil, *Mémoires*, I, 367; *Mercure françois*, IV (1616–17), 157–8.

76 Beaucaire, *Mémoires de Richelieu*, II, 171.

77 Déagent, *Mémoires*, p. 45.

78 Ibid., pp. 46–7, 70; *Relation exacte*, pp. 452, 467; Montpouillan, *Mémoires*, p. 30; *Journal d'Arnauld, 1614–1620*, pp. 167, 240–42; Pontchartrain, *Mémoires*, pp. 305–6, 376–8; Brienne, *Mémoires*, pp. 12–13; Duccini, *Concini*, p. 310.

79 *Relation exacte*, p. 482.

80 Maréchal d'Estrées, *Mémoires*, pp. 308–9.

81 Déagent, *Mémoires*, pp. 50–61; Brienne, *Mémoires*, p. 12.

82 Henri de Mesmes, sieur d'Irval, civil lieutenant in the Paris *prévoté* court, came from a Paris *parlementaire* family, and was a third estate deputy to the Estates General of 1614. J. Michael Hayden, *France and the Estates General of 1614* (Cambridge, 1974), pp. 95, n.28, 103, 122, 145, n.33, 267; François Bluche, *Les Magistrats du Parlement de Paris au XVIIIe siècle* (Paris, 1960), pp. 78, 89, 93, 274. On the de Mesmes family, see Robert Harding, *Anatomy of a Power Elite* (New Haven, 1978), pp. 186–7.

83 *Relation exacte*, pp. 452–6, 463; Montpouillan, *Mémoires*, pp. 28–36; *Journal d'Arnauld 1614–1620*, p. 35; Batiffol, "Le Coup d'état," *Rev hist* 97 (1908), 60–1.

84 Montpouillan, *Mémoires*, p. 33; Déagent, *Mémoires*, pp. 49, 56; Beaucaire, *Mémoires de Richelieu*, II, 175; *Relation exacte*, p. 453; Fontenay-Mareuil, *Mémoires*, I, 363–4.

85 D'Estrées, *Mémoires*, pp. 327–8; Bassompierre, *Mémoires*, II, 105–10; Duccini, *Concini*, pp. 69–103.

86 Fontenay-Mareuil, *Mémoires*, I, 376–8; Pontchartrain, *Mémoires*, p. 387; Jean Charay, ed., *Vie du maréchal Jean-Baptiste d'Ornano* (Grenoble, 1971), pp. 15, 35–6, 44, 46.

87 *Relation exacte*, pp. 458–9; Montpouillan, *Mémoires*, pp. 37–8; Déagent, *Mémoires*, pp. 66–7, 69; *Mercure françois*, IV (1617), 198–9; *Journal d'Arnauld 1614–1620*, pp. 282–3; Beaucaire, *Mémoires de Richelieu*, II, 192; Marvick, *Louis XIII*, pp. 199–200.

88 *Relation exacte*, p. 465; *Journal d'Arnauld 1614–1620*, pp. 280, 316, 358–9, 376–7; Beaucaire, *Mémoires de Richelieu*, II, 191–2; *Mercure françois*, V (1617), 229; Bassompierre, *Mémoires*, II, 131–2; Pontchartrain, *Mémoires*, pp. 400–1; Rohan, *Mémoires*, pp. 513–14; Anselme, *Histoire généalogique*, VII, 431–2, 439; François Bluche, ed., *Dictionnaire au Grand Siècle* (Paris, 1990), 1612; Michaud, *Biographie universelle*, XLIII, 681–3; Duccini, *Concini*, pp. 358–61; Fernand Bournon, *La Bastille* (Paris, 1893), p. 86.

89 Jean-Claude Pascal, author of the most recent study of Luynes, shares this view of his role in the murder. Idem, *L'Amant du Roi* (Monaco, 1991), pp. 162–200.

90 Duccini, *FaireVoir*, pp. 324–39; Beaucaire, *Mémoires de Richelieu*, II, 214.

91 Duccini, *Concini*, pp. 350–61, 373–9, 383–9; idem, *FaireVoir*, pp. 328–9, 335, 338–9, 345,

363–74, 508; Jeffrey Sawyer, "Pamphleteers Construct Concini," *Cahier du Dix-Septième*, 3 (1989), 261–78; Moote, *Louis XIII*, pp. 95–6.

92 Duccini, *Concini*, pp. 390–411; idem, *FaireVoir*, p. 374; Michaud, *Biographie universelle*, XXVII, 285–7.

93 Beaucaire, *Mémoires de Richelieu*, II, 194. "Et, partant, ce fut un conseil précipité, injuste et de mauvais exemple, indigne de la majesté royale et de la vertu du Roi, qui n'eut point aussi de part en cette action; car il commanda simplement qu'on l'arrêtât prisonnier et qu'on de lui méfit point, si ce n'étoit qu'il mit le premier la main aux armes, de sorte qu'on ne le pût arrêter qu'en le blessant."

94 Déagent, *Mémoires*, pp. 46–7.

95 Fontenay-Mareuil, *Mémoires*, I, 378, 385.

96 Pontchartrain, *Mémoires*, p. 388.

97 Bassompierre, *Mémoires*, II, 125–9; *Relation exacte*, pp. 472–3; *Journal d'Arnauld 1614–1620*, pp. 298–301; Héroard, *Journal*, II, 2461; Fontenay-Mareuil, *Mémoires*, I, 385; Batiffol, "Le Coup d'état," *Rev hist* 97 (1908), 281–6.

98 Beaucaire, *Mémoires de Richelieu*, II, 172–3, 176–7, 200–1.

99 Rohan, *Mémoires*, p. 512; Fontenay-Mareuil, *Mémoires*, I, 377–8; Mézeray, *L'Histoire de la mère et du fils*, II, 217–19; *Recueil des pièces les plus curieuses qui ont esté faites pendant le règne du Connestable M. de Luynes* (Paris, 1628), *Le Comtadin Provençal* (1620), pp. 94, 105, 109; *Veritez Chrestiennes au Roy Très Chrestien* (1620), pp. 126–48; *Raisons de la Royne Mère* (1620), pp. 268–70; *Méditations de l'hermite Valérien* (1620), p. 319; *L'Ombre de Monseigneur le duc de Mayenne* (1622), p. 584.

100 Batiffol, "Le Coup d'état," *Rev hist* 97 (1908), 282–6; Moote, *Louis XIII*, pp. 100–1; Carmona, *Marie de Médicis*, pp. 322–5, 335; Marvick, *Louis XIII*, pp. 205–7; Pierre Chevallier, *Louis XIII* (Paris, 1979), pp. 171–2.

101 Duccini, *Concini*, pp. 381–8; Georges Mongrédien, *Léonora Galigai* (Paris, 1968), pp. 194, 200–1; Georges Delamare, *Le Maréchal d'Ancre* (Paris, 1961), pp. 267–83; Carmona, *Marie de Médicis*, pp. 337–8, 340; Henri d'Almeras, *Concini, Maréchal d'Ancre* (Paris, 1928), p. 183; Pascal, *L'Amant du Roi*, p. 218; Françoise Kermina, *Marie de Médicis* (Paris, 1979), p. 245; Philippe Delorme, *Marie de Médicis* (Paris, 1998), p. 199.

102 Beaucaire, *Mémoires de Richelieu*, II, 217; Rohan, *Mémoires*, p. 512; Fontenay-Mareuil, *Mémoires*, I, 389; Crèvecoeur, *Un document nouveau*, pp. 15–16; Duccini, *Concini*, pp. 381, 388.

103 *Recueil, Le Comtadin provençal*, pp. 88–9; *La Chronique des Favoris*, p. 475; Beaucaire, *Mémoires*, II, 171–8.

104 *Mercure françois*, IV (1617), 225–30; *Journal d'Arnauld 1614–1620*, pp. 308–9; Pontchartrain, *Mémoires*, p. 393; *Relation exacte*, pp. 469, 475–6. The memoirs of Brienne, Montpouillan, Bassompierre, Fontenay-Mareuil, Rohan, d'Estrées, and Montglat do not mention Léonora's death.

105 Déagent, *Mémoires*, pp. 45–6.

106 Duccini, *Concini*, pp. 364, 380; idem, *FaireVoir*, p. 327; Bonney, *The King's Debts*, p. 92.

107 *Relation exacte*, p. 469; *Journal d'Arnauld 1614–1620*, pp. 287–8; Beaucaire, *Mémoires de Richelieu*, II, 189–90.

108 Ibid., II, 212.

109 Héroard, *Journal*, II, 2473.

110 Marvick, *Louis XIII*, p. 209; Duccini, *Concini*, pp. 382–3.

111 Moote, *Louis XIII*, p. 100; Marvick, *Louis XIII*, pp. 210–14.

4

The rewards of favor

The queen's "Ballet of Psyche" was first performed on 17 February 1619 in the grand salon of the Louvre. The curtain fell to the floor to reveal a formal garden with flower beds, sculptures, great stone vases, and fountains on a painted backdrop and on the stage. Two large swans appeared pulling a golden chariot in which Venus and Cupid sat. Venus complained that she was being ignored because of the beautiful Psyche, who now came on stage surrounded by ten lutists singing her praises to Jupiter, and he commanded the winds to bring her to his palace. Eight small boys dressed in feathers with wings on their backs made an entrance as the winds, blowing here and there and sweeping Psyche along with them. After several set changes, the heavenly palace of the gods appeared as a painted backdrop of billowing clouds where the gods, led by Jupiter, gathered together to deify Psyche for her beauty. Three doors in the clouds opened, and sixteen goddesses entered to sing and dance on stage and down the runways. They wore crystalline headdresses and white satin gowns embroidered with gold, pearls, and diamonds that glowed in the flickering candlelight. Their long gauzy sleeves reached to the floor, floating and swaying as they danced, and the performance ended when they danced in a line, hand-to-hand, linked by a golden chain.[1]

The sixteen goddesses were court ladies. First in line was Anne of Austria dancing Juno, the queen of heaven, followed by Themis, Minerva, Diana, Ceres, Astracea, and Thetis danced by her Bourbon in-laws, the king's sister Christine, the duchesses de Longueville, Montpensier, Vendôme, and Elbeuf, and the marquise de Verneuil. The eighth goddess, Flora, was danced by Luynes's wife, who appeared on stage as the first non-royal, a significant honor she had also received in the queen's ballet, "Beauty and the Nymphs," performed the previous year on 25 February 1618.[2]

Marie de Rohan, the daughter of Hercule, duc de Montbazon, married Luynes in the Louvre on 13 September 1617. The ceremony was performed by the new archbishop of Tours, Bertrand Deschaux, within whose diocese she had grown up.[3] Royal weddings usually took place in the queen's chapel in an old corner tower of the Louvre next to her apartments on the second floor.[4] Luynes was honored with a royal wedding attended by the king and his family, and the celebrations afterward included the whole court.[5] There was almost certainly a banquet that evening, and festivities for two days, probably a ball one evening and a play or ballet the next, after which the court traveled south to stay at Lésigny-en-Brie, Luynes's new château near Fontainebleau.[6] He had wanted to marry the king's natural half-sister, Catherine-Henriette de Vendôme, who considered the marriage a mésalliance and refused, so he had chosen a duke's daughter instead.[7] He married Marie for her rank and beauty, not her dowry, which was never paid. Marie was a pretty, 17-year-old blonde who was intelligent, vivacious, and charming with an infectious gaiety that chased away boredom and endeared her wherever she went for the rest of her life. She was a marriage prize, and the court had been speculating for years about whom she would marry.[8] The king's favor had provided Luynes with a marriage to one of the prettiest, most charming young ladies at court, and an alliance with one of the great feudal noble families of France.

The wedding announcement in the *Mercure françois* mentioned a speech in Luynes's honor made during the festivities by a sieur Drion, and published separately as a pamphlet. Drion compared Agrippa, the favorite of Caligula, to Luynes, the favorite of Louis XIII. Agrippa had been threatened by Tiberius, Caligula's predecessor as emperor of Rome, just as Luynes had been threatened by Concini, the Queen Mother's favorite. Both were saved by the timely death of their tormentors, and liberally rewarded by the emperors whom they had loyally served.[9] This chapter discusses Luynes's rewards.

Richelieu incorporated the *Mercure françois* account into his memoirs, commenting that when Luynes married, "Everyone sang his praises, but since these praises had no real foundation, all that could be said in his favor was that he had been a companion to the king as Agrippa had been to Caligula, without considering that he (Agrippa) would come to an unhappy end because of his vanity, or that God would take so exemplary a revenge that it was almost a forewarning of the short duration of Luynes's fortune."[10] Richelieu had again twisted praise of Luynes into criticism.

François de Silly, comte de La Rocheguyon, was a royal favorite who had been named master of the king's hunting dogs in 1615, and he acted as Luynes's go-between in asking for Marie's hand in marriage. He had danced in "Renaud," probably becoming acquainted with Luynes in this way. He was asked to act as a go-between because he was a distant cousin of the Rohan-Montbazon, and his mother was Madame de Guercheville, the Queen Mother's first lady of honor.[11] Anti-Luynes pamphleteers declared that an ungrateful Luynes had ignored La Rocheguyon instead of rewarding him as he deserved, but in fact, La Rocheguyon was named a knight in the Order of Saint Esprit in December 1619 and a duke in January 1621.[12]

The marriage contract was signed two days before the wedding ceremony in the presence of the king and queen. It stipulated that Marie was to have a dowry of 200,000 livres divided into three payments, 50,000 livres when the engagement was announced, 100,000 livres a year later, and 50,000 livres two years after that with 5 per cent interest on the delayed payments. Marie was also to have a lifetime annual income of 10,000 livres from 5 pieces of property that had belonged to her mother and her grandmother.[13] The king gave Luynes a wedding gift of 200,000 livres, which acted as a settlement from the groom's family since the dowry usually matched the groom's settlement, and the king increased his pension to 32,000 livres a year. Average ducal dowries were 200,000 to 400,000 livres, so Marie's dowry was on the low side.[14]

Her father's financial difficulties determined the amount of her dowry. Thirty years later Marie brought a lawsuit against her father, stating that he had never paid her dowry or the interest on it. By this time, the total amounted to 600,000 livres, which she wanted paid to her. She also stated that her father had not paid her the stipulated income of 10,000 livres a year, only 7,334 livres or three-quarters, keeping the rest for himself, and she wanted the arrearages paid. She secured a judgment from the Parlement of Paris in 1651, ordering payment of the sums stipulated in her marriage contract, but she never got the money. She signed a provisional agreement in 1654 with her father in which he gave her lands in Anjou and Touraine, the châteaux of Montbazon and Couzières, and the *hôtel* de Montbazon in Paris to cancel the debt, but when she tried to take possession of this property, she discovered that it had already been seized by creditors. Her father died bankrupt a year later with the debt still unpaid.[15] Luynes never protested the dowry's non-payment, which was common in great families, because he was wealthy enough to overlook it. He was proud of his wife's high rank, and insisted that she keep the privilege of the *tabouret*, which allowed the holder to sit on a folding stool in the presence of the queen. The Rohan family enjoyed this privilege, and Marie would have lost it by marrying him. Visible signs of rank were important, and the privilege of the *tabouret* caused numerous quarrels.[16]

Luynes's first child, a daughter named Anne-Marie for the queen and her mother, was born on 26 January 1619.[17] Her parents wanted a grand marriage for her, so a match was arranged with Charles Louis de Lorraine, duc de Joyeuse, second son of the duc de Guise. The Lorraine had the rank of foreign princes. The marriage contract was read to the king on 22 January 1620, and Luynes agreed to pay a dowry of 600,000 livres with the king adding a wedding gift of 100,000 livres.[18] The proposed marriage was attacked as a mésalliance in a pamphlet urging the duc de Guise to oppose it.[19] Both children were only a year old, so the marriage ceremony was postponed until they were adults, but it never took place. Luynes died in 1621, and Anne-Marie, no longer the daughter of a royal favorite, was not considered of sufficient rank to be a suitable match for a son of the house of Lorraine. The duc de Guise fled France in 1631 to avoid arrest, taking his son with him, and the boy died unmarried in Florence in 1637, while Anne-Marie died unmarried in 1646. There was another daughter born to Luynes and Marie sometime during the winter of 1620, but she died ten years later.[20]

On Christmas night 1620, Luynes's son and heir was born. He was named Louis-Charles for the king and his father, and Paris church bells rang in celebration, while cannon were fired at the château of Caen where Luynes and the king were visiting. The baby was baptized in Paris with the king acting as his godfather and Marie de Médicis as his godmother, and the whole court participated in the celebrations, rumored to have cost the king 80,000 livres. The king had celebrated the birth and baptism of Luynes's son as if he were his own.[21] Louis-Charles d'Albert, duc de Luynes, carried on the family line. He married three times, fathered numerous children, and died in 1690 at the age of seventy.[22] What other rewards besides a wife did Luynes receive?

Luynes's fortune through 1617

A classic criticism of royal favorites was that they were greedy. The anti-Luynes pamphleteers declared that Luynes had accumulated a huge fortune of ten to twelve million livres by adding to Concini's already enormous fortune, which the king had given him.[23] After Luynes's death, the king joked that his favorite had casually remarked one day that he needed four million gold écus (twelve million livres), a quip intended to demonstrate his greed.[24] The judicial decision condemning Léonora to death had ordered her fortune to revert to the crown, and a month later by royal letters in August 1617, the king had given her property to Luynes, who was obliged to pay her debts.[25] The pamphleteers noted that Luynes had then acquired pensions, land from the royal domaine, and cash from the treasury to double the amount of Concini's fortune.[26] He had also secured fortunes for his brothers who pillaged over four million livres from the royal treasury in three years. Court rumors persisted that Luynes and his brothers together had amassed between ten and thirty million livres in property and offices.[27] The pamphleteers described the three "Luynards" as a plague of locusts and a three-headed dog ravaging France.[28] They declared that Luynes was even greedier than Concini.[29] How much of Concini's fortune did Luynes actually get?

The pamphleteers had accused Concini and his wife of pillaging the state to create an enormous fortune, an accusation repeated endlessly by royal propagandists after their deaths and asserted by historians ever since. The pamphleteers declared that Concini had accumulated a fortune in cash of twelve million livres in addition to offices, lands, jewelry, and investments worth as much, and that he had drained fourteen million livres from the royal treasury in seven years. The Venetian ambassador declared that Concini had amassed a fortune of at least fifteen million livres. The *Mercure françois* deplored his extravagance, claiming that he had spent 280,000 livres a year in cultivating the good will of Spain, and 80,000 pistoles a night in gambling.[30]

Jean-François Dubost has noted that these claims about Concini's huge fortune are ridiculous. Rumors circulated after his death that Concini had spent 6,000 livres a day or 2,190,000 livres a year. Such an income would have needed a fortune of at least forty million livres, which would have been impossible to accumulate in seven years. Pamphleteers always described Concini's fortune as two or three times bigger than the largest contemporary fortunes acquired over fifteen or twenty years.[31] Luynes could not have inherited such an enormous fortune because it did not exist. Concini told Bassompierre that he had amassed a fortune of over seven million livres.[32] Crèvecoeur estimated his fortune at 8.4 million livres.[33] How much of this did Luynes get?

He had inherited little from his father. Luynes's annual income in 1614 was about 4,400 livres. As the head of two fauconnerie departments, he received a salary of 700 livres each for a total of 1,400 a year, plus an annual royal pension of 2,000 livres, and 1,000 livres a year from his lands in Provence, a total of 4,400 livres. He inherited two of his father's fiefs, Luynes and Mornas, worth perhaps 27,500 livres, and his brothers inherited the other two fiefs, Cadenet and Brantes, worth about the same. When the value of his household offices are added to his lands, his fortune in 1614 was about 41,500 livres, which was typical for a provincial noble serving in a royal household.[34]

When Luynes became the favorite-in-chief in 1615, he added another 11,000 livres a year to his income. These figures are approximate and conservative, but he received an income of about 2,000 livres a year as first ordinary gentleman of the king's bedchamber; 2,500 livres as governor of Amboise; 2,500 livres as captain-governor of the Tuileries; and 2,000 livres in salary as a councillor of state with another 2,000 livres for living expenses.[35] The king gave him the money to buy these offices. Luynes's annual income, therefore, rose to 15,400 livres in 1615. The next year he added a salary of 1,200 livres a year as grand falconer, plus 3,000 livres maintenance, an unknown salary as bird keeper of the king's bedchamber, and 2,500 livres as captain-governor of the Louvre, which brought his income to at least 22,100 livres a year.[36]

Luynes more than quadrupled his annual income in 1617. He became first gentleman of the king's bedchamber for an annual salary of 3,500 livres;

captain of the royal guard company of one hundred men-at-arms for a salary of 3,500 livres a year; and captain-governor of the Bastille for another 3,000 livres a year. Supplementary payments averaging as much as 10,000 livres a year were attached to each of these offices for an additional annual total of 30,000 livres. The king increased Luynes's annual pension to 32,000 livres when he married, and he was named lieutenant-general of Normandy for a salary of 6,000 livres a year with unknown cash gifts from the Estates of Normandy. He became governor of the Norman fortress of Pont de l'Arche for an annual salary of about 2,500 livres, another office belonging to Concini.[37] With Luynes's larger pension, they added 80,500 livres to his annual income, which rose to 102,600 livres in 1617.

This income, however, was not large enough for Luynes to display the magnificence expected of a favorite-in-chief.[38] Anne de Montmorency, the influential favorite of Henri II, had landed revenues of 138,465 livres in 1563, and equally substantial revenues from other sources.[39] Three-quarters of the revenues of great court nobles came from sources other than land, and increasingly their revenues came from the crown.[40] Henri III's favorites, the ducs de Joyeuse and Epernon, also had large incomes. Joyeuse's income rose from 26,950 livres in 1581 to 152,650 in 1586, while that of Epernon went from 45,000 livres in 1581 to 191,900 livres in 1588. Most of this money came from royal pensions, salaries from royal offices, cash gifts from the royal treasury, and various types of loans and investments.[41] Luynes as the new favorite-in-chief needed a larger income.

He got about 1.9 million livres from Concini's fortune, which was less than a quarter of an estimated fortune of 8.4 million livres. Victor Cousin believed that Luynes had received 2.4 million from Concini's fortune.[42] L'Huillier, a royal attorney in the Paris *Chambre des Comptes*, estimated the amount at about 2 million livres, while an anonymous observer put it at 2.5 million livres.[43] Jean-François Dubost has noted that Luynes may have received as little as 1.5 million livres.[44] These were not the huge sums described by the anti-Luynes pamphleteers. Why did he receive so little?

Luynes received less than a quarter of Concini's fortune because the royal letters granted him only what had belonged to Léonora, not to her husband. They had a legal property separation, and Concini had put all of their property in her name, which Luynes got, but they kept at least 60 percent of their fortune in liquid assets, an unusually high percentage, most of which Luynes did not get. Concini had nearly two million livres worth of notes due, payment orders on the royal treasury, and other forms of paper cash in his pockets when he died, none of which Luynes got. Nor did he get the 300,000 livres that Concini was owed by the Rouen tax receiver.[45] Léonora had been liquefying assets for their return to Italy, and she had put between 1,020,000 and 1,030,000 livres into state investments in Florence and Rome, which Luynes never got. He did not receive the 321,000 livres she had invested with French financiers either. Most of it, 200,000 livres, went to reimburse Vitry for his office of guard captain, which was given to his brother, while another 72,000 livres went to pay fines and debts. Luynes did not get any of the money that Léonora had invested with bankers and financiers.[46]

He had refused to accept as a gift the jewelry found on Léonora when she was arrested, which the king gave to the queen. This jewelry included a pearl necklace worth 105,000 livres, and a casket whose contents and value are unknown. Léonora declared that she had lost 600,000 livres in jewelry at the time of her arrest, probably stolen by the men going through her belongings. Robert Arnauld d'Andilly reported that she lost 900,000 livres worth of jewelry, a sum that may have included the casket that the queen received.[47] Léonora and her husband had put much of their wealth into jewelry, gold and silver plate, precious objects, and cash kept in locked chests in their various residences. Pillaging mobs took all that was in their Paris houses.

Their mansion on the rue de Tournon was sacked by a mob in September 1616 with an estimated loss of 150,000 livres, and the abbé de Marolles reported seeing the house stripped down to its walls. The mob took all the furniture, even the iron grills, and cut down the trees in the garden. Léonora received 450,000 livres in compensation from the crown, which she used to refurnish the house, but it was almost certainly sacked again at Concini's death six months later when his body was burned at its door. Arnauld d'Andilly reported that the small house Concini kept on the rue d'Autriche next to the walls of the Louvre was also sacked on the day of his death by royal guards, who stole 900,000 livres worth of furnishings including a number of locked chests that took 12 mules and 2 wagons to move. The amount may have been exaggerated, but probably at least 500,000 livres worth of furnishings and chests were taken. Luynes, therefore, did not get the contents, worth at least 650,000 livres, of either Paris house.[48] He did not get the contents of the château at Lésigny either because Léonora had shipped its furnishings to Italy via Amsterdam, intending to sell the château and their Paris mansion. The château's luxurious furnishings, including 3 tapestries worth 25,000 livres, must have been comparable in value to the furnishings of their Paris mansion, thus worth about 150,000 livres.[49] Luynes had lost at least 800,000 livres in furnishings, probably more. Over 5 million livres of Concini's fortune had disappeared. What did Luynes get?

He received the fief and château of Lésigny-en-Brie, which had been valued at 300,000 livres.[50] He may have used part of the king's wedding gift to furnish it, or when the king visited Lésigny in late August, he may have given Luynes the money to furnish it. Luynes also received the mansion on the rue de Tournon, purchased by Léonora in 1606 for 42,000 livres, and sold by him in 1621 for 186,625 livres. A pamphleteer declared that he had been so embarrassed by the public outcry at his possession of this house that he sold it to the crown to use as an ambassadorial residence. In fact, for 175,000 livres the year before, Luynes had bought a better house closer to the Louvre in a more aristocratic neighborhood. This larger house had more extensive gardens, was in better condition, and had no unpleasant memories of what happened to unpopular royal favorites.[51] Luynes also received the marquisat d'Ancre in Picardy, which Léonora had bought for 330,000 livres in 1610. The Queen Mother had given her 450,000 livres to make the purchase, and she used the other 120,000 livres to make improvements to the property, increasing its value. Luynes changed the name of the marquisat and its village to Albert. He also kept, furnished, and occasionally used the small house on the rue d'Autriche next to the palace walls worth perhaps 10,000 livres. Its back door opened onto the Louvre gardens, and a covered walkway led from the house into the palace, making it a convenient retreat.[52]

Finally, Luynes got the furnishings of Léonora's three-room apartment in the Louvre worth as much as 150,000 livres. This would have brought the sum in furnishings to 950,000 livres, or nearly the 1,000,000 that Concini had said he still possessed after his house had been sacked in September 1616.[53] Léonora had 20 locked chests full of valuable objects in her apartment. The chests contained gold and silver plate; jewelry; gold and silver objets d'art including candlesticks, reliquaries, vases, pitchers, basins, framed mirrors, and even chamber pots; Chinese and Turkish carpets; and tapestries of all sizes. There were numerous dresses, skirts, cloaks, blouses, shirts, sleeves, waist-coats, and pants as well as horse, coach, and bed coverings, bed hangings and curtains, all in precious materials such as velvet, satin, and taffeta, most of them bejeweled or embroidered in gold and silver. The apartment was luxuriously furnished with expensive furniture in rare woods, chairs upholstered in velvet, bed hangings of embroidered silk, oriental carpets, and tapestries, and gold and silver objects worth as much as 48,000 livres. Luynes may have used some of these furnishings in his new, larger apartment in the Louvre, acquired in May 1617 from Madame de Guercheville, who had accompanied the Queen Mother to Blois.[54] The total value of the property and furnishings that Luynes got from Concini, therefore, was about 1,097,000 livres.[55] Crèvecoeur estimated this amount at 850,000 livres, excluding the contents of Léonora's apartment in the Louvre, and Dubost estimated it at 800,000 livres, again excluding the furnishings of the Louvre apartment.[56]

Luynes was also given five offices that had belonged to Concini and his wife. He had been immediately sworn into Concini's office of first gentleman of the king's bedchamber valued at 240,000 livres, retaining at the same time his office of first ordinary gentleman of the king's bedchamber. In 1623, the office of first gentleman was worth 300,000 livres, and in 1625, it sold for 360,000 livres.[57] Within a few months of Concini's death, Luynes had received his Norman offices of provincial lieutenant-general worth at least 200,000 livres, and governor of the fortress of Pont de l'Arche on the Seine below Rouen, worth 60,000 livres in 1611.[58] A few years later, Luynes secured Concini's strategically important Norman fortress of Quillebeuf at the mouth of the Seine east of Le Havre. Its value is unknown, but it may have been worth as much as 100,000 livres by 1620. Luynes did not get all of Concini's Norman offices, however, because the governorship of Caen went to the king's half-brother, the grand prior de Vendôme.[59] Luynes also got Léonora's office of mistress of the queen's robes, which he gave to his sister Antoinette du Vernet in December 1618.[60] This office was comparable to that of first gentleman of the king's bedchamber, but offices in the queen's household were less valuable, so it may have been worth 200,000 livres. Luynes, therefore, had obtained offices worth about 800,000 livres from Concini and his wife.[61]

When this sum is added to the value of Concini's property, the total is 1,897,000 livres or about 1.9 million livres from which Luynes was expected to pay Léonora's debts. Her creditors, however, never got in full what they were owed. A pamphleteer complained that Luynes had paid only half her debts.[62] Great nobles, always in debt, were notorious for not paying their debts. There was no moral pressure on Luynes to pay the debts of an unpopular female favorite who had been executed, and probably not much legal pressure either since he was now a favorite. It is surprising that he paid any of her debts.

When the offices the king had given Luynes in 1615 and 1616 are added to his fortune of 1,897,000 livres, it became even larger. The château of Amboise was worth 300,000 livres, the office of royal guard captain 200,000 livres, and the office of grand falconer 135,000 livres.[63] This was a total of 635,000 livres, to which 140,000 livres, the capitalized salaries of his other 1615 and 1616 offices, may be added for a total of 775,000 livres.[64] When this sum is added to Luynes's inherited fortune of 41,500 livres, his total fortune in 1617 was 2,713,500 livres, or 2.7 million, which came mostly from the crown. The average fortune of a courtier in this period was 806,000 livres.[65]

So, Luynes had acquired a substantial fortune in three years, but it was not the huge fortune of millions described by the pamphleteers. From Concini's wife, he had obtained three empty houses, two in Paris and one in the suburbs, none of them distinguished, and the furnishings of her three-room apartment in the Louvre. He did not get any of her jewelry, investments, or cash, and he had to pay her debts. The Concini fortune helped Luynes's political future, but it did not have the enormous importance that the pamphleteers and some historians have claimed.[66] Luynes had also been given five offices that had belonged to

Léonora and her husband. Luynes's offices in 1617 included first gentleman and first ordinary gentleman of the king's bedchamber; grand falconer and keeper of the king's bedchamber birds; captain-governor of the Tuileries, Louvre, and Bastille; captain of the royal guard company of one hundred men-at-arms; governor of Amboise; councillor of state and honorary councillor of the Parlement of Paris;[67] lieutenant general of Normandy; and governor of the Norman fortresses of Pont de l'Arche and Quillebeuf. Royal household offices were prestigious and allowed regular access to the king and his family, but Luynes wanted a power base outside the court, so he sought a provincial government. He wanted the status, prestige, patronage, and power that went with a provincial government.

A fortune of 2.7 million livres was large, but there were other court fortunes as large or larger including Concini's. Between 1589 and 1624, the average of the fortunes of royal princes was 2.4 million livres, and that of noble courtiers 1.5 million livres.[68] The Gondi de Retz were worth over 5 million livres in 1603.[69] Henri IV's minister-favorite, the duc de Sully, had a fortune of 2.2 million livres in 1610.[70] Henri II de Bourbon, prince de Condé, was worth about 3 million livres in 1618.[71] In the late 1580s, the duc d'Epernon had a fortune of about 3 million livres, which had increased half again as much by the time of his death in the 1640s.[72] Louis Gouffier, duc de Roannez, had a fortune of 2.25 million livres in 1625.[73] The duc de Nevers when he died in 1637 left property worth 8 million livres, four times the family fortune in 1551 when the duke had about 2 million livres with landed revenues of 115,085 livres.[74] Henri de Lorraine, duc de Guise, had landed revenues of 130,000 livres in the 1570s, and a fortune of at least 2.6 million livres, which does not include his income from investments or royal lands held in usufruct.[75] The fortune of Henri de Lorraine, duc de Mayenne, was estimated at 2.1 million livres in 1610.[76]

So, Luynes's fortune at the time of his marriage put him among the wealthiest of the great court nobles, but his fortune was not unique. In fact, it was not the size of his fortune that had shocked contemporaries, but rather the speed with which it had been acquired, and its source in the property and offices of his predecessor, an unpopular royal favorite whom he had helped to murder. It was widely believed that Concini's fortune was larger than it was, and that Luynes had gotten all of it, so he was widely believed to be wealthier than he really was. His contemporaries were shocked when he tripled his fortune during the next four years, but he was no greedier than other courtiers. Everyone at court hoped to become rich at the crown's expense.

Luynes's fortune after 1617

The imprisoned prince de Condé resigned his government of Guyenne at the king's request. Luynes wanted a provincial government, but he did not want Guyenne because Bordeaux was too far away from Paris, and his favor depended upon seeing the king often. So, he persuaded Henri de Lorraine, duc de Mayenne, to trade his government of the Ile-de-France for that of Guyenne and the Bordeaux fortress of the Château Trompette. Luynes became governor and lieutenant general of the Ile-de-France, with a reservation on the offices of governor and lieutenant general of Paris, which he secured in 1620 after the incumbent died. Mayenne also resigned to Luynes the governments of the Picard fortresses and towns of Noyon, Coucy, Chauny, and Soissons.[77] The king in December 1618 named Luynes's wife first lady of honor and superintendent of the queen's household, an office suppressed by Henri IV, recreated for her, and suppressed again in 1623. Richelieu, who loathed her, wrote in his memoirs that she quickly became Anne's favorite.[78]

Luynes persuaded the king to make his mother exchange her first-tier government of Normandy for the more distant, second-tier provincial government of Anjou. She did not want to do this, and Richelieu wrote that she had to be threatened with imprisonment in Luynes's château of Amboise or in a convent before she would agree. Her resignation of the government of Normandy became part of the Treaty of Angoulême in April 1619 reconciling her with her son. Luynes, already lieutenant general of Normandy, now became its governor, which he offered to Charles de Lorraine, duc de Guise, in exchange for his government of Provence with its Mediterranean fortresses and royal galleys. Guise refused, so he offered Normandy to the king's half-brother, César de Vendôme, in exchange for his important government of Brittany, but he refused. Finally, Luynes offered Normandy to Henri II d'Orléans, duc de Longueville, in exchange for his government of Picardy, a heavily fortified frontier province bordering the Spanish Netherlands. Picardy, Brittany, and Provence were all strategically important provinces with heavy concentrations of troops. Longueville accepted, and in August 1619, Luynes was sworn in as governor and lieutenant general of Picardy and the Boulonnais, which had been confiscated from the duc d'Epernon. He also became governor of the Picard fortresses of La Fère, Ham, and Saint Quentin.

Luynes gave his father-in-law Montbazon the government of the Ile-de-France in 1619 in exchange for the government of Amiens, and kept for himself the office of lieutenant general of the Ile-de-France. Amiens was the capital of Picardy, and Luynes's marquisat of Albert was nearby. He also gave Montbazon the governorships of the Picard fortresses of Noyon, Chauny, Coucy, and Soissons after he had acquired the more important governments of Calais and

Boulogne. Montbazon was already governor of the city and fortress of Nantes, and he became lieutenant general of Basse-Normandie in 1620. Luynes named his brother Cadenet lieutenant general of Picardy, and commander of the Normandy regiment garrisoning the Parisian fortress of Vincennes. He gave his cousin Ornano the offices of lieutenant general of Haute-Normandie, and governor of the Norman fortress of the Pont de l'Arche.[79]

So, within three years Luynes had created a significant power base for himself in northern France adjacent to the capital and the court. He had become governor of Picardy and six Picard fortress towns, Amiens, Calais, Boulogne, La Fère, Ham, and Saint Quentin, with four more through his father-in-law, Noyon, Chauny, Coucy, and Soissons. Luynes's brother Cadenet had become lieutenant general of Picardy, and Luynes's client Mauny had been named governor of Caen in 1620. Luynes's father-in-law was governor of the Ile-de-France, while he himself was lieutenant general. Luynes also became governor and lieutenant general of Paris, and captain-governor of three Parisian fortresses, the Louvre, Tuileries, and Bastille, while his brother Cadenet commanded the garrison of a fourth, Vincennes, and his client the baron de Paluau was governor of a fifth, Saint-Germain-en-Laye. Luynes's brother Brantes and his brother-in-law Du Vernet were lieutenants of the Bastille, and Brantes soon became its governor. Luynes's father-in-law and his cousin Ornano were lieutenant generals of Normandy. Ornano was governor of the Norman fortress of Pont de l'Arche and the city of Rouen, while Luynes himself was governor of the fortress of Quillebeuf, and his client Desplan was governor of the fortress of Meulan. These three Seine fortresses gave Luynes control of the river from Paris to its mouth. Court nobles watched in dismay as he acquired these fortresses in and around Paris, fearing his intentions.[80]

With the king providing the purchase money, these new offices significantly increased Luynes's fortune. The government of Picardy was worth about 500,000 livres, and the lieutenant generalship of the Ile-de-France another 300,000 livres. The governments of Amiens and Calais were worth 300,000 and 360,000 livres, respectively, for a total of 660,000 livres.[81] The governments of Boulogne and Paris were worth about 300,000 livres each for a total of 600,000 livres.[82] The governments of La Fère, Ham, and Saint Quentin were worth about 100,000 livres each for a total of 300,000 livres.[83] The office of superintendent of the queen's household was worth about 300,000 livres.[84] These offices added 2,660,000 livres or another 2.7 million to Luynes's fortune.[85]

Luynes satisfied another ambition in August 1619 when he became a duke. He had recently purchased the *comté* of Maillé on the Loire about ten miles west of Tours, and the king issued royal letters in August erecting it into the duchy of Luynes. Perched on a ridge overlooking the river, Maillé was an eleventh-century castle rebuilt during the thirteenth century. It has remained much the same ever since, a square stone château with an open courtyard and a feudal facade of four towers on the river side and four towers on the land side. The village of Maillé lay at its feet. The new duchy consisted of approximately fifty parishes reaching to the walls of Tours and surrounding the city on three sides. It was about the same size as the duchy of Montbazon across the Loire, which was composed of forty to fifty parishes. The square keep of the château de Montbazon, all that now remains, dated from the eleventh century. The Rohan had bought this château in the fifteenth century, so Luynes's father-in-law was a neighbor.[86] Luynes knew the region well because of the years he had spent at the château of Le Lude northwest of Tours and the château of Amboise east of Tours. The value of his duchy is unknown, but it was worth at least several hundred thousand livres.[87] The king in 1620 gave him as a gift an exemption from the royal tax of *lods et ventes* on his new duchy.[88] Luynes also bought six fiefs in 1618 of which the value of only one is known, 51,000 livres, and he undoubtedly bought more land during the next three years.[89]

Luynes was received as a duke and a peer in the great hall of the Parlement of Paris on 14 November 1619. The judges had assembled at eight o'clock that morning, and Luynes arrived fifteen minutes later accompanied by his brother Cadenet, the prince de Condé, the duc de Montbazon, and Charles du Plessis de Liancourt, the head of the small stables when Luynes was a stable page. Other members of his entourage included Lesdiguières's son-in-law, Charles de Créquy, whose son soon would marry Luynes's niece; Charles de Schomberg whose father was superintendent of finance; and the sieurs de Praslin, Bassompierre, Alincourt, and Mauny. A large number of court nobles were in the audience. The royal attorney of the Parlement, Omer Talon, made a speech in which he declared that Luynes had been rewarded with the titles of duke and peer for his services to the monarchy. The first president of the Parlement announced that the royal letters creating the new duchy had been registered, and Luynes swore an oath of loyalty as a duke and peer. Then the doors of the great hall were thrown open, and the new duke and his friends emerged jubilantly to ride off in their carriages. It was a great day for Luynes. He had joined one of the most exclusive clubs in France.[90]

On 31 March 1621, the king named Luynes constable of France, and he was sworn into office two days later. The office of constable had been worth 240,000 livres in the sixteenth century, and was probably now worth at least 300,000 livres.[91] The constable was commander-in-chief of the army under the king who was the supreme commander. Although not a field commander, the constable had authority and precedence over the marshals of France, and was first-ranked among the great officials of the crown. His privileges included being addressed as "Monseigneur" and extensive military patronage. The office may have been a feudal relic, but it was prestigious and profitable.[92] So, Luynes had become a duke and a constable, titles that Concini had wanted but had never got.[93] Luynes had acquired the office of constable by default, however, because the duc de Lesdiguières, who had the reputation and expertise to exercise it, had refused to convert to Catholicism.[94] Luynes's widely criticized appointment provoked pamphlets and satiric doggerel protesting his military inexperience, and declaring that Lesdiguières, Mayenne, or Guise would have been a better choice. The king and Richelieu permanently abolished the office of constable in 1627.[95]

Guillaume Du Vair, keeper of the seals, died suddenly on 3 August 1621 at Tonneins on the Garonne river while on campaign with the king, and that evening the king named Luynes a temporary replacement. The keeper of the seals exercised the functions of the absent chancellor, which included presiding over royal council meetings, and Luynes eagerly accepted, although this was the first time that a constable had been named keeper of the seals. Luynes may have wanted a relative or client to hold this office because he had not yet bought it himself by the time of his death four months later.[96]

Luynes's fortune when he married was 2.7 million livres, although when the cost of the offices he gave relatives is deducted, it was 2,253,500 livres or about 2.25 million.[97] The offices he acquired after 1617 were worth 2,660,000 livres, increasing his fortune to 4,913,500 livres or about 4.9 million. Another 1,326,000 livres may be added since the office of constable was worth 300,000 livres, and he had 51,000 livres in land; 375,000 livres in jewelry;[98] 400,000 livres in investments;[99] and at least 200,000 livres in furnishings for his two châteaux, Paris mansion, Louvre apartment, and house on the rue d'Autriche.[100] Luynes's documented fortune, therefore, was 6,239,500 livres, or about 6.2 million at the time of his death in 1621. This is an incomplete, conservative estimate that does not include his duchy and other lands,[101] cash on hand,[102] investments or loans, and offices of unknown value. When these are added, his fortune would have been closer to 8 million livres.[103] Luynes had accumulated a fortune nearly as large as that of Concini in the same length of time, seven years (1615–21).

Luynes's documented annual income in 1621 was 586,564 livres. He received 70,000 livres a year in royal pensions, and 40,000 livres in investments (*rentes*), a surprisingly low sum given his position.[104] His provincial government provided a salary of about 60,000 livres, plus variable allowances for living expenses and troop maintenance as well as unknown gifts and bribes.[105] The salt revenues for Picardy, which the king had given him, were worth 279,314 livres in 1623.[106] The revenues from his duchy of Luynes were probably at least 20,000 livres a year, plus another 1,000 for his Provençal fiefs.[107] The revenues from his other lands are unknown. He received 4,200 livres a year as grand falconer, 3,500 livres as first gentleman of the king's bedchamber, and 2,000 as first ordinary gentleman; 4,000 as councillor of state; 5,000 as governor of the Louvre and Tuileries, and 3,000 as governor of the Bastille, plus supplementary payments attached to these offices for at least another 30,000 livres. His salaries as governor of Amiens, Calais, Boulogne, and Paris were probably about 3,000 a year or 12,000 livres total, and about 2,500 a year each for the lesser fortresses of La Fère, Ham, and Saint Quentin or 7,750 total.[108] His annual salary as constable was around 30,000 livres, and he received a salary of 3,000 livres a year in 1620 and 1621 as a knight of Saint Esprit.[109] More than 40 percent of his income, therefore, came from royal salaries and pensions. In addition, his wife received 8,800 livres a year as superintendent of the queen's household, plus unknown gifts.[110] The total is 586,564 livres, which does not include all of his landed revenues, cash gifts from the king,[111] loans to the state and other investments, and bribes. When these are added, Luynes's income would have been well over 700,000 livres a year. His debts and expenses are unknown.

Debunking myths

There are several widely accepted myths about Luynes's greed and ambition. Contemporaries thought him enormously wealthy because he had inherited Concini's huge fortune. In fact, he had inherited less than one-quarter of Concini's not so enormous fortune. He was said to have modeled himself on Concini whom he surpassed in greed and ambition, and court nobles quipped that the tavern had only changed its sign, which has been repeated by historians ever since.[112] They have also repeated Richelieu's assertion that Luynes's rise to fame and fortune gave him delusions of grandeur. Luynes, however, was no greedier or more ambitious than other courtiers, and he was too shrewd to make the mistake of behaving like another Concini.

In fact, Luynes modeled himself on a long line of royal favorites. The word *favori* had first been used in the early sixteenth century.[113] Nicolas de Brichanteau, marquis de Beauvais-Nangis, remarked that the age of favorites in France had begun with the rise of the royal court as an avenue to wealth during the reign of François I.[114] A pattern of favorite acquisitions had developed that included accumulating a large fortune; securing an important household office such as first gentleman of the king's bedchamber; making an illustrious marriage; providing generously for family members; acquiring provincial and fortress governments; lands; a large clientele; the titles of duke and peer; high-ranking military offices such as marshal, constable, or admiral; and high-ranking government offices including a seat on the royal council. The careers of Montmorency,

Joyeuse, Epernon, Concini, Luynes, and Richelieu all fit this pattern.[115]

Luynes's documented fortune of 6.2 million livres at the time of his death was equivalent in size to that of many other favorites, ministers, and financial officials. Sully, Henri IV's minister-favorite, had accumulated a fortune of 5 million by the time of his death in 1641.[116] Claude Bullion, superintendent of finance under Richelieu, had amassed a fortune of nearly 8 million when he died in 1640.[117] Henry II de Bourbon, prince de Condé, enjoyed a fortune of 16.5 million at his death in 1646.[118] Nicolas Fouquet, superintendent of finance under Mazarin, had amassed a fortune of 15.5 million when he was arrested for embezzlement in 1661.[119] Abel Servien, another financial superintendent, had a fortune of 4.4 million when he died in 1659.[120] Colbert, Louis XIV's minister of finance, had accumulated a fortune of nearly 5 million at his death in 1683.[121] The two great minister-favorites, Richelieu and Mazarin, had amassed fortunes of 20 million and 38 million, respectively, at their deaths in 1642 and 1661.[122]

Louis Batiffol noted that Luynes's fortune, compared with those of men who had similar opportunities, was smaller than theirs, probably because he had less time to acquire it.[123] Luynes accumulated his fortune at a time when the royal treasury was empty, which made him appear greedier than Concini. Ironically, the anti-Luynes pamphleteers began accusing him of excessive greed and ambition only after the Queen Mother had emptied the treasury to give Concini his fortune. Richelieu would acquire a fortune of twenty million livres in eighteen years (1624–42), while Mazarin amassed a fortune nearly double that size in the same length of time, eighteen years (1643–61). Luynes had accumulated a large fortune, but it was not unusually large.

Jean-Pierre Labatut has noted that Louis XIII's generosity to Luynes was unexceptional.[124] The crown distributed large cash gifts to great nobles during Henri IV's reign and Louis XIII's minority in order to secure their obedience. From 1600 to 1610, the crown distributed 2 million livres a year in pensions to the *grands*, which it increased to 3 million in 1610, 4 million in 1611, 5 million in 1613, 1614, and 1617, and more than 5 million a year from 1618 to 1621.[125] From 1611 to 1617, 11 great nobles received more than 15 million livres in cash gifts from the crown. The prince de Condé received 3,665,990; the comte de Soissons 1.5 million; the prince de Conti 1.4 million; the duc de Guise 1.7 million; the duc de Nevers 1.6 million; the duc de Longueville 1.2 million; the ducs de Mayenne, father and son, more than 2 million; the duc de Vendôme more than 600,000; the duc d'Epernon nearly 700,000; and the duc de Bouillon more than 1 million.[126] The Peace of Loudun in 1616 cost the crown at least 17 million livres, perhaps as much as 20 million, distributed among the rebellious great nobles.[127] Everyone took as much as he could get from the crown. In this context, Luynes's fortune does not seem excessively large, and he does not appear outrageously greedy.

Favorites were early modern success stories. As self-made men, they had turned the social hierarchy on its head, threatening everyone else's rank and status in so doing, and they were never liked for this reason.[128] They were always portrayed as social-climbing opportunists, greedy and ambitious without principles or goals beyond promoting themselves, and this was how Luynes's enemies portrayed him. Concini was depicted as a squirrel who had ambitiously climbed to the top of the tallest tree, and then had greedily stored food in its trunk for the winter. Favorites were resented for diverting the flow of royal patronage away from other nobles, and Concini was especially resented as a foreigner who had diverted the flow away from French nobles. Courtiers were regarded as greedy and ambitious, and those who succeeded spectacularly like royal favorites became the object of universal envy and resentment.[129] Luynes was no greedier or more ambitious than other courtiers, only more successful.

The usual explanation for his greed and the speed with which he acquired his fortune was that the king's favor had gone to his head. Richelieu wrote that Luynes "was too weak to remain firm under the pressure of such great good fortune in which he immediately lost himself, allowing himself to be carried away as if by a flood."[130] He declared that the ambitious Luynes had begun to act as if he were king, and sought to become the prince d'Orange, comte d'Avignon, duc d'Albret, and king of Austrasie (the eastern kingdom of the Gauls with Metz as its capital), and to annex Toul, Metz, and Verdun (the urban governments of his enemy, the duc d'Epernon) to form a new kingdom.[131] An anti-Luynes pamphleteer reported that he had offered to lend the king five million livres in exchange for the government of Brittany, and that he wanted the governments of Navarre and Béarn, which belonged to the d'Albret family, because then all he needed to become a prince of the blood was to change the "r" in his name from Albert to Albret.[132] Pamphleteers reported that the king's favor had so turned his head that Luynes made his father-in-law and other great nobles wait for hours in the antechamber to his rooms, and that he wore his hat in the presence of the king and prince de Condé who were bareheaded. He used the familiar form of address with everyone, including those who had a higher rank or were older, and insisted that everyone address him as "Monseigneur."[133]

Luynes was a skilled courtier who had been at court since he was thirteen years old. Such flagrantly imprudent behavior by an experienced courtier seems unlikely. Contemporaries described Luynes as courteous, kind, and affable, someone who was charming and deferential. This description conflicts with that of Richelieu and the pamphleteers, who insisted that he was arrogant, pretentious, and rude. Luynes knew that the king was jealous of his authority, and that he would not tolerate being pushed aside or having his authority usurped in public. Luynes knew that if he were foolish enough to imitate the arrogant bravado of Concini, he would lose the king's favor and might well share Concini's fate. He was too astute to repeat Concini's mistakes.

It had been rash, however, for Luynes to put together such a large power base so quickly because he seemed to have boundless ambition. Recognizing the strategic importance of controlling the governments around Paris, he traded until he got what he wanted, which frightened the great nobles. He chose Picardy, Concini's government, and became both governor and lieutenant general of Picardy, although Concini had been only lieutenant general. He acquired six Picard fortress governorships, Amiens, Calais, Boulogne, Ham, La Fère, and Saint Quentin, although Concini had only held four, Amiens, Péronne, Roye, and Montdidier, which had caused criticism at the time.[134] To make matters worse, Luynes made his cousin a Norman lieutenant general and governor of the Seine fortress of Pont de l'Arche. He held the fortress of Quillebeuf himself, while a client held that of Meulan, and his father-in-law was the other Norman lieutenant general. Concini had also been lieutenant general of Normandy, and had held several urban governments in that province, but he had relinquished Picardy and its fortresses before acquiring them. Luynes did not. In addition, he held the offices of lieutenant general of the Ile-de-France and governor and lieutenant general of Paris, and controlled five Parisian fortresses.

Henri IV had adopted a successful policy of refusing to allow provincial governors to hold the governorships of cities and fortresses in their provinces. A governor could hold urban governorships in other provinces, but not in his own. This policy was meant to discourage revolts by provincial governors because if they rebelled against the king, they had to contend with the hostile governors of their own provincial cities and fortresses. As additional security, the king refused to name the same man as governor of a city and its fortress, but instead named different governors.[135]

Concini, however, disregarded this policy to the dismay of the great nobles, and Luynes did the same. He jointly held city and fortress governorships, and he began to acquire these governorships for his relatives. He soon controlled ten urban governorships in Picardy, and with their fortress garrisons and his troops as governor, he controlled a significant military force in a sensitive northern province on the Spanish Netherlands border. This made the great nobles nervous. They feared that he was another Concini, whom they had suspected of intriguing with Spain to establish his own kingdom in the north, or trying to depose the young king and seize the throne for himself.[136] The Queen Mother denounced Luynes for holding too many governorships, and a pamphlet in her name called for a law prohibiting favorites from holding fortress governorships.[137] To avoid being compared with Concini, Luynes should have chosen a different provincial government, secured urban governorships in

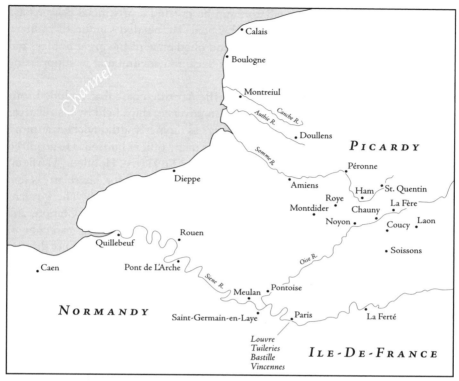

Figure 4 Luynes's Power Base: Picardy, Normandy, Ile-de-France.

other provinces, and refused the office of constable. His recklessness made him unpopular. Why did he make this mistake?

There was a sense of urgency about everything Luynes did, as if he knew that his time in the sun was short. He knew that royal favorites did not last long, a legacy of Concini's murder, and he must have felt threatened by his unpopularity, realizing what it could mean. Luynes was forty in 1618, and he knew that time and circumstances were not on his side. He was deeply committed to his family's welfare, which even Richelieu grudgingly admitted.[138] So, he tried to accumulate as much as he could as fast as he could, and since most vacancies were created by death, he got what had belonged to Concini. His haste was understandable if not wise.

During the early seventeenth century, the constant strife of rival court factions endangered a fragile peace. There were noble intrigues and conspiracies at court in 1602, 1605–1606, and 1610, flaring into open revolt from 1614 to 1617. The Queen Mother and her supporters rebelled in 1619 and 1620, while the Protestant great nobles rebelled in 1621. Luynes's chosen role was that of a peacemaker and conciliator, and he created a provincial power base as a political necessity to accomplish this goal. He needed significant military power of his own to secure the respect and obedience of the great nobles, and his power base in the north around Paris became instrumental in suppressing the Queen Mother's revolt.

Richelieu created a power base on the Atlantic coast that included four provincial governments and eighteen urban governorships held by his relatives and clients. His power base was twice as large as Luynes's, although he was more discreet in creating it, and he did not hold as many offices himself. He acquired the urban governments of Calais in Picardy, and Le Havre, Honfleur, Harfleur, Montvilliers, Pont de l'Arche, and Rouen in Normandy for his relatives and clients, while a cousin became lieutenant general of Normandy. The government of Anjou and its fortress governorships of Angers, Saumur, Chinon, and Ponts-de-Cé were held by his kin and clients, while he became governor of Brittany, and secured the government of the Touraine and the governorships of Brest, Nantes, Brouage, Oléron, Ile-de-Ré, Aunis, and La Rochelle for his kin and clients. The only coastal province to elude him was Poitou. Richelieu assembled a much larger provincial power base than Luynes in the same length of time, seven years (1626–33), and he, too, created it as a political necessity.[139]

This chapter has refuted three myths about Luynes, namely, that he inherited Concini's enormous fortune; that he modeled himself on Concini; and that his sudden rise to power went to his head, making him arrogant and rude. Luynes's fortune put him among the wealthiest of court nobles, but it was not unique, and it did not come from Concini. Contemporaries thought that it did, and that he was wealthier than he really was. Known for his charm and affability, Luynes followed a well-established career path of royal favorites. He was no greedier or more ambitious than other courtiers, and he was too experienced and shrewd to openly abuse his power and position. Historians have been repeating these myths about him ever since they first appeared in Richelieu's memoirs. Luynes's greed and ambition have been exaggerated.

Notes

1 B.N., imprimés Lb 36, *Discours du ballet de la Reyne, tiré de la fable de Psyché* (1619); *Mercure françois*, 25 vols. (Paris, 1605–44) V (1619), 104–8; Jean Héroard, *Journal*, ed. Madeleine Foisil, 2 vols. (Paris, 1989), II, 2596; Paul LaCroix, *Ballets et mascarades de cour de Henri III à Louis XIV*, 6 vols. (Geneva, 1868), II, 200–11.

2 Ibid., II, 139–45; Achille Halphen, ed., *Journal d'Arnauld d'Andilly 1614–1620* (Paris, 1857), pp. 399–400; Héroard, *Journal*, II, 2521.

3 Ibid., II, 2487; Joseph Bergin, *The Making of the French Episcopate* (New Haven, 1996), pp. 431, 606.

4 Louis Batiffol, *Le Louvre sous Henri IV et Louis XIII* (Paris, 1930), pp. 31–2.

5 Paul Phélypeaux de Pontchartrain, *Mémoires concernant les affaires de France sous la régence de Marie de Médicis*, eds. Michaud and Poujoulat, 2nd ser., vol. 5 (Paris, 1837), p. 395; Georges Poisson, *La Duchesse de Chevreuse* (Paris, 1999), pp. 9–57.

6 *Mercure françois*, V (1617), 97.

7 Fontenay-Mareuil, François Du Val, marquis de. *Mémoires du Messire Du Val*, ed. Louis Monmerqué, 2 vols. (Paris, 1826), I, 399–400; Henri de Rohan, *Mémoires du duc de Rohan*, eds. Michaud and Poujoulat, 2nd ser., vol. 5 (Paris, 1837), p. 513; Berthold Zeller, *Le Connétable de Luynes* (Paris, 1879), p. 43; Armand Baschet, *Le Roi chez la Reine* (Paris, 1866), pp. 303–6; Louis Batiffol, *Le Roi Louis XIII à vingt ans* (Paris, 1910), p. 487, n. 3; Jean-Paul Desprat, *Les Bâtards d'Henri IV* (Paris, 1994), pp. 189–90.

8 François Malherbe, *Oeuvres*, ed. Ludovic Lalanne, 5 vols. (Paris, 1862–9), III, 134, 137, October 1610; B.N., Clairambault 1132, fol. 89; Victor Cousin, *Madame de Chevreuse* (Paris, 1856), pp. 7–8; Ruth Kleinman, *Anne of Austria* (Columbus, OH, 1985), p. 49.

9 Ibid.; B.N., imprimés Lb 36, *Discours fait à Monsieur de Luynes par le sieur Dryon* (Paris, 1917), pp. 6–60, esp. 15–18.

10 Charles, comte Horric de Beaucaire, ed., *Mémoires du Cardinal de Richelieu*, 10 vols. (Paris, 1907–13), II, 262–3. "Tout résonnoit d'éloges à sa gloire; mais, comme il n'y avoit rien à lui dire pour fonder ses louanges, il se remarqua que tout ce qu'on put avancer en sa faveur fut de l'accomparer au roi juif Agrippa, qui fut favori de l'empereur Caligula, qui succéda à Tibère, ne considérant pas qu'il avoit en une si malheureuse fin pour sa vanité, que Dieu vengea exemplairement, qu'il faisoient quasi un pronostic de la court durée de sa fortune."

11 Margaret McGowan, *L'Art du ballet de cour en France* (Paris, 1963), pp. 105, n. 27, 118, n. 9; A.N., VII 11 (1622), fols. 1–7; Père Anselme de Sainte Marie, *Histoire généalogique et chronologique de la Maison Royale de France*, 3rd. edn, 9 vols. (Paris, 1726–33, New York, 1967), IV, 756; *Journal d'Arnauld 1614–1620*, p. 130, n. 2; Eugène Griselle, *Etat de la maison du Roi Louis XIII* (Paris, 1912), pp. 57, 281.

12 *Recueil des pieces les plus curieuses qui ont esté faites pendant le règne du Connestable M. de Luynes* (Paris, 1628), *Le Comtadin Provençal* (1620), p. 93, *Les Chevaliers de l'Ordre de Saint Esprit*, pp. 30–3; B.N., imprimés Lb 36, *Seconde partie et response à la Chronique des Favoris* (1622), p. 15; Anselme, *Histoire généalogique*, VI, 738; DBF, fasc. 111, 1011.

13 Jean-Antoine Pithon-Curt, *Histoire de la noblesse du Comté Venaissin*, 4 vols. (Paris, 1743–50), IV, 173; B. Inguimbertine, ms. 1847, fols. 187–187v; B.N., Ms. fr. 17345, fols. 286–90; Louis Batiffol, *La Duchesse de Chevreuse* (Paris, 1913), p. 9.

14 B.N., Dossiers bleus 8, fols. 62, 112; Clairambault 1132, fol. 90v; Jean-Pierre Labatut, *Les Ducs et pairs de France au XVIIe siècle* (Paris, 1972), pp. 145, 147.

15 B.N., Ms. fr. 17345, fols. 286–90; Batiffol, *La Duchesse de Chevreuse*, p. 10 (pp. 275–6 in 1920 edition); Daniel Dessert, *Argent, pouvoir et société au Grand Siècle* (Paris, 1984), p. 364. Luynes may have absolved Montbazon from paying the dowry as part of his acquisition of the government of Amiens. *Journal d'Arnauld 1614–1620*, p. 440.

16 Fontenay-Mareuil, *Mémoires*, I, 399–400; Henri de Loménie de Brienne, *Mémoires du comte de Brienne*, eds. Michaud and Poujoulat, 3rd ser., vol. 3 (Paris, 1838), p. 14; Labatut, *Les Ducs et pairs*, pp. 84, 203, 366, 393–4.

17 Pontchartrain, *Mémoires*, p. 403.

18 Ibid., p. 411; Eugène and Jules Halphen, eds., *Journal inédit d'Arnauld d'Andilly 1620* (Paris, 1888), p. 9; *Mercure françois*, VI (1620), 268; B. Inguimbertine, ms. 1847, fols. 163–7, marriage contract of 25 February 1620.

19 *Recueil*, *Lettre de Monseigneur le Cardinal de Guise à Monseigneur le Duc de Guise sur l'alliance que Luynes pretendait faire de sa fille avec le dernier fils dudit sieur duc* (1620), pp. 77–8.

20 Fontenay-Mareuil, *Mémoires*, I. 499; Anselme, *Histoire généalogique*, IV, 266; Pithon-Curt, *Histoire*, IV, 173; Sharon Kettering, *Judicial Politics and Urban Revolt* (Princeton, 1978), pp. 116–18; François-Alexandre Aubert de La Chesnaye-Desbois, *Dictionnaire de la noblesse*, 19 vols. (Paris, 1863–76), I, 234.

21 Batiffol, *Le Roi Louis XIII à vingt ans*, p. 487; idem, *La Duchesse de Chevreuse*, pp. 13–14.

22 Anselme, *Histoire généalogique*, IV, 167–8.

23 *Recueil*, *Les Admirables Proprietez de l'Aluyne* (1620), p. 50; *Le Comtadin Provençal*, pp. 95–8; *Advertissement à Monsieur de Luynes* (1617), pp. 5, 11; *La Chronique des Favoris* (1622), p. 475; B.N., imprimés Lb 36, *Seconde partie et responce*, pp. 17–18.

24 Héroard, *Journal*, II, 2821, 10 April 1622.
25 B.N., Dossiers bleus 8, fol. 53v; Dupuy 853, fols. 109–12; R. de Crèvecoeur, *Un document nouveau sur la succession des Concini* (Paris, 1891), pp. 15–16; Louis Batiffol, "Le Coup d'état du 24 avril 1617," *Rev hist* 97 (1908), 275 n.5; Fernand Hayem, *Le Maréchal d'Ancre et Léonora Galigai* (Paris, 1910), pp. 224–6.
26 *Recueil, L'Ombre de Monseigneur le duc de Mayenne* (1622), p. 381; *Le Comtadin Provençal*, pp. 95–6; *Méditations de l'hermite Valérien* (1621), p. 321; B.N., imprimés Lb36, *Seconde partie et responce*, pp. 17–18.
27 *Recueil, Le Comtadin provençal*, p. 96; *Méditations de l'hermite Valérien*, p. 318; *Le Tout en Tout de la Cour* (1620), p. 70; *Requeste presentée au Roy Pluton* (1620), p. 74; *La Chronique des Favoris*, p. 475; François de Bassompierre, *Journal de ma vie. Mémoires du maréchal de Bassompierre*, ed. Edouard de Chanterac. 4 vols. (Paris, 1870–77), II, 383.
28 *Recueil, Le Jugement de Minos* (1620), pp. 291–303; *Le Monstre à Trois Testes* (1620), p. 67; *Le Tout en Tout de la Cour*, p. 70; *Les Soupirs de la Fleur de Lys* (1622), pp. 406–8; *La Chronique des Favoris*, p. 475.
29 *Recueil, Requeste presentée au Roy Pluton*, p. 75; *Advertissement à Monsieur de Luynes*, pp. 5, 11; B.N., imprimés Lb36, *La Disgrace du Favory de la Fortune* (1617), pp. 1–9; *Discours fait à Monsieur de Luynes par Dryon* (1617), pp. 11–12.
30 *Mercure françois*, IV (1617), 161–2; Hélène Duccini, *Concini* (Paris, 1991), p. 213; idem, "Un campagne de presse sous Louis XIII: l'affaire Concini (1614–1617)," *Histoire sociale, sensibilités collectives et mentalités*, ed. Robert Mandrou (Paris, 1985), pp. 292–301; Jean-François Dubost, *La France italienne XVIe-XVIIe siècle* (Paris, 1997), p. 298.
31 Ibid., pp. 300–1; Hélène Duccini, *Faire Voir, Faire Croire* (Paris, 2003), p. 133.
32 Bassompierre, *Mémoires*, II, 108–9.
33 Crèvecoeur, *Un document nouveau*, p. 20.
34 B.N., Pièces originales 21, fol. 122v; Eugène Griselle, *Ecurie, vénerie, fauconnerie et louveterie du Roi Louis XIII* (Paris, 1912), pp. 28–9; Sophie de Laverny, *Les Domestiques commensaux du roi au XVIIe siècle* (Paris, 2002), p. 256. Luynes's salaries have been capitalized at ten for a value of 14,000 livres and added to 27,500. The known value of his father's property was 55,000 livres, which has been halved to 27,500.
35 B.N., Dossiers bleus 8, fols. 92v, 99, 125; Dupuy 92, fol. 113; Pièces originales 21, fol. 139; *Journal d'Arnauld 1614–1620*, pp. xx, 56–7, 59, 222; Jonathan Dewald, *Pont-St-Pierre 1398–1789* (Berkeley, 1987), p. 181. Arnauld d'Andilly received 2,000 livres in salary, and 2,000 livres in maintenance as a councillor of state in March 1618. The salary of the king's first *écuyer* in 1620 was 3,000 livres. Labatut, *Les Ducs et pairs*, p. 145.
36 B.N., Dossiers bleus 8, fol. 125; Griselle, *Ecurie*, p. 28; Pithon-Curt, *Histoire de la noblesse*, IV, 170–1; Dewald, *Pont-St-Pierre*, p. 181; Jeroen Duindam, *Vienna and Versailles* (Cambridge, 2003), p. 120.
37 B.N., Dossiers bleus 8, fols. 57v, 61–2, 92v, 99; Pièces originales 21, fol. 89; Ms. fr. 7854, fol. 276; *Mercure françois*, V (1617), 97, 160; Anselme, *Histoire généalogique*, VI 230–31; Griselle, *Etat de la maison du Roi*, p. 10; Robert Harding, *Anatomy of a Power Elite* (New Haven, 1978), pp. 139; Dewald, *Pont-St-Esprit*, p. 181; Fernand Bournon, *La Bastille* (Paris, 1893), pp. 47, 49, 53, n. 3, 86; Bernard Barbiche, *Sully* (Paris, 1978), p. 171; Duindam, *Vienna and Versailles*, pp. 118–20. Luynes in 1617 also received the Norman *baillages* of Verneuil and Evreux, whose value and income are unknown.
38 Jacqueline Boucher, *La Cour de Henri III* (La Guerche-de-Bretagne, 1986), p. 84.
39 Mark Greengrass, "Property and Politics in Sixteenth-Century France: The Landed Fortune of Constable Anne de Montmorency," *Fr Hist* 2 (1988), 375.
40 Labatut, *Les Ducs et pairs*, pp. 271–82; Georges d'Avenel, *La Noblesse française sous Richelieu* (Paris, 1901), p. 173.
41 Nicolas Le Roux, *La Faveur du Roi* (Paris, 2001), pp. 472–3.
42 Victor Cousin, "Le Duc et le connêtable de Luynes," *Journal des Savants* (May 1861), 269.
43 B.N., Dupuy 853, fols. 109–110, 117; Dupuy 92, fol. 113.

44 Dubost, *La France italienne*, p. 302.
45 Ibid., pp. 300, 302; Crèvecoeur, *Un document nouveau*, pp. 10–11, 16, 19; Duccini, *Concini*, pp. 273,320, 388; Hayem, *Le Maréchal d'Ancre*, p. 236. Hayem published the trial interrogations of Léonora (B.N., Cinq Cents de Colbert 221), which provide much of what is known about her financial affairs. Ibid., pp. 217–312.
46 Duccini, *Concini*, p. 273; Françoise Bayard, *Le Monde des financiers au XVIIe siècle* (Paris, 1988), p. 365; Crèvecoeur, *Un document nouveau*, pp. 10–11, 20; *Journal d'Arnauld 1614–1620*, p. 288; Louis Batiffol, *La Vie intime d'une reine de France au XVIIe siècle* (Paris, 1906), pp. 381–6; Hayem, *Le Maréchal d'Ancre*, pp. 275–6, 309.
47 Ibid., p. 275; *Journal d'Arnauld 1614–1620*, pp. 287–8; Duccini, *Concini*, p. 314; Dubost, *La France italienne*, p. 300; Batiffol, *La Vie intime*, p. 380; *Relation exacte de tout ce qui s'est passé à la mort du mareschal d'Ancre*, eds. Michaud and Poujoulat, 2nd ser., vol. 5 (Paris, 1837), p. 469.
48 Bassompierre, *Mémoires*, II, 91–2; *Mercure françois*, IV (1616), 201–5; Fontenay-Mareuil, *Mémoires*, I, 353–4; *Les Mémoires de Michel de Marolles, abbé de Villeloin*, 3 vols. (Paris, 1656), I, 28; Hayem, *Le Maréchal d'Ancre*, p. 288; Crèvecoeur, *Un document nouveau*, pp. 10–11, n.3, 17–18; *Journal d'Arnauld 1614–1620*, p. 289; Batiffol, *La vie intime*, pp. 357, n.2, 358; Duccini, *Concini*, pp. 73, 235–6.
49 *Journal d'Arnauld 1614–1620*, p. 289; Hayem, *Le Maréchal d'Ancre*, p. 309; Crèvecoeur, *Un document nouveau*, p. 19; Duccini, *Concini*, pp. 76, 273, 372. The duc de Montmorency spent 100,000 livres decorating his Paris town house in 1613. Malherbe, *Oeuvres*, III, 319. The prince de Condé spent 120,000 livres for this purpose at the same time. Katia Béguin, *Les Princes de Condé* (Paris, 1999), p. 30.
50 B.N., Pièces originales 21, fols. 87–8; Hayem, *Le Maréchal d'Ancre*, p. 309; *Journal d'Arnauld 1614–1620*, p. 314; Héroard, *Journal*, II, 2483; Batiffol, *La Vie intime*, pp. 359–60; Duccini, *Concini*, pp. 76, 435. The property had cost 100,000 livres, and Léonora had added another 200,000 livres in repairs and improvements.
51 Crèvecoeur, *Un document nouveau*, p. 17, n.3, 18; B.N., imprimés Lb 36, *Seconde partie et responce*, p. 19; Bassompierre, *Mémoires*, II, 152; Batiffol, *La Vie intime*, p. 359, n.1; idem, "Louis XIII et le duc de Luynes," *Rev hist* 103 (1910), 252 and nn. 3,4; Duccini, *Concini*, p. 380.
52 Hayem, *Le Maréchal d'Ancre*, p. 235; Crèvecoeur, *Un document nouveau*, pp. 16–18; Henry Sauval, *Histoire et recherches des antiquités de la ville de Paris*, 3 vols. (Paris, 1733), II, 600; Batiffol, *La Vie intime*, pp. 357–8; Duccini, *Concini*, pp. 85–6, 88–9, 434.
53 Bassompierre, *Mémoires*, II, 109.
54 "Le Procès de la maréchale d'Ancre," *Documents d'histoire (XVIIe, XVIIIe et XIXe siécles)*, ed. Eugène Griselle (Paris, 1910), pp. 26–32, 172–86; *Journal d'Arnauld 1614–1620*, p. 304; Batiffol, *La Vie intime*, pp. 352–3.
55 Luynes received the château of Lésigny, valued at 300,000 livres, the mansion on the rue de Tournon, valued at 186,625, the Paris house on the rue d'Autriche valued at 10,000, the marquisat d'Ancre/Albert valued at 450,000, with 150,000 in Louvre apartment furnishings, for a total of 1,096, 625 livres, rounded off to 1,097,000.
56 Crèvecoeur, *Un document nouveau*, p. 19; Dubost, *La France italienne*, p. 300.
57 Ibid., p. 299; B.N., Dossiers bleus 8, fols. 92v, 99; Griselle, *Etat de la maison du Roi*, p. 10; *Relation exacte*, p. 469; Pontchartrain, *Mémoires*, p. 304; Laverny, *Les Domestiques*, pp. 178, 181; Batiffol, *Le Roi Louis XIII*, p. 486; idem, "Louis XIII et le duc de Luynes," 103 (1910), 250; Anselme, *Histoire généalogique*, IV, 252–3, VI, 230–1; Duccini, *Concini*, pp. 83, 103, 321; Berthold Zeller, *Richelieu et les ministres de Louis XIII de 1621 à 1624* (Paris, 1880), p. 232.
58 The market prices of provincial governorships and lieutenant generalships varied with the size, location, profitability, and importance. These offices were often given as rewards or gifts, inherited, or exchanged for other offices and honors without money changing hands. The lieutenant generalships of Poitou and Anjou sold for about 100,000 livres in 1613 and 1619, and that of Brittany for 400,000 livres in 1618. Malherbe, *Oeuvres*, III, 329–30; *Journal d'Arnauld 1614–1620*, pp. 352, 429. The government of Anjou sold for 300,000 livres in 1619. Fontenay-Mareuil, *Mémoires*, I, 443. The government of Poitou sold for 331,000 livres

in 1651. Labatut, *Les Ducs et pairs*, p. 275. The government of Berry and fortress of Bourg sold for 300,000 livres in 1616, and a marshal's baton. Fontenay-Mareuil, *Mémoires*, I, 336. The government of Brittany sold for 600,000 livres in the 1590s, and was worth about 500,000 livres in 1633. Harding, *Anatomy of a Power Elite*, p. 125; Joseph Bergin, *Cardinal Richelieu. Power and the Pursuit of Wealth* (New Haven, 1985), pp. 88, 311. Poitou, Berry, and Anjou were second-tier provinces. Brittany, Picardy, and Normandy were first-tier provinces worth more. Normandy had two lieutenant generalships, reducing their value.

59 B.N., Dossiers bleus 8, fol. 92v; *Journal d'Arnauld 1614–1620*, p. 295; *Relation exacte*, p. 465; Fontenay-Mareuil, *Mémoires*, I, 374, 376; *Mercure françois*, IV (1617), 159–60; Dubost, *La France italienne*, p. 299.

60 Griselle, *Etat de la maison du Roi*, p. 89; *Journal d'Arnauld 1614–1620*, p. 390.

61 The office of first gentleman of the king's bedchamber has been valued at 240,000 livres; the two Norman fortresses at 160,000; the office of lieutenant-general at 200,000; and that of *dame d'atour* at 200,000, for a total of 800,000 livres. The office of captain of the Bastille has not been included because it did not come from Concini.

62 B.N., imprimés Lb 36, *Seconde partie et responce*, p. 18; Batiffol, "Le Coup d'état," *Rev hist* 97 (1908), 275, n.5.

63 B.N., Dossiers bleus 8, fols. 61, 99; *Journal d'Arnauld 1614–1620*, p. 222; Beaucaire, *Mémoires de Richelieu*, I, 308; Malherbe, *Oeuvres*, III, 218, 417. An office of captain in the royal bodyguards sold for 180,000 livres in 1611. Vitry's office of captain was valued at 200,000 livres in 1617.

64 These were the offices of first ordinary gentleman of the king's bedchamber at 2,000 livres a year; captain of the Tuileries and captain of the Louvre at 2,500 livres each a year; governor of the Bastille at 3,000 livres a year; and councillor of state at 4,000 livres a year for a total of 14,000 livres. The formula used here is a capital base of twenty times landed revenues and ten times other revenues. Luynes's salaries of 14,000 livres have been capitalized at ten times for 140,000 livres. See Labatut, *Les Ducs et pairs*, p. 259; Vincent Pitts, *La Grande Mademoiselle at the Court of France 1627–1693* (Baltimore, 2000), pp. 263–8, 276, n. 1, 336, n. 1; Jonathan Dewald, *The Formation of a Provincial Nobility* (Princeton, 1980), p. 116, n.5. Labatut and Pitts used the formula of thirty times landed revenues, but I have used Dewald's more conservative formula of twenty times.

65 Labatut, *Les Ducs et pairs*, p. 248.

66 Duccini, *Concini*, p. 388; Poisson, *La Duchesse de Chevreuse*, p. 17; Jean-François Solnon, *La Cour de France* (Paris, 1987), p. 197.

67 B.N., Dossiers bleus 8, fol. 92v; Anselme, *Histoire généalogique*, VI, 230–31.

68 Labatut, *Les Ducs et pairs*, pp. 248–9.

69 Ibid., p. 263.

70 Isabelle Aristide, *La Fortune de Sully* (Paris, 1989), p. 92.

71 Béguin, *Les Princes de Condé*, p. 31.

72 Le Roux, *La Faveur du Roi*, pp. 474–5; Nicolas Fessenden, "Epernon and Guyenne: Provincial Politics under Louis XIII" (PhD dissertation, Columbia University, 1972), pp. 271–8.

73 Labatut, *Les Ducs et pairs*, p. 264.

74 Ibid., p. 261; Harding, *Anatomy of a Power Elite*, p. 144.

75 Stuart Carroll, *Noble Power during the French Wars of Religion* (Cambridge, 1998), p. 25.

76 Malherbe, *Oeuvres*, III, 134.

77 B.N., Dossiers bleus 8, fol. 99; Dupuy 92, fol. 113; Pontchartrain, *Mémoires*, p. 400; Anselme, *Histoire généalogique*, VI, 231; *Mercure françois*, V (1618), 259; *Journal d'Arnauld 1614–1620*, pp. 374, 440; Roger Doucet, *Les Institutions de la France au XVIe siècle*, 2 vols. (Paris, 1948), I, 233.

78 B.N., Cinq Cents Colbert 91, fol. 44; *Journal d'Arnauld 1614–1620*, p. 390; Griselle, *Etat de la maison du Roi*, p. 103; Beaucaire, *Mémoires de Richelieu*, III, 8; Kleinman, *Anne of Austria*, p. 49; Batiffol, *La Vie intime*, p. 137.

79 B.N., Dossiers bleus 8, fol. 99; Pontchartrain, *Mémoires*, pp. 395, 407–8; Beaucaire, *Mémoires*

de Richelieu, II, 309, 352, III, 11; Bassompierre, Mémoires, II, 144; Brienne, Mémoires, p. 15; Journal d'Arnauld 1614–1620, pp. 374, 421, 440, 454–5; Fontenay-Mareuil, Mémoires, I, 336, 493; Richard Bonney, The King's Debts (Oxford, 1981), p. 94, n. 3; Mercure françois, VI (1620), 11, 16; Eusèbe Pavie, La Guerre entre Louis XIII et Marie de Médicis (Angers, 1899), p. 88.

80 Ibid., p. 579; Mercure françois VI (1620), 22; Pontchartrain, Mémoires, pp. 395, 398, 400–2, 404, 412; Rohan, Mémoires, p. 516; Beaucaire, Mémoires de Richelieu, II, 296; Fontenay-Mareuil, Mémoires, I, 452. Luynes also received fortified places in the new Paris city wall. B.N., Dossiers bleus 8, fol. 100; Dupuy 92, fol. 113.

81 B.N., Dupuy 92, fol. 114v; Malherbe, Oeuvres, III, 244; Roland Mousnier, La Vénalité des offices sous Henri IV et Louis XIII, 2nd edn (Paris, 1971) p. 342. The comparable governorships of Saumur in 1621, and Le Havre in 1626, were worth 300,000 livres. Raoul Patry, Philippe de Duplessis-Mornay (Paris, 1933), p. 588; Bergin, Cardinal Richelieu, p. 311. A Brittany lieutenant-generalship was worth about 400,000 livres in 1618, but Brittany was a larger, more important province than the Ile-de-France. Luynes sold Calais in 1620 for about 425,000 livres. Journal d'Arnauld 1614–1620, p. 352; Journal d'Arnauld 1620, p. 8.

82 The comparable government of Dieppe was worth 300,000 livres in 1619. Fontenay-Mareuil, Mémoires, I, 451. Arnauld said Dieppe was worth 250,000 livres in 1619. Journal d'Arnauld 1614–1620, p. 440.

83 The comparable governments of the fortified châteaux of Chinon, Angers, and Brouage were worth about 100,000 livres each in 1619. Fontenay-Mareuil, Mémoires, I, 336, 443; Journal d'Arnauld 1614–1620, pp. 410, 429.

84 The office of superintendent of the queen's household was worth 600,000 livres in the 1670s. Marcel Marion, Dictionnaire des institutions de la France aux XVIIe et XVIIIe siècles (Paris, 1968), p. 356. It was probably worth half that 60 years earlier.

85 Richelieu's offices were worth 2.6 million livres. Bergin, Cardinal Richelieu, p. 247. Mazarin's offices were worth 2,278,000 livres or 2.3 million. Daniel Dessert, "Pouvoir et fortune au XVIIe siècle: la fortune de Mazarin," Revue d'histoire moderne et contemporaine 23 (1976), 167–8.

86 B.N., Dupuy 850, fols. 97–9; Anselme, Histoire généalogique, VI, 256–7; Labatut, Les Ducs et pairs, p. 273.

87 The duchy of Montbazon was valued at 600,000 livres in 1678. Labatut, Les Ducs et pairs, p. 285. Concini in 1616 had offered 633,000 livres for the domaine of Alençon in Normandy to be erected into a duchy. Duccini, Concini, p. 283. Richelieu paid 600,000 livres for the duchy of Fronsac in 1633. Bergin, Cardinal Richelieu, p. 294. For the values of duchies in the seventeenth century, see Labatut, Les Ducs et pairs, pp. 285–6.

88 Ibid., p. 277.

89 B.N., Pièces originales 21, fols. 89, 91, 93, 95, 119.

90 Journal d'Arnauld 1614–1620, pp. 454–6. Luynes became governor of Paris at Liancourt's death in October 1620, having acquired this office the year before.

91 A salary of 24,000 livres has been capitalized at ten to reach the figure of 240,000 livres as the office's value. Doucet, Les Institutions de la France, I, 112.

92 B.N., Dossiers bleus 6, fol. 101; Anselme, Histoire généalogique, VI, 230–1; Eugène Halphen, Journal inédit d'Arnauld d'Andilly 1621 (Paris, 1891), pp. 19–20; Héroard, Journal, II, 2748–9; Batiffol, "Louis XIII et le duc de Luynes," Rev hist 103 (1910), 255–7; Marion, Dictionnaire des institutions, pp. 129–30.

93 Duccini, Concini, pp. 242, 283, 266.

94 Charles Bernard, Histoire des guerres de Louis XIII (Paris, 1633), I, 116–20; Fontenay-Mareuil, Mémoires, I, 501–2; Zeller, Le Connétable de Luynes, pp. 43–7; Charles Dufayard, Le Connétable de Lesdiguières (Paris, 1892), pp. 440–56.

95 Brienne, Mémoires, pp. 19–20; Rohan, Mémoires, p. 524; Recueil, L'Ombre de Monsieur le Connestable (1622), pp. 426–38; L'Advis au Roy sur le restablissement de l'office de Connestable (1620), pp. 5–16. A satiric quatrain went, "Je suis ce que le Roi m'a fait, Je fais ce que je veux en France, Car le Roi j'y suis en effet, Et lui ne l'est qu'en apparence." Brienne, Mémoires, p.

19. "I am what the king made me. I do what I want in France because I am the king in reality, and he only appears to be king."

96 B.N., Dossiers bleus 8, fol. 101; Dupuy 92, fol. 115; Ms. fr. 18148, fols. 298–300; *Journal d'Arnauld 1621*, p. 68; Anselme, *Histoire généalogique*, VI, 538–9; Doucet, *Les Institutions de la France*, I, 108; Brienne, *Mémoires*, pp. 21–2.

97 Luynes gave his office of captain of the king's one hundred men-at-arms, worth 200,000 livres, to his brother Cadenet. Pithon-Curt, *Histoire de la noblesse*, IV, 183; Pontchartrain, *Mémoires*, pp. 400–1. He gave his office of lieutenant-general of Normandy, worth 200,000 livres, and governor of Pont de l'Arche, worth 60,000 livres, to his cousin Ornano. The combined value of these offices was 460,000 livres, deducted from 2,713,500 livres for a total of 2,253,500 livres.

98 Harding, *Anatomy of a Power Elite*, p. 174.

99 Batiffol, "Louis XIII et le duc de Luynes," 253. Luynes had an annual income of 40,000 livres in *rentes* at his death, which capitalized at ten was 400,000 livres.

100 This figure is an estimate, but Luynes elegantly furnished his residences. A.N., MCVII 11 (22 March 1622), inventory after death of the *hôtel* de Luynes; *Recueil, L'Ombre de Monseigneur le duc de Mayenne*, p. 379; Harding, *Anatomy of a Power Elite*, p. 174; Labatut, *Les Ducs et pairs*, p. 302. Dukes were expected to live in great luxury and did so. Ibid., pp. 300–10.

101 Luynes owned at least five other fiefs, and in February 1620, the king gave him a tract of land running from the Paris city gate of Saint Victor to that of Saint Bernard on which to build houses. He was later given more land running from the Saint Bernard gate along the river for this purpose. Batiffol, "Louis XIII et le duc de Luynes," *Rev hist* 103 (1910), 252, n. 6. Land speculation was profitable because the prices of land and houses within the Paris city walls rose steadily during the seventeenth century, and numerous royal officials engaged in land speculation. Roland Mousnier, *Paris, capitale au temps de Richelieu et de Mazarin* (Paris, 1978), pp. 118–19.

102 A large sum in cash was found in the fortress of Amiens after Luynes's death, used to pay the garrison of 1,500 soldiers and 800 workmen. *Mercure françois*, VII (1621), 888; Batiffol, *La Duchesse de Chevreuse*, pp. 41–2. Scipion Dupleix reported that Luynes had 700,000 livres in cash at the time of his death. Idem, *Histoire de Louis le Juste, XIII du Nom* (Paris, 1635), p. 295. Richelieu kept cash reserves of 4,080,000 livres. Bergin, *Cardinal Richelieu*, p. 246. Mazarin kept cash reserves of 8,704,794 livres. Dessert, "Pouvoir et finance," 165.

103 If Luynes at his death had 700,000 livres in cash, 400,000 livres in *rentes*, and a duchy worth at least 400,000 livres, he would have been worth 7,739,500 livres or 7.7 million. See notes 87, 99, and 102 above.

104 Batiffol, "Louis XIII et le duc de Luynes," *Rev hist* 102 (1909), 255.

105 Harding, *Anatomy of a Power Elite*, p. 139; Roland Mousnier, *The Institutions of France under the Absolute Monarchy, 1598–1789*, 2 vols., *The Organs of State and Society*, trans. Arthur Goldhammer (Chicago, 1984), II, 474.

106 A.N., MC XXXIX 55, 1623; Labatut, *Les Ducs et pairs*, p. 275.

107 The comparable duchy of Montbazon had revenues of 20,000 livres in 1678. A royal ordinance in 1582 had declared that no land could be erected into a peerage without revenues of 24,000 livres a year, but this was not always enforced. Labatut, *Les Ducs et pairs*, pp. 143, 285. For the revenues of seventeenth-century duchies, see ibid., p. 285.

108 Dewald, *Pont-St-Pierre*, p. 181; B.N., Mélanges Colbert 324. Governors of smaller cities and fortresses typically received 2,000 to 3,000 livres a year in salary.

109 The salary of sixteenth-century constables was 24,000 livres a year. Doucet, *Les Institutions de la France*, I, 112; Wilmer McCorquodale, "The Court of Louis XIII" (PhD dissertation, University of Texas, 1994). p. 185.

110 Griselle, *Etat de la maison du Roi*, p. 103; Sharon Kettering, "The Household Service of Early Modern French Noblewomen," *Fr Hist Stud* 20 (1997), 72–8. Madame de Guercheville, the Queen Mother's lady of honor, received gifts of a large diamond cross and 300,000 livres. Batiffol, *La Vie intime*, pp. 138–9. Idem, "Louis XIII et le duc de Luynes," *Rev hist* 102 (1909),

26: Du Vair complained about the 200,000 livres gift Luynes wanted to give his wife.

111 Luynes received 111,600 livres from the king as a gift in 1616. Duindam, *Vienna and Versailles*, p. 119. He received 99,000 livres from the royal treasury on 1 June 1620 to cover his military expenses while on campaign with the king, and the same sum again on 8 Feburary 1621. B.N., Pièces originales 21, fols. 99, 109. He had also received 18,000 livres from the royal treasury in May 1620. *Journal d'Arnauld 1620*, p. 17.

112 François de Paule de Clermont, marquis de Montglat, *Mémoires*, ed. Petitot, 2nd ser., vol. 49 (Paris, 1825), p. 28; Dupleix, *Histoire de Louis le Juste*, p. 108; Batiffol, "Louis XIII et le duc de Luynes," *Rev hist* 103 (1910), 259–60; Gabriel Hanotaux and the duc de La Force, *Histoire du Cardinal de Richelieu*, 6 vols. (Paris, 1893–1947), vol. II, part 2, 313–14; *Journal d'Arnauld 1614–1620*, pp. 295–6, n. 3. This quip was credited to Bouillon and Montglat among others.

113 Arlette Jouanna, "Faveur et favoris," *Henri III et son temps*, ed. Robert Sauzet (Paris, 1992), p. 153; J.H. Elliott and L.W.B. Brockliss, *The World of the Favourite* (New Haven, 1999).

114 Nicolas de Brichanteau, marquis de Beauvais-Nangis, *Histoire des favoris françois depuis Henri II jusqu'à Louis XIII* (Paris, 1665), p. 3.

115 Brigitte Bedos-Rezak, *Anne de Montmorency* (Paris, 1990), pp. 76–107; Le Roux, *La Faveur du Roi*, pp. 461–577; Lucien Romier, *Jacques d'Albon de Saint André* (Paris, 1909), pp. 175–218; Pierre Chevallier, *Louis XIII* (Paris, 1979), p. 188.

116 Aristide, *La Fortune de Sully*, p. 411.

117 Jean-Pierre Labatut, "Aspects de la fortune de Bullion," *XVIIe siècle* 60 (1963), 11.

118 Béguin, *Les Princes de Condé*, p. 53.

119 Daniel Dessert, *Fouquet* (Paris, 1987), p. 353.

120 Idem, "Fortune politique ... la succession du superintendant Abel Servien," *La France d'Ancien Régime*, eds. Jean Jacquart et al., 2 vols. (Toulouse, 1984), I, 207–14.

121 Jean Villain, *La Fortune de Colbert* (Paris, 1994), p. 322.

122 Bergin, *Cardinal Richelieu*, p. 248; Claude Dulong, *La Fortune de Mazarin* (Paris, 1990), p. 133.

123 Batiffol, "Louis XIII et le duc de Luynes," *Rev hist* 103 (1910), 250. Batiffol noted that Victor Cousin had made the same observation.

124 Labatut, *Les Ducs et pairs*, p. 148.

125 Mousnier, *La Vénalité des offices*, p. 436.

126 Beaucaire, *Mémoires de Richelieu*, II, 139–40.

127 Mousnier, *La Vénalité des offices*, p. 436; Duccini, *Concini*, p. 216.

128 Duccini, *Concini*, p. 409; Arlette Jouanna, *Le Devoir de révolte* (Paris, 1989), p. 232.

129 Edouard Fournier, *Variétés historiques et littéraires*, 10 vols. (Paris, 1855–63), III, 241–71, "Le Satyrique de la cour" (1624); V, 75–95, "Catéchisme des courtisans" (1649); IX, 351–8, "Le Courtisan à la mode" (1625); Pauline Smith, *The Anti-Courtier Trend in Sixteenth Century French Literature* (Geneva, 1966), pp. 11–55, 152–218, 224–6.

130 Beaucaire, *Mémoires de Richelieu*, III, 183. "Il étoit d'un esprit médiocre et timide; peu de foi, point de générosité, trop foible pour demeurer ferme à l'assaut d'une si grande fortune, en laquelle il se perdit incontinent, s'y laissant emporter comme en torrent, sans aucune retenue; ..."

131 Ibid., III, 180, 183.

132 *Recueil, Méditations de L'hermite Valérien*, p. 317.

133 Ibid., *Le Comtadin Provençal*, pp. 101–2; B.N., imprimés Lb 36, *Seconde partie et responce*, pp. 23–5; Batiffol, "Louis XIII et le duc de Luynes," *Rev hist* 103 (1910), 257–9; idem, *Le Roi Louis XIII*, pp. 547–8.

134 Duccini, *Concini*, pp. 93–4, 196, 209–13, 222–6.

135 Mousnier, *The Institutions of France*, II, 475.

136 Duccini, *Concini*, pp. 262–73. The *Mercure françois* reported that Concini intended to establish an independent government between the Loire and the English Channel, so he acquired fortress and city governorships and filled provincial offices with his men. Ibid., IV (1617), 160.

137 Bonney, *The King's Debts*, pp. 94, 100; *Recueil, Manifeste de la Royne Mère envoyé au Roy* (1620), p. 264.

138 Beaucaire, *Mémoires de Richelieu*, III, 190.

139 Bergin, *Cardinal Richelieu*, pp. 80–94, 134; Jouanna, *Le Devoir de révolte*, p. 233.

5

Friends of the favorite

Louis XI had founded the military Order of Saint Michel in 1469 to reinforce the great nobles' loyalty to the monarchy. The original thirty-six knights swore allegiance and fidelity to the king as the head of the order and received a royal pension. Every year on the feast day of Saint Michel, they dined with the king and attended mass.[1] Membership in the order was considered an honor for a century, but during the religious wars so many knighthoods were awarded that they lost their value. Montaigne remarked that when he was a young man, there was nothing he wanted more than to join the order, but by the time he became a knight in 1572, so many had been awarded that they were no longer prestigious.[2] Hundreds of knights joined the order during the late sixteenth century. For instance, 716 new knights were received during the six years from 1578 to 1584, and even more claimed to be members.[3] Luynes's father joined the order in 1569, while his great-grandfather had joined a century earlier. The monarchy distributed all these knighthoods to pacify the provincial sword nobility, and to weaken the patronage power of the great nobility, although without much success.[4]

Henri III founded the Order of Saint Esprit in 1578, a new smaller order modeled on that of Saint Michel and meant to attach the great nobles more securely to the crown. They and their clients had become a threat to royal authority, and the creation of a new Catholic military order was meant to reinforce their loyalty to a Catholic monarchy.[5] Twenty-seven *grands* were received into the order during the first meeting on 31 December 1578 in the church of the Augustinian friars at Paris. Membership was limited to one hundred drawn from the highest ranks of the nobility, including nine clerics and four officers with the rank of commanders, and eighty-seven chevaliers or knights.[6] They swore an oath of loyalty to the king and the Roman Catholic Church, received royal pensions, and attended annual chapter meetings. The king named the candidates for membership, while the order rigorously investigated their backgrounds. Successful candidates needed documentary proof of three generations of male nobility on their father's side, and proof that they were practising Catholics who had never committed a crime.[7] Luynes's proofs provide useful information about his origins.[8] The Order of Saint Esprit became the most prestigious military order in France.

Sixty-four new members, that is, five clerics and fifty-nine knights, were received into the order in 1619, the largest induction of new members in decades.[9] A lengthy description of the three-day reception ceremony, which took place with considerable pomp and pageantry from 31 December 1619 through 2 January 1620, was the first entry in the 1620 edition of the *Mercure françois*.[10] At three o'clock on the afternoon of 31 December, the knights gathered in a Paris mansion facing the Seine, and walked in stately procession to the nearby church of the Augustinian friars. The queen and her ladies were already seated in the packed church. Positions in the procession were determined by Henri III's statutes creating the order, which decreed when, where, and how the ceremony should take place and what should be worn.[11] A crowd of courtiers and Parisians gathered to watch the magnificently dressed knights go by. They made an eye-catching spectacle in the half-light of a cold wintry day.

The archers of the Paris municipal guard marched first, followed by the hundred Swiss guards and a dozen men playing trumpets, fifes, and drums wearing the king's blue velvet livery. Then the order arrived, announced by two heralds in green cloaks. The newly nominated knights came first, marching by twos according to the date of their nominations, and wearing doublets and breeches of white and silver silk sparkling with precious stones, white velvet court shoes, black hats and cloaks. The officers of the order appeared next followed by the knights by rank in twos according to the dates of their receptions. A hundred royal guards stood on either side of the street. Green and gold were the order's colors, and the knights wore the order's long black velvet cloak covered with gold flames topped by a green collar. They also wore the order's large gold eight-pointed Maltese cross, engraved on one side with a dove representing the Holy Ghost and on the other with a portrait of Saint Michael, which hung around their necks on a wide blue ribbon of moiré silk, the famous cordon bleu.[12]

The king marched at the end of the procession preceded by the prince de Condé, and when Louis entered the church, the organ began to play. He sat in the first chair of the choir, and his chair and the altar were covered with green and gold cloth decorated with gold flames and lined with orange taffeta. Vespers were celebrated by the Cardinal de La Rochefoucauld, grand almoner and commander of the order, who sat on the king's right. The prince de Condé, the king's cousin, sat on his left. Condé had been received as a knight at the king's coronation in October 1610, when Louis as grand master of the order had taken his oath and received his cloak and cross.[13]

Before vespers, the king sat on a throne before the altar surrounded by the order's officers to receive the new clerics, and after vespers, he again sat there to receive the new knights. Each came forward when his name was called, knelt before the king, and swore an oath of loyalty to him and the Roman Catholic Church on the order's statutes.[14] Each kissed the king's hand, donned a cloak and cross, and was escorted to a seat among the knights. This solemn, impressive ceremony lasted until eight o'clock that evening, and ended with a trumpet fanfare. Héroard, the king's doctor, reported that Louis had returned to the Louvre about 6 pm, and was in bed by 7:30.[15]

On New Year's Day, 1 January 1620, the knights gathered at ten o'clock in the morning, and walked in procession by twos to the church, wearing their cloaks and crosses and carrying white candles, to attend a high mass for the order's members. At two o'clock that afternoon, they dined in the refectory of the Augustinian friars, and three hours later returned to the candle-lit church to attend vespers, which lasted until eight o'clock that evening. The king's doctor reported his return to the Louvre about 6 pm.[16]

On the third and final day, 2 January 1620, the knights assembled in the same mansion facing the Seine, and walked in full regalia carrying their white candles to the church of the Augustinian friars to attend a mass for the knights who had died, especially those within the past year. Their crosses and coats of arms were displayed on benches draped in black cloth, and their relatives had been invited to attend the mass, which ended at two o'clock. There was another magnificent banquet in the refectory, and afterward a chapter meeting. The newspaper account concluded with this meeting, and did not report when it ended or if there had been a vespers service. That evening at the Louvre, there were fireworks and a ballet in which an overly ambitious Phaeton was thrown from the Pont Neuf into the Seine to drown, a reworking of the Concini theme.[17] The reception for the knights of Saint Esprit had been an opulent, expensive event.[18] Since the order's revenues were inadequate to pay for this spectacle, why was it held? Who paid for it?[19] Who were the new knights, and why were they chosen?

The power of ceremonies

The newspaper description of the reception was the official account intended for courtiers and educated Parisians. The monarchy published a sanitized, embellished version of court ceremonies to an audience unaware of what had actually happened.[20] So, there are differences between the official accounts of court ceremonies and the private accounts of participants and observers who described what really went on behind the scenes. For instance, Héroard noted in his journal that the king had returned to the Louvre each evening before the ceremony's end as reported in the *Mercure françois*. Did the king leave early? Was the doctor mistaken about the time he returned, or did the newspaper account embellish the event's solemnity and importance by making it last longer than it really did?

The *Mercure françois* reported that there was a chapter meeting on the afternoon of 2 January in the small refectory of the church of the Augustinian friars. In reality, according to the minutes of the order, the king had cancelled it because he was tired and irritable. Héroard reported that he had returned to the Louvre at 5:15 pm.[21] So, the chapter meeting was not held on the last day, although it was reported in the *Mercure françois* as having taken place. There was no vespers service either. The knights must have assembled later at the Louvre to watch the fireworks and the ballet, although neither of these events was reported in the *Mercure françois*. Héroard reported that the king went to bed at 10 pm, so he had probably watched the entertainment with the knights.[22]

Private accounts of the 1619 reception include minutes of the order's meetings, and memoirs of contemporary participants and observers who paint a less harmonious picture than the newspaper account.[23] Numerous precedence quarrels occurred because of the court's obsession with rank and status. The discord began on 5 December 1619 during a chapter meeting called by the king in his study at Saint-Germain-en-Laye, which Luynes attended as a guest. There is only a brief mention of this meeting in the newspaper account.[24] The king called the meeting because too many individuals had been nominated for membership in the order. Fontenay-Mareuil estimated that more than 150 brevets had been distributed promising places.[25] When a list was made at the meeting, there were actually 119 nominations. Henri IV had promised places to 13 individuals, Marie de Médicis to 38, and Louis to 68. It was decided that 59 knights and 5 clerics should be received for a total of 64, who were then selected.[26] The names of those excluded remained on a list of candidates to be received at a later date, and they were offended and angry.

There were two disputes during the 5 December chapter meeting. Cardinal de La Rochefoucauld, first-ranked among the clerics, protested the seating order, and only agreed reluctantly to sit on the king's left because the prince de Condé was already sitting on his right. (The right was more prestigious than the left.) The Cardinal sat on the king's right during the reception, and Condé on the left. The clerics insisted on being received first by claiming precedence as the First Estate, so it was decided that the new clerics should be received by the king before vespers, and the new knights after vespers. The order's minutes relate that the king had another throne set up in the back of the church by the main entrance, and that he sat there when he entered the church, not in the choir as the newspaper account reported. He went forward to the throne by the altar to receive the new members, and then returned to the throne at the back of the church.[27]

The presence of the second throne at the back was not reported in the *Mercure françois*. The order's statutes specified that the reception should take place in the front of the church with the king sitting on a throne before the altar, and there was no mention of a second throne in the back.[28] A throne at the back, however, allowed the king a respite from the proceedings. It was tiresome listening to sixty-four men repeating the same long oath one after the other, followed each time by the singing of the *Vene Creator Spiritus*, and then listening to the same long speech every time they received their cloaks, and again their crosses. The order's minutes relate that Louis had become so impatient by the time all the dukes had been sworn in that a group of twelve non-dukes were brought forward to be received. That was too many, so the remaining nominees took their oaths in unison in groups of six to save time, and as soon as they had finished, the bored, exhausted king left the church in haste, which was not reported in the *Mercure françois* either.[29]

There were two additional chapter meetings before the reception ceremony. On 20 December, the nominees' proofs of nobility were verified during a meeting at the Paris residence of Cardinal de La Rochefoucauld, which the king did not attend. There was another meeting on 23 December at the Louvre for the king to confirm the final list of nominees and their ranks.[30] It was decided then that foreign princes should march according to the date of their nominations, not the date of their duchies' creation as specified in the order's statutes.[31] Henri II d'Orléans, duc de Longueville, a royal prince, refused to be received because he would have had to follow Charles de Lorraine, duc de Guise, a foreign prince nominated before him whose duchy was newer than his. Foreign princes always followed royal princes. Guise was a supporter of Condé and Luynes, while Longueville belonged to the Queen Mother's party, which probably explains the change.[32] An angry Longueville refused to cede precedence or attend the reception, and the Queen Mother's revolt began a few months later in his government of Normandy.

During the New Year's Day banquet, another quarrel occurred over who was to hand the king a napkin. Louis de Bourbon, comte de Soissons, grand master of the king's household and a teenager who was second prince of the blood, insisted that his office gave him this right, and snatched the napkin away from an underling to hand to the king himself. This enraged Condé, his much older uncle who claimed precedence as first prince of the blood, and who tried to snatch the napkin away from Soissons. The king had to intervene, telling his brother Gaston to hand him the napkin, and Condé and Soissons to calm down. Soissons supported the Queen Mother, while Condé was an ally of Luynes, and their rivalry was exacerbated by a bitter feud between Condé and Soissons's mother.[33] The quarrel did not end there. After the banquet, their friends and clients gathered at their Paris mansions. The duc de Guise, a close friend of Condé, rushed to his support, while the duc de Mayenne, who supported the Queen Mother, hurried to join Soissons. Luynes was an ally of Condé, so their enemies rallied to Soissons's side. A brawl seemed likely, but the crowd dispersed without bloodshed.[34]

Court ceremonies created, expressed, and maintained a hierarchy of dominance and deference, providing a detailed demarcation of the rank and power of court nobles and their relationship to the king. Rank in the Order of Saint Esprit, for example, was considered an indication of rank at court. The biographer of Charles de Blanchefort de Créquy noted proudly that he had been seventh in rank at his reception as a knight of Saint Esprit, marching immediately after members of the royal family and the house of Lorraine.[35] Ceremonial pomp demonstrated the king's authority and power, and was meant to awe and impress. The stately procession of new knights through the streets of Paris, announced by drum rolls and trumpet fanfares, was meant to demonstrate to Parisians and courtiers alike that Louis XIII's government was strong, stable, and successful. So, there was a procession on three successive days, although it was cold in January, and the knights in their finery were not warmly dressed.

The Saint Esprit reception was also meant to demonstrate that the young king held the reins of power firmly in his own hands, and that his mother's dominance was over. He had been reconciled with her in September, but she had stubbornly refused to return to court, and was conspicuously absent from the Saint Esprit ceremony. Court noblewomen complained because she and the queen had not been sitting beside Louis at the reception.[36] Her absence emphasized that she was no longer regent, while the great nobles' oaths of loyalty to the king emphasized that they were no longer rebels. The precedence quarrels were not mentioned in the *Mercure françois* because the king wanted to project an image of strength and unity, not squabbling weakness. Spectacles and pageantry enhanced the monarchy's image by demonstrating consensus and disguising conflict. So, the crown paid for the reception ceremony as part of its ongoing campaign to gain the cooperation of the great nobility.[37]

Luynes and the king used the distribution of knighthoods to reward faithful servants of the crown, especially those who had helped them to get rid of Concini, and they withheld knighthoods to punish those who continued to support the Queen Mother. Luynes also used knighthoods to reward his relatives and clients, and to attract new clients. It was almost certainly his idea to induct a large number of new members into the order, and to hold a lavish reception ceremony for them. Fontenay-Mareuil remarked that Luynes had been very keen to join the order himself, and to have his friends join.[38] He probably hoped that being received into the order, and the marks of honor shown him during the ceremony, would improve his image at court.

The nominees were escorted to the king to swear their oaths of loyalty by a knight on either side. The princes and dukes were escorted by the ducs de Ventadour and Montbazon, Luynes's father-in-law. The first large group of non-dukes was escorted by Luynes himself and his old friend, Charles du Plessis de Liancourt, who had headed the small stables when he was a stable page. Liancourt had investigated Luynes's proofs of rank and religion aided by another knight, Claude de Harville, sieur de Palaiseau, governor of the fortresses of Calais and Compiègne in Luynes's government of Picardy. The elderly Palaiseau retired a short while later. Luynes had become a duke six weeks earlier with Liancourt in attendance, and since he had already been sworn in with the dukes, albeit as the last one, he could now escort the non-dukes as a new knight.[39] This honor should have gone to someone whose duchy and knighthood were older. There were also complaints because Luynes's brother-in-law, Louis de Rohan, comte de Rochefort, was received first after the dukes, although as one of the last nominees, he should have been received last. This was noted with disapproval because his uncle, Alexandre de Rohan, marquis de Marigny, was among the last to be received.[40]

The king had enthusiastically adopted Luynes's idea for the reception ceremony, which he discussed at a council meeting.[41] When Luynes realized how many promises of membership had been made, however, he left the selection of nominees to a chapter meeting in order not to offend anyone. He asked only that four of his nominees be chosen, Jean de Varigniez, sieur de Blainville; Louis de La Marck, marquis de Mauny; René du Bec, marquis de Vardes; and Charles, sieur de Rambures. They were all received as new members.[42]

The efforts of Nicolas de Brichanteau, marquis de Beauvais-Nangis, to get his name on the list of nominees is illuminating. Beauvais-Nangis was known to the king and Luynes because he was Vitry's uncle.[43] He discussed the matter with the marquis de Beuvron, who also wanted his name on the list. Beuvron knew the chancellor of the order who promised to help, and said that Luynes had spoken well of them. Beauvais-Nangis went to see Luynes, who was encouraging and told him to speak to the secretary in charge of the list, Antoine de Potier, sieur de Sceaux. He saw Sceaux who said that he would mention his name to the king after he had a written request from Luynes. Beauvais-Nangis brought him the request, but nothing happened. When the name of Sceaux's brother, René de Potier, comte de Tresmes, a royal guard captain, was included on the list, Beauvais-Nangis went to see him, and he promised to speak to his brother. Beauvais-Nangis left court for several months, and when he returned, he found that his name and those of Vaubecourt, Beuvron, and the marquis de Neubourg and Villars had been included on the list. So, he visited Luynes once again to thank him for his help. Beauvais-Nangis was the only one of the five to be actually received into the order, however, probably because of his family connection to Vitry and his visits to Luynes. The incident demonstrates Luynes's extensive patronage power.[44]

As we shall see, Luynes was responsible for nineteen nominations including himself. The king was responsible for twenty,[45] and the royal family for nine,[46] a total of twenty-nine nominations for the king and his family. The thirty-nine nominees of Luynes and the king were a little more than half of the original list of sixty-eight, leaving twenty-nine disappointed, angry individuals. The Queen Mother's original list of nominees was cut from thirty-eight to two, and Henri IV's from thirteen to two, leaving another forty-seven unhappy individuals. The king and Luynes participated together in the selection of nominees, but the final choice was the king's. The nominees' names had to be inscribed on the list in his handwriting, and he had to verify the final list as head of the order.[47] Six of Luynes's nominees had danced in the king's ballets, and nine were members of his household, while one belonged to his queen's household and one to his brother's household.[48] So, the king already knew and approved of Luynes's nominees before their selection, demonstrating again the power balance in their relationship.

Luynes's nominees included two prelates and sixteen knights. The prelates were Bertrand Deschaux, archbishop of Tours, who had married him, and Christophe Lestang, bishop of Carcassonne, who had acted as his envoy to the Queen Mother in the Concini affair. The knights, besides himself, included his brothers Cadenet and Brantes, his cousin Ornano, his brother-in-law Rohan de Rochefort, and his wife's uncle Rohan de Marigny. The knights also included five fortress governors who were Luynes's clients, Charles, sieur de Rambures, governor of Dourlens in Picardy; René du Bec, marquis de Vardes, governor of La Chapelle in Picardy; Louis de Crevant, marquis d'Humières, governor of Ham and Compiègne in Picardy; Jacques d'Estampes, sieur de Valençay, governor of Calais in Picardy; and Antoine de Buade, baron de Paluau, governor of Saint-Germain-en-Laye near Paris. Luynes also nominated Charles de Créquy, comte de Canaples, who would marry his niece six months later; Jean de Varigniez, sieur de Blainville, a new client; and Louis de La Marck, marquis de Mauny, a former client of the Queen Mother now his client. Luynes nominated as well La Rocheguyon, who had brokered his marriage, the baron de Termes, brother of his old patron Bellegarde, and Henri de Schomberg, brother-in-law of his recently deceased patron, the comte Du Lude.[49] Luynes remembered and rewarded those who had helped him in the past.

The *Mercure françois* reported that nobles angry at being rejected rode south to join the Queen Mother in revolt at Angers.[50] Her supporters who had been refused membership in the order included the three sons of the duc d'Epernon, who had helped to arrange her escape from Blois. Epernon's sons were received by Richelieu into the order in 1633, along with Henri de La Trémoille, duc de Thouars; François-Annibal d'Estrées, marquis de Coeuvres; Jean de Nettancourt, comte de Vaubecourt; and Georges de Brancas, marquis then duc de Villars, brother-in-law of d'Estrées and half-brother of the duc de Mayenne.[51] They all supported the Queen Mother, and their exclusion from membership in 1619 had encouraged them to join her in revolt.[52]

Richelieu's harshness would make him many enemies among the great nobility, so he used Luynes's tactic of inducting new members into the Order of Saint Esprit to placate them.[53] On 4 May 1633, Richelieu staged a lavish reception ceremony for forty-eight new knights to reward those who had served him well, especially his relatives and clients, and to solicit new clients. Richelieu observed in his memoirs that the king needed to reward his loyal servants from time to time, and since he had not inducted any new members into his military order in thirteen years, he had held a reception at Fontaine-bleau during Pentecost for new knights, who were thus rewarded for their service to the crown.[54]

The king himself may have proposed this reception. There were several changes in the 1633 ceremony that only he could have made because Richelieu had not been present at the 1619 reception. This time the ceremony was held in May rather than in the dead of winter, and in the more comfortable château of Fontainebleau rather than in the church of the Augustinian friars. There were no processions through the cold, dirty streets of Paris, and instead of driving an exhausting thirty minutes each way across the city in a lumbering coach from the Louvre to the church, the king now left the ballroom or chapel to walk down a gallery to his own apartments.[55]

According to Brienne, Richelieu had been advised to postpone the recep-tion because too many places had been promised, but he ignored this advice and went ahead, anyway. The king had already promised places to numerous individ-uals of whom Brienne was one. Brienne wrote in his memoirs that Richelieu had made certain to include his own relatives and clients who were promoted over "good and faithful servants of the king." Brienne added that many loyal servants like himself were not received, and had to be content with the king's promise that they would be received in future.[56] In other words, Richelieu removed names from the king's list of nominees. Brienne noted that in 1619 the king had allowed him to purchase the office of provost-master in the order and paid for most of it. He added, "I feel myself obliged to say that Luynes, who treated me courteously, helped me with his good offices, although I was not in his confidence, and I have never liked depending on favors."[57] Brienne resigned this office to a cousin in 1621. Although nominated to a knighthood in the order of Saint Esprit, he was never received, much to his chagrin.[58]

Thirteen of the forty-eight new members in 1633 were Richelieu's relatives and clients, and so were three of the order's officers.[59] Eleven of the new knights came from recently rebellious provinces, and were either already Richelieu's clients or influential nobles whom he hoped to make clients.[60] He probably also hoped to secure the support of the eight nobles excluded in 1619 by receiving them in 1633.[61] These additional nominees meant that Richelieu was responsible for the selection of twenty-seven of the forty-eight new members, more than half of the total. The king was responsible for ten, and the queen for one.[62] Richelieu had more nominees than Luynes, and significantly more proportionally because the 1633 group of candidates was smaller.

Richelieu had adopted Luynes's tactic of distributing Saint Esprit knight-hoods to secure the support of the great nobility. Luynes and the king had together participated in their selection, but Richelieu now chose more than half the nominees himself, and he had twice as many as the king. It is well-known that Richelieu increasingly dominated the royal council and the upper levels of royal government after 1630. The king's favor was still important, but it was not as decisive as Richelieu's favor, which the 1633 Saint Esprit reception demonstrates.[63]

Luynes's clientele

During the first week of December 1619, the prince de Condé discussed the reception ceremony with the king, and expressed concern about the diversity of the nominees' backgrounds. They were not all from the high nobility as the order's statutes specified.[64] Condé probably had in mind some of Luynes's nominees. The pamphleteers accused Luynes of naming new knights from obscure families by the dozens, describing them as "low-born poltroons."[65] One pamphlet listed nineteen deserving nobles whose names had been omitted from the list including Vaubecourt, Beuvron, Neubourg, and Villars, all named by Beauvais-Nangis.[66] The pamphleteers accused the "Luynards," that is, Luynes and his brothers, of ignoring the great nobles and advancing upstarts and unworthy men. They were accused of promoting themselves and their greedy, low-ranking relatives and friends at the expense of the king, his family, and the *grands*.[67] "Friend" and "servant" in contemporary usage often meant "client."[68]

The pamphleteers accused Luynes of filling the royal council and high government offices with so many clients that a "cabal of luynistes" surrounded the king, giving him bad advice, driving everyone else away, and corrupting the government.[69] They declared that the three "Luynards" had seized every vacant office, benefice, and pension for themselves and their friends. The duc de Rohan said that Luynes had brought a swarm of relatives to court from

Avignon.[70] The pamphleteers accused Luynes of giving more than a hundred pensions to relatives and friends, who were pillaging the state and getting rich at the expense of the people.[71] Luynes and his brothers were described as "three pumpkins sprouting in one night and ruining everything." The word "pumpkin" meant someone of low birth who advanced through favoritism.[72] (Pumpkins displace other plants in a garden.) Richelieu wrote in his memoirs, "He (Luynes) had only a single virtue that could be opposed to all his bad qualities, that he enriched his relatives and servants, believing that a part of his wealth belonged to those who belonged to him."[73]

The king quipped after Luynes's death that he had never known anyone who had so many relatives. They arrived by the boatload from the Midi and never had anything silk to wear, i.e., they were poor.[74] This quip summarizes the complaints about Luynes's "friends." There were too many of them; they had no qualifications besides being his relatives and clients; they were penniless provincial nobodies promoted above their station; and they greedily took advantage of their opportunities at the expense of everyone else. As an unpopular foreigner with no relatives in France, Concini did not have many dependents to reward.[75] Luynes, however, had spent his life at court, and he was French with a large family. He had numerous dependents to reward, making him look even greedier than Concini. How large was Luynes's clientele? Who belonged to it, and what did they receive?

About thirty-five of Luynes's clients belonged to the inner core of a much larger clientele. Aristocratic clienteles may be visualized as a series of concentric rings reaching out from a small inner core composed of noble *fidèles*, clients who had fidelity relationships with their patron characterized by absolute devotion and loyalty until death. The more numerous ordinary clients in the outer rings had less enduring relationships based on obligatory reciprocity.[76] Henri I, duc de Montmorency-Damville, governor of Languedoc, had a clientele of about 250, with an inner core of 50, plus 200 clients in the outer rings. Charles de Lorraine, duc de Mayenne and governor of Burgundy, had an inner core of 25 to 30, plus outer rings of 200 to 300 clients, who increased briefly to 400 or 500 during the 1590s, when he was chief of the Holy Catholic League. Gaspard de Pontevès, comte de Carcès, head of the Catholic League in Provence, had a clientele of several hundred in 1588 with a loyal nucleus of about twenty to thirty.[77]

Henri III's favorite, the duc de Joyeuse, had a clientele of several hundred in the outer rings and an inner core of about thirty. Another favorite of Henri III, the duc d'Epernon, had a clientele of several hundred in addition to his ordinance and infantry companies.[78] Louis de Valois, comte d'Alais, duc d'Angoulême, and governor of Provence, had a provincial clientele of about 125 in 1645, with an inner core of 25. In addition, he kept companies of horse and foot guards, an ordinance company, and two provincial gendarmes companies of 50 to 100 men each. When these military clients are added to his household of about 100, Alais had a clientele of 400 to 500.[79] The clienteles of Henri II, prince de Condé, and his son Louis II, the Grand Condé, were even larger with a nucleus of about 175 noble families. The Grand Condé had a household of 522 in 1644, and 546 in 1660, although four years later his household had been cut in half to 273. After 1660, he maintained two infantry regiments, two ordinance companies, one cavalry regiment, and one guard company. The clienteles of the princes de Condé, father and son, numbered over 500.[80]

Besides an inner core of about 35 *fidèles*, Luynes would have had a much larger clientele of several hundred clients including 50 to 100 guards. In his memoirs, Bassompierre repeated a sarcastic remark that the king had made in November 1621, when they were on campaign in the Midi. Luynes had entered the king's lodgings preceded by his Swiss guards and his body guards, probably a company of each, followed by a crowd of courtiers and army officers. When the king saw him, he snapped, "Look, Bassompierre, here comes the king."[81] Great court nobles often traveled with large military retinues for prestige, and sometimes for safety as in Concini's case. The duc de Mayenne met the king at Tours in June 1619 with 200 gentlemen, while Luynes was accompanied by 300 noblemen when he met the Queen Mother at Tours in September 1619. The duc de Lesdiguières arrived at court in January 1620 surrounded by 300 mounted noblemen, while the duc de Nevers appeared with 150 to 200 gentlemen in March 1621. The duc de Guise arrived at court with 500 to 600 horsemen in 1611, and nearly 1,000 in March 1617, although such large musters were exceptional.[82]

Besides these entourages, great court nobles usually maintained households of 100 or more. The comte Du Lude had a household of 91,[83] while the duc d'Epernon had a household of 70 to 80, plus 40 guards, and the duc de Nevers had a household of 82.[84] Richelieu kept a household of 180, a guard company of 150 foot soldiers, and a mounted guard company of 100.[85] When they are added to the men in his provincial governments, Richelieu had a clientele the size of those of the princes de Condé. François de Lorraine, duc de Guise, had a household of 164 in 1561, plus an ordinance or gendarmes company of 250.[86] Léonard-Philibert, vicomte de Pompadour, had a household of about 100 at his château of Pompadour in 1630.[87] Charles de Lorraine, duc de Guise, governor of Provence, had a household of 100 at his Marseille townhouse in 1631, and he kept a company of light horse, plus smaller ordinance and guard companies.[88]

It is likely, therefore, that Luynes had a household of about 100 in addition to his guards. When they are added to his 35 *fidèles*, he would have had a clientele of about 235, plus clients from his estates. Since little is known about his lands, it is impossible to estimate the number of clients from this source. The strength of their loyalty is questionable, too, since his lands had been recently purchased or acquired through confiscation, and had not been in his family for generations, which tended to produce stronger bonds of personal loyalty. Luynes would have had clients from his provincial and Parisian governments as well, but nothing is known about them either. They would have been taken over from other patrons, which tended to produce looser bonds of loyalty. So, Luynes maintained a clientele of at least 300, the number of men who accompanied him to Tours in September 1619.[89] This was an average-sized clientele for a great court noble. The clienteles of Montmorency, Mayenne, Carcès, Joyeuse, and Epernon were about the same size, while those of Richelieu, Alais, and Condé were larger. How many of Luynes's clients were his relatives?

Nineteen of his inner core of thirty-five *fidèles*, a little more than half, were relatives who included his wife, her father, her uncle, her brother, his own two brothers, a sister, his two brothers-in-law, a niece and her husband, a nephew, five maternal cousins, and the son of a cousin.[90] The duc d'Epernon had eighteen relatives among his clients including three sons, a brother, two sisters, two nieces, a nephew, three cousins, a sister-in-law, four illegitimate sons, and an illegitimate daughter.[91] Twenty-two of Richelieu's maternal kin were his clients. Although his paternal kin were less numerous, some of them must also have been his clients, so he may have had as many as twenty-five to thirty relatives who were clients.[92] Luynes had about the same number of kin who were clients as Epernon, and somewhat fewer than Richelieu. Luynes's kin composed only about five per cent of his clientele, and he had few paternal kin as clients because his father had been an only child. Luynes did not bring an army of relatives to court, whatever the king or Rohan claimed.

The pamphleteers were correct when they declared that most of Luynes's kin and clients did not belong to the great nobility. By court standards, they were provincial nobodies, although they came from respectable families of the provincial sword nobility. Only his in-laws were great court nobles. The diversion of royal patronage to Luynes's clients caused anger and resentment among nobles expecting to be recipients. Pontchartrain wrote in his memoirs that court nobles had loudly protested the king's generosity to Luynes's relatives and friends in January 1618, and that they had complained again in July. In January 1619, they had accused Luynes of monopolizing the flow of royal patronage, and in February they began to speak openly against him. A year later they were daring to criticize him in front of the king.[93]

Luynes's brothers and maternal cousins benefited greatly from his generosity, but his other dependents received more modest rewards. He arranged profitable marriages for his brothers. On 14 January 1620, Honoré d'Albert, sieur de Cadenet, had married a wealthy heiress, Claire-Charlotte d'Ailly, comtesse de Chaulnes, baronne de Péquigny, dame de Rayneval and Magny, and vidame d'Amiens, whose lands were in Luynes's government of Picardy. The king gave them a wedding gift of 200,000 livres, and some months later by royal letters Chaulnes became a duchy, and Cadenet became the duc de Chaulnes.[94] In December 1619, he was named a knight of Saint Esprit, and took an oath of loyalty as a marshal of France with an annual salary of 10,000 livres. He was already a member of the royal council, and he was receiving 22,000 livres a year in royal pensions by 1622.[95] He became camp master of the Normandy regiment, formerly Concini's regiment, and he garrisoned the château of Vincennes with twelve companies of this regiment. Luynes gave him the captaincy of the king's one hundred men-at-arms, and Chaulnes became lieutenant general of Normandy in 1619. He levied and commanded the regiment of Picardy in 1620, and became captain-governor of the city and fortress of Amiens.[96] His spectacular rise caused much envy at court.

On 6 July 1620, Léon d'Albert, sieur de Brantes, had married Marguerite-Charlotte de Luxembourg, heiress of Henri, duc de Luxembourg-Piney, prince de Tingry, and comte de Ligny. Besides these lands, she had inherited an annual income of 120,000 livres in investments (*rentes*), a Paris mansion and its furnishings. Brantes took the name and arms of Luxembourg, and by royal letters became the duke of Luxembourg-Piney.[97] He became a knight of Saint Esprit, governor of the Bastille, and captain of the king's guard company of light horse purchased for 300,000 livres, plus his captaincy in the regiment of royal guards. He also became a colonel of the Orgeval artillery regiment, and governor of the Guyenne fortress of Blaye purchased for him by the king for 384,000 livres. He briefly became a royal council member after Luynes's death.[98]

The pamphleteers declared that Chaulnes and Luxembourg were peasants trying to appear as gentlemen. They had arrived at court wearing unfashionable out-of-date clothes, and had only succeeded because they had married well. According to the pamphleteers, the king gave Chaulnes 1,000,000 livres when he married, plus an income of 18,000 livres a year from the Paris salt tax, and twice that from the Picardy salt tax. The king was supposed to have given Luxembourg the even more startling sum of 1,800,000 livres when he married.[99] None of this was true, but Louis Batiffol cited it as evidence of Luynes's greed, and historians have repeated it ever since.[100] Luynes did not reward his relatives as extravagantly as the pamphleteers claimed, but he was generous to his brothers and cousins.

Luynes's cousin, François II de Raimond de Mourmoiron, sieur de Modène, came from an old sword noble family of the Comtat Venaissin. He became the baron de Modène after his first cousin Marie, the wife of Jean-Baptiste d'Ornano, ceded him this title. He participated in the conspiracy to kill Concini, and attended Luynes's wedding, becoming a useful political client. He was trusted by Luynes, who sent him on a diplomatic mission to Savoy, and by the king who sent him on a mission to Rome. As a councillor of state, Modène took a seat on the large council in January 1620, and on the small council in June. For his service, he was rewarded with the office of grand provost in the king's household, and the governorships of Fougère and Concarneau in Brittany. He became tainted, however, by his connection to Ornano, and for this reason he was arrested with Ornano in 1626 and sent to the Bastille. When Ornano died a few months later, Modène was released, sent from court, and died six years later in Avignon. The pamphleteers declared that he had accumulated a large fortune while at court, but this seems unlikely given the modest landholdings described in his will. His son Esprit was a page and then a chamberlain in the household of Gaston d'Orléans.[101]

Jean-Baptiste d'Ornano, comte de Montlor, a title given him by his wife, was a maternal cousin of Luynes three times removed. His wife, Marie, had inherited the titles of comte de Montlor (Montlaur), marquis de Maubec, and baron d'Aubenas from her father, Louis de Raimond de Mourmoiron. She gave the first title to her husband, kept the second for herself, styling herself the marquise de Montlaur, and gave the third to her cousin Modène. The Ornano were a family of Corsican nobles who had emigrated to France a half-century earlier. After inheriting his father's offices of colonel of the Corsican regiment and governor of Pont-Saint-Esprit, Ornano went to court in 1610 where he attracted the attention of the Queen Mother, who arranged his marriage. The marriage contract, dated 4 February 1611, listed Modène as a witness. Ornano's will in 1616 named Modène as the executor of a modest estate of 3,750 livres in investments (*rentes*), and revenues from the barony of Lunel and the seigneury of Galargues in Languedoc. Through Luynes's patronage, Ornano became lieutenant general of Haute-Normandie, governor of the Pont de l'Arche and Rouen, a councillor of state, and captain of an ordinance company. The king gave him a gift of 30,000 livres, and he became a knight of Saint Esprit, while his wife danced in the queen's ballet of 1619. His good fortune was envied at court.

Ornano, however, also wanted a marshal's baton, which eluded him, although three were awarded in the autumn of 1619. He complained to Luynes, who secured his appointment as governor of the king's brother, and despite the Queen Mother's opposition, Ornano took the oath of office on 3 December 1619. He and his wife acted as surrogate parents to Gaston, who became very fond of them, and later gave the widowed marquise a lifetime pension. Ornano's brother, Joseph-Charles, was named master of Gaston's wardrobe, while his other brother, Henri-François-Alphonse d'Ornano, sieur de Mazargues, became Gaston's master of horse, and was given command of the regiment of Mazargues. Henri inherited his brother's offices of colonel of the Corsican regiment and governor of Pont-Saint-Esprit, and was named governor of Tarascon with a royal pension of 2,000 livres.

Ornano lost his office as Gaston's governor in May 1624, but remained his household superintendent and first gentleman of his bedchamber. Richelieu gave Ornano a marshal's baton in April 1626 to secure his cooperation, but he wanted a seat on the royal council, too, insisting that Luynes had recommended him for a seat. That was too much for Richelieu, who had Ornano arrested in May 1626, along with his brothers and Modène. He sent Ornano's wife from court to La Ferté-Bernard in the Maine, and Ornano himself to the prisons of Vincennes where he died of kidney failure in September 1626. His brothers and Modène were then released and sent from court.[102]

Luynes's mother, Anne de Rodulf (Rodulph), came from a fifteenth-century Provençal noble family. Through her son's patronage, her kinsman Pierre de Rodulf, sieur de Saint Jean, was named lieutenant of the Bastille, and a few years later governor of Blaye. Luynes arranged the marriage in February 1620 of Gabrielle, daughter of his cousin Antoine de Rodulf, sieur de Saint Paulet, to a captain in the regiment of Normandy.[103] Luynes's eldest sister, Marie, had married Claude de Grimoard de Beauvoir du Roure, sieur de Bonneval and Combalet, in 1599. Luynes's niece, Anne du Roure de Combalet, was named the queen's maid of honor, and danced in her ballet of February 1619. Anne married Charles de Créquy, comte de Canaples, a grandson of the duc de Lesdiguières, in a lavish wedding on 1 June 1620. Her new husband received 100,000 livres from the king, 100,000 from Luynes, and 100,000 from his father-in-law, and the promise that he would inherit his father's office of camp master in the royal guards regiment when his father received the next marshal's baton. It was said at court that Canaples had only married Luynes's niece to gain favor. A network of marriage alliances, therefore, linked the Du Roure, Ornano, Raimond de Mourmoiron, and Albert de Luynes families.[104]

On 28 November 1620, Anne du Roure's brother, Antoine, who was Luynes's nephew, married Richelieu's favorite niece, Marie de Vignerod de Pont du Courlay, later the duchesse d'Aiguillon. Antoine was a 20-year-old captain in the regiment of Normandy, a small man with broken veins in his face. His premature death at the siege of Montpellier in September 1622 became a welcome release for his wife, who despised him. Richelieu wrote in his memoirs that Luynes had proposed the match to obtain his support in managing the Queen Mother. Richelieu said that he did what he could to stop the marriage because he thought it would make him enemies at court, and because his niece had loathed Antoine on sight, but Antoine was smitten, so the marriage went ahead. The marriage contract stipulated that Luynes would give his nephew 150,000 livres; the Queen Mother would give Richelieu's niece 60,000 livres; and her uncle would give her jewelry and furnishings worth 40,000 livres.[105]

In 1605, Luynes's second sister, Antoinette, had married Barthélemy du Vernet, an obscure Languedocian nobleman who was named an ordinary gentleman of the king's bedchamber, a lieutenant of both the Bastille and Vincennes, and a captain in the regiment of Normandy. Antoinette became the queen's mistress of robes in December 1618.[106] Luynes's third sister, Louise, had married Antoine de Villeneuve, sieur de Mons, who came from a cadet branch of an old Provençal sword noble family. He was named governor of Les Baux in Provence, and of Honfleur, Pont l'Evêque, and Auge in Normandy, and he became *premier maître d'hôtel* in the household of Gaston d'Orléans as well as an army camp master, and he received a pension of 6,000 livres. Luynes's youngest sister, Anne, entered the Ursuline convent at Pont-Saint-Esprit in 1614 at age thirty-seven, and became the mother superior in 1618. The king wanted to give her the abbey of Maubuisson in 1620, but she refused and died at Pont-Saint-Esprit in 1623.[107] Luynes had married five of his six siblings, an unusually large number. He was generous to his family, but not extravagant as the pamphleteers claimed.

Luynes also helped his in-laws, although less than might be expected. His wife became superintendent of the queen's household and her first lady of honor. Her father, the duc de Montbazon, already master of the king's hunt (*grand veneur*), governor of Nantes, and a knight of Saint Esprit, now became governor of the Ile-de-France and the Picard fortresses of Noyon, Chauny, Coucy, and Soissons. In 1620, he was named the Queen Mother's *chevalier d'honneur* and lieutenant general of lower Normandy, and after Luynes's death, he became governor and lieutenant general of the city of Paris. His brother, Alexandre de Rohan, marquis de Marigny, was named a knight of Saint Esprit and captain of the king's one hundred men at arms, while Montbazon's son, Louis de Rohan, comte de Rochefort, became a knight of Saint Esprit, and accompanied Chaulnes on his ambassadorial mission to England in January 1621.[108]

Luynes had created in and around Paris a large clientele composed of royal household officials, fortress governors, and army officers. He himself became grand falconer, first gentleman, and first ordinary gentleman of the king's bedchamber. Five of his relatives joined the king's household, and five joined Gaston d'Orléans's household.[109] Thirteen of his clients joined the king's household, and four joined Gaston's household.[110] Luynes placed fourteen dependents in the queen's household including his wife, sister, two nieces, four clients, six wives and daughters of kin and clients.[111] He placed a total of forty-one kin and clients in royal households, forty-two including himself. Luynes was accused of purging the Queen Mother's clients and replacing them with his own.[112] This was probably untrue, but he did replace the king's confessor and Gaston's governor with his own clients. Luynes was also falsely accused of filling the

Queen Mother's household with his spies and clients, which she never would have tolerated, but he did send cavalry companies commanded by Jean-Jacques de Mesmes, sieur de Roissy, to guard the roads leading to Blois. Roissy was the father of the *prévôté* lieutenant who had refused to arrest Concini. Filling royal households with dependents was a common practice among high household officials.[113]

Luynes made household appointments to reward loyal service, and to gain influence with the king and his family. Salaries were low, about 3,000 to 3,500 livres a year, but the supplementary benefits included pensions, living allowances, gifts, bribes, tax exemptions, and investment opportunities, perhaps another 10,000 livres a year. Household officials could receive as much as 30,000 livres a year. A *maître d'hôtel* of the king's household had an income of 36,000 livres in 1623, while Luynes's client Sauveterre, first valet of the king's wardrobe, had an annual income of 30,000 livres in 1626.[114] Luynes placed kin and clients such as Sauveterre in royal households as eyes and ears to provide him with information, and as voices to influence opinions and attitudes. For this reason, he replaced the Queen Mother's choice of her son's confessor, Pierre Coton, with his own confessor, Jean Arnoux, who defended his interests for three years. When he began to criticize him to the king, however, Luynes got rid of him. Luynes was not the only one who surrounded the king and his family with dependents. Richelieu was notorious for purging the queen's household of those whom he distrusted and filling it with his own spies and clients, who reported everything she said and did. She loathed him for this and made no secret of it.[115]

Luynes enjoyed extensive military patronage as constable. He was able to place his kin and clients in the king's military household, and in the regiments of Picardy, Normandy, Mazargues, and Rambures. His nephew Antoine du Roure, his brother-in-law Barthélemy du Vernet, and the husband of his cousin Gabrielle de Rodulf were captains in the Normandy regiment commanded by his brother Chaulnes. The Queen Mother protested that Luynes's kin and clients were monopolizing fortress governorships.[116] Richelieu remarked, "There is not a fortress in France which Luynes and his friends do not hope to buy, thereby doubling the price ... They have secured in this way some eighteen of the most important fortresses, filling them with large garrisons in peacetime and doubling their arsenals ... They maintain soldiers at court, have stationed at Vincennes the regiment of Normandy commanded by the sieur de Chaulnes and created for him, acquired as many companies as they can in the regiment of guards, bought the company of the king's light horse, and in the name of the sieur de Brantes bought the (king's) company of gendarmes."[117] Richelieu's appraisal was surprisingly accurate. Seven of Luynes's kin,[118] and twelve of his clients held fortress governorships for a total of nineteen.[119] His brother

Chaulnes commanded the Normandy regiment and the king's company of one hundred men-at-arms, while his brother Luxembourg commanded the king's guard company of light horse. Luynes had created a strategically important network of clients in and around Paris, which did not, however, include anyone holding an episcopal office because he did not have any male kin who were clerics.[120]

Luynes had to defer to the king's wishes, so he did not have an entirely free hand in distributing patronage. Ornano had wanted the governorship of the Château Trompette at Bordeaux, but the king gave it to the duc de Mayenne instead. Luynes had wanted the government of Caen, but the grand prior de Vendôme got it instead. Luynes sought the archbishopric of Sens for his client Ruccellai, but Octave de Saint Lary de Bellegarde got it instead.[121] Despite what his enemies claimed, however, Luynes's clientele was not excessively large by great noble standards, and his clients were not extravagantly rewarded, although his control over the distribution of royal patronage and his gifts to dependents were greatly resented. Other court nobles had to wait patiently for death or disgrace to create a vacancy, and then they had to watch Luynes's family and friends take the place, which was infuriating. Similar grievances had caused a great noble revolt in 1614, and the murder of a royal favorite in 1617. Not surprisingly, anger and resentment at Luynes's control over the distribution of royal patronage drove nobles south to join the Queen Mother's revolt in 1619 and again in 1620.

Notes

1 Charles Herman, "Knights and Kings in Early Modern France: Royal Orders of Knighthood, 1469–1715" (PhD dissertation, University of Minnesota, 1990), pp. 45–66; Philippe Contamine, "L'Ordre de Saint-Michel," *Bulletin, Société nationale des antiquaires de France* (1976), 212–38.

2 Michel de Montaigne, *The Complete Essays of Montaigne*, trans. Donald Frame (Stanford, 1957), Book II: 12, p. 434; Book II: 7, pp. 275–8.

3 Herman, "Knights and Kings," pp. 57–9; Nicolas Le Roux, *La Faveur du Roi* (Paris, 2000), p. 732.

4 Jean-Marie Constant, "Un groupe socio-politique: la noblesse seconde," *L'Etat et les aristocraties*, ed. Philippe Contamine (Paris, 1989), pp. 279–304; J.H.M. Salmon, "A Second Look at the *noblesse seconde*," *Fr Hist Stud*, 25 (2002), 575–93.

5 Jacqueline Boucher, *Société et mentalités autour de Henri III*, 4 vols. (Lille, 1981), IV, 1354–7.

6 Père Anselme de Sainte Marie, *Histoire généalogique et chronologique de la Maison Royale de France*, 9 vols. (Paris, 1726–33, New York, 1967), IX, 9, 15–20, 51–73; Jeroen Duindam, *Vienna and Versailles* (Cambridge, 2003), pp. 284–5.

7 Anselme, *Histoire généalogique*, IX, 11–12, 15.

8 B.N., Dossiers bleus 8, fols. 112–17.

9 Anselme, *Histoire généalogique*, IX, 105–25.

10 *Mercure françois*, 25 vols. (Paris, 1605–44), VI (1620), 1–24; Pierre Boitel de Gaubertin, *Relation historique des pompes et magnifiques cérémonies observées à la réception des chevaliers de L'Ordre du Saint Esprit* (Paris, 1620).

11 Anselme, *Histoire généalogique*, IX, 13, 20–1; Herman, "Kings and Knights," pp. 71–92; B.N., Clairambault 1135, fols. 1–23, statutes of the order in 1629.

12 Jean-Pierre Labatut, "Louis XIV et les chevaliers de l'Ordre du Saint Esprit," *XVIIe siècle*, 128 (1980), 267–77.

13 Anselme, *Histoire généalogique*, IX, 131–2.

14 Herman, "Knights and Kings," pp. 73–4.

15 Jean Héroard, *Journal*, ed. Madeleine Foisil, 2 vols. (Paris, 1989), II, 2059.

16 Ibid., II, 2660; *Mercure françois*, VI (1620), 7–8; Anselme, *Histoire généalogique*, IX, 13.

17 Boitel de Gaubertin, *Relation historique*, pp. 237–8; Wilmer McCorquodale, "The Court of Louis XIII" (PhD dissertation, University of Texas, 1994), p. 179.

18 *Mercure françois*, VI (1620), 1–9.

19 McCorquodale, "The Court of Louis XIII," p. 168.

20 Duindam, *Vienna and Versailles*, pp. 161, 218.

21 B.N., Ms. fr. 16802, fol. 180; McCorquodale, "The Court of Louis XIII," pp. 179–80; Héroard, *Journal*, II, 2059, II, 2660.

22 Ibid.

23 B.N., Ms. fr. 16802, fols. 148–78; McCorquodale, "The Court of Louis XIII," pp. 171–86. The memoirists were Fontenay-Mareuil, Beauvais-Nangis, Pontchartrain, and Brienne.

24 B.N., Ms. fr. 16802, fols. 151–63; *Mercure françois*, VI (1620), 1.

25 François Du Val, marquis de Fontenay-Mareuil, *Mémoires du Messire Du Val*, ed. Louis Monmerqué, 2 vols. (Paris, 1826), I, 458.

26 The 59 new knights were added to 28 existing ones, making 87 knights, the largest number possible under the statutes, and with the 9 clerics and 4 officers, a total of 100.

27 B.N., Ms. fr. 16802, fols. 177–8; Fontenay-Mareuil, *Mémoires*, I, 459; McCorquodale, "The Court of Louis XIII," p. 176.

28 Anselme, *Histoire généalogique*, IX, 13.

29 McCorquodale, "The Court of Louis XIII," p. 177; B.N., Ms. fr. 16802, fols. 177–8; *Mercure françois*, VI (1620), 1–24.

30 B.N., Ms. fr. 16802, fols. 165–71.

31 Ibid., fols. 148–9; McCorquodale, "The Court of Louis XIII," pp. 173–4; Anselme, *Histoire généalogique*, IX, 13.

32 Ibid., IX, 159; Fontenay-Mareuil, *Mémoires*, I, 459; Labatut, "Louis XIV et les chevaliers," p. 271.

33 Achille Halphen, ed., *Journal d'Arnauld d'Andilly 1614–1620* (Paris, 1857), pp. 457–8; B.N., Ms. fr. 25198, fols. 4–5; Paul Phélypeaux de Pontchartrain, *Mémoires concernant les affaires de France sous la régence de Marie de Médicis*, eds. Michaud and Poujoulat, 2nd ser., vol. 5 (Paris, 1837), p. 460; Eugène Griselle, *Etat de la maison du Roi Louis XIII* (Paris, 1912), p. 10; McCorquodale, "The Court of Louis XIII," p. 178; Eusèbe Pavie, *La Guerre entre Louis XIII et Marie de Médicis, 1619–1620* (Angers, 1899), pp. 56–7, 82–5.

34 *Mercure françois*, VI (1620), 268–9.

35 Nicolas Chorier, *Histoire de la vie de Charles de Créquy de Blanchefort* (Grenoble, 1683), p. 149; Jeroen Duindam, *Myths of Power* (Amsterdam, 1994), pp. 98–125.

36 Chorier, *Histoire de Créquy*, p. 269.

37 Duindam, *Vienna and Versailles*, pp. 161–219.

38 Fontenay-Mareuil, *Mémoires*, I, 458.

39 McCorquodale, "The Court of Louis XIII," p. 177; Anselme, *Histoire généalogique*, IX, 13, 83, 123; B.N., Dossiers bleus 8, fol. 112; *Mercure françois*, VI (1620), 5.

40 Ibid., 5–6, 23; Fontenay-Mareuil, *Mémoires*, I, 460.

41 Nicolas de Brichanteau, marquis de Beauvais-Nangis, *Mémoires*, eds. Louis Monmerqué and A.H. Taillandier (Paris, 1862), p. 154.

42 Fontenay-Mareuil, *Mémoires*, I, 459; Anselme, *Histoire généalogique*, IX, 141, 148, 150, 152.

43 Anselme, *Histoire généalogique*, VII, 439; Beauvais-Nangis, *Mémoires*, pp. iv–v; Le Roux, *La Faveur du Roi*, p. 430.

44 Beauvais-Nangis, *Mémoires*, pp. 154–6; Anselme, *Histoire généalogique*, IX, 143, 302, 352.

45 The king's nominees were Henri de Gondi, cardinal de Retz; Philippe de Gondi, comte de

FRIENDS OF THE FAVORITE 137

Joigny; Henri de Gondi, duc de Retz; his brother-in-law, Léonor de la Magdelaine, marquis de Ragny; Gaston d'Orléans, Louis de Bourbon, comte de Soissons; César de Bourbon, duc de Vendôme; Charles de Valois, duc d'Angoulême; Courtenvaux; Bellengreville; Vitry; his brother Du Hallier; their uncle Beauvais-Nangis; Pardallian de Montespan; Bassompierre; La Curée; Potier de Tresmes; La Vieuville; Rambouillet; Philippe de Béthune, comte de Selles.

46 The queen nominated Emmanuel de Crussol, duc d'Uzès. The queen mother nominated Henri de Lorraine, duc de Mayenne, and Martin du Bellay, marquis de Thouarcé. Condé's nominees were Louis d'Aloigny, marquis de Rochefort; Charles de Lorraine, duc de Guise; Guise's younger brother, Claude de Lorraine, duc de Chevreuse; and their cousin, Charles de Lorraine, duc d'Elbeuf. Henri IV's nominees were Bertrand de Vignolles, and André de Cochefilet, baron de Vaucelas.

47 Beauvais-Nangis, *Mémoires*, p. 155.

48 *Journal d'Arnauld 1614–1620*, p. 399; Margaret McGowan, *L'Art du ballet de cour en France, 1581–1643* (Paris, 1963), pp. 105, n. 27, 118, n. 9. The ballet dancers were Humières, La Rocheguyon, Rohan de Rochefort, Blainville, Paluau, and Brantes. The king's household members were Termes, La Rocheguyon, Lestang, Humières, Cadenet, Brantes, Paluau, Valençay, and Blainville. Mauny was the queen's master of horse, while Ornano was governor of Gaston d'Orléans.

49 Anselme, *Histoire généalogique*, II, 87, IV, 61–4, V, 768, VII, 392, 550, 733–4, VIII, 68, IX, 132–55; Joseph Bergin, *The Making of the French Episcopate* (New Haven, 1996), pp. 606, 657; Jacques Humbert, *Le Maréchal de Créquy* (Paris, 1962), pp. 77–8; Griselle, *Etat de la maison du Roi*, pp. 10–12; Jean-Pierre Labatut, *Les Ducs et pairs de France au XVIIe siècle* (Paris, 1972), pp. 76–8, 81, 138–9, 145, 251, passim; *Journal d'Arnauld 1614–1620*, pp. 430–1 and n. 3.

50 *Mercure françois* VI (1620), 269, 271; Pontchartrain, *Mémoires*, pp. 410, 413.

51 Anselme, *Histoire généalogique*, IV, 600; V, 151, 270, 288; VII, 470; IX, 74, 158, 160–3; *Mémoires du maréchal d'Estrées*, ed. Petitot, 2 d ser., vol. 16 (Paris, 1822), pp. 170–73.

52 B.N., Ms. fr. 25198, fols. 1–17; McCorquodale, "The Court of Louis XIII," p. 175.

53 Richard Bonney, *Political Change in France under Richelieu and Mazarin, 1624–1661* (Oxford, 1978), pp. 284–317.

54 Armand Jean du Plessis de Richelieu, *Mémoires de Richelieu*, eds. Michaud and Poujoulat, 2nd ser., vol. 8 (Paris, 1837), p. 455.

55 McCorquodale, "The Court of Louis XIII," p. 190.

56 Henri de Loménie de Brienne, *Mémoires du comte de Brienne*, ed. Petitot, 2nd ser., vol. 36 (Paris, 1824), pp. 44–5.

57 Idem, *Mémoires du comte de Brienne*, eds. Michaud and Poujoulat, 3rd ser., vol. 3 (Paris, 1838), p. 16. "Je me crois obligé de dire ici que Luynes en usoit honnêtement avec moi, m'aida de ses bons offices; et cependant j'avois très-peu de part à sa confiance, parce que je n'ai jamais voulu dépendre des favoris."

58 Anselme, *Histoire généalogique*, IX, 312.

59 The new members were Richelieu; his brothers-in-law, Urbain de Maillé, marquis de Brézé, and François de Vignerot, marquis du Pont de Courlay; his cousins, Charles du Cambout, baron de Pontchâteau; Charles de La Porte, marquis de La Meilleraye; and Louis de Moy, sieur de La Meilleraye. Richelieu's brother Alphonse was the king's grand almoner and an officer of the order, while Richelieu's clients included Henri d'Escoubleau de Sourdis, archbishop of Bordeaux, and his brother Charles d'Escoubleau, marquis de Sourdis; Claude de Rébé, archbishop of Narbonne; Louis de Nogaret, cardinal de La Valette, archbishop of Toulouse; Charles de Schomberg, duc du Hallwin; Jean de Gallard de Béarn, comte de Brassac; and François, maréchal d'Estrées. Two of the order's officers were his clients, Claude le Bouthillier, treasurer, and Claude de Bullion, chancellor. Anselme, *Histoire généalogique*, IX, 157–79, 303, 340; Joseph Bergin, *Cardinal Richelieu* (New Haven, 1985), pp. 69–118; Sharon Kettering, *Patronage in Sixteenth-and Seventeenth-Century France* (Aldershot, 2002), III, 424–5.

60 They included Charles de Schomberg, governor of Languedoc; Claude de Rébé, archbishop

of Narbonne; Languedoc lieutenant generals Charles de Lévis, duc de Ventadour, Louis duc d'Arpajon, and Hector de Gelas, marquis de Leberon; François de Bonne de Créquy, duc de Lesdiguières, governor of Dauphiné; Charles-Henri, comte de Clermont, constable of Dauphiné; Just-Henry, comte de Tournon, seneschal of Auvergne; Henri de Beaudean, comte de Parabère, governor of Poitou; Henri de La Trémoille, duc de Thouars; Léonard-Philibert, vicomte de Pompadour, lieutenant general of the Limousin. Anselme, *Histoire généalogique*, IV, 156–79; William Beik, *Absolutism and Society in Seventeenth-Century France* (Cambridge, 1985), pp. 223–44.

61 They were the ducs de Longueville and Thouars; Epernon's three sons; the marquis d'Estrées and de Villars; the comte de Vaubecourt; Henri de Lorraine, comte d'Harcourt. Anselme, *Histoire généalogique*, IX, 156–79; Bonney, *Political Change*, p. 288.

62 The king's nominees were Guillaume de Simiane, marquis de Gordes; Antoine, duc d'Aumont; François de Cossé, duc de Brissac; Charles, comte de Lannoy; Claude de Rouvroy, duc de Saint Simon; his brother Charles de Rouvroy, marquis de Saint Simon; Roger du Plessis, sieur de Liancourt; Gabriel de Rochechouard, marquis then duc de Mortemart; Jean-François de Gondi, archbishop of Paris; Louis de Valois, comte d'Alais, later duc d'Angoulême. The queen's appointee was François de Béthune, comte, then duc d'Orval. Anselme, *Histoire généalogique*, IX, 156–79.

63 Orest Ranum, *Richelieu and the Councillors of Louis XIII* (Oxford, 1963), pp. 2, 8–9, 13, 18, 22, 29.

64 Pontchartrain, *Mémoires*, p. 459.

65 *Recueil des pièces les plus curieuses qui ont esté faites pendant le règne du Connestable Luynes* (Paris, 1628), *Le Qu'as-tu-veu de la Cour* (1620), p. 44, *Noel* and *Pasquil des Chevaliers* (1620), pp. 34–8; B.N., imprimés Lb 36, *Seconde partie et responce à la Chronique des Favoris* (1622), p. 9.

66 *Recueil, Pasquil des Chevaliers* (1620), p. 38.

67 Ibid., *Requeste presentée au Roy Pluton par Conchino Conchini* (1620), p. 74, *Manifeste de la Royne Mère* (1620), p. 272, *Méditations de l'hermite Valérien* (1621), p. 315; Henri de Rohan, *Mémoires du duc de Rohan*, eds. Michaud and Poujoulat, 2nd ser., vol. 5 (Paris, 1837), p. 511.

68 Sharon Kettering, "Patronage in Early Modern France," *Fr Hist Stud* 17 (1992), 839–62; idem, "Friendship and Clientage in Early Modern France," *Fr Hist* 6 (1992), 139–58.

69 *Recueil, Manifeste de la Royne Mère*, pp. 267–8, 270, 273; *Rejouissance de toute la France sur la mort du Connestable* (1622), p. 166.

70 Ibid., *La Chronique des Favoris* (1622), pp. 442, 475; Rohan, *Mémoires*, p. 516.

71 *Recueil, Le Comtadin Provençal*, p. 97; *Le Tout en Tout de la Cour* (1620), p. 70; *Les Soupirs de la Fleur de Lys* (1622), pp. 406–8.

72 François de Bassompierre. *Journal de ma vie. Mémoires du maréchal de Bassompierre*, ed. Edouard de Chanterac. 4 vols. (Paris, 1870–77), II, 174; Le Roux, *La Faveur du Roi*, pp. 175–6.

73 Charles, comte Horric de Beaucaire, ed., *Mémoires du Cardinal de Richelieu*, 10 vols. (Paris, 1907–13), III, 190. "Il n'avoit qu'une seule vertu qu'on puisse opposer à toutes ses mauvaises qualités, c'est qu'il fit du bien à tous ses parents et à tous ses serviteurs, estimant une partie de ses richesses consister en celles de ceux qui lui appartenoient..."

74 Héroard, *Journal*, II, 2059, II, 2821, April 10, 1622.

75 Hélène Duccini, *Concini* (Paris, 1991), p. 269.

76 Kettering, "Patronage in Early Modern France," 844–52; idem, "Gift-Giving and Patronage in Early Modern France," *Fr Hist* 2 (1988), 131–51.

77 Mark Greengrass, "Noble Affinities in Early Modern France," *European History Quarterly* 16 (1986), 276–8; Henri Drouot, *Mayenne et le Bourgogne*, 2 vols. (Paris, 1937), I, 103–15, II, 66, 73–87, 96–102, 112–30; Sharon Kettering, "Clientage during the French Wars of Religion," *The Sixteenth Century Journal* 20 (1989), 225–31.

78 Le Roux, *La Faveur du Roi*, pp. 249, 505–19.

79 Sharon Kettering, *Patrons, Brokers, and Clients in Seventeenth-Century France* (New York, 1986), pp. 87, 92–3.

80 Katia Béguin, *Les Princes de Condé* (Paris, 1999), pp. 157–8, 161, 199, 209, 269–78, 395–440;

Jean Mariéjol, *Henri IV et Louis XIII*, in *Histoire de France*, ed. Ernest Lavisse, 9 vols. (Paris, 1911), vol. VI, part 2, 146.

81 Bassompierre, *Mémoires*, II, 383.

82 *Journal d'Arnauld 1614–1620*, pp. 305, 428, 447; Eugène and Jules Halphen, eds., *Journal inédit d'Arnauld d'Andilly 1620* (Paris, 1888–1909), pp. 5–6; Eugène Halphen, ed., *Journal inédit d'Arnauld d'Andilly 1621* (Paris, 1871), p. 15; Kettering, *Patrons, Brokers, and Clients*, pp. 216–17; Mariéjol, *Henri IV et Louis XIII*, VI, 146.

83 A. D., Maine-et-Loire, E2189, fols. 1–69.

84 Nicolas Fessenden, "Epernon and Guyenne" (PhD dissertation, Columbia University, 1972), pp. 255–7; Emile Baudson, *Charles de Gonzague, duc de Nevers* (Paris, 1947), p. 167.

85 Maximin Deloche, *La Maison du Cardinal de Richelieu* (Paris, 1912), pp. 485, 363–4.

86 Stuart Carroll, *Noble Power during the French Wars of Religion* (Cambridge, 1998), p. 63.

87 Yves-Marie Bercé, "Les Conduites de fidélité," *Hommage à Roland Mousnier: Clientèles et fidélités en Europe à l'époque moderne*, ed. Yves Durand (Paris, 1981), p. 130.

88 A.A.E., Fonds France 1701, fol. 228, Guise to Richelieu, March 12, 1631; Sharon Kettering, *Judicial Politics and Urban Revolt in Seventeenth-Century France* (Princeton, 1978), p. 133.

89 Between 400 and 500 men accompanied Luynes when he rode into Rouen in November 1617. *Journal d'Arnauld 1614–1620*, p. 323.

90 They included Marie de Rohan; Hercule de Rohan, duc de Montbazon; Alexandre de Rohan, marquis de Marigny; Louis de Rohan, comte de Rochefort; Honoré d'Albert, duc de Chaulnes; Léon d'Albert, duc de Piney-Luxembourg; Antoinette du Vernet; Barthélemy du Vernet; Claude du Roure, sieur de Bonneval, husband of Luynes's sister Marie. Their daughter, Anne du Roure, married Charles de Créquy, comte de Canaples. Their son married Richelieu's niece, Marie de Vignerod de Pontcourlay. Antoine de Villeneuve de Mons married Luynes's sister, Louise. Luynes's maternal cousins included Pierre de Rodulph, sieur de Saint Jean; Jean-Baptiste d'Ornano and his two brothers; François Raimond de Mourmiron, baron de Modène; and Modène's son Esprit. Anselme, *Histoire généalogique*, IV, 61, 63–4, 266, 272, 274, 293; VI, 538–9; Jean-Antoine Pithon-Curt, *Histoire de la noblesse du Comté Venaissin*, 4 vols. (Paris, 1743–50), III, 14–15, 18–19; IV, 168–9; Edmé de Juigné de Lassigny, *Histoire de la maison de Villeneuve en Provence*, 3 vols. (Lyon, 1912), I, 138, 232–3; Jean Charay, ed., *Vie du maréchal Jean-Baptiste d'Ornano* (Grenoble, 1971), pp. 12, 14–16; Albert Bonneveau-Avenant, *La Duchesse d'Aiguillon* (Paris, 1879), pp. 89–99.

91 Fessenden, "Epernon and Guyenne," pp. 226–34.

92 Sharon Kettering, "Patronage and Kinship in Early Modern France," *Fr Hist Stud* 16 (1989), 424–5; Bergin, *Cardinal Richelieu*, pp. 14–22, appendix two.

93 Pontchartrain, *Mémoires*, pp. 398, 400, 402, 404; Duindam, *Vienna and Versailles*, pp. 230, 249; *Journal d'Arnauld 1620*, p. 13.

94 Héroard, *Journal*, II, 2663; *Mercure françois*, VI (1620), 469; A.N., M.C. XXXVI 109, January 13, 1620; *Journal d'Arnauld 1620*, p. 5; *Journal d'Arnauld 1621*, pp. 12–13; Anselme, *Histoire généalogique*, IV, 272–3, 337–9; Pithon-Curt, *Histoire de la noblesse*, IV, 182; Beaucaire, *Mémoires de Richelieu*, III, 8; Labatut, *Les Ducs et pairs*, pp. 145, 250–2.

95 Héroard, *Journal*, II, 2655; B.N., Pièces originales 21, fol. 51v; *Journal d'Arnauld 1614–1620*, pp. 394, 457; Pontchartrain, *Mémoires*, p. 402; Louis Batiffol, "Louis XIII et le duc de Luynes," *Rev hist* 103 (1910), 253, ns.3,5; Paul Bondois, *Le Maréchal de Bassompierre* (Paris, 1925), p. 467.

96 Pontchartrain, *Mémoires*, pp. 395, 415; *Journal d'Arnauld 1614–1620*, pp. 317–18, 440; A.N., M.C. VII 11, fols. 1–7, March 22, 1622; B.N., Dossiers bleus 8, fols. 61, 99, 101; Dupuy 92, fols. 113–113v; Fontenay-Mareuil, *Mémoires*, I, 419; Beaucaire, *Mémoires de Richelieu*, III, 11; Pithon-Curt, *Histoire de la noblesse*, IV, 183.

97 B. Inguimbertine, Carpentras, ms. 1847, fols. 196–200, July 5, 1620; *Journal d'Arnauld 1620*, p. 21; *Journal d'Arnauld 1621*, p. 8; Pithon-Curt, *Histoire de la noblesse*, IV, 186; Beaucaire, *Mémoires de Richelieu*, III, 99, n. 3; Fontenay-Mareuil, *Mémoires*, I, 468; Bassompierre, *Mémoires*, II, 202.

98 *Journal d'Arnauld 1614–1620*, pp. 358, 376, 418–19; *Journal d'Arnauld 1620* p. 47; Beaucaire, *Mémoires de Richelieu*, III, 11; B.N., Dupuy 92, fols. 113v; Anselme, *Histoire généalogique*, III, 732–3, IV, 274–5; Fontenay-Mareuil, *Mémoires*, I, 492.

99 B.N., imprimés Lb36, *La Magie des Favoris* (1619), pp. 1–30; *Seconde partie et responce*, pp. 20–21; *Recueil, L'Ombre de Monsieur le Connestable* (1622), pp. 426–38; *Le Comtadin Provençal* (1620), pp. 97–8; *La Chronique des Favoris* (1622), pp. 446–7, 464–5.

100 Batiffol, "Louis XIII et le duc de Luynes," *Rev hist* 102 (1909), 253–4; idem, *Le Roi Louis XIII à vingt ans* (Paris, 1910), p. 546; Michel Carmona, *Marie de Médicis* (Paris, 1981), pp. 347–8; Pierre Chevallier, *Louis XIII* (Paris, 1979), p. 190; A. Lloyd Moote, *Louis XIII* (Berkeley, 1989), p. 103; Duccini, *Concini*, pp. 259, 388; Joseph Bergin, *The Rise of Richelieu* (New Haven, 1991), p. 200.

101 B. Inguimbertine, ms. 1847, fol. 194; A. D. Vaucluse, ms. E22, Modène's will, 1630; *Journal d'Arnauld 1614–1620*, pp. 312, 317, 345, 378; *Journal d'Arnauld 1620*, p. 5; *Journal d'Arnauld 1621*, p. 13; Pontchartrain, *Mémoires*, pp. 394, 396, 398, 402; Bassompierre, *Mémoires*, II, 152–3; Pithon-Curt, *Histoire de la noblesse*, III, 3, 14–15, 18–20, 107–9; Pavie, *La Guerre*, p. 58; Anselme, *Histoire généalogique*, IX, 138; Charay, *Vie du maréchal Jean-Baptiste d'Ornano*, pp. 114–15, n. 10, 147; B.N., imprimés Lb36, *Seconde partie et responce*, p. 20; *Recueil, Le Comtadin Provençal*, p. 98; J.L. Prompsault, *Histoire de Modène* (Carpentras, 1883), pp. 34–6. Modène also received revenues from the comté de Castres. Batiffol, *Le Roi Louis XIII*, p. 496, n. 2.

102 Charay, *Vie du maréchal Jean-Baptiste d'Ornano*, pp. 158–60, 171–4, his marriage contract and will; idem, *Vie du maréchal Alphonse d'Ornano* (Aubenas-in-Vivarais, 1971), p. 192; Etienne Algay de Martignac, *Mémoires du Gaston d'Orléans*, ed. Petitot, 2nd ser., vol. 31 (Paris, 1824), pp. 46–9; *Journal d'Arnauld 1614–1620*, pp. 319–20, 351–2, 385–6, 399–400, 450–51; Beaucaire, *Mémoires de Richelieu*, III, 122 and n. 1; Anselme, *Histoire généalogique*, VII, 391–3; *Mercure françois* X (1623–5), 471; Pavie, *La Guerre*, p. 579; Georges Dethan, *La Vie de Gaston d'Orléans* (Paris, 1992), pp. 42–5, 53–62.

103 B. Avignon, ms. 3421, fols. 184–5, 270; B. Inguimbertine, Carpentras, ms. 1847, fols. 25–56; Pithon-Curt, *Histoire de la noblesse*, III, 109, 112; René Borricand, *Nobiliaire de Provence*, 3 vols. (Aix, 1974–6), II, 1040; Anselme, *Histoire généalogique*, IV, 266.

104 A.N., M.C. VII 9, May 31, 1620; *Journal d'Arnauld 1614–1620*, pp. 399–400; *Journal de Arnauld 1620*, pp. 17, 19; Héroard, *Journal*, II, 2692; Fontenay-Mareuil, *Mémoires*, I, 469; Charay, *Vie du Jean-Baptiste d'Ornano*, pp. 14–15; Pithon-Curt, *Histoire de la noblesse*, III, 14–15, IV, 169; Anselme, *Histoire généalogique*, IV, 291–3, VII, 392; Labatut, *Les Ducs et pairs*, p. 251; Humbert, *Le Maréchal de Créquy*, pp. 77–8.

105 Beaucaire, *Mémoires de Richelieu*, III, 89–90 and n. 1; Bassompierre, *Mémoires*, III, 122–3 and n. 1; *Journal d'Arnauld 1620*, pp. 41–2, 58; Gédéon Tallemant des Réaux, *Historiettes*, ed. Antoine Adam, 2 vols. (Paris, 1960–61), I, 304; Bonneveau-Avenant, *La Duchesse d'Aiguillon*, pp. 79–99, marriage contract pp. 86–8.

106 A.N., M.C. VII 11, fols. 1–7, March 22, 1622; Pontchartrain, *Mémoires*, pp. 400–1; *Journal d'Arnauld 1614–1620*, p. 390; Griselle, *Etat de la maison du Roi*, p. 89; Pithon-Curt, *Histoire de la noblesse*, IV, 169; Anselme, *Histoire généalogique*, IV, 266.

107 Pithon-Curt, *Histoire de la noblesse*, IV, 169; Juigné de Lassigny, *Histoire de la maison de Villeneuve*, I, 138, 232–3; Eugène Griselle, *Maisons de la Grande Mademoiselle et de Gaston d'Orléans* (Paris, 1912), p. 8; *Les Bouches-du-Rhône. Encyclopédie départementale*, ed. Paul Masson, 17 vols. (Paris, 1913–37), IV, 497–502; Kettering, *Judicial Politics*, p. 209; Claude-Alain Sarre, *Vire sa soumission* (Paris, 1997), pp. 85–7.

108 *Journal d'Arnauld 1614–1620*, p. 353, n. 1; *Journal d'Arnauld 1620*, pp. 59–60; Anselme, *Histoire généalogique*, IV, 61, 64.

109 Luynes's two brothers and his brother-in-law Du Vernet were ordinary gentlemen of the king's bedchamber. His brother Chaulnes was captain of the king's one hundred men at arms, while his brother Luxembourg was a captain in the regiment of royal guards, then captain of the king's light horse. Luynes's first cousin Modène was *grand prévôt*, and his father-in-law Montbazon was *grand veneur*. His cousin Ornano was Gaston d'Orléans's governor, while one

of Ornano's brothers was Gaston's master of hunt, and the other was master of his wardrobe. Modène's son was a page, then a chamberlain in Gaston's household, while Luynes's brother-in-law, Villeneuve, was first *maître d'hôtel*.

110 The duc de Bellegarde, *Grand Ecuyer*, and Liancourt father and son, *Premier Ecuyer*, were political allies. Luynes's client, Jean de Varigniez, sieur de Blainville, became master of the king's wardrobe in 1620, and first gentleman of his bedchamber in 1622. Arnoux, the Jesuit confessor of Luynes and the king, was replaced in 1621 by Séguiran, another Jesuit appointee. Charles-Hercules de Crevant, marquis d'Humières, became a first gentleman of the king's bedchamber. Antoine de Buade, baron de Paluau, succeeded his father as *premier maître d'hôtel* of the king's household. Esprit d'Alart, sieur d'Esplan, was *grand maréchal des logis* of the king's household and governor of Meulan. Sauveterre was first valet of the king's wardrobe. Marcillac was an ordinary gentleman of the king's bedchamber. Bassompierre was colonel of the Swiss guards, and Tronson was a royal secretary. Luynes's former patron, François de Daillon, comte Du Lude, was Gaston d'Orléans's governor, first gentleman of his bedchamber, and superintendent of his household. Luynes's old friend, André Contades, was Gaston's under governor, and an ordinary gentleman of the royal stables, councillor of state, knight of Saint Michel, and governor of the city and fortress of Angoulême. Luynes's other clients in Gaston's household included his appointments secretary and first *valet de chambre*. Griselle, *Etat de la maison du Roi*, pp. 3, 10–12, 26, 46, 327; idem, *Maison de Gaston d'Orléans*, p. 2; *Mercure françois*, XII (1626), 374; Anselme, *Histoire généalogique*, VIII, 507, V, 768; Tallemant des Réaux, *Historiettes*, I, 845, n. 2; *Journal d'Arnauld 1620*, p. 16; *Journal d'Arnauld 1621*, p. 13; Bassompierre, *Mémoires*, II, 289, n. 2; Rohan, *Mémoires*, p. 511; Batiffol, *Le Roi Louis XIII*, p. 496; Charay, *Vie du maréchal Jean-Baptiste d'Ornano*, pp. 61, n. 48, 63.

111 Luynes's wife was the queen's household superintendent and first lady of honor. His sister, Antoinette du Vernet, was her mistress of robes. His nieces Dianne du Vernet and Anne du Roure de Combalet, and his inamorata Claude de Mailly de Clinchamps, were maids of honor. The wives of his clients Mauny, Contades, and Marcillac, with the latter's daughter, became ladies and maids of honor. Eléonore Du Buisson and Mademoiselle de Chassans, kin of clients, were chamber ladies. The marquis de Mauny was the queen's master of horse, while Marcillac was a gentleman of her stables, and the abbé Ruccellai a member of her *cabinet*. Griselle, *Etat de la maison du Roi*, pp. 89–90, 93–4, 103, 228, 323, 327–8; Eugène Halphen, ed., *Journal inédit d'Arnauld d'Andilly 1622* (Paris, 1898), pp. 16–17.

112 Fontenay-Mareuil, *Mémoires*, I, 386.

113 *Recueil, Le Comtadin Provençal*, p. 100; Fontenay-Mareuil, *Mémoires*, I, 392, 425; *Journal d'Arnauld 1614–1620*, pp. 352 and n. 1; 361, 377, 437; Pavie, *La Guerre*, pp. 36–41; Sophie de Laverny, *Les Domestiques commensaux du roi de France au XVIIe siècle* (Paris, 2002), pp. 75–83; Le Roux, *La Faveur du roi*, pp. 127, 208, n. 1, 479, 498, n. 5; Griselle, *Etat de la maison du Roi*, pp. 28, 67–8, 105; Roland Mousnier, *L'Homme rouge ou la vie du Cardinal de Richelieu* (Paris, 1992), p. 160.

114 Duindam, *Vienna and Versailles*, pp. 111–12, 118–20; Berthold Zeller, *Richelieu et les ministres de Louis XIII de 1621 à 1624* (Paris, 1880), p. 226; *Mercure françois*, XII (1626), 375.

115 *Journal d'Arnaud 1614–1620*, pp. 312, 348, 382, 389, 446; Pontchartrain, *Mémoires*, pp. 394, 401; Fontenay-Mareuil, *Mémoires*, pp. 385–6; Kleinman, *Anne of Austria*, pp. 70–85, 96–101; idem, "Social Dynamics at the French Court: The Household of Anne of Austria," *Fr Hist Stud* 16 (1990), 520; Wendy Gibson, *Women in Seventeenth-Century France* (New York, 1989), p. 150.

116 *Recueil, Manifeste de la Royne Mère envoyé au Roy* (1620), p. 264.

117 Beaucaire, *Mémoires de Richelieu*, III, 11. "Les gouvernements et les places … il n'y en a aucune qu'ils ne marchandent, qu'aux dépens du Roi ils ne mettent au double prix de sa valeur … jusqu'au nombre de dix-huit les plus importantes. Ils y entretiennent, en pleine paix, de très fortes garnisons, en redoublent les arsenaux … Ils se fortifient de gens de guerre entretenus dans la cour, tiennent le régiment de Normandie, commandé par le sieur de Chaulnes et créé en sa faveur sur pied dans le Bois-de-Vincennes, acquierent le plus de compagnies qu'ils

peuvent dans le régiment des Gardes, achètent la compagnie des chevau-légers du Roi et, au nom du sieur de Brantes, marchandent la compagnie de ses gens d'armes."

118 Luynes held the fortress governorships of Amboise, Quillebeuf, Bastille, Louvre, and Tuileries. His father-in-law held those of Nantes, Noyon, Chauny, Coucy, and Soissons. His brother Chaulnes was acting governor of Vincennes and governor of Amiens. His brother Luxembourg was governor of the Bastille and Blaye. His brother-in-law Du Vernet was lieutenant of the Bastille and Vincennes. His cousin Rodulf de Saint Jean was a lieutenant of the Bastille. His cousin Modène was a governor of Fougère and Concarneau, and his cousin Ornano was governor of Pont de l'Arche.

119 Contades was governor of Angoulême; Desplan of Meulan; Paluau of Saint-German-en-Laye; d'Humières of Ham and Compiègne; Charles, sieur de Rambures, of Doulens and Crotoy, plus being camp marshal and camp master in the royal regiment bearing his name. Jacques d'Estampes, sieur de Valençay, governor of Calais, had been *grand maréchal des logis* in the king's household. Eustache de Conflans, vicomte d'Ouchy, IV, was governor of Saint Quentin and an army lieutenant general. René du Bec, marquis de Vardes, was governor of La Capelle in Picardy. Most of these fortresses were in Picardy, Luynes's government. Charles Le Normand, sieur de Beaumont, an army camp master, was governor of La Fère. He replaced the baron de Paluau as *premier maître d'hôtel* of the king's household. Louis de La Marck, marquis de Mauny, was governor of Caen. Marcillac, a 1617 conspirator, became governor of Sommières. The older brother of Blainville, who was a lieutenant in the Caen *baillage* court and master of the king's wardrobe, became governor of Libourne. Luynes's client de La Chesnaye became governor of Royan. The government of Montreuil in the Pas-de-Calais went to Luynes's client Migneux. Anselme, *Histoire généalogique*, II, 87; VI, 149; VII, 550; VIII, 68; IX, 124, 141, 144, 150, 151, 155; Griselle, *Etat de la maison du Roi*, pp. 12, 146; Beaucaire, *Mémoires de Richelieu*, III, 191, n. 3; Bassompierre, *Mémoires*, II, 285 and n. 1; *Journal d'Arnauld 1614–1620*, pp. 308, n. 2, 424 and n. 2; *Mercure françois*, VI (1620), 316, 346, XII (1621), 375; David Buisseret, *Henry IV* (London, 1984), p. 92; Fontenay-Mareuil, *Mémoires*, p. 529; Pavie, *La Guerre*, pp. 100, 209.

120 Bergin, *Making of the French Episcopate*, p. 444.

121 *Recueil, Le Comtadin Provençal*, pp. 89–85, 106–7, "Méditations de l'hermite Valérien, pp. 318–23, 327–8, *La Chronique des Favoris*, p. 475; B.N., imprimés Lb 36, *Seconde partie et responce*, p. 27; *Journal d'Arnauld 1614–1620*, p. 319; François de Malherbe, *Oeuvres*, ed. Antoine Adam (Paris, 1971), p. 1055, n. 2; Bergin, *Making of the French Episcopate*, pp. 572–3, 615.

6

Luynes and the court nobility

The château of Blois stands on a hillside on the north bank of the Loire not far from Amboise. Around midnight on the night of 21–22 February 1619, a man could be seen climbing a ladder to one of the château's terraces, and then a second ladder to a window far above on which he knocked and entered. A short while later, he reemerged from this window and began to descend the ladder, followed by a stout middle-aged woman with a heavy box in her arms, and four men and a woman. Soon, they were all standing on the terrace more than sixty feet below the window.

To reach the street, they had planned a second descent by ladder, but the stout woman declared that she was too tired to go farther. So, her companions used a cloak to half-lower, half-slide her down the embankment, and then came down the ladder themselves. When they were all standing in the street below, two of the men linked arms with the stout lady, and they walked together down the street. An officer of the city guard mistook her for a whore because she was walking between two men without a torch and called out to her, and she joked about this with her companions. Reaching the bridge over the river, they were dismayed to find that the coach they had been expecting was not there, but discovered it hidden in a little lane off to the side. Hurrying to it, the two ladies and two of the men got in, and the other men mounted horses to ride alongside. The coach lumbered off down the road toward the château of Loches where the duc d'Epernon was waiting for them. Suddenly, the coach stopped. The stout lady had left her box behind on the ground, and someone had to go back to get it. Torches were lit when the coach was well outside the town. In this way Marie de Médicis escaped from Blois, clutching a fortune in jewelry.[1] Her famous exploit has been recounted many times.[2] Why did she escape?

The Queen Mother enjoyed the same income and lifestyle at Blois as she had in the Louvre, but she was in disgrace far from the court and Paris, and she felt snubbed and ignored. The final straw was not being invited to return to court to attend her daughter Christine's wedding. She was bored,

and she missed being regent, although her interest in the routine of government was limited, and she could be erratic, vain, and stubborn.[3] She hated
being confined to Blois, and considered herself the victim of Luynes and his
brothers, malicious enemies who had become the king's trusted advisers. In
letters to her son on 23 February, 10 March, 4 and 11 April 1619, published
in the *Mercure françois* and later as pamphlets, she declared that she had escaped
because she felt oppressed and dishonored as a captive. She worried that she
might be even more narrowly confined, and declared that she feared for her life.
A year later, she insisted that fear for her safety was the reason she would not
return to court, alluding to Concini's murder. She declared that the king had
been listening to evil advisers, the "Luynards," and mismanaging the country,
which would be plunged into civil war if he persisted. She had escaped to warn
him, and to assist him in governing as she told several of his ministers in letters
also published as pamphlets.[4] The king's reaction to her announcement can be
imagined. He was extremely irritated.

Louis was hunting at Saint-Germain-en-Laye when he heard the news,
and he left immediately for Paris where he called a council meeting to decide
what to do. In letters to his mother in March and April, which were published,
he said that he held her in high esteem, but that she was surrounded by evil
advisers to whom she had mistakenly listened. He strongly defended Luynes,
and accused the duc d'Epernon of kidnapping her, a tactic which absolved her
of voluntary participation and opened the door to negotiations. He deplored
her ill-judged conduct, which he said dishonored them both and would cause a
civil war, and he said that when she complained about the government's actions,
she complained about him. He announced that he was coming to visit her,
which sounded more like a threat than a promise.[5]

Richelieu considered Luynes to be the implacable enemy of the Queen
Mother, and blamed him for her quarrel with her son. He wrote in his memoirs
that because the reconciliation of mother and son threatened his interests, Luynes
kept them apart. He refused to be reconciled with her himself, or to allow her
reconciliation with her son, and he blocked her return to court because he
feared her influence on the king.[6] Richelieu wrote that "the Queen Mother,
dispirited by her bad treatment, suffered it patiently because of the disorders
in the state and the widespread grievances in France ... she feared for the king
and was distressed at the plight of the kingdom ... she wondered if she should
go to Paris, if she would be safe there ... but she decided that she could not
go there without danger."[7] Accepting Richelieu's account based on that of the
Queen Mother, Gabriel Hanotaux, Georges Pagès, and Richard Bonney have
blamed Luynes's ambition and greed for the quarrel between mother and son
causing the civil war of 1619–20.[8] Rejecting this explanation, Louis Batiffol and
A. Lloyd Moote have insisted that Luynes did not mistreat the Queen Mother.

Figure 5 Portrait of the Queen Mother, Marie de Médicis, by Thomas de Leu.

He was not vindictive toward her, and he did not turn the king against her. The king himself distrusted his mother, and did not want her in his government.[9] Which interpretation is correct?

The Queen Mother left Epernon's château of Loches after a few days for his more secure, fortified château of Angoulême, thereby presenting the king and Luynes with a dilemma. Neither of them wanted her back at court, sitting on the royal council and meddling in political affairs, which was what she wanted, but they did not want her stirring up trouble in Angoulême either. What was to be done with her? The king decided to raise troops and march on Angoulême to confront Epernon and recapture his mother, specifically an army in Champagne under the duc de Guise, one in Guyenne under the duc de Mayenne, another in the Limousin under Henri de Schomberg, comte de Nanteuil, and one in Poitou-Saintonge under his own command. At the same time, he sent Philippe de Béthune, comte de Selles, and Cardinal de La Rochefoucauld to Angoulême to try to negotiate a reconciliation with her.

The court nobility did not know whom to support. They had been loyal to the Queen Mother as regent, but she had favored Concini whom they hated, and she appeared weak and easily influenced by her champion, the volatile, belligerent Epernon. Their lawful monarch was the young king, who had gotten rid of Concini and restored his father's ministers to office with Luynes's help. Luynes was the unpopular new favorite, but at least he was French, not Italian. The court nobility hesitated because they knew that backing the loser could end their court careers, as it had done for Honoré d'Albert. To remain the favorite, Luynes needed to secure their support and the Queen Mother's acceptance, or at least her neutrality. This chapter discusses how he did so.

Marie de Médicis signed the Treaty of Angoulême in late April 1619, agreeing to exchange her government of Normandy for that of Anjou, which was less important and farther away from Paris. She received the fortress governorships of Angers, Ponts-de-Cé, and Chinon on the Loire, although she had wanted either Nantes or Amboise as well. Montbazon held the first and Luynes the second, so she got neither. She was given the fortress garrisons, her own guard company, two companies of gendarmes, and two light horse companies for her protection, although she wanted more troops. She was to have complete control over her household. She was allowed to come and go freely, and the sieur de Roissy's cavalry companies were withdrawn. Her income and lifestyle remained the same, her debts were paid, and her supporters were not punished. The king invited her to return to court with the understanding that she would not participate in politics, but she would not commit herself on this.

The treaty's generous terms were ratified when the king met his mother at Montbazon's château of Couzières near Tours on 5 September 1619. Luynes had been reconciled with her on the previous day, having sworn loyalty to her on his knees. She made a lavish ceremonial entry into Angers as its new governor in mid-October at the crown's expense.[10] She still wanted Luynes's dismissal, however, and a seat on the royal council before she would agree to return to court, thus ending the threat of civil war. The king did not want her in his government, but he wanted her back at court where he could keep an eye on her. Mother and son were at an impasse.

Marie's discontent grew during the next few months. In October 1619, the prince de Condé was released from prison. She had ordered his arrest three years earlier, but she had not been consulted about his release. The king issued a declaration in November apologizing for Condé's imprisonment, and she bitterly protested this indirect attack upon her regency to no avail. In December, Luynes's cousin and client Ornano was sworn in as Gaston's governor, replacing her client the comte de Breves without her consent. At the end of the month, Luynes's brother Chaulnes was sent on an ambassadorial mission to England to discuss the marriage between her youngest daughter, Henriette Marie, and the Prince of Wales. She had not been consulted about this mission either, although the marriage, which she did not favor, had been under discussion off and on since 1612. Finally, only two of her candidates were received into the Order of Saint Esprit, fewer even than Condé had. She felt slighted and ignored.

The king was annoyed because she remained at Angers, stubbornly refusing to return to court despite his letters urging her to do so. Now she went public, publishing pamphlets defending her conduct, just as she had earlier published her letters to him justifying her escape from Blois.[11] She was widely regarded as the mistreated victim of Luynes, who again served as a lightning rod to deflect criticism from the king. Court nobles began to support her because they were disillusioned with the way in which Luynes was distributing patronage, and they helped her to raise money and levy troops. She wrote letters to foreign monarchs explaining her conduct, which were published as pamphlets, and she began talks with the Protestants, whose stronghold was in the southwest near Angoulême. She ignored the envoys whom Luynes and the king sent requesting her return to Paris.[12] A military confrontation seemed likely.

By June 1620, the Queen Mother had secured two million livres with which to buy munitions and pay troops. Her great noble supporters included the Vendôme brothers, the prince de Conti, the comte de Soissons, the ducs de Longueville, Rohan, Mayenne, Nemours, Retz, Bouillon, Châtillon, Roannez, La Trémoille-Thouars, La Force, Montmorency, Epernon and his three sons, Cardinal Guise, the maréchaux de Boisdauphin and Roquelaure, and the comtes de Saint Paul, Saint Aignan, d'Aubeterre, and La Suze. Through their governments and clienteles, they were able to incite rebellion in Anjou, Maine, Aunis, Saintonge, Poitou, the Limousin, Angoumois, Brittany, the Vendomois,

Normandy, Burgundy, Champagne, Languedoc, and Béarn. This was most of
the Loire valley, the west and southwest, and large areas north and east of
Paris, a huge sweep of territory making the Queen Mother a dangerous foe in
the spring and summer of 1619.[13] She also published pamphlets accusing the
king of ignoring the traditional governing class, mistreating her, and promoting
those who were unworthy such as Luynes and his brothers.[14]

In June 1620, a rebellion erupted in Normandy provoked by the Queen
Mother's supporters, the king's cousin, the duc de Longueville, who was provincial governor, and the grand prior de Vendôme, the king's half-brother, who was
governor of Caen. The king took a royal army of 9,000 into that province in July
to confront the rebels. He entered Rouen without resistance on 10 July, and
named his brother Gaston provincial governor, and Luynes's cousin Ornano
governor of Rouen. With Luynes and Condé beside him, he rode into Caen
on 15 July, and named Luynes's client Mauny as its governor. Since Ornano
was lieutenant general of upper and Montbazon of lower Normandy, Luynes's
clients filled the key offices in the new provincial government.[15]

The king turned south in late July, and with 16,000 foot soldiers and
1,500 horse, he marched toward the Loire. By 4 August, he was a league away
from La Flèche, which surrendered without a fight. He then marched toward
Angers to attack his mother's army of 8,000 infantry and 1,200 cavalry. The
two armies met on 7 August at Ponts-de-Cé, a village of one street on the tip
of an island in the Loire facing Angers. Outnumbered two to one, the Queen
Mother's forces turned and ran.[16] A week later on 13 August, the king, his
brother, Condé, and Luynes met the Queen Mother at the château of Brissac
across the river from Angers to discuss terms for the Treaty of Ponts-de-Cé,
also known as the Treaty of Angers. She was declared innocent of treason, and
given 300,000 livres to pay her military expenses. There was a general amnesty
for her supporters who would not lose their freedom, offices, or pensions,
and the Treaty of Angoulême remained in effect.[17] The terms were generous,
but the Queen Mother still refused to return to court. She finally returned in
January 1621, and began attending council meetings a year later on 31 January
1622, six weeks after Luynes's death.[18]

The second view of Luynes's behavior, therefore, appears to be the
correct one. Luynes did not turn the king against his mother. The king himself
took the initiative in using force against her, and he was the moving spirit in
the 1620 campaign, acting against Luynes's advice when he invaded Normandy.
This chapter argues that Luynes and the king tried hard to convince the Queen
Mother to return to court so they could keep an eye on her. It may not have
been a genuine reconciliation, but she was in no physical danger. She stubbornly
refused to return, however, because she blamed Luynes for her exile and the
deaths of her favorites, and she wanted him disgraced and punished. Luynes's

survival depended upon neutralizing her and securing the acceptance of the court nobility. So, with the king's help, he created a court party to counteract her influence, and France slipped into civil war.

Luynes's court party

During 1619 and 1620, Luynes successfully recruited thirty-seven court nobles sympathetic to the new regime to form a party opposing that of the Queen Mother. Contemporaries described such groups as parties, so that term has been used here, although the group was really a faction, not a party, because it lacked self-recognition, a stable permanent membership, an internal hierarchical organization, and a common political ideology beyond support for the new regime.[19] Factional alliances were fluid and ever-changing, and their unstable membership was based on self-interest and personal ties, although members could share common ideological beliefs as well.[20]

Luynes's supporters included both allies and clients. Allies had a horizontal, equal relationship with a patron because they already had wealth, status, and power which they were seeking to augment by serving him. Luynses's court party was an alliance of equals. The allies in his court party significantly outnumbered his clients, who were dependent upon him for their position in a vertical, unequal relationship. Luynes used his patronage power to advance his kin and create a large noble clientele until February 1619, after which he used it to create a court party whose members were recruited for their political usefulness.

Luynes's court party included his kin, in-laws, clients, former patrons, and their kin. It included court nobles who had a personal relationship with the king, such as his relatives, favorites, and friends, many of whom had danced in his ballets, and it included nobles who were the friends and clients of other party members such as the prince de Condé. It also included disgruntled former supporters and enemies of the Queen Mother. Most were young, ambitious, and eager to make a name for themselves, and they were attracted by the promise of patronage and advancement. They were a diverse group bearing some of the most illustrious names in France. Now, who were they?

Luynes's brothers Chaulnes and Luxembourg, and his cousins Modène and Ornano were members. All but Ornano received seats on the royal council. Chaulnes raised 4,000 troops for the Picardy regiment that fought under his command against the Queen Mother, while Modène acted as a camp master under Condé, who commanded the royal army in Anjou. Ornano fought in Normandy, and Luxembourg was sent as an envoy to the Queen Mother. Luynes's in-laws also belonged to his court party, including his father-in-law, the duc de Montbazon; his brother-in-law, the comte de Rochefort; and his uncle-by-marriage, the marquis de Marigny. Rochefort and Luxembourg had danced in the king's ballets. Rochefort was taken prisoner in Nantes by the Queen Mother's forces in July 1620, while his father, Montbazon, the city's governor, was away levying troops for the king in the Ile-de-France. Chaulnes, Ornano, Rochefort, and Marigny became knights of Saint Esprit.[21] Montbazon had been a member for years.

Luynes's former patrons, now allies, and their dependents were also members of his court party. They included the *Grand Ecuyer*, Roger de Saint Lary de Bellegarde, and his younger brother, César-Auguste, baron de Termes, who were both knights of Saint Esprit. Termes was killed at the siege of Clairac two years later, while Bellegarde was named a duke in 1619, and given a seat on the royal council. Luynes's allies included Henri de Schomberg, whose sister Jeanne had married François de Daillon, comte Du Lude, in whose household Luynes had served as an ordinary gentleman. Schomberg led a royal army against the Queen Mother in the spring of 1619. He was named superintendent of finance and grand master of artillery that autumn, and received as a knight of Saint Esprit in December. His son Charles had been an *enfant d'honneur* or childhood playmate of the king, who transferred the title of Charles's new wife, Anne, duchesse d'Hallwin, to him and added that of a peer. The comte Du Lude was named governor of the king's brother, an office exercised by his son, Timoléon, after he became ill. When Du Lude died in September 1619, his son retired from court to live quietly in the country.[22]

Luynes's former patrons included the *Premier Ecuyer*, Charles du Plessis de Liancourt, who died in October 1620, and was succeeded in office by his son Roger, a childhood playmate of the king and a favorite who had danced in his ballets. Roger married Henri de Schomberg's daughter. His half-brother, François de Silly, comte de La Rocheguyon, was the go-between who had arranged Luynes's marriage, and he had also danced in the king's ballets. A member of the king's household, La Rocheguyon was named a knight of Saint Esprit in 1619 and a duke in 1621. Madame de Guercheville, the Queen Mother's first lady of honor, was the mother of both Liancourt and La Rocheguyon by different husbands, but she was in Angers, and they were at court eager to advance their careers. François V, comte de La Rochefoucauld, was another favorite of the king, his household official, and a knight of Saint Esprit. He had given up a coveted ambassadorial mission to Spain in 1616 to dance in a royal ballet. In June 1620, he raised 3,000 foot soldiers for the royal army, and two years later became a duke and the governor of Poitou. La Rochefoucauld had married the daughter of Charles du Plessis de Liancourt, so he was Roger's brother-in-law, and his younger brother, the baron d'Estissac, also supported Luynes and the king.[23]

Great nobles with large clienteles, provincial governors with troops under their command, and experienced soldiers willing to fight for the king were the most desirable allies. Henri II de Bourbon, prince de Condé, the king's cousin and second in line for the throne, was an important new ally. He commanded the royal army at the battle of Ponts-de-Cé in August 1620. Condé had led the noble revolt against Concini until he was imprisoned by the Queen Mother in September 1616. Luynes secured his release three years later, and drove him in his own carriage to Chantilly to meet the king, who gave him the government of Berry and a seat on the royal council. Luynes had a talent for turning potential enemies into friends. It was suggested that Condé's widowed sister, the princesse d'Orange, marry Luynes's brother, but she died in January 1619. Condé attended the ducal receptions of Luynes and his brothers, and Luynes's reception as constable, while Luynes and the queen served as godparents of Condé's baby daughter, baptized in the Louvre on 20 June 1620.[24] Condé had enormous personal prestige, and he became Luynes's ally against their common enemy, the Queen Mother.

Charles de Lorraine, duc de Guise and governor of Provence with a large clientele, was Condé's close friend and joined him in supporting Luynes. He led a royal army against the Queen Mother in 1619, and was given a seat on the royal council as a reward. His eldest son, François, was to marry Condé's baby daughter by a contract signed in February 1620, but the marriage never took place. Guise's infant son was to marry Luynes's baby daughter by a marriage contract signed in January 1620, but that marriage never took place either. Guise's younger brother, Claude de Lorraine, prince de Joinville and duc de Chevreuse, a dancer in the king's ballets, joined his brother in supporting Luynes. He married Luynes's widow in 1622, and received his offices of grand falconer and first gentleman of the king's bedchamber. His cousin, Charles II de Lorraine, duc d'Elbeuf, also supported Luynes. Elbeuf was the king's brother-in-law, having married his natural half-sister in 1619, and he became military commander of Normandy and captain of a cavalry company. Guise, Chevreuse, and Elbeuf were members of the order of Saint Esprit, and witnesses to the May 1620 marriage contract between Anne du Roure, Luynes's niece, and Charles de Céquy, comte de Canaples, Lesdiguières's grandson. The other witnesses included Luynes's wife, his two brothers, his cousin Ornano, his patron Belle-garde, and his ally Condé and his wife.[25] The Rohan-Condé-Lorraine connection elevated Luynes's status at court.

Luynes had arranged the marriage of his niece, Anne du Roure, to Charles, comte de Canaples, in the hope of persuading Charles's grandfather, the duc de Lesdiguières, to join the party opposing the Queen Mother. Lesdiguières, governor of the Dauphiné and a marshal of France, had an excellent military reputation and a large clientele. He was sworn in as a duke in February 1620, and his grandson married Luynes's niece that June. Canaples inherited his father's office of camp master in the royal guards regiment. Later his own father, Charles de Blanchefort de Créquy, Lesdiguières's son-in-law, would inherit his title of duke. Créquy had wanted to become a duke in his own right, but the Queen Mother had opposed it. Créquy was a good friend of Condé, and he joined Luynes's court party, becoming a knight of Saint Esprit in 1619 and a marshal in 1621. He led the royal army that marched into Caen in July 1620, then rode south with Condé to Anjou. His son Canaples commanded a royal guards regiment at the battle of Ponts-de-Cé, and became a camp master in the Normandy regiment. Lesdiguières hoped to be named constable, but he was a Protestant, so the office went to Luynes. After his death, Lesdiguières abjured and became constable.[26]

Nicolas de Neufville, marquis d'Alincourt, who had recently married Canaples's sister Madeleine, joined his brother-in-law in supporting Luynes and the king. His father, Charles de Neufville, marquis de Villeroy, was governor of Lyon and the Lyonnais where he had a large clientele, and he was a good friend of Lesdiguières. Alincourt would inherit his father's offices. One of Alincourt's sisters married Pierre Brûlart, vicomte de Puysieux, secretary of state, and the other married Jean II de Souvré, marquis de Courtenvaux, a favorite of the king and a childhood playmate. Courtenvaux raised troops in the Touraine for the royal army in the summer of 1620, and accompanied Chaulnes on his ambassadorial mission to England the following January. He, his father, and his brother were the only courtiers to attend Luynes's funeral.[27]

Other witnesses to the Canaples-Du Roure marriage contract included Henri de Gondi, cardinal de Retz; Charles de Choiseul, marquis de Praslin; and François, marquis de Bassompierre. All three participated in the 1620 campaign. Retz was bishop of Paris, master of the king's oratory, and president of the royal council. He convinced his nephew to switch sides, and the duc de Retz went over to the king with 1,500 infantry just before the battle of Ponts-de-Cé. Praslin, lieutenant general of Champagne, was an old soldier who had fought for Henri IV, and then in 1620 for his son under Condé's command. His own son had been a childhood playmate of the king. Named a marshal of France in October 1619, Praslin attended Luynes's ducal reception that November.[28]

François de Bassompierre was an ambitious favorite who danced in the king's ballets. Concealing his dislike and jealousy of Luynes, he accompanied him to Couzières in September 1619, Compiègne in October, and his ducal reception in November. Having successfully solicited Luynes's patronage, Bassompierre received a gift of 10,000 livres, and was named colonel of the king's Swiss guards in October 1619, and a knight of Saint Esprit that December. He was a good friend of Schomberg and Créquy, and he had served with Créquy as a camp master in the royal army in Champagne under Guise's command in the spring of 1619. Bassompierre was given command of this army in 1620, and marched with it to Anjou where he served as a camp master under Condé. He commanded the Swiss guards at the surrender of La Flèche in August. Bassompierre, Créquy, Praslin, and Schomberg accompanied Luynes to his reconciliation with the Queen Mother at Couzières, while Bassompierre and Praslin escorted the Queen Mother to meet the king at Brissac. Luynes would suggest that Bassompierre marry his niece, although nothing came of it.[29]

Charles de Gonzague, duc de Nevers, and Charles de Cossé, duc de Brissac, also joined Luynes's court party. Nevers, a friend of Condé, was the governor of Champagne where he had a large clientele, and he was given a seat on the royal council. His son commanded an infantry regiment in the army of Champagne, and marched with it to Anjou in 1620. Nevers supported Luynes and the king because he wanted their help in winning his claim to the duchy of Mantua against the Medici, and in creating a Christian militia with which to reconquer the eastern Mediterranean. Luynes gave him 100,000 livres for this project. The Queen Mother had promised him 1,200,000 livres, but had never given him the money. Luynes probably hoped that Nevers would influence his brother-in-law, the duc de Mayenne, to change sides. Nevers had been married to Mayenne's sister, Catherine, who had died in March 1618. Luynes may have also hoped, futilely, that Mayenne's cousins, Guise, Chevreuse, and Elbeuf, would persuade him to switch sides.[30]

Luynes obtained the support of Charles de Cossé, comte de Brissac, by having the Parlement of Paris register the royal letters elevating his title to that of duke in July 1620. These letters had been issued in 1611, but their registration had been blocked by the Queen Mother. Brissac, lieutenant general of Brittany, now became the acting provincial governor, replacing César de Vendôme who supported the Queen Mother. Brissac's son fought with the royal army in Anjou. The treaty of Ponts-de-Cé was signed at his château, and the king in gratitude gave him a cash gift to refurbish it.[31]

Luynes also secured the support of three disgruntled members of the Queen Mother's party, the abbé Ruccellai, Louis de La Marck, marquis de Mauny, and Antoine de Lauzière, marquis de Thémines. Ruccellai was driven from the Queen Mother's household by Richelieu. Mauny was a close friend of Ruccellai, and he became angry when Richelieu's older brother was given the governorship of Angers that he had wanted, so he left, too. The marquis de Thémines, who was captain of the Queen Mother's guards and another friend of Ruccellai, had to leave after he killed Richelieu's older brother in a duel on 8 July 1619. The three arrived at court in mid-July and became Luynes's clients. Mauny was named a knight of Saint Esprit, received the government of Caen in July 1620, and an office in the queen's household. Ruccellai had acquired the abbey of Signe in Champagne from Concini, and Luynes now secured an

Figure 6 Political Parties in 1620.

abbey confiscated from the duc de Rohan for him, and he unsuccessfully tried to secure the archbishopric of Sens for him. When his father had arrested Condé on the Queen Mother's orders, Thémines had been present. Condé's enmity toward him for this reason was probably why he withdrew from court to live on his estates. Thémines levied troops in Guyenne for the royal army in 1620, and helped to seize the city of Moissac for the king. The duc de Rohan described this trio of Richelieu's enemies as "very powerful enemies of the Queen Mother."[32] They all joined Luynes's court party.

Luynes tried to recruit supporters from among the opposition. In March 1619, he recalled Richelieu from exile to rejoin the Queen Mother's household, hoping that his moderating influence would temper Epernon's belligerence. Richelieu persuaded her to sign the Treaty of Angoulême a month later. Luynes arranged the marriage of his nephew to Richelieu's niece in November 1620, and veered toward supporting his candidacy for a cardinal's hat, proposed by the king in August. Luynes had earlier sought to secure Epernon's support by offering his son a cardinal's hat, and the Vatican now chose Epernon's son. Luynes had also suggested the marriage of his niece to Epernon's second son, the marquis de La Valette, but his proposal was rejected. An earlier proposal that Luynes's brother Brantes marry Epernon's niece had also been rejected. Luynes allowed Epernon to keep his government of Metz and his office of infantry colonel, but his generosity did not persuade Epernon to change sides. The duke remained firmly committed to the Queen Mother. Luynes also tried, unsuccessfully. to secure the support of the grand prior de Vendôme by giving him two lucrative abbeys.[33]

Pontchartrain observed that there was a party at court composed of the unaligned provincial governors with large clienteles, specifically Lesdiguières in the Dauphiné, Villeroy and his son Alincourt in the Lyonnais, Montmorency in Languedoc, Bellegarde in Burgundy, Roquelaure in Guyenne, and Epernon in the Angoumois, Aunis, and Saintonge.[34] Luynes secured the support of Bellegarde, Lesdiguières, and Alincourt, while the others joined the Queen Mother's party.

Therefore, Luynes could add his allies' provinces of Burgundy, the Lyonnais, and the Dauphiné to his own governments of Picardy, the Ile-de-France, the city of Paris, and Normandy, as well as Condé's government of Berry, Brissac's government of Brittany, Nevers's government of Champagne, and Guise's government of Provence. Luynes and the king controlled Tours and the Touraine in the Loire valley through Courtenvaux and his father, plus the Loire fortresses of Amboise, Brissac, Saumur, and Nantes.[35] Luynes with the king's help had created a large block of territory opposing that of the Queen Mother, and the men controlling this territory were willing to raise troops and fight for them. They included Condé; Guise, his brother Chevreuse, and his cousin Elbeuf; Lesdiguières, his son-in-law Créquy, and grandson Canaples; Brissac and his son; Nevers and his son; Bellegarde and his brother; Bassompierre; Praslin; Schomberg and his son; Montbazon and his son; Alincourt; La Rochefoucauld; Courtenvaux; Chaulnes; Luxembourg; Modène; and Ornano.

Luynes's supporters were rewarded generously with royal patronage including household, provincial, and military offices, titles, court privileges, cash gifts, and ambassadorial appointments. Chaulnes, Praslin, Créquy, and Bassompierre received marshal's batons, while Bellegarde was given 36,000 livres by the king in 1619.[36] Nine dukes were created from 1619 through 1621, and they included Luynes, Chaulnes, Luxembourg, Bellegarde, La Roche-guyon, La Rochefoucauld, Brissac, Schomberg, and Lesdiguières. Other honors included membership in the order of Saint Esprit; privileges such as the *tabouret* and royal-style weddings and baptisms; and honors of the court, which included being presented to the king and queen, riding in their carriages, attending the king's *levers* and *couchers*, being received in the royal apartments, going hunting and hawking with the king, and attending his ballets, receptions, and balls.[37]

Honors of the court provided access to the king, offering opportunities to secure patronage and exercise power, so Luynes carefully controlled their distribution. Chaulnes, Modène, Bellegarde, Schomberg, Condé, Guise, and Nevers, for example, were invited to sit on the royal council by the king, while Guise, Condé, Créquy, and Bassompierre were given army commands, and Schomberg became artillery grand master and superintendent of finance. Chaulnes and Bassompierre were made marshals and sent on ambassadorial missions to England and Spain, while Modène was sent as an extraordinary ambassador to Savoy.[38]

Distributing patronage to secure support, however, proved to be a double-edged sword because those who went empty-handed became embittered. The duc d'Epernon was furious when his son, the archbishop of Toulouse, did not receive a cardinal's hat as Luynes had suggested he might. It went instead to Cardinal de Retz, president of the royal council and a friend of Luynes. In retaliation, Epernon aided the Queen Mother's escape, which explains why Luynes secured a cardinal's hat for his son in 1620, although he disappointed Richelieu, who got his hat in September 1622.

Epernon had become angry when Luynes sided with Guillaume Du Vair, keeper of the seals, in a precedence quarrel over seating at a royal council meeting. Their quarrel exploded into violence a week later on Easter Sunday 1618 in the Paris church of Saint Germain de l'Auxerrois. Epernon as a duke insisted that he had precedence over Du Vair, a high-ranking royal official, so he pulled Du Vair from his seat in the church, marched him outside, and returned to take the seat himself. Du Vair complained to Luynes who spoke to the king, and he threatened to arrest Epernon for treason, ordering him to leave court immediately for his government of Metz. A year later in retaliation, Epernon rode to Loches to meet the Queen Mother. He was punished by having his governments of Boulogne and the Boulonnais confiscated and given to Luynes, and by having his sons refused membership in the Order of Saint Esprit.[39]

The duc de Mayenne became angry when Villars, his client, and La Ferté-Senneterre, the client of his friend Soissons, were refused membership in the Order of Saint Esprit, although both Mayenne and Soissons themselves were received. Mayenne did not want to exchange his government of the Ile-de-

France for Guyenne, but felt he could not refuse because Luynes had requested it. He had been given 150,000 livres by the king to cover his military expenses in raising an army to use against Concini, but this sum had only partially covered his costs and had not been paid in full, although he had repeatedly asked Luynes for the money. Disenchanted with the new regime, Mayenne left to join the Queen Mother at Angoulême in April 1619. He returned to court after the Couzières reconciliation, but left again to join her at Angers in March 1620.

Quarrels helped to determine party affiliation. Mayenne was a close friend of the comtesse de Soissons, who was a bitter enemy of Condé, while the Vendôme brothers supported the Queen Mother after quarrelling with both Luynes and his uncle-by-marriage Marigny. Failing to obtain patronage determined party affiliation, and drove angry resentful nobles to join the Queen Mother. Pontchartrain noted that widespread envy of Luynes also created support for the Queen Mother.[40] The king's childhood friends flocked to Luynes's support including Courtenvaux, Blainville, Humières, the younger Liancourt, and the sons of Praslin and Du Lude.[41] Court nobles joined Luynes's party for a variety of reasons, but the prospect of receiving patronage was probably the most important reason.

Manipulating factional rivalries

Luynes and the king had to control the conflict among court factions in order to govern successfully, and did so by using the classic strategy of divide-and-rule. They played off rival factions to gain the upper hand, and balanced them against each other so that no single faction became too powerful.[42] Luynes used the carrot and stick to manipulate the court nobility, offering them patronage for their cooperation, withdrawing it for their lack of cooperation, and using it to play off or co-opt his rivals and enemies. He performed the favorite's traditional function of interviewing those who wanted patronage and making recommendations to the king, and he created a court party in this way. He became a channel of communication and a buffer between the king and the court nobility. Serving as the king's spokesman, messenger, go-between, and troubleshooter, Luynes performed the boring, unpleasant tasks that the king did not want to do such as interviewing foreign ambassadors.[43]

Luynes was always looking for new supporters. In January 1617, he asked a client to find out whether Beauvais-Nangis favored him or Concini, and in February he asked another client to inquire whether Bassompierre was loyal to him. He wrote a letter on 3 November 1618 to the marquis de Nérestan(g), captain of a royal ordinance company and a former friend of Concini, soliciting his support. In May 1621, he removed the government of Laon from the maréchal d'Estrées, a friend of the Queen Mother, to give it to one of his own clients. Earlier, he had sought to reinforce Bassompierre's loyalty by offering him marriage with his niece.[44] The Venetian ambassador noted that during a dinner at Fontainebleau in May 1621, Luynes had chatted with a crowd of nobles standing behind his chair and dealt with their requests as he ate.[45] As we have seen, he used nominations to the order of Saint Esprit to reward his kin and clients. A pamphlet, *Harangue faite au Roy par la Reine Mère* (1622), warned the king about the greed and ambition of Luynes's court party, who included great nobles, ministers, and high-ranking government officials.[46]

Luynes and the king traveled down the Loire by boat in May 1621, and stopped at the fortified château of Saumur where Du Plessis-Mornay was the Huguenot governor. He had been offered 100,000 écus (300,000 livres) and a marshal's baton to relinquish his office but had refused. Luynes requested an interview, and told Du Plessis-Mornay that he was speaking on the king's behalf. He apologized for having to deliver the bad news that he was going to lose his governorship. He said, however, that the king did not intend to seize it permanently, and would never do so without his consent. Luynes added that the king no longer had confidence in his Protestant subjects, so he found it necessary to place a Catholic garrison at Saumur to safeguard travel on the Loire. The king had given its command to the Catholic comte de Sault, Lesdiguières's grandson, for the duration of the campaign against the Huguenots. Luynes swore to Du Plessis-Mornay that his governorship would be returned to him after three months, but he never got it back.[47]

Luynes often performed such unpleasant tasks for the king. In the autumn of 1618, he invited the duc de Rohan to his rooms in the Louvre, and told him that the king knew he supported the Queen Mother, but added that he had asked the king to forgive him because they were related by marriage. Luynes declared that it would be necessary for Rohan to tell him everything he knew about the Queen Mother's affairs in order to allay the king's anger. Rohan was outraged and refused to say anything, declaring that he was not a spy. In response, Luynes lost his temper and told him that he would have to leave court. The king punished Rohan by confiscating one of his abbeys, and ordering the demolition of one of his fortified châteaux. In 1622, Rohan's government of Poitou was given to La Rochefoucauld.[48]

The source of Luynes's power was his control over the distribution of royal patronage, a mixed blessing.[49] Robert Arnauld d'Andilly, for instance, was disappointed when he did not receive his uncle's office of intendant of finance after his death in October 1617. Luynes had promised him this office, but he had still not received it a year later when he asked Madame de Luynes to arrange an interview for him with her husband. Going to their rooms that evening, Arnauld made an impassioned plea to receive his uncle's office, but Luynes put him off, evidently intending to give it to someone else. Furious, Arnauld thanked Madame de Luynes for allowing him the opportunity to discover that he could expect nothing from her husband and left in a huff. Although Luynes arranged for him to be named deputy to the superintendent of finance, Arnauld never forgave him.

Arnauld saw Luynes for the last time in November 1621 at the château of Piquecos while on campaign in the southwest. Expecting to deliver a report to Schomberg, who was the superintendent of finance, he entered the room about midnight to find no one there except Luynes and Cardinal de Retz who were playing a game of *trictrac* (backgammon). Arnauld had turned to leave when Luynes said to him, "Monsieur d'Andilly, what would you say if I told you that today someone told me that you are not my friend?" Arnauld answered, "Monseigneur, how would you respond to your own question? You might say that you have made a list of your friends, and that my name is at the top of your list, while all those whom you have advanced before me are below mine on the list." Luynes was so surprised at this that he said nothing, doffing his hat so that Arnauld could not see his face. Arnauld never saw him again because soon afterward Luynes died of scarlet fever.[50] Distributing royal patronage was a double-edged sword making Luynes as many enemies as friends.

Condé's friendship proved to be another mixed blessing. Contemporaries knew that Luynes had secured Condé's release from prison in October 1619 to use him as a counterweight to the Queen Mother's influence. After Concini's murder, Condé had been transferred from the Bastille to the more agreeable château of Vincennes, and his wife had been allowed to join him. They had walked daily in the woods around the château, and the next summer Luynes's brother Cadenet became their jailor and friend. Luynes himself visited Condé in March 1619, a few weeks after the Queen Mother's escape, and Béthune had to dissuade him from releasing Condé then. He arranged Condé's release nine months later.[51]

After February 1619, Luynes sent a steady stream of personal envoys to assure the Queen Mother of his good intentions and to persuade her to return to court. They included the archbishop of Sens, Père de Bérulle, Cardinal de La Rochefoucauld, Père Suffren who was her confessor, Père Arnoux who was the confessor of Luynes and the king, Blainville who had been Concini's friend and was now Luynes's client, and Bellegarde and Montbazon who were friends of both the Queen Mother and Concini; Bellegarde was Epernon's nephew. Luynes also sent his brothers Chaulnes and Luxembourg, his cousins Modène and Ornano, and his friends Béthune, Jeannin, and Schomberg to see her. He convinced the king to be reconciled with his mother at Couzières in September 1619, and he went down on his knees himself to her at this time.[52] She still refused to return to court. On 20 October 1619, five days after her formal entry into Angers, Luynes drove in his own carriage to Vincennes to escort the newly liberated Condé and his wife to Chantilly to be reconciled with the king. A flurry of pro-Condé pamphlets celebrated this event. On 14 November as a mark of gratitude, Condé accompanied Luynes to his ducal reception in the Parlement of Paris. Luynes's entourage also included Cadenet, Praslin, Schomberg's son, Bassompierre, Créquy, Alincourt, Mauny, Montbazon, and Liancourt.[53]

Condé was arrogant, ambitious, and aggressive by nature, and he exerted a strong influence over the young king by appealing to the bellicose side of his nature. The king had always delighted in playing at war, and Condé encouraged his interest. Luynes was more cautious and conciliatory. By freeing Condé, Luynes had acquired an ally against the Queen Mother, but he had also acquired a rival for the king's favor, and there were no other princes of the blood at court to offset Condé's influence.[54] Luynes did not want to destroy the Queen Mother's influence because he hoped to use it against Condé, and he did not want to destroy Condé's influence because he hoped to use it against the Queen Mother, but he wanted to control the use of their influence, and he did not want either of them to become more powerful than he was.

The Queen Mother returned to court in January 1621. She and the king had been asked by Luynes to serve as the godparents of his infant son born at Christmas, and she could not refuse without insulting them both.[55] So, she came back to Paris, probably with secret relief. She visited Luynes's wife and new baby several times, and attended an Italian comedy in Luynes's apartments in the Louvre. She was obsequiously flattering to him, but she did not accompany Luynes and the king on their southwestern campaign in May. Instead, she visited Richelieu at his abbey of Coussay in Anjou, briefly saw the king during the siege of Saint Jean d'Angély in June, and spent the rest of the summer at Angers, returning to Paris in September. Luynes and the king reluctantly allowed her return because they thought she had been neutralized as a political force.[56]

Condé had been nullified as well. He had asked the king's permission to retire to his government of Berry on 2 October 1620 after the king had announced his intention to go on campaign in Béarn. Why Condé did so is unknown, but he may have wanted to be named commander-in-chief of the royal army, or to have greater influence in government, perhaps by acting as regent during the king's absence. He did not obtain either post. He was ambitious and tended to be impulsive, but whatever his reason, he made a mistake in leaving court.[57] Luynes reluctantly agreed to support the king's campaign against the Protestants, and was rewarded by being sworn in as constable on 2 April 1621. Condé returned to court to attend this ceremony, and immediately afterward the king announced his intention of going on campaign in the southwest, pointedly telling him that he did not have to go. Luynes had obviously been whispering in the king's ear. Condé returned to his government of Berry, and was conspicuously absent during the siege of Saint Jean d'Angély that summer, although he seized several Huguenot châteaux in the Loire valley for the king. He was again conspicuously absent during the siege of Montauban that autumn. When he learned of Luynes's death, he hurried to meet the king at Angoulême, and entered Paris at his side on 28 January 1622, resuming his seat on the royal council at this time.[58]

Historians have overlooked Luynes's creation of a court party to oppose the Queen Mother. This party included nineteen great nobles who were his allies and three nobles who his were clients,[59] seven of his relatives and in-laws,[60] and eight former patrons and their dependents.[61] Luynes had created a party of thirty-seven court nobles, many of whom were *grands* belonging to illustrious families, which is significant because the Queen Mother's supporters included some of the greatest names in France. Only Luynes's kin and clients were not great nobles. His supporters were generously rewarded. Seventeen became knights of Saint Esprit; nine received titles of duke; four received marshal's batons; seven were given seats on the royal council; four got army commands; three received provincial governments; and the rest got diplomatic assignments, household offices, fortress governorships, royal pensions, and cash gifts. Luynes used his control over the distribution of royal patronage to create a court party of *grands* willing to raise troops and fight for the king, and the Queen Mother's revolt collapsed in the face of their determination.

Secretary of state Nicolas de Neufville de Villeroy wrote a memorandum in 1611 for the Queen Mother as regent in which he stated that successful royal government depended upon controlling the great nobles by separating them, playing them off against each other, and placating them with patronage.[62] Luynes and the king followed his advice in suppressing the Queen Mother's revolt, and their victory secured them the great nobles' respect and cooperation without having to make financial concessions, an achievement often overlooked by historians. Luynes's skill at manipulating the court nobility has been overlooked as well, although the king's contributions to their success should not be underestimated. He steadfastly supported Luynes by giving him a free hand in the distribution of patronage, and his support was essential to the recruitment of noble allies, many of whom were his favorites and friends. He boldly challenged his mother on the battlefield, and his military victories in Normandy and Anjou convinced the nobility to abandon her and support him. His mystique as king attracted their support, while Luynes did the actual legwork of recruiting them. The king and Luynes worked together as a team to defeat the Queen Mother, and they would govern France together the same way.

Notes

1 Guillaume Girard, *The History of the Life of the Duke of Espernon*, tr. Charles Cotton (London, 1670), pp. 347–50; J. Russell Major, "The Revolt of 1620," *Fr Hist Stud* 14 (1986), 391; François Du Val, marquis de Fontenay-Mareuil, *Mémoires du Messire Du Val*, ed. Louis Monmerqué, 2 vols. (Paris, 1826), I, 431–6; Achille Halphen, ed., *Journal d'Arnauld d'Andilly 1614–1620* (Paris, 1857), pp. 447–8; Paul Phélypeaux de Pontchartrain, *Mémoires concernant les affaires de France sous la régence de Marie de Médicis*, eds. Michaud and Poujoulat, 2nd ser., vol. 5 (Paris, 1837), p. 403.

2 Louis Batiffol, *Le Roi Louis XIII à vingt ans* (Paris, 1910), pp. 346–51; Michel Carmona, *Marie de Médicis* (Paris, 1981), pp. 379–80; Pierre Chevallier, *Louis XIII* (Paris, 1979), pp. 213–5; Jean-Luc Chartier, *Le Duc d'Epernon*, 2 vols. (Paris, 2000), II, 225–52; Roland Mousnier, *L'Homme en rouge ou la vie du Cardinal de Richelieu* (Paris, 1992), pp. 174–7; Françoise Kermina, *Marie de Médicis* (Paris, 1979), pp. 262–5.

3 Joseph Bergin, *The Rise of Richelieu* (New Haven, 1991), p. 166 and n. 19; Batiffol, *Le Roi à vingt ans*, p. 330; Carmona, *Marie de Médicis*, pp. 373–4, 377.

4 *Mercure françois*, 25 vols. (Paris, 1605–44), V (1619), 137–9, 161–71, 174–6; B.N., imprimés Lb 36, 1174–5, 1178–80, 1184–5, 1187, 1192, 1199, 1200; see *Catalogue de l'histoire de France*, 16 vols. (Paris, 1968–69), I, 492–6.

5 *Mercure françois*, V (1619), 145–8; B.N., Ms. fr. 20741, fols. 25v, 26v, 38v; CC Colbert 97, fol. 19v; A.A.E., Fonds France 772, fol. 75; *Journal d'Arnauld 1614–1620*, p. 404; Eugène Griselle, "Louis XIII et sa mère," *Rev hist* 105 (1910), 308–21; B.N. Lb 36, *Lettre du Roy envoyée à la Royne Mère le 28 mai 1619* (Paris, 1619).

6 Eusèbe Pavie, *La Guerre entre Louis XIII et Marie de Médicis* (Angers, 1899), pp. 620–1; Berthold Zeller, *Le Connêtable de Luynes* (Paris, 1879), p. 57; Armand Jean du Plessis de Richelieu, *Mémoires de Richelieu*, eds. Michaud and Poujoulat, 2nd ser., vol. 7 (Paris, 1837), p. 217.

7 Fontenay-Mareuil, *Mémoires*, I, 392; Charles, comte Horric de Beaucaire, ed., *Mémoires du Cardinal de Richelieu*, 10 vols. (Paris, 1907–31), II, 381, III, 1–17. "La Reine mère, qui avoit l'esprit lassé des mauvais traitements qu'elle recevoit, mais les souffrait avec patience, savoit tous ces désordres qui se passoient dans l'Etat, et les plaintes universelles de la France venoient à ses oreilles … Elle consulte si elle doit aller à Paris et si elle peut prendre sûreté dans la mauvaise volonté de ceux qu'elle avait pensée s'acquérir en oubliant leurs fautes. Sur cette question les esprits partagent; les uns estimant ce voyage nécessaire, d'autres le croyoient inutile et le publient dangereux pour elle; son sens la porte au sentiment des derniers," Ibid., III, 12–13.

8 Gabriel Hanotaux and the duc de La Force, *Histoire du Cardinal de Richelieu*, 6 vols. (Paris, 1893–1947), II, 313–15; Georges Pagès, *Naissance du Grand Siècle* (Paris, 1948), pp. 93–6; idem, *La monarchie d'Ancien Régime* (Paris, 1928), pp. 68–70; Richard Bonney, *The King's Debts* (Oxford, 1981), pp. 94–5.

9 Batiffol, *Le Roi à vingt ans*, p. 375 and n. 3; idem, "Louis XIII et le duc de Luynes," 43–9; A. Lloyd Moote, *Louis XIII* (Berkeley, 1989), pp. 110–13.

10 *Mercure françois*, VI (1619–20), 313–33, October 14, 1619; A.A.E., Fonds France 772, passim; B.N., imprimés Lb 36, *Accord et réconciliation du Roy avec La Reine sa mère* (1619); *Articles accordés par MM. Le Cardinal de La Rochefoucauld et de Béthune au nom du Roi à la Reine mère le 20 mai* (1619); *Les Triomphes et magnificences faits à l'entrée de la Reine mère en la ville de Tours le 6 septembre* (1619); *Récit et véritable discours de l'entrée de la Reine mère dans la ville d'Angers faite le 16 octobre* (1619); *Négociation commencée au mois de mars de l'année 1619 avec la Reine mère Marie de Médicis par Monsieur le comte de Béthune* (Paris, 1672); *Articles concluded and agreed upon by the Lords, the Cardinal de La Rochefoucauld and de Béthune, in the name of the King of France to the Queen Mother* (London, 1619); Fontenay-Mareuil, *Mémoires*, I, 448–9; *Journal d'Arnauld 1614–1620*, p. 361; Pavie, *La Guerre*, pp. 20–1, 50–2, 62–3, 69–70; Bergin, *Rise of Richelieu*, pp. 183–4; Batiffol, *Le Roi à vingt ans*, pp. 350–64; idem, "Louis XIII et le duc de Luynes," *Rev hist* 103 (1910), 47.

11 *Mercure françois*, V (1619), 137–9, 161–4, 174–6; *Recueil des pièces les plus curieuses qui ont esté faites pendant le règne du connestable M. de Luynes* (Paris, 1628), pp. 83–110, *Le Comtadin Provençal*

(1620); pp. 126–48, *Véritez Chrestiennes au Roy* (1620), pp. 278–91, *La Sibylle françoise* (1620); Batiffol, *Le Roi à vingt ans*, p. 357.

12 Ibid., pp. 364–70; Pavie, *La Guerre*, pp. 73–8, 91–4, 108–19.

13 Ibid., pp. 108–73; Batiffol, *Le Roi à vingt ans*, p. 372.

14 *Recueil*, B.N., Lb 36, *Lettre de la Royne Mère envoyée au Roy* (July 1620), pp. 259–60, *Manifeste de la Royne Mère envoyé au Roy* (July 1620), pp. 261–8, *Raisons de la Royne Mère* (July 1620), pp. 269–78.

15 *Mercure françois*, VI (1620), 285–318; "Au voyage du Roi" (1620) in *Archives curieuses de l'histoire de France*, eds. F. Danjou and M.L. Cimber, 2nd ser., vol. 2 (Paris, 1838), pp. 203–40; Gabriel Vanel, ed., *Journal de Simon Le Marchand bourgeois de Caen* (Caen, 1903), pp. 86–99; Pavie, *La Guerre*, pp. 253–93.

16 Ibid., pp. 346–504; Mousnier, *L'Homme rouge*, pp. 186–8; *Mercure françois*, VI (1620), 319–38.

17 Ibid., pp. 338–9; A.A.E., Fonds France 773, fols. 100–6; Pavie, *La Guerre*, pp. 594–669. The Queen Mother was promised 600,000 livres for her expenses. Ibid., p. 579.

18 B.N., imprimés Lb 36, *Traité de la paix par l'amiable accord du Roy avec la Reine sa mère* (1620); also in *Archives curieuses*, 97–102; Eugène Halphen, ed., *Journal inédit d'Arnauld d'Andilly 1622* (Paris, 1898), p. 13.

19 For a description of faction, see Robert Shephard, "Court Factions in Early Modern England," *Journal of Modern History* 64 (1992), 721–45; Arlette Jouanna, *Le Devoir de révolte. La Noblesse française et l'état moderne* (Paris, 1989), pp. 368–84.

20 Roger Mettam, *Power and Faction in Louis XIV's France* (London, 1988), pp. 48–54, 81–101; Peter Campbell, *Power and Politics in Old Regime France* (London, 1996), pp. 156–76; Jeroen Duindam, *Vienna and Versailles* (Cambridge, 2003), pp. 248–9.

21 *Journal d'Arnauld 1614–1620*, p. 394; Eugène and Jules Halphen, eds., *Journal inédit d'Arnauld d'Andilly 1620* (Paris, 1888), p. 5; Pontchartrain, *Mémoires*, p. 415; Pavie, *La Guerre*, pp. 178, 237–8, 253, 258, 326–8, 346, 555.

22 Père Anselme de Sainte Marie, *Histoire généalogique et chronologique de la Maison Royale de France*, 9 vols. (Paris, 1726–33, New York, 1967), III, 914, IV, 307–8, VII, 519, VIII, 192; Jean-Pierre Labatut, *Les Ducs et pairs de France au XVIIe siècle* (Paris, 1972), pp. 78, 122, 170, 198; Pavie, *La Guerre*, pp. 183, 392; Eugène Halphen, ed., *Journal inédit d'Arnauld d'Andilly 1621* (Paris, 1892), p. 10; *Journal d'Arnauld 1614–1620*, pp. 340, 352 and notes; Gédéon Tallement des Réaux, *Historiettes*, ed. Antoine Adam (Paris, 1960–61), II, 144–50.

23 Anselme, *Histoire généalogique*, IV, 428–9, 756; Margaret McGowan, *L'Art du ballet de cour en France 1581–1643* (Paris, 1963), pp. 105, n.27, 118, n.9; DBF, fasc. 112, 1011–14; Beaucaire, *Mémoires de Richelieu*, II, 129–30.

24 *Journal d'Arnauld 1614–1620*, pp. 316, 318, 405, 452; *Journal d'Arnauld 1620*, p. 20; Eugène Halphen, ed., *Journal inédit d'Arnauld d'Andilly 1621* (Paris, 1871), pp. 8, 10; Fontenay-Mareuil, *Mémoires*, I, 453; *Mercure françois*, VI (1619), 334; François de Bassompierre. *Journal de ma vie. Mémoires du maréchal de Bassompierre*, ed. Edouard de Chanterac, 4 vols. (Paris, 1870–77), II, 146; Pavie, *La Guerre*, pp. 61, n.2., 177, 237–8, 360, 469.

25 *Journal d'Arnauld 1620–1621*, p. 9; Pontchartrain, *Mémoires*, pp. 380–1, 411; Fontenay-Mareuil, *Mémoires*, I, 424; A.N., M.C., VII 9, May 31, 1620; Tallement des Réaux, *Historiettes*, I, 145–52; Anselme, *Histoire généalogique*, III, 488, 493; Hélène Duccini, *Concini* (Paris, 1991), pp. 241, 342; Pavie, *La Guerre*, pp. 178, 237–8, 360; Sharon Kettering, *Judicial Politics and Urban Revolt* (Princeton, 1978), pp. 111–18; DBF, VIII, 1111–12; René de Boulle, *Histoire des ducs de Guise*, 4 vols. (Paris, 1850), IV, 384–7.

26 Pontchartrain, *Mémoires*, pp. 412–13, 415; Fontenay-Mareuil, *Mémoires*, I, 469; Anselme, *Histoire généalogique*, IV, 284, 293; *Journal d'Arnauld 1614–1620*, p. 447; Louis Videl, *Histoire de la vie du connestable de Lesdiguières* (Paris, 1638), pp. 331–8, 355–7, 361, 371, 382–3; Nicolas Chorier, *Histoire de la vie de Charles de Créquy de Blancfort* (Grenoble, 1683), pp. 137–9, 150; Charles Dufayard, *Le Connétable de Lesdiguières* (Paris, 1892), pp. vii–xxii, 377–9, 418–9, 440–60, 486; Jacques Humbert, *Le Maréchal de Créquy* (Paris, 1962), pp. 77–8; Pavie, *La Guerre*, pp. 278–9, 340, 346, 472, 618–9.

27 Pontchartrain, *Mémoires*, p. 393; *Journal d'Arnauld 1620*, pp. 59–60; Chorier, *Histoire de Créquy*, pp. 144–6; Anselme, *Histoire généalogique*, III, 641–2; Pavie, *La Guerre*, p. 238; Joseph Nouillac, *Villeroy* (Paris, 1908), pp. 278, 555.

28 Anselme, *Histoire généalogique*, III, 895; Joseph Bergin, *The Making of the French Episcopate* (New Haven, 1996), p. 632; DBF, VIII, 1212–13; *Journal d'Arnauld 1614–1620*, pp. 444, 447, 454; Pavie, *La Guerre*, pp. 462–3, 595; Eugène Griselle, *Etat de la maison du Roi Louis XIII* (Paris, 1912), p. 49.

29 Bassompierre, *Mémoires*, II, 145, 288, 403; Chorier, *Histoire de Créquy*, pp. 137–8, 148–9; Anselme, *Histoire généalogique*, III, 895; *Journal d'Arnauld 1614–1620*, pp. 399, 432, 447, 452, 454–6; Paul Bondois, *Le Maréchal de Bassompierre* (Paris, 1925), pp. 183–252, esp. 190–1; Pavie, *La Guerre*, pp. 228, 236–8, 347, 360; Jean Castarède, *Bassompierre, maréchal, gentilhomme, rival de Richelieu* (Paris, 2002), pp. 72–123.

30 David Parrott, "A 'prince souverain' and the French crown: Charles de Nevers," *Royal and Republican Sovereignty in Early Modern Europe*, eds. Robert Oresko et al. (Cambridge, 1987), pp. 149–87, 157; Emile Baudson, *Charles de Gonzague, duc de Nevers* (Paris, 1947), pp. 134–53, 172–94; Anselme, *Histoire généalogique*, III, 713; Pavie, *La Guerre*, pp. 181–2, 347, 587; *Journal d'Arnauld 1614–1620*, pp. 421, 423, 433; Victor Tapié, *La Politique étrangère de la France et le début de la Guerre de Trente Ans (1616–1621)* (Paris, 1934), pp. 280, 332; Robert Harding, *Anatomy of a Power Elite* (New Haven, 1978), pp. 148–9.

31 B.N., imprimés Lb 36, *L'Entrevue du Roi et de la Reine sa mère au château de Brissac* (1620); Pavie, *La Guerre*, pp. 184, 238, 271, 343; Anselme, *Histoire généalogique*, III, 713, IV, 323–4. The château has a Louis XIII staircase and a Louis XIII stone bridge.

32 *Journal d'Arnauld 1614–1620*, pp. 430–1, 437; Henri de Rohan, *Mémoires du duc de Rohan*, eds. Michaud and Poujoulat, 2nd ser., vol. 5 (Paris, 1837), pp. 514–15; Fontenay-Mareuil, *Mémoires*, I, 427, 446–7, 503; François de Malherbe, *Oeuvres*, ed. Antoine Adam (Paris, 1971), p. 1055, n. 2; Bergin, *Rise of Richelieu*, pp. 189–93; idem, *The Making of the French Episcopate* (New Haven, 1996), p. 572; Griselle, *Etat de la maison du Roi*, pp. 90, 103, 336; Pavie, *La Guerre*, pp. 10–11 and notes; Berthold Zeller, *Richelieu et les ministres de Louis XIII de 1621 à 1624* (Paris, 1880), p. 26.

33 Fontenay-Mareuil, *Mémoires*, I, 467; *Journal d'Arnauld 1620*, pp. 45, 58; Antoine Degert, "Le Chapeau du Cardinal de Richelieu," *Rev hist* 118 (1915), 255–88; Bergin, *Rise of Richelieu*, pp. 178–208, 215–29; Pavie, *La Guerre*, pp. 185–6; Mousnier, *L'Homme rouge*, pp. 158–64, 177–9, 202–4.

34 Pontchartrain, *Mémoires*, p. 385.

35 The governor of Saumur was Du Plessis-Mornay, a royalist Protestant who supplied the king with troops and munitions. Pavie, *La Guerre*, pp. 240–1, 374–6, 515.

36 Labatut, *Les Ducs et pairs*, p. 276.

37 François Bluche, *Les Honneurs de la Cour* (Paris, 1957), pp. 1–4; idem, *Louis XIV* (Paris, 1986), pp. 448–73; Duindam, *Vienna and Versailles*, pp. 124, 216; idem, *Myths of Power* (Amsterdam, 1994), pp. 119–21; Jean-François Solnon, *La Cour de France* (Paris, 1987), pp. 362–7.

38 *Journal d'Arnauld 1614–1620*, pp. 345, 378; Fontenay-Mareuil, *Mémoires*, I, 414–15.

39 Ibid., pp. 359–60, 362–8, 414, 427; Girard, *The History of Espernon*, pp. 308–14; Rohan, *Mémoires*, p. 514; Pontchartrain, *Mémoires*, p. 404; Mousnier, *L'Homme rouge*, pp. 202–3.

40 Pontchartrain, *Mémoires*, pp. 404, 411–12; *Journal d'Arnauld 1614–1620*, pp. 353, 416; *Journal d'Arnauld 1620*, p. 11; Chorier, *Histoire de Créquy*, pp. 154–5; Pavie, *La Guerre*, pp. 57, 82–5, 87–8, 106–9, 113–15, 157.

41 Griselle, *Etat de la maison du Roi*, p. 49; Moote, *Louis XIII*, p. 82.

42 Mettam, *Power and Faction*, pp. 51–4; Campbell, *Power and Politics*, pp. 16–29; Duindam, *Vienna and Versailles*, pp. 242–54.

43 *Recueil*, *Méditations de l'hermite Valérien* (1621), p. 325; J.H. Elliott and L.W.B. Brockliss, eds., *The World of the Favourite* (New Haven, 1999), pp. 13–23, 71–8, 81–122, 279–304; Joseph Bergin and Lawrence Brockliss, eds., *Richelieu and His Age* (Oxford, 1992), pp. 13–43; A. Lloyd Moote, *Louis XIII* (Berkeley, 1990), p. 104; Hanotaux, *Histoire du Cardinal de Richelieu*,

II, part 2, 209, 448–9; Mousnier, *L'Homme rouge*, p. 155; Nicolas Le Roux, *La Faveur du Roi* (Paris, 2000), passim.

44 Nicolas de Brichanteau, marquis de Beauvais-Nangis, *Mémoires*, eds. Louis Monmerqué and A.H. Taillandier. (Paris, 1862), pp. 151–2; Bassompierre, *Mémoires*, II, 112, 288; Léon Geley, *Fancan et la politique de Richelieu 1617 à 1627* (Paris, 1884), p. 84; Eugène Griselle, *Louis XIII et Richelieu* (Paris, 1911, Geneva, 1974), pp. 367, 369–70.

45 Zeller, *Le Connêtable de Luynes*, p. 188.

46 Fontenay-Mareuil, *Mémoires*, I, 382; Bassompierre, *Mémoires*, II, 385; B.N., imprimés Lb 36, *Harangue faite au Roy par la Reine Mère* (1622), pp. 8–13.

47 Eugène Halphen, ed., *Journal inédit d'Arnauld d'Andilly 1621* (Paris, 1891), pp. 29–33; Raoul Patry, *Philippe Du Plessis-Mornay* (Paris, 1933), pp. 587–9.

48 Rohan, *Mémoires*, pp. 23–7, 513–15.

49 Charles Bernard, *Histoire des guerres de Louis XIII contre les religionnaires rebelles* (Paris, 1633), p. 243.

50 *Mémoires de Messire Robert Arnauld d'Andilly*, ed. Petitot, 2nd ser., vols. 33–4, 2 vols. (Paris, 1824), I, 379–83, 391–2. "Monsieur d'Andilly, que diriez-vous de ce qu'un homme de qualité m'a dit aujourd'hui que vous n'étiez point de mes amis? … Monseigneur, que lui avez-vous répondu? … Vous pouviez, monseigneur, lui répondre que si vous aviez fait un mémoire de vos amis et de vos serviteurs, je m'y serois trouvé en tête, et que tant de personnes qui ont passé devant moi seroient demeurées dernière" Ibid., I, 398–9.

51 Fontenay-Mareuil, *Mémoires*, I, 452; Pavie, *La Guerre*, pp. 57–9. Tapié, *La Politique étrangère*, p. 328.

52 *Journal d'Arnauld 1614–1620*, passim 1619–1620; *Journal d'Arnauld 1620*, passim; Bergin, *Rise of Richelieu*, pp. 178–97; Pavie, *La Guerre*, pp. 50–2, 63–5, 69–70, 145, 176–238.

53 Pontchartrain, *Mémoires*, p. 395; *Mercure françois*, VI (1619), 334; Fontenay-Mareuil, *Mémoires*, I, 418–19, 452; *Journal d'Arnauld 1614–1620*, pp. 316–17, 409, 452, 454–5; Rohan, *Mémoires*, p. 515; Chorier, *Histoire de Créqy*, pp. 153–5; Pavie, *La Guerre*, pp. 61, 176, 211; B.N., imprimés Lb 36, *La Réception véritable faite par le roi à Monseigneur le prince de Condé au château de Chantilly* (1619); *La Liberté donné par le roi a Monseigneur le prince de Condé* (1619); *Le Manifeste de Monseigneur le prince de Condé, envoyé aux bons Français* (1619).

54 Victor Cousin, "Le Duc et connêtable de Luynes," *Journal des Savants* (October 1862), 623, 630–5; Henri d'Orléans, duc d'Aumale, *Histoire des princes de Condé pendant les XVIe et XVIIe siècles*, 7 vols. (Paris, 1863–93), II, 124–6; Jouanna, *Le Devoir de révolte*, pp. 215–16; Pavie, *La Guerre*, 189–90, 205–6.

55 Batiffol, *Le Roi à vingt ans*, p. 487; idem, *La Duchesse de Chevreuse* (Paris, 1913), pp. 13–14.

56 Zeller, *Le Connêtable de Luynes*, pp. 18–19, 58–62; Degert, "Le Chapeau du Cardinal de Richelieu," 257; Mousnier, *L'Homme rouge*, p. 204.

57 Bassompierre, *Mémoires*, II, 209, 288; Aumale, *Histoire des princes de Condé*, II, 133–6; Cousin, "Le Duc et connêtable de Luynes," *Journal des Savants* (August 1862), 491; (September 1862), 559–60.

58 Ibid., II, 149–60; Zeller, *Le Connêtable de Luynes*, pp. 50–1, 54; *Journal d'Arnauld 1621*, pp. 12, 40, 63–5.

59 The allies were Condé, Guise, Chevreuse, Elbeuf, Nevers and his son, Brissac and his son, Lesdiguières, his son-in-law Créquy, and grandson Canaples, La Rocheguyon, Alincourt, Praslin, Bassompierre, Courtenvaux, La Rochefoucauld and his brother, and Cardinal de Retz. The clients were Ruccellai, Mauny, and Thémines.

60 Luynes's relatives were Chaulnes, Luxembourg, Modène, Ornano, Montbazon, Rochefort, Marigny, and Canaples a nephew-by-marriage.

61 Luynes's former patrons were Bellegarde and his brother Termes; Du Lude and his son; Liancourt and his son; Schomberg and his son.

62 Salvo Maestellone, *La Reggenza de Maria de' Medici* (Florence, 1962), pp. 229–36, copy of the 1611 memorandum; J. Russell Major, *Representative Government in Early Modern France* (New Haven, 1980), pp. 398–400; Nouillac, *Villeroy*, pp. 517–29.

7

Luynes the minister

Luynes took the oath of office as constable on Friday 2 April 1621 in the long gallery of the Louvre overlooking the Seine. Arriving at about eleven o'clock in the morning, he entered to find the gallery packed with spectators and members of the royal council including the president, chancellor, keeper of the seals, old and new superintendents of finance, four secretaries of state, and eleven councillors of state. Present as well were the marshals of France, knights of Saint Esprit, foreign ambassadors, and a large group of Luynes's friends and relatives including the prince de Condé, several dukes, Luynes's brothers, cousins, and in-laws, and his old friend Sauveterre. Luynes made his way through the throng, accepting congratulations on all sides, and walked to the far end of the gallery to stand before a throne on a low riser.

The king, who had been at mass, now entered the gallery accompanied by the Scots guards and his brother Gaston. He walked to the far end of the gallery, and took his seat on the throne. In a ceremony rich with feudal symbolism, Luynes knelt on a pillow before the throne, his hands clasped between those of the king, while the chancellor read the oath of office, which Luynes repeated after him. A sword was presented to the king by Jean de Varigniez, sieur de Blainville, master of the wardrobe, the king's childhood friend, and Luynes's client. The king drew the sword from an outer scabbard of Moroccan leather stamped with Luynes's arms in gold, and an inner velvet scabbard covered with precious stones and gold and silver embroidery. He tapped Luynes three times on the shoulder with the naked blade, kissed the sword, and handed it to him as a gift for his loyal service. The sword was worth more than 30,000 écus (90,000 livres) because its blade was gold, and its gold hilt was studded with diamonds. The king's brother fastened the sword's scabbard and belt around the waist of Luynes, who was still on his knees before the king, holding the sword in front of him. He put the sword into its scabbard, kissed the king's hands, and thanked him for his generosity. The king stood, invited Luynes to stand, and they left the room together, followed by everyone else. The king went off to lunch, and three days later he and Luynes left for Fontainebleau where they stayed three weeks. On 28 April 1621, they mounted up and rode south to Orléans to begin their campaign against the Huguenots.[1]

Richelieu wrote in his memoirs that Luynes was named constable because his clients on the council insisted that a commander-in-chief be appointed to lead the army in the southwest. Lesdiguières was the obvious choice, but he was a Protestant so the office went to Luynes, and Lesdiguières had to be satisfied with being named general camp marshal of the army.[2] Brienne and Arnauld d'Andilly said that Condé had sought to strengthen his friendship with Luynes by suggesting to the king that he be given the constable's sword, although Brienne remarked that everyone thought it strange that someone who had no experience of military command should be given the first sword of France.[3] Condé later criticized Luynes's performance as constable, but they were no longer friends by then.[4] The king told Richelieu after Luynes's death that he had not wanted to appoint him constable, but that he had gotten the office by trickery.[5] This was the king's often used excuse for unpopular appointments. More plausibly, he may have promised Luynes the office and regretted it later, but Luynes forced him to keep his promise.[6] Luynes was able to persuade him to make this appointment because the king wanted him to go with him on campaign in the southwest, and the office of constable was his price for agreeing to go. The balance of power in the relationship was in Luynes's favor this time.

As one of thirty councillors of state, Luynes had been a low-ranking member of the royal council without portfolio. Now, he became a minister with portfolio because as constable he was first among the crown's great officials, and he thus became a minister favorite.[7] Brienne wrote in his memoirs that Luynes had at first given the impression that he was content to be a personal favorite, and that he was not interested in attending council meetings. He soon told Brienne, however, that he could arrange for him to play a more important role in government if he would keep a journal on what had been said in council meetings and let him read it. Brienne was offended, and told Luynes that it would be better if he attended the meetings himself and heard the debates in person. So, Luynes began to attend council meetings, and to discuss the debates afterward with his friends and fellow council members Déagent and Tronson.[8]

After Du Vair's death on 3 August 1621, Luynes temporarily assumed the office of keeper of the seals, which allowed him to preside over council meetings in the absence of the president, Cardinal de Retz, and the chancellor, Nicolas de Brûlart de Sillery. The chancellor was an old man who had remained in Paris to act as the regency government with the queen and Jeannin. Cardinal de Retz was ill, only joining the king in the southwest that autumn and dying in 1622. Brienne reported that Luynes conscientiously presided over every council meeting and did not interrupt reports.[9] He had probably begun to attend council meetings because the king did, and then had become interested in the debates. Within five years, Luynes had developed from a personal into a political favorite, and then into a minister favorite.

Luynes had sought the prestigious office of constable to gain the respect of the *grands*, and his lavish reception ceremony was part of his campaign to counter the pamphlets attacking him.[10] Being named constable, however, backfired because he was widely regarded as too inexperienced to hold the office. His appointment provoked considerable protest, and actually increased his unpopularity among the great nobles.[11] Luynes's reception as constable, attended by the royal council, highlights the questions discussed in this chapter. How were important decisions made? What role did Luynes play in decision-making? What role have historians said that he played?

Luynes's clients on the royal council

There was only one royal council in theory, but it met in so many different guises that in reality there were two basic types, councils of political affairs and councils of judicial and financial administration. The *Conseil des affaires* dealt with political affairs, and its members included the king, his favorites, members of the royal family, dukes, marshals headed by the constable, cardinals, and great officials of the crown who were ministers, particularly the chancellor, keeper of the seals, superintendent of finance, and controller general of finance. The council also included four secretaries of state and thirty councillors of state. There was a smaller council known as the *Conseil secret*, *Conseil étroit*, or *Conseil de cabinet*, which met more often than the large council. It had about a half-dozen members who were the king's favorites and principal ministers with seats on the large council. Its membership tended to change with every shift and turn in royal policy and favor.

Louis XIII regularly attended meetings of the *Conseil des affaires*, and decided nothing without its advice. He would cut short hunting trips to attend these meetings, which were usually held in the mornings in his study two or three times a week.[12] They were held more often during crises and could last all day. He did not attend administrative council meetings, which were held several times a week in the afternoons. The king would sit at the head of the council table with his hat on, and the ministers and councillors of state would sit along the sides with their hats on. The secretaries of state were seated if they were councillors of state. Otherwise, they stood and served in rotation as reporters of the meetings in which they actively participated. Standing at the back of the room and along the sides with their heads bare were ministerial deputies, intendants of finance, masters of requests, and officials making reports. The dukes and marshals could also attend council meetings, but usually did not.

Important political issues were discussed at meetings of the large council. The king would solicit the opinion of each member in turn by rank, and the debates could be lively. When everyone had been heard, there would be a voice vote, and a plurality would decide the issue unless the king himself expressed a strong opinion, which could change the vote in his favor. The ministers tended to support the king's firmly expressed opinions, but it was not always clear if he had persuaded them to adopt a decision or if they had persuaded him.[13] The council at this time was not dominated by one individual as it would be later.

In October 1618, Robert Arnauld d'Andilly returned to court from Sedan with a letter from the duc de Bouillon to the king, which he gave to Luynes. He had delivered the king's letter to the duke a month earlier. That afternoon Luynes's client Sauveterre came to inform Arnauld that the king had requested his presence in the grand salon of the château. When he entered, he found an impromptu council meeting in session, with the king sitting in an armchair surrounded by chancellor Brûlart de Sillery, keeper of the seals Du Vair, superintendent of finance Jeannin, councillor of state Luynes, intendant of finance Déagent, and four secretaries of state, all of whom were standing. The king asked Arnauld to report on his trip, and he talked for over an hour after which the chancellor asked him questions.[14]

Luynes regularly attended meetings of the large and small councils, and he had clients on both who were members of his personal advisory group.[15] In fact, the pamphleteers complained that he had filled the royal councils with his clients.[16] Pontchartrain observed that the great nobles had protested in January 1619 that they were unable to play their traditional advisory role because Luynes was allowing only his relatives and clients to sit on the royal council.[17] Richelieu wrote in his memoirs in 1621 that the council was full of Luynes's *affidés*.[18] Who were these "friends"?

Luynes had four "friends" besides himself on the large council, and they also attended meetings of the small council. They included Guichard Déagent, sieur de Saint Marcellin, a client who became an intendant of finance and a council member in April 1617, and joined the small council at the same time. Déagent was disgraced in December 1618, and left court for Grenoble six months later. He was replaced on the large council on 6 January 1619 by Luynes's brother Chaulnes, who also joined the small council. Henri de Schomberg, comte de Nanteuil, an ally who was the brother-in-law of Luynes's former patron Du Lude, was named superintendent of finance on 3 September 1619. Four days later, he took a seat on the council above Chaulnes, and was soon attending small council meetings. Luynes's cousin Modène joined the council on 12 January 1620, and six months later he began attending small council meetings.

Luynes's brother Luxembourg was invited by the king to sit on the large council a week after Luynes's death, probably as a gesture of sympathy for his bereavement. With Chaulnes and Modène, however, he lost his seat on the council a few months later. The king never invited Luynes's other cousin, Ornano, to join.[19]

A few days after Concini's murder, a new *Conseil des affaires* met in the king's study. Those attending included chancellor Brûlart de Sillery; keeper of the seals Guillaume Du Vair; superintendent of finance Pierre Jeannin; and secretary of state for foreign affairs Nicolas de Neufville de Villeroy, who exercised his office jointly with his son-in-law, also the chancellor's son, Pierre de Brûlart, vicomte de Puysieux. Pierre would replace his father-in-law Villeroy in office at his death in December 1617. Also present were Antoine de Loménie de La Ville-aux-Clercs, who exercised his office jointly with his son, Henri de Loménie de Brienne; Paul Phélypeaux de Pontchartrain, who was followed in office in 1621 by his brother Raymond Phélypeaux, sieur d'Herbault; and Antoine de Potier, sieur de Sceaux, whose cousin, Nicolas Potier d'Ocquerre de Gesvres, replaced him in 1622. Attending as well were Déagent, intendant of finance replacing Gilles Maupeou who had become controller general of finance; Guillaume de l'Aubespine, baron de Châteauneuf, councillor of state and intendant of finance; other former council members; and a large crowd of nobles.[20]

After getting rid of Concini, the king and Luynes summoned a new council excluding the Queen Mother's supporters, and including some of Henri IV's former ministers who were known as the *barbons* or greybeards. They provided continuity, and their appointment was popular both at court and in Paris. They included Sillery, Du Vair, Jeannin, Villeroy, and Pontchartrain, all of whom had first been appointed to the council by Henri IV, and then removed by the Queen Mother and Concini in 1616. Their recall on 30 April 1617 signaled the end of the old regime. The greybeards received this nickname because Villeroy was seventy-four in 1617; Jeannin was in his middle seventies; Brûlart de Sillery was in his late sixties; Du Vair was in his early sixties; and Pontchartrain, Brienne, and Sceaux were over fifty. They were conservatives, and the chancellor's son Puysieux may be included among them for this reason, although he was younger. There were frequent changes in the council's membership over the next few years. Villeroy, Du Vair, Pontchartrain, Sceaux, and Luynes died, while Déagent was disgraced, and Jeannin resigned as superintendent of finance, although he kept his seat on the council until his death in 1623.[21]

There were three main factions on the council during Luynes's years in power, his clients, the *barbons*, and the *grands*, although faction membership could overlap. The *grands* were a group of great nobles who had been given seats on the council for their loyalty to the king during the Queen Mother's revolt. They included the prince de Condé and the ducs de Guise, Nevers, Bellegarde,

Montbazon, and Chaulnes. Members of the royal family and dukes were entitled by rank to attend council meetings, but they did not do so regularly unless invited by the king, who asked his cousin Condé to attend regularly. The prince had arrived at court in October 1619, left for an unknown reason in October 1620, and only returned after Luynes's death. He would probably have become the head of a council faction if he had stayed longer. The Queen Mother would also have become the head of a faction if she had been allowed to resume her seat, and Luynes did not want either of them on the council for this reason.

Luynes did not have enough clients on the large council to dominate it, and while he had clients on the small council, they were never a majority. He was unable to form a coalition of council members to dominate discussions because the *barbons* were loyal to the king, not to him personally, which was also true of the *grands*. In any event, the king would not have tolerated his open domination of meetings. Despite what Richelieu and the pamphleteers claimed, Luynes did not control the council by packing it with his clients. He had no clients among the secretaries of state, most of whom later became Richelieu's clients.[22] Luynes exercised influence outside council meetings.

The small council met to review matters to be discussed later at meetings of the large council. The king called a meeting of the small council on 19 November 1617 to discuss issues before the Rouen Assembly of Notables, which had been convened to deal with problems arising from the nobles' revolt.[23] The meeting included Déagent, Luynes, Jeannin, and secretary of state Loménie de La Ville-aux-Clercs acting as the reporter. The king called a small council meeting in his study on 17 December 1617 to discuss the Rouen assembly's deliberations, and those attending included Brûlart de Sillery, Du Vair, Luynes, Jeannin, and Déagent. In late April 1618, the king called a small council meeting in the queen's study to discuss Du Lude's appointment as governor of his brother Gaston. Attending were Du Vair, Jeannin, Luynes, and Déagent. On 14 October 1621, the king and Luynes called a small council meeting at the château of Piquecos to discuss the terms of the duc de Rohan, the Protestant commander-in-chief, for ending the siege of Montauban. Those attending included Cardinal de Retz, Chaulnes, Schomberg, and secretary of state Puysieux acting as the reporter. The king called a small council meeting on military strategy at the fortress of Libourne on 31 December 1621, two weeks after Luynes's death, which was attended by Cardinal de Retz, Schomberg, Marillac, Bassompierre, and marshals Praslin, Chaulnes, and Créquy.[24]

When the king was on campaign, the marshals regularly attended council meetings, and the royal council became a *Conseil de guerre* or council of war. The marshals were the highest-ranking generals beneath the constable, and their number varied from eleven in 1610 to fourteen in 1630.[25] On 20 April 1621, the king called a meeting of the large council at Fontainebleau with all the marshals attending to ratify his decision to go to war against the Huguenots, which the council approved. Council meetings were held more frequently when the king was on campaign. There were meetings every day in June 1620 during the Normandy campaign, and nearly every day in May and June 1621 during the siege of Saint Jean d'Angély. After the town surrendered on 23 June, the king called a council meeting to discuss strategy. Those attending included Luynes, the maréchaux de Lesdiguières, Praslin, Chaulnes, and Brissac, Cardinal Guise, the ducs de Chevreuse and d'Elbeuf, Schomberg, Du Vair, and the secretaries of state.[26]

The membership of the small council overlapped with that of Luynes's own advisory group of clients. As we have seen, Luynes had assembled a group of conspirators to help him get rid of Concini. They had included his brothers, his cousin Modène, Déagent, Marcillac, and Tronson, who became the nucleus of his advisory group, and continued to advise him after Concini's death. Déagent, Chaulnes, Modène, and Schomberg sat on the small council, while Tronson, a councillor of state, sat on the large council. Luynes's other political clients, Luxembourg, Ornano, Contades, Ruccellai, Blainville, Sauveterre, Desplan, and Marcillac, did not sit on the councils, but he consulted a few informally at a time, and they gave him advice. The group's membership was fluid, and occasionally included other clients such as Bassompierre and Père Arnoux. Luynes's political clients also provided him with information, and acted as his envoys, messengers, and go-betweens.[27]

Except for Déagent and Schomberg, Luynes's clients held household, not government offices. Ornano and Contades were governor and under governor of the king's brother, while Modène and Blainville were the king's grand provost and wardrobe master.[28] Luxembourg was captain in a royal guards regiment, then captain of the king's guard company of light horse, while Chaulnes was captain of the king's one hundred men-at-arms. The abbé Ruccellai obtained a position in the queen's study.[29] Louis Tronson, sieur du Coudray, was a secretary in the king's household.[30] Jacques de Beziade de Sauveterre was first valet of the king's wardrobe, an office that Luynes had secured for him. He had been an usher in the Queen Mother's bedchamber until she had dismissed him for defending Luynes.[31] Bernard de Crugy, sieur de Marcillac, had been a member of Condé's household before joining the Queen Mother's household, but he was dismissed after he became a Concini conspirator, and Luynes secured him a place as an ordinary gentleman of the king's bedchamber. Esprit d'Alart, sieur d'Esplan, had been one of the duc de Luxembourg's guards before becoming Luynes's client, and later grand marshal of lodgings in the king's household. Bassompierre was colonel of the king's Swiss guards; Père Arnoux was the confessor of both Luynes and the king; and Ornano became governor of the king's brother, Gaston d'Orléans.[32]

Luynes consulted his personal advisory group on issues before the council for discussion, and also asked the opinion of the greybeards, especially Brûlart de Sillery, Du Vair, and Jeannin. Then he would talk to the king, who sometimes made a decision on the basis of their conversation, but usually the issue was discussed in a small council meeting, and often in a large council meeting, before the king made a decision. Luynes preferred one-on-one conversations or small meetings with a few friends to council discussions. As a backroom politician, he preferred to work behind-the-scenes. For instance, the Venetian ambassador told Luynes in April 1621 that he had learned of a potential Swiss alliance detrimental to Venetian interests. Luynes replied, "Truth to tell, I know nothing about this alliance. I want to speak to the king and my friends about it. Let me look into this affair, and do not speak about it to others."[33]

There was a precedence quarrel over seating at a large council meeting in late April 1618. Epernon complained that Du Vair, who was keeper of the seals, had sat across from the chancellor instead of below him on the same side as he should have, and insisted that the other side was reserved for dukes when they chose to attend. After the meeting, Epernon, Montmorency, and Montbazon, who were dukes, went to see the king in his study to complain about Du Vair's behavior. The king asked the opinions of Brûlart de Sillery and Du Vair who were present, and a heated debate followed. The king finally went off to lunch, leaving Luynes behind to resolve the dispute. That afternoon Luynes and Déagent met privately to discuss the matter with the chancellor and keeper of the seals, and that evening the king met with all four of them in his study. Jeannin, who had been away from court, was consulted when he returned. That night the king called Montmorency and Epernon to his bedside to tell them he had decided that the chancellor should review the rules on precedence, and that Epernon should leave court immediately for his government of Metz.[34] Epernon was so furious at being reprimanded by the king that he helped the Queen Mother to escape a year later.

The news arrived in Paris of her escape on the morning of 23 February 1619. The king was hunting at Saint Germain, but Luynes was still in Paris, and he was visibly upset by the news. He did not know what to do, so he asked the advice of Brûlart de Sillery and Jeannin. They recommended caution, saying that she still might be persuaded to return, and they warned against doing anything in haste that might provoke a civil war. Jeannin advocated sending envoys to discuss the situation with her.

The king came back to Paris on the afternoon of 23 February. That evening he called a council meeting in his study, and the council met all day from 25 February through 1 March. The king wanted to take immediate military action against his mother, and he was so firm on this that Luynes had to support him in public to retain favor. The greybeards urged caution and voiced concerns about a coalition of great nobles joining the Queen Mother, or a simultaneous revolt by the Protestants. They advised negotiating with her. Du Vair took a hard line because of his recent quarrel with Epernon, and joined the king in advocating military action.

After five days of meetings, a compromise was reached. The council decided that commissions would be issued to levy troops as the king wanted, and that at the same time letters and envoys would be sent to the Queen Mother to negotiate a reconciliation as the conservatives wanted. Letters would also be sent to the provincial parlements, the provincial governors, and the fortress governors requesting their assurances of loyalty to the king.[35] Luynes must have supported this more moderate plan because he immediately sent envoys to the Queen Mother. He had been acting as a mediating force between the hawks and doves on the council, privately consulting the conservatives and taking their advice, while publicly supporting the king. He often served as an intermediary between the king, the greybeards, and the great nobles.

The Austrian ambassador, the comte de Furstenberg, had been granted a personal interview with the king on 5 December 1619. The election of the Catholic Ferdinand II as the new Holy Roman Emperor had provoked a German Protestant revolt, and the emperor wanted French aid in crushing it. The council met that afternoon to decide what to do. Condé advocated levying an army to send to Germany, which Schomberg, Jeannin, and Puysieux opposed as too risky. They advised the king to offer to mediate instead, and he took their advice. Luynes said nothing at this meeting, but the next day he visited the ambassador to assure him of the king's regret at not being able to offer more aid because of his own Protestant problems.[36] Evidently, Luynes had discussed the matter in private with the king, and he was now acting as his messenger and go-between in trying to soften the blow of French rejection. Luynes seemingly agreed with the decision not to intervene, but Louis Batiffol has cited his interview with Furstenberg as an example of his incompetence because he garbled what had been said at the meeting. Luynes, however, may have deliberately changed what had been said in order to make the council's decision more agreeable to the ambassador.[37]

On the morning of 29 June 1620, Bassompierre had gone to the Louvre to take his leave of the king before assuming command of the royal army in Champagne. In the courtyard, he was handed a note from the comte de Soissons announcing that he and his mother had decided to leave court that night to join the Queen Mother at Angers. Bassompierre hurriedly climbed the stairs to the king's apartments to inform him of their departure. Luynes was present, and the king announced that he was going hunting in the Bois de Boulogne, and would spend the night there at the château of Madrid. He declared that he would invite Soissons to visit him at the château that evening and arrest him.

Both Luynes and Bassompierre told the king that it would be unwise to arrest him without definite proof. Luynes told the king to go hunting, and said that he and Bassompierre would remain in Paris to discover what was going on and decide what to do. The king should send them his guard company of light horse that afternoon to make the arrest if necessary. He agreed and rode off.

Luynes asked Bassompierre to dine with him and his brother Chaulnes to discuss what to do. Bassompierre, however, had already agreed to dine with Nevers and Praslin, so he told Luynes that he would meet him afterward at his Paris residence. Modène, Contades, Schomberg, Chaulnes, and Luynes were waiting for him when he arrived, and Luxembourg rode up as captain of the king's guard company of light horse. Luynes asked Bassompierre what he thought should be done, and he replied that they had two choices. Either the king would have to allow Soissons to leave unhindered as if he were unimportant, or he would have to arrest him, which could be done at his residence, the city gates, or in the suburbs rather than at the château of Madrid. Bassompierre told Luynes that it was his decision to make. Luynes was uncertain about what to do, and his friends did not know either. Bassompierre told him disapprovingly that it was getting late, and that he would have to make up his mind. Glaring at him, Luynes said bluntly, "That's easy for you to say. If you had to hold the pot by the handle as I do, you would be just as anxious and uncertain."[38]

Bassompierre recommended asking the royal ministers for their advice, so Luynes summoned them to a meeting at the residence of chancellor Brûlart de Sillery. When Schomberg arrived, he said that Cardinal de Retz was too ill to come. Bassompierre offered to go ask his opinion, and visit the grand prior de Vendôme at the same time to learn his intentions. Returning, he reported that the grand prior really was leaving that night for Angers, and that Cardinal de Retz had no opinion, probably because he was afraid of giving bad advice. Although the cardinal was a friend of Luynes, he was a weak man with little political influence. When Bassompierre returned to the chancellor's residence, he found Jeannin there, and Jeannin advised allowing Soissons to go unmolested because "the count and and the countess [his mother] brought only ostentation and smoke to the Queen Mother's party, not advantage or profit."[39]

Luynes took Jeannin's advice. He dismissed the company of light horse, and allowed Soissons and his friends to depart unhindered. They left Paris by the Saint Jacques gate at a little after eleven o'clock that night. Returning to the Louvre the next afternoon, the king called a meeting of the large council to ratify Luynes's decision, which he presented as his own.[40] Luynes had consulted his clients and the conservatives before advising the king. He had a consultative political style, always asking the opinions of those whom he trusted before making recommendations to the king, a habit that made him seem indecisive and uncertain.

Luynes's role in decision-making

The affable Luynes was conciliatory by nature. Flexible and adaptable, he was more apt to negotiate than to confront or challenge. His was a voice of caution in the inner circle of a king who loved playing soldiers, and whose advisers included such hotheads as Condé, Guise, Epernon, and Créquy. Their solution to any problem was to take immediate military action. Luynes, in contrast, was a self-proclaimed peacemaker and moderate who regularly consulted the conservative greybeards.[41] After news of the Normandy revolt arrived in Paris on 1 July 1620, the king called all-day council meetings on 2 and 3 July to decide what to do. Chancellor Brûlart de Sillery told the king to remain in Paris and let his generals conduct the campaign in Normandy because Paris was full of troublemakers who would be rioting in the streets as soon as he left the city. The chancellor said that the campaign could be lengthy, and that the Queen Mother's troops at Metz and Angers could march on the capital to occupy it. He said that whoever lost Paris, lost France, and that Paris was more important than Normandy, which could be reconquered from Paris. He added that Normandy would not fall to the rebels because its fortified cities of Rouen, Dieppe, Le Havre, and Caen were in reliable royalist hands. He said that the king should stay in Paris to safeguard the city, and the other conservatives and Luynes agreed with him.

Condé advised the opposite. He said that the king should attack the rebels immediately before they gained strength. He declared that Normandy was a suburb of Paris, and that the Louvre should be defended at Rouen and Caen. This was exactly what the king was hoping to hear because he wanted to lead an army into Normandy. He declared that Normandy was a test, and if he could defeat the rebels there, he could intimidate the rebels in Anjou, Angoulême, and Guyenne into laying down their arms. The king was so firm on this that Luynes was forced to agree with him to retain favor. Luynes often appeared indecisive because he had to change his opinions to agree with those of the king, who announced to the Parlement of Paris on 4 July that he was marching to Normandy. Luynes found himself riding toward Rouen on 7 July with the king, his brother, and Condé, and they entered the city on 10 July. The next day a lengthy council meeting was held to discuss taking Caen. After listening to his ministers' hesitations and fears, the exasperated king declared, "Péril deça, péril dela, péril sur terre, péril sur mer. Allons droit à Caen." ("Peril is everywhere. Let's go to Caen."). That ended the meeting. Accompanied by Condé and Luynes, he rode into Caen on 15 July.[42]

Triumphant after his victory at Ponts-de-Cé, the king in September marched his army through Rohan's government of Poitou and Epernon's government of Saintonge into Mayenne's government of Guyenne.[43] All three had supported the Queen Mother, and the king wanted to emphasize that they now owed loyalty and obedience to him. Arriving in Bordeaux on 18 September, he announced his intention of resolving the Protestant problem in Béarn. He had inherited this small principality in the foothills of the Pyrénées from his father along with the neighboring kingdom of Navarre. Béarn had allowed only Protestant worship within its borders since 1569, and had confiscated the property and revenues of the Catholic Church. The king's edict of 25 June 1617, restoring Catholic worship and Church property in Béarn, had been ignored. The king now decided to enforce his edict in person, since he had a victorious army within easy marching distance, and to attach these principalities to France as provinces.[44]

When the king arrived in Bordeaux, he summoned the Protestant governor of Béarn, the duc de La Force, a supporter of the Queen Mother, to appear before him on 25 September. The Béarnais still refused to enforce the king's edict, and La Force was unable to convince him that they would do so voluntarily. So, the king called a council meeting on 9 October to ratify his decision to march south to Pau to enforce his edict. The meeting was attended by Mayenne, Luynes, Praslain, Epernon, Du Vair, Schomberg, Créquy, and Bassompierre. Mayenne opposed the campaign on military grounds. Several rivers had to be crossed before reaching Béarn where resistance was entrenched; the roads were bad; the countryside was wild; winter was approaching; and there would be supply problems.[45] The king dismissed these objections, and the council ratified his decision to march on Béarn, which Schomberg and Créquy strongly supported. Council members in favor of the campaign who were not at the meeting included Condé, Guise, Nevers, Brûlart de Sillery, Puysieux, Jeannin, and Cardinal de Retz, who all belonged to the Catholic party at court. The king left Bordeaux on 10 October, and rode into Pau on 15 October accompanied by a large entourage of nobles.[46]

Although he had said nothing at the meeting, Luynes opposed the invasion of Béarn. Fontenay-Mareuil remarked that it was widely known at court that Luynes wanted peace, and that he opposed attacking the Huguenots, which the English ambassador reported in a February 1620 dispatch. Luynes reproached Bassompierre in October 1620 for advising the king to punish his enemies, i.e., the Béarnais, because he had advised the king to forgive them. The king told the papal nuncio in January 1621 that Luynes did not want to go to war against the Huguenots, which the Venetian ambassador reported in a March dispatch, and the Spanish ambassador in London had reported in a February dispatch.[47] Luynes may not have accompanied the king to Béarn because Héroard's journal records that the king did not visit Luynes once during the two weeks he was gone from 10 October when he left until 25 October when he returned, and the king normally saw him at least once a day.[48] Richelieu blamed Luynes's reluctance to go on love for his heavily pregnant wife because he wanted to be in Paris for her confinement. This was untrue, however, because Luynes was in Picardy with the king from 14 December to 12 January, and the baby was born in Paris on Christmas day.[49]

It was widely recognized at court that Luynes had hoped to secure the edict's enforcement through negotiation, not war. He had several private interviews with the duc de La Force in an attempt to find acceptable terms for Béarn's compliance, i.e., a way for the Parlement of Pau to register the edict restoring Catholicism. Predictably, Condé wanted to march immediately on Pau, not negotiate. Luynes had written to La Force on 23 September 1620 that "I would rather die than be forced to go to Béarn." La Force was uncooperative because he thought the approaching winter and Luynes's distaste for war would solve the problem, a view seemingly substantiated when Luynes ordered some of the king's bedchamber personnel, guards, gendarmes, and light horse to return to Paris, and told the king that he should go, too.[50]

La Force's view of the king's lack of seriousness about the Béarn campaign was reinforced by a ballet that he attended two days after arriving in Bordeaux. The ballet was performed on 27 September in the grand salon of the Château Trompette with the king in the audience. Celebrating his recent victory over his mother, it was danced by Luynes, the duc de Luxembourg, the prince de Condé, the duc de Mayenne, Gaston d'Orléans, and "other seigneurs of the court." Twelve boys, dressed as Turks in white damask and turbans, came on stage to recite a poem praising the king's valor. They were followed by a rodomontade, a big, blustering braggart who swaggered around the stage with exaggerated gestures and movements, to announce that he was the brave captain who had triumphed over earth and hell, only to be defeated in battle by Louis XIII. Eight knights dressed as Moors now ran on stage, swords in hand, to do acrobatic dancing. They twisted, leaped, jumped, and spun down the runways and on to the dance floor, declaring that Louis XIII would become a celestial body because he was greater than Mars. Finally, six shepherdesses (danced by men) came on stage in flowery costumes to sing praises of the king's prowess accompanied by lutes, and they, too, danced down the runways to the floor, ending the performance.[51] This frothy spectacle helped to convince La Force that the king was not serious about invading Béarn.

The duke realized too late the firmness of the king's intentions and the strength of the Catholic party, notwithstanding that Luynes had warned him he had many enemies on the royal council.[52] Soon afterward, the king removed La Force as governor of Béarn. Luynes's assurance that this would not happen indicates his own lack of influence in the matter; the king had ignored his advice. Luynes told La Force to speak to the king about his government, and an opportunity came when they were riding toward Pau together, but the king only said, "Serve me well."[53] When Luynes realized that La Force was disgraced, and that the Béarn campaign was a fait accompli, he supported it to retain favor. His initial opposition, however, indicates that his was a much needed voice of caution in the king's inner circle, reinforcing his reputation for timidity.

Luynes influenced the king's decision-making privately in one-on-one conversations, demonstrated by the famous quarrel between Cardinal Guise and the duc de Nevers, who were engaged in a lawsuit before the *Grand Conseil* over control of the priory of La Charité. The *Grand Conseil* was the judicial authority of the royal council exercised separately as a court.[54] Cardinal Guise, accompanied by his brothers the ducs de Guise and Chevreuse, and their cousin the duc d'Elbeuf, had accidentally encountered Nevers in Paris on 24 March 1621, and the meeting became violent. The angry cardinal pulled a sword from beneath his cloak, and started to hit the duke with it. Once Nevers was on the ground, he began to kick him, and his two brothers and their cousin surrounded the unarmed Nevers' with drawn swords. Gentlemen from both entourages rushed forward, and a mêlée followed.

Nevers was so humiliated that he challenged the cardinal to a duel, and Guise declared that he would fight. Nevers withdrew to his château in Champagne accompanied by the ducs de Mayenne, Longueville, Roannez, Retz, and several hundred horsemen. Guise remained in Paris with his brothers, his cousin, the prince de Condé, and the duc de La Valette, who rallied their supporters. The court was split over whom to support. When a rumor flew around Paris that the Guises were going to follow Nevers to Champagne, the king sent a guard captain to place them under house arrest, and two hours after midnight on 29 March, the guard captain with a company of light horse escorted the cardinal to the Bastille. Héroard's journal reported that on 28 March, the evening before the cardinal's arrest, the king had remained in Luynes's rooms until well after midnight waiting for news, and did not go to sleep until four in the morning.[55] Luynes and the king made the surprise decision to arrest the cardinal without consulting the council because Guise and Condé were council members. The quarrel ended three months later when the cardinal died of scarlet fever while on campaign with the king.[56]

In the civil war of 1619–20, Nevers had supported the king against the Queen Mother, but neither the king nor Luynes had trusted him very much.[57] Cardinal Guise had supported the Queen Mother. The king decided to arrest the cardinal because he had been the aggressor in the quarrel, but his politics were probably a consideration. A complicating factor was the support of his brothers, his cousin, and his friend Condé for the king during the civil war, while Nevers's friends the ducs de Mayenne, Longueville, Retz, and Roannez had supported the Queen Mother. If Nevers, Mayenne, Retz, and Longueville joined the discontented comte de Soissons and grand prior de Vendôme who

Figure 7 Portrait of Louis XIII, *c*.1622–25, by Peter Paul Rubens.

were being encouraged by the Queen Mother, there could be another revolt. The king had to resolve the Guise-Nevers quarrel before leaving Paris.

Luynes's skill in manipulating the court nobility and the *grands* was once again demonstrated. Almost certainly on his advice, the king wrote a soothing note to Nevers absolving him of blame and demanding that he and Mayenne return to court. He placated the comte de Soissons by promising that he could marry his brother Gaston's daughter, a marriage that never took place, and gave the grand prior de Vendôme 100,000 livres to compensate him for losing his government of Caen. The duc de Guise was mollified by having his brother moved to the more agreeable château of Vincennes and then released. Cardinal Guise joined the king on campaign with his brother the duc de Chevreuse, who was publicly reconciled with Nevers in March 1622. Condé returned to his government of Berry, and the king left for Orléans to go on campaign after making Mayenne a general.[58]

The king and Luynes together had made the decision to arrest the cardinal and placate his supporters with concessions. They had operated as a team for which the precedents were the Concini conspiracy and their staging of court ballets. The Concini conspirators had provided the king with options, and he had made the final decisions. Luynes had presented his ballet production plans to the king, who had reviewed them and suggested changes. In a similar manner, Luynes consulted his clients and the greybeards before offering the king political advice, which he adopted or rejected after he consulted the royal councils. In 1617 and 1618, the king had visited Luynes once a day in the evenings. In 1620 and 1621, he was seeing him two or three times a day, especially before and after council meetings, and he often did not see him at all on days when the council did not meet. They still hunted occasionally, but mostly they discussed the council's agenda and the war's progress in long private conversations.[59]

Luynes had a significant influence on the king's political thinking, but his influence was not paramount. It was tempered by the give-and-take of council debates, the opinions of the other ministers, the advice of the marshals, the personal interests of the great nobles, and the king's personality.[60] The king knew his own mind, demonstrated by his decisions to execute Concini, dismiss Richelieu, and march on Normandy and Béarn. Luynes was not an independent actor. His freedom of action was hampered by his need to retain the king's favor. He could not outshine the king, act as if he were king, vehemently disagree with him, or provoke his jealousy. He could only make suggestions and offer advice, and there were others to whom the king also listened.

It was widely known at court that the king was jealous of his authority, and that he would snipe at Luynes when he thought he was encroaching upon it.[61] In November 1621, when the English ambassador arrived for an interview, the king had snapped, "He is going to have an interview with King Luynes."[62] In council meetings, the king sometimes openly expressed disgust at Luynes's opinions, for example in March 1621.[63] In February 1620, highly irritated, he had told Luynes to shut up because he did not know what he was talking about after Luynes had publicly opposed his campaign against the Protestants.[64] The Venetian ambassador told Luynes in June 1619 that he should take control of the council and dominate it to secure the decisions he wanted. Luynes shook his head and said that was impossible. Louis Batiffol interpreted this to mean that he was too incompetent to control the council, but it is more likely Luynes meant that to have done so would have angered the king. When Luynes's views were disputed in council meetings, he would say, "The king should decide because be knows more about it than we do. We should not contradict him." Batiffol interpreted this to mean that Luynes was too indecisive to have an opinion.[65] It is more likely that he was flattering the king, and that the decision had already been made in private.

Because of the king's jealousy, Luynes did not usually give speeches in public. He did so, however, at the opening of the Estates of Normandy in Rouen on 18 November 1617. He addressed the Estates as the new provincial lieutenant general, although he was not sworn in for another month. Sitting at a table facing a room full of deputies, he declared:

> Messieurs, you have in this assembly an advantage that does not occur often. What you decide will be at once presented to the king, who is on his way to this city as if [it were] a second Paris. Let me assure you that His Majesty will strive to give you every sort of satisfaction on your remonstrances. His Majesty knows the importance of this great province and its affection for his service, which has made him want to hold here one of the most illustrious assemblies ever convoked in this kingdom. We hope that His Majesty will remedy all the problems of this province, and those shared by the state in general. For my part, I shall never miss any opportunity to serve and protect your interests, as I am obligated by the duty of my office, with which it has pleased His Majesty to honor me, and by the friendship and good will that you have sworn to me, which I beg you with all my heart to continue. I shall serve you in every way. You will learn from the letters of the King and his commissioners what His Majesty wants.[66]

This short, eloquent speech, full of graceful compliments, demonstrates Luynes's use of charm and flattery to manipulate and influence, especially in praising the province and its deputies. There was an implicit warning, however, in his remark that the king was on his way to Normandy and would strive to satisfy the province's grievances, undoubtedly tax complaints. The veiled warning was that the province should strive in turn to satisfy the king's financial needs by approving the tax subsidies requested in the commissioners' letters. When Luynes declared his commitment to defend the interests of the province, the implicit message was that if the province cooperated, it would be rewarded. Luynes's speech was subtle, showing political astuteness and pragmatism. The salient point is that he made this speech before the king arrived in Rouen. There is no evidence that he gave any speeches after the king arrived. The Assembly of Notables opened a few weeks later and met through January 1618. The assembly was probably held in Rouen so Luynes could be sworn in as lieutenant general of Normandy, and he may have been expected to address it, but he did not.[67]

When Luynes spoke formally in public, he was often the spokesman for the king, who stuttered badly and hated speaking in public. During the council debate of 20 April 1621 on the Huguenot campaign, Brûlart de Sillery and Jeannin spoke against it, but Luynes defended it, saying what the king had almost certainly told him to say, since he had previously opposed the campaign. His argument went as follows:

> Monsieur de Luynes, continuing still the King's favourite, advised him [the king] to go to war against his subjects of the reformed religion in France, saying he would neither be a great prince as long as he allowed so puissant [powerful] a party to remain within his dominions, nor could he justly style himself the most Christian king as long as he permitted such "heretics" to be in that great number they were, or to hold those strong places which by public edict were assigned to them: and therefore that he should extirpate them as the Spaniards had done the Moors ...[68]

Luynes's letters are full of flowery compliments and polite courtesies, but little else.[69] Louis Batiffol has remarked that Luynes usually spoke little in council meetings, and seldom said anything of substance when he did. He often refused to talk to foreign ambassadors, telling them to speak to Puysieux who was the secretary of state for foreign affairs. Because Luynes said nothing, Batiffol concluded that he had nothing to say, and that he did not understand the issues well enough to comment.[70] Another interpretation of his silence is possible.

Luynes was a "no fingerprints" politician, that is, he was secretive about what he thought and did. Political sophisticates are often secretive because power politics is a game of misdirection. After watching the frenetic search for damaging papers among the belongings of Concini and his wife to use at her trial for treason, Luynes was unlikely to have committed anything significant to paper. Since he was semi-literate, he did not have the habit of committing his thoughts to paper, and he did not have a government office that required him to do so. He said little to foreign ambassadors, especially to the hostile Italian and Spanish ambassadors, because he did not trust them, and he said little in council meetings because he had already discussed the issues in private with the king, who preferred to appear dominant in public. Favorites usually stayed in the shadows when exercising political influence.[71]

Skilled at court intrigue, Luynes was good at dissembling, which was essential to success in court politics.[72] He dissembled through his silence, hiding behind a mask of charm and affability. He was a shrewd politician, although remaining in the shadows made him appear ineffectual. Gabriel Hanotaux observed that Luynes had both intelligence and sang-froid, while Denis Avenel commented on his good sense, crafty mind, and savoir-faire.[73] Luynes feared that mistakes blamed on the favorite as the traditional scapegoat would create for him a lethal unpopularity. He and everyone prominent at court in 1617, including Richelieu, feared being murdered as Concini had been.[74] His death was a constant reminder of the price that could be paid for mistakes.

Historiography on Luynes's role

Whose hand was at the tiller? Who made the decisions? Was it the king, Luynes, or some other minister? A. Lloyd Moote and Louis Batiffol have insisted that Louis XIII was a strong monarch who made important decisions himself. Moote has argued that Luynes influenced the king, but never controlled him. Luynes was too self-interested and opportunistic, too much the wheeler-dealer, to be in charge of the government.[75] Batiffol has argued that Luynes was too timid, hesitant, and ineffectual to be the principal decision-maker. Until disgraced in 1619, Déagent was the capable hand guiding both Luynes and the king.[76] Roland Mousnier accepted Batiffol's judgment that Luynes was incompetent, ignorant, and unstable, noting that he was only interested in his personal success and his family, while "politics were conducted by the king in his council."[77] According to Victor Tapié, Puysieux replaced Déagent as the king's most influential adviser, and made foreign policy with the help of Luynes and the king. Tapié acknowledged that Luynes influenced policy-making, but said that how much has remained a mystery because Luynes did so in private conversations with the king and left no trace on paper.[78] Luynes's silence has always been a problem for historians.

Gabriel Hanotaux considered Luynes too indecisive and vacillating to be an effective minister, and contrasted Richelieu's strong rule with the timid, unsuccessful policies of the mediocre Luynes. Hanotaux regarded Luynes as responsible for all the mistakes made during these years, particularly for going to war against the Protestants. In so doing, however, without realizing it, Hanotaux assumed that Luynes was the dominant influence and that the king did what he said.[79] A.D. Lublinskaya has noted that Hanotaux's work is full of such "insoluble contradictions." Hanotaux admitted that the Huguenots were a serious threat, so Luynes had to confront them, although this admission contradicted his condemnation of Luynes for starting the war against them. Hanotaux thought that Luynes's foreign policy was unsuccessful, but he acknowledged that Richelieu had followed this same policy until 1630.[80]

Victor Cousin made the argument that Luynes was the precursor of Richelieu because the Cardinal adopted and used many of the policies that Luynes had helped to develop in 1620 and 1621.[81] Cousin portrayed Luynes as a strong minister, crediting him with all important policy decisions without offering sufficient evidence for this. Berthold Zeller also portrayed Luynes as a capable first minister who made policy, but diminished the king's importance in so doing.[82] Lublinskaya agreed with Cousin and Zeller that Luynes was an effective first minister, and that his reputation had been destroyed by a historical tradition based on Richelieu's memoirs.[83] Pierre Chevallier insisted that Luynes had dominated the king and his council.[84]

The historiography on Luynes's role in decision-making, therefore, is divided into two opposing views. In the one, a strong dominant king made decisions with the help of Déagent and Puysieux, while Luynes was an ineffectual favorite. In the other, a strong dominant favorite made decisions for an inexperienced young king. Both views are overstated. Luynes had more influence than Batiffol, Hanotaux, or Mousnier recognized, and the king played a bigger role in decision-making than Cousin, Zeller, Lublinskaya, or Chevallier allowed. This chapter has argued that the king and Luynes operated together as a team in governing France, and that neither was dominant all the time. They were partners who took the advice of others in making decisions. As Moote noted, Luynes influenced the king but did not control him. Moote overemphasized Luynes's character defects as the reason for this, and a better explanation would be his consultative political style. Luynes consulted the *barbons* and his own personal advisory group before making recommendations to the king, and together he and the king made decisions with the help of the royal councils. This style of group decision-making had developed during the Concini conspiracy. No one person was consistently dominant.

Influential decision-makers included the king, Luynes, his clients Déagent, Modène, Schomberg, and Chaulnes, and the *barbons*, especially Jeannin, Brûlart de Sillery, his son Puysieux, and Du Vair. Because of insufficient evidence, it is often difficult to know how each voted on specific issues, which is the classic problem of ministerial government. No minutes were taken during council meetings, and no detailed descriptions of them exist. For instance, the king rode into Agen on 10 August 1621, and called a council meeting the next day to decide whether or not to besiege Montauban. The *Mercure françois* described the arguments made during this council meeting for and against the siege in great detail without identifying who the hawks and doves were. Richelieu later observed that Mayenne and the king were hawks. Not surprisingly, the council decided in favor of the siege because the king wanted it. Victor Tapié, Georges Pagès, and Orest Ranum have noted that determining ministerial responsibility, and the extent of individual influence, is difficult if not impossible.[85] It can be safely said, however, that Luynes's personal relationship with the king and his clients on the council gave him significant influence over decision-making.

There were some similarities between Luynes's political style and that of Richelieu. The cardinal and the king were partners who worked together in governing France, and the king may have more readily accepted a partnership with Richelieu because he had previously had one with Luynes. Richelieu learned from Luynes how to manage the king by forming a strong emotional bond with him, and by making him feel appreciated, valued, and understood, not indirectly as Concini had tried to do by bullying him through the Queen Mother. Richelieu saw the king often, and together they discussed the council's agenda before and after meetings. Luynes had established the precedent for their political partnership.

There were some important differences, however. Richelieu officially became first minister (*premier ministre*) by letters patent in 1629, although he had been using this title for several years. Luynes never used this title. Richelieu was a political favorite, and he did not have the same type of personal relationship with the king that Luynes had. He did not have a consultative political style, and he never consulted the other ministers or participated in group decision-making to the extent that Luynes did. Richelieu was the king's openly acknowledged principal adviser, and he acted in public as his first minister, which Luynes never did. Richelieu dominated the council after 1631, formulating and coordinating royal policy, which the king then reviewed and approved. Richelieu had far greater decision-making power than Luynes had ever had.[86]

Notes

1 B.N., Dupuy 487, fols. 32–6; imprimés Lb 36, *Les Cérémonies royales faictes en baillant par la maison du Roy l'espée du Connestable à Monseigneur le duc de Luynes le 2 avril* (1621); *Mercure françois*, 25 vols. (Paris, 1605–44), VII (1621), 277; Jean Héroard, *Journal*, ed. Madeleine Foisil, 2 vols. (Paris, 1989), II, 2749–53; Eugène Halphen, ed., *Journal inédit d'Arnauld d'Andilly 1621* (Paris, 1891), pp. 19–20; B.I.F., Collection Godefroy 519, fols. 137–9; Henri Griffet, *Histoire du règne de Louis XIII*, 3 vols. (Paris, 1758), I, 283.

2 Charles, comte Horric de Beaucaire, ed., *Mémoires du Cardinal de Richelieu*, 10 vols. (Paris, 1907–13), III, 129–30; Berthold Zeller, *Le Connêtable de Luynes* (Paris, 1879), pp. 46–7.

3 Henri de Loménie de Brienne, *Mémoires du comte de Brienne*, eds. Michaud and Poujoulat, 3rd ser., vol. 3 (Paris, 1838), pp. 19–20; *Mémoires de Messire Robert Arnaud d'Andilly*, ed. Petitot, 2nd ser., vols. 33–4, 2 vols. (Paris, 1824), I, 396.

4 François Du Val, marquis de Fontenay-Mareuil, *Mémoires du Messire Du Val*, ed. Louis Monmerqué, 2 vols. (Paris, 1826), I, 503.

5 Pierre Grillon, ed., *Les Papiers de Richelieu*, 5 vols. (Paris, 1975–82), II, 567, 6 October 1627; Elizabeth Marvick, *Louis XIII* (New Haven, 1986), p. 220.

6 Zeller, *Le Connêtable*, pp. 43–4; Louis Batiffol, "Louis XIII et le duc de Luynes," *Rev hist*, 102 (1909), 255–6.

7 Ibid., 261; Bernard Barbiche, *Les Institutions de la monarchie française à l'époque moderne* (Paris, 1999), p. 283.

8 Brienne, *Mémoires*, p. 13.

9 Ibid., pp. 21–2.

10 Charles Bernard, *Histoire des guerres de Louis XIII*, 3 vols. (Paris, 1633), I, 117.

11 Fontenay-Mareuil, *Mémoires*, I, 498–9, 501–2.

12 Ibid., I, 384.

13 Barbiche, *Les Institutions*, pp. 279–90; Roland Mousnier, *Le Conseil du Roi de Louis XII à la Révolution* (Paris, 1970), pp. 5–13; idem, "Le Conseil du Roi de la mort de Henri IV au gouvernement personnel de Louis XIV," in *La Plume, la faucille et le marteau* (Paris, 1970), pp. 141–78; idem, *The Institutions of France under the Absolute Monarchy 1598–1789*, 2 vols., *The Organs of State and Society*, trans. Arthur Goldhammer (Chicago, 1984), II, 130–79; idem,

L'Homme rouge ou la vie du Cardinal de Richelieu (Paris, 1992), pp. 150–5; Georges Pagès, "Le Conseil du Roi sous Louis XIII," *Revue d'histoire moderne* 12 (1937), 293–324; Orest Ranum, *Richelieu and the Councillors of Louis XIII* (Oxford, 1963), pp. 45–75; Edmund Dickerman, *Bellièvre and Villeroy* (Providence, RI, 1971), p. 91.

14 *Mémoires Arnauld d'Andilly*, I, 382.

15 Fontenay-Mareuil, *Mémoires*, I, 383; Henri de Rohan, *Mémoires du duc de Rohan*, eds. Michaud and Poujoulat, 2nd ser., vol. 5 (Paris, 1837), 511–12; Achille Halphen, ed., *Journal d'Arnauld d'Andilly 1614–1620* (Paris, 1851) p. 372; Batiffol, "Louis XIII et le duc de Luynes," 254.

16 *Recueil des pièces les plus curieuses qui ont esté faites pendant le règne du Connestable M. de Luynes* (Paris, 1628), *Rejouissance de toute la France sur la mort du connestable* (1622), pp. 166, 168; *Méditations de l'hermite Valérien* (1621), pp. 325–6; B.N., imprimés Lb 36, *Seconde partie et responce à la Chronique des Favoris* (1622), p. 17; *Apologie ou response à la Chronique des Favoris* (1622), p. 12.

17 Paul Phélypeaux de Pontchartrain, *Mémoires concernant les affaires de France sous la régence de Marie de Médicis*, eds. Michaud and Poujoulat, 2nd ser., vol. 5 (Paris, 1837), p. 402.

18 Beaucaire, *Mémoires de Richelieu*, III, 129.

19 *Journal d'Arnauld 1614–1620*, pp. 302, 394, 439 and n. 2 , 446–9, 447 and n. 1 ; Eugène and Jules Halphen, eds. *Journal inédit d'Arnauld d'Andilly 1620* (Paris, 1888), p. 5; Louis Batiffol, *Le Roi Louis XIII à vingt ans* (Paris, 1910), pp. 493–6; Berthold Zeller, *Richelieu et les ministres de Louis XIII de 1621 à 1624* (Paris, 1880), p. 6.

20 *Relation exacte de tout ce qui s'est passé à la mort du mareschal d'Ancre*, eds. Michaud and Poujoulat, 2nd. ser., vol. 5 (Paris, 1837), p. 467; *Journal d'Arnauld 1614–1620*, pp. 291, 295 and n. 1; Brienne, *Mémoires*, pp. 12–13; Pontchartrain, *Mémoires*, p. 391; Fontenay-Mareuil, *Mémoires*, I, 377; Hélène Duccini, *Concini* (Paris, 1991), pp. 109–13, 310–11; Richard Bonney, *The King's Debts* (Oxford, 1981), pp. 75, 95–7, 285–90; Mousnier, *Les Institutions*, II, 136–46; François Bluche, *Richelieu* (Paris, 2003), pp. 352–6; Joseph Nouillac, *Villeroy* (Paris, 1908), pp. 278, 554; Henri Ballande, *Rebelle et conseiller: Jeannin* (Paris, 1981), pp. 229–36; Père Anselme de Sainte Marie, *Histoire généalogique et chronologique de la Maison royale de France*, 9 vols. (Paris, 1726–33, New York, 1967), IV, 765, 769, VI, 558–61; Michel Antoine, "L'Entourage des ministres aux XVIIe et XVIIIe siècles," *Origines et histoire des cabinets des ministres en France*, ed. Michel Antoine et al. (Paris, 1975), pp. 15–21.

21 Beaucaire, *Mémoires de Richelieu*, II, 197–9; Fontenay-Mareuil, *Mémoires*, I, 377, 382; Pontchartrain, *Mémoires*, p. 391; *Journal d'Arnauld 1614–1620*, p. 295; *Relation exacte*, p. 467.

22 Ranum, *Richelieu and the Councillors of Louis XIII*, passim.

23 For accounts of the 1617 Assembly of Notables, see J. Russell Major, *Representative Government in Early Modern France* (New Haven, 1980), pp. 412–15; Roland Mousnier, *La Vénalité des offices sous Henri IV et Louis XIII,* 2nd edn (Paris, 1971), pp. 631–8; Bonney, *The King's Debts*, pp. 96–8.

24 *Journal d'Arnauld 1614–1620*, pp. 326, 340, 369; François de Bassompierre, *Journal de ma vie. Mémoires du maréchal de Bassompierre*, ed. Edouard de Chanterac, 4 vols. (Paris, 1870–77), II, 346, 397.

25 Eugène Halphen, ed., *Journal inédit d'Arnauld d'Andilly 1621* (Paris, 1891), p. 23; Roger Doucet, *Les Institutions de la France au XVIe siècle*, 2 vols. (Paris, 1948), I, 114; John Lynn, *Giant of the Grand Siècle* (Cambridge, 1997), pp. 298–9.

26 Héroard, *Journal*, II, 2698–2703, 2755–9; *Mercure françois*, 25 vols. (Paris, 1605–44), VII (1621), 509–11.

27 *Mémoires Arnauld d'Andilly*, I, 382–5, 391–3.

28 Eugène Griselle, *Etat de la maison du Roi Louis XIII* (Paris, 1912), pp. 11, 192; idem, *Ecurie, vénerie, fauconnerie et louveterie du Roi Louis XIII* (Paris, 1912), p. 20; Eugène Halphen, ed., *Journal inédit d'Arnauld d'Andilly 1622* (Paris, 1898), p. 13, n. 3 ; Etienne Algay de Martignac, *Mémoires de Gaston, duc d'Orléans*, ed. Petitot, 2nd ser., vol. 31 (Paris, 1824), pp. 45–6.

29 *Journal d'Arnauld 1622*, p. 16.

30 Orest and Patricia Ranum, eds., *Mémoires de Guillaume Tronson* (Paris, 2003), pp. 16–17;

Mercure françois, XII (1626), 375–7.

31 Griselle, *Etat de la maison du Roi*, pp. 39, 74; B.N., Dupuy 487, fol. 36. B.I.F., Collection Godefroy 519, fol. 137.

32 Beaucaire, *Mémoires de Richelieu*, I, 333, n. 2 ; II, 172, n. 3 ; Henri d'Orléans, duc d'Aumale, *Histoire des princes de Condé*, 7 vols. (Paris, 1863–96), III, 42–5; *Mercure françois*, XII (1626), 375–7; J. Michael Hayden, *France and the Estates General of 1614* (Cambridge, 1974), p. 154; Gédéon Tallemant des Réaux, *Historiettes*, ed. Antoine Adam, 2 vols. (Paris, 1960–61), I, 845, n. 2 ; Griselle, *Etat de la maison du Roi*, pp. 3, 46; Rohan, *Mémoires*, p. 511.

33 Gabriel Hanotaux and the duc de La Force, *Histoire du Cardinal de Richelieu*, 6 vols. (Paris, 1893–1947), II, part 2, 435; Batiffol, *Le Roi Louis XIII*, p. 506. "A dire le vrai, je ne sais pas un mot de l'histoire de cette ligue ... Je veux en parler au roi et mes amis; laissez-moi un peu arranger cette affaire à moi tout seul et, de grâce, n'en parlez à personne."

34 *Journal d'Arnauld 1614–1620*, pp. 362–6.

35 Ibid., p. 404; Fontenay-Mareuil, *Mémoires*, I, 437–9; Pontchartrain, *Mémoires*, pp. 403–4; Héroard, *Journal*, II, 2598–9; Eusèbe Pavie, *La Guerre entre Louis XIII et Marie de Médicis* (Angers, 1899), pp. 22–3; Ballande, *Jeannin*, pp. 239–41; *Oeuvres mêlées du président Jeannin*, ed. Petitot, 2nd ser., vol. 16 (Paris, 1822), pp. 57–9; Hanotaux, *Histoire du Cardinal de Richelieu*, II, part 2, 276.

36 Héroard, *Journal*, II, 2654; *Mercure françois*, VI (1619), 342–53; Victor-Lucien Tapié, *La Politique étrangère de la France et le début de la Guerre de Trente Ans (1616–1621)* (Paris, 1934), pp. 425–9.

37 Héroard, *Journal*, II, 2654–5; Batiffol, *Le Roi Louis XIII*, pp. 507–9.

38 Bassompierre, *Mémoires*, II, 155. "Vous en parlés bien a vostre ayse; sy vous teniés la queue de la poile comme moy, vous seriés aussy en peine comme moy."

39 Ibid., II, 156. "Je m'en reviens cheux monsieur le chancelier et trouvay que Mr le president Jannin avoit par de fortes raysons persuadé de les laisser aller sans rien dire ny empescher leur dessein, disant que Mr le Comte ny madame la Comtesse n'apportoint que de la fumée et ostentation au party de la reine et nul avantage ou proffit; ..."

40 Ibid., II, 151–7; Héroard, *Journal*, II, 2697; Pavie, *La Guerre*, pp. 227–31.

41 Joseph Bergin, *The Rise of Richelieu* (New Haven, 1991), p. 225; Eusèbe Pavie, *La Guerre*, p. 250.

42 *Mercure françois*, VI (1620), 281–5; Héroard, *Journal*, II, 2699–2701; *Journal d'Arnauld 1620*, pp. 20–1; "Véritables relations de ce qui s'est passé au voyage du Roy" (1620) in *Archives curieuses de l'histoire de France*, eds. F. Danjou and M.L. Cimber, 2nd ser., vol. 2 (Paris, 1838), 203–6; B.N., imprimés Lb 36, *Récit véritable de ce qui s'est passé au Palais à la séance du Roi samedi le 4 juillet* (1620); Beaucaire, *Mémoires de Richelieu*, III, 48; Pavie, *La Guerre*, pp. 232–5; Hanotaux, *Histoire du Cardinal de Richelieu*, II part 2, 338.

43 For the king's route, see Héroard, *Journal*, II, 334; A. Lloyd Moote, *Louis XIII* (Berkeley, 1989), map 2.

44 A.A.E., Fonds France 773, fol. 149–57; Bernard, *Histoire des guerres de Louis XIII*, I, 74–84; Léonce Anquez, *Histoire des assemblées politiques des réformes en France (1573–1622)* (Paris, 1859, Geneva, 1970), pp. 299–313, 325–31; Mousnier, *L'Homme rouge*, pp. 199–201; Hanotaux, *Histoire du Cardinal de Richelieu*, II, part 2, 428–31; Moote, *Louis XIII*, pp. 121–4; Pierre Chevallier, *Louis XIII* (Paris, 1979), pp. 223–6; Pierre Tucoo-Chala, *Histoire du Béarn* (Paris, 1970), pp. 49–57; J.A. Clarke, *Huguenot Warrior: Henri de Rohan* (The Hague, 1966), pp. 70–3.

45 Mayenne had moral doubts about the campaign because he told the duc de La Force several times that "we are doing wrong." Jacques Nompar de Caumont, duc de La Force *Mémoires*, ed. Marquis de la Grange, 4 vols. (Paris, 1843), I, 119.

46 Bassompierre, *Mémoires*, II, 212–13; *Journal inédit d'Arnauld 1620*, p. 55; Fontenay-Mareuil, *Mémoires*, I, 499; Bernard, *Histoire des guerres de Louis XIII*, I, 75; Nicolas Chorier, *Histoire de la vie de Charles de Créquy* (Grenoble, 1683), pp. 174–5; Mousnier, *L'Homme rouge*, p. 195; Hanotaux, *Histoire du Cardinal de Richelieu*, II, part 2, 429.

47 Fontenay-Mareuil, *Mémoires*, I, 498–9; Charles Howard Carter, *The Secret Diplomacy of the Habsburgs 1598–1625* (NewYork, 1964), p. 205; Sidney Lee, ed., *The Autobiography of Edward, Lord Herbert of Cherbury* (London, 1906), pp. 200–1; Victor Cousin, "Le Duc et connêtable de Luynes," *Journal des Savants* (September 1862), 558–9; Batiffol, "Louis XIII et le duc de Luynes" 103 (1910), 41–2; idem, *Le Roi Louis XIII*, p. 515 and n. 4 ; Bassompierre, *Mémoires*, II, 219.

48 Héroard, *Journal*, II, 2718–9. Arnauld stated that Luynes and his brother Chaulnes were members of the king's entourage when he entered Pau on 15 October, but he could have been mistaken. *Journal d'Arnauld, 1620*, p. 55.

49 Ibid., p. 259; Héroard, *Journal*, II, 2729–24; Beaucaire, *Mémoires de Richelieu*, III, 103; Cousin, "Le Duc et connêtable de Luynes" (September 1862), 559.

50 *Catalogue of the collection of autograph letters of Alfred Morrison*, ed. AlphonseThibaudeau, ser. 1, vol. 3 (London, 1873–97), 269; Beaucaire, *Mémoires de Richelieu*, III, 103–4.

51 B.N., imprimés Lb 36, *Ballet dansé en la présence du roi, princes et seigneurs de la cour, en la ville de Bordeaux, au Chasteau-Trompette, le 27 septembre* (1620); Paul LaCroix, *Ballets et mascarades de la cour*, 6 vols. (Geneva, 1868–70), II, 244–9; Margaret McGowan, *L'Art du ballet de cour en France* (Paris, 1963), p. 181.

52 Fontenay-Mareuil, *Mémoires*, I, 494; Auguste de Caumont, duc de La Force, *Le Maréchal de La Force (1558–1652)* (Paris, 1950), pp. 205–6.

53 La Force, *Mémoires*, I, 119–20.

54 Doucet, *Les Institutions*, I, 202–9.

55 Héroard, *Journal*, II, 2747.

56 *Journal d'Arnauld 1621*, pp. 13–19, 49–50; Beaucaire, *Mémoires de Richelieu*, III, 137–9; Fontenay-Mareuil, *Mémoires*, I, 513; *Mercure françois*, VII (1621), 508, 570–1; Claude Malingre, *Histoire de la rebellion excitée en France par les rebelles de la religion prétendue réformée* (Paris, 1626), pp. 130–3.

57 David Parrott, "A 'prince souverain' and the French crown: Charles de Nevers," *Royal and Republican Sovereignty in Early Modern Europe*, eds. Robert Oresko et al. (Cambridge, 1997), p. 166.

58 Zeller, *Le Connêtable de Luynes*, pp. 53–4; Emile Baudson, *Charles de Gonzague, duc de Nevers 1580–1637* (Paris, 1947), pp. 204–5; B.N., imprimés Lb 36, *Accord de la querelle de MM les duc de Nevers et prince de Joinville, fait par le Roi, 19 mars* (1622).

59 Héroard, *Journal*, II, passim.

60 Moote, *Louis XIII* (Berkeley, 1989), p. 104.

61 "Le pourtrait du Roy" (1618) in *Archives curieuses*, 2nd ser., vol. 2 (Paris, 1838), 401–20; B.N., Ms. fr. 17363, fol. 230; FrançoisVI, duc de La Rochefoucauld, *Mémoires*, ed. Petitot, 2nd ser., vols. 51–2, 2 vols. (Paris, 1826), I, 337.

62 Bassompierre, *Mémoires*, II, 385.

63 *Journal d'Arnauld d'Andilly 1621*, pp. 10–11.

64 Lee, *Autobiography of Cherbury*, pp. 200–1; Batiffol, *Le Roi Louis XIII*, p. 501 and n. 2.

65 Ibid., pp. 505–6.

66 *Journal d'Arnauld 1614–1620*, p. 325. "Messieurs, vous avez en cette assemblée un avantage qui s'y rencontre peu souvent, c'est que tout ce que vous résoudrez sera incontinent après présenté au Roy, qui s'achemine en cette ville comme en son second Paris, et m'asseure que Sa Majesté s'efforcera de vous donner toute sorte de satisfaction sur vos remonstrances. Elle sayt l'Importance de cette grande Province et son affection extrême à son service, ce que lui a fait désirer d'y tenir l'une des plus célèbres assemblées qui se puisse convoquer en son Royaume; tellement que nous avons sujet d'espérer que Sa Majesté remédiera tout ensemble, et aux maladies particulières de cette Province, et à celles qui luy sont communes avec l'Estat en général. Pour mon regard, je ne manqueray pas d'embrasser en toutes occasions ce qui sera de vos intérests, comme y estant obligé par le devoir de la charge dont il a pleu à Sa Majesté de m'honorer, et encore par l'amitié et bienveüillance que vous me témoignez, laquelle je vous supplie de tout mon coeur de me continüer, et je vous serviray tous, et en

général, et en particulier. Vous entendrez par les lettres du Roy et par Messieurs les Commissaires ce qui est des Intentions de Sa Majesté."
67 Fontenay-Mareuil, *Mémoires*, I, 405.
68 Lee, *Autobiography of Cherbury*, p. 116.
69 B.N., CC Colbert 97, fols 53, 81, 94–5, 100, 102, 121; Clairambault 374, fol. 290; 377, fols. 147–9; B.N., Ms. fr. 3687, fols. 173v–174v; 3690, fols. 160, 274; 3795, fol. 100; 4069, fols. 162–3; 4102, fols. 18–20; 20155, fol. 404.
70 Batiffol, "Louis XIII et le duc de Luynes" 103 (1910), 32–4; idem, *Le Roi Louis XIII*, pp. 499–505.
71 J.H. Elliott and L.W.B. Brockliss, *The World of the Favourite* (New Haven, 1999), p. 282; James Boyden, *The Courtier and the King* (Berkeley, 1995), p. 151; Graham Darby, "Lerma before Olivares," *History Today* (July 1995), 31; Patrick Williams, *The Great Favourite* (Manchester, 2006), pp. 9–10.
72 Roger Mettam, *Power and Faction in Louis XIV's France* (Oxford, 1988), pp. 51–2; Xavier Le Person, *"Pratiques" et "Practiqueurs." La vie politique à la fin du règne de Henri III* (Geneva, 2002), passim.
73 Hanotaux, *Histoire du Cardinal de Richelieu*, II, part 2, 209; Denis Avenel, ed., *Lettres, instructions diplomatiques et papiers d'état du Cardinal de Richelieu*, 8 vols. (Paris, 1853–77), VII, 430, 455.
74 Françoise Hildesheimer, *Richelieu* (Paris, 2004), pp. 226, 296, 301, 388.
75 Moote, *Louis XIII*, pp. 103–5.
76 Batiffol, "Louis XIII et le duc de Luynes" *Rev hist* 102 (1909), 250–8; idem, *Le Roi Louis XIII*, pp. 488–95.
77 Mousnier, *L'Homme rouge*, p. 155.
78 Tapié, *La Politique étrangère*, pp. 231–2.
79 Hanotaux, *Histoire du Cardinal de Richelieu*, II, part 2, 357–8, 382–6, 406–12.
80 A.D. Lublinskaya, *French Absolutism: The Crucial Phase 1620–1629*, trans. Brian Pearce (Cambridge, 1968), pp. 149–51.
81 Cousin, "Le Duc et connétable de Luynes" (May 1861), 262.
82 Zeller, *Le Connêtable de Luynes*, pp. i–iii, 4–5, 10–11.
83 Lublinskaya, *French Absolutism*, pp. 148–9.
84 Chevallier, *Louis XIII*, pp. 177–208.
85 Tapié, *La Politique étrangère*, p. 316; Georges Pagès, *Les Institutions monarchiques en France sous Louis XIII* (Paris, 1933), p. 40; Ranum, *Richelieu and the Councillors of Louis XIII*, pp. 76, 97; *Mercure françois*, VII (1621), 817–20; Beaucaire, *Mémoires de Richelieu*, III, 154; Héroard, *Journal*, II, 2773; Charles Bernard, *Histoire des guerres de Louis XIII contre les religionnaires rebelles* (Paris, 1622), I, 204–5.
86 Ranum, *Richelieu and the Councillors of Louis XIII*, pp. 1–26; Moote, *Louis XIII*, pp. 135–74; Mousnier, *L'Homme rouge*, pp. 221–33; Louis Batiffol, *Richelieu et le Roi Louis XIII* (Paris, 1935), p. 19; Barbiche, *Les Institutions*, pp. 269–72.

8

The siege of Montauban

The red-brick city of Montauban on the river Tarn was the second largest Protestant city in the southwest. Unable to capture the first, La Rochelle, the king decided to occupy Montauban for its strategic importance as the gateway to Languedoc. Montauban, however, refused to admit the approaching royal army of 25,000 men, dragging 45 cannons behind it. The duc de Rohan, commander of the Huguenot forces, arrived in the fortified city on 18 June 1621 to supervise the preparation of its defenses for a siege. The royal army positioned itself around Montauban on three sides so that no one could get in or out, leaving the northeast corner open because of the rough terrain. The siege area was divided into three sections so far apart that it took an hour by horse to go from one to the other. The army had too few troops to surround the city entirely.

Rohan supervised the reinforcement of Montauban's sturdy walls, and the construction of firing bastions above its gates. The duc de La Force was put in command of a defensive garrison of 5,000 soldiers and 44 cannons, greatly inferior in numbers to the king's army but equal in firepower, and a siege was not a pitched battle. Enough munitions, grain, wine, and livestock had been stockpiled to last a year. Rohan broke through the royalist lines in late July, heading for Castres southeast of Montauban to recruit reinforcements, and the royal army began its siege in mid-August. The city resisted fiercely withstanding three major assaults. Three months later, the royal army was still unable to breach its walls or force open its gates, and had endured heavy losses from the repeated attacks. Rohan's reinforcements of about 1,500 men broke through the royalist lines on 28 October to enter the city. With winter approaching, the king and Luynes decided to lift the siege a few days later.[1]

On the evening of 22 September, hoping to breach a wall, a royal engineer decided to explode a large mine that had been under construction for weeks. François de Bassompierre protested because of the late hour, but the duc de Chaulnes, Luynes's brother, insisted because he wanted to lead the attack. There was a huge explosion, and Bassompierre ran for his life. The badly placed mine contained too much gunpowder, and the front of the wall rose to a great height. A thousand pounds of plaster and building material fell back over the royalist trenches. Bassompierre took refuge in a wooden barrel, which cracked under the weight of the debris, and he had to dig his way out. He ran to the gaping crater, climbing over corpses to get there, just in time to see the royalists rush the wall, which had not been breached. They were beaten back by heavy gunfire. During the next three days, Bassompierre worked hard to reorganize the royalist lines by securing replacements, repairing damaged trenches, bringing up more artillery, and repelling sorties by the Montalbanais. His head was grazed by a shell, and he bled profusely, but he was not seriously wounded.

On 26 September, Bassompierre was summoned by the king to siege headquarters at Piquecos, a red-brick château on a hill overlooking a valley north of Montauban. He mounted his horse and rode off, his clothing covered with mud and his head encrusted with blackened, dried blood. He was almost unrecognizable, but the king and Luynes received him without saying a word, and gave him command of the king's guard company of light horse, replacing Luynes's brother who had fallen ill. As they stood chatting, the queen and three of her ladies entered the room. She asked Luynes who that dirty man was, and Luynes jokingly replied that he was a provincial seigneur by the name of the comte de Curton. The queen exclaimed, "Jésus, but he is ugly!" Luynes said in an aside to the king, "Sire, present Monsieur de Bassompierre to the queen and her ladies as the comte de Curton." The king went along with the joke and said, "Here is a really dirty fellow who should stay at home in the country!" When Bassompierre laughed, the ladies recognized him and fussed over his head wound.[2] This anecdote highlights the questions asked here. Why did Luynes agree to go on campaign against the Protestants? Who decided to besiege Montauban, and why did the siege fail? What was Luynes's role in the siege?

The 1621 campaign and sieges

The 1621 campaign against the Huguenots lasted from 5 April, when the king and Luynes left Paris for Fontainebleau, until 15 December when Luynes died. The king and Luynes travelled from Fontainebleau to Orléans on 28 April, and then by boat down the Loire to Saumur, arriving on 11 May. Two days later the king decided to besiege the fortified Protestant town of Saint Jean d'Angély, which had refused to open its gates to the approaching royal army. The siege began on 16 May and lasted until 23 June. The king and Luynes travelled overland on 17 May from Saumur to Thouars, Parthenay, Fontenay-le-Comte, Niort, and Chizé, arriving on 4 June at the château of Vervant near Saint Julien, which became siege headquarters. Most of the Huguenot towns along the way

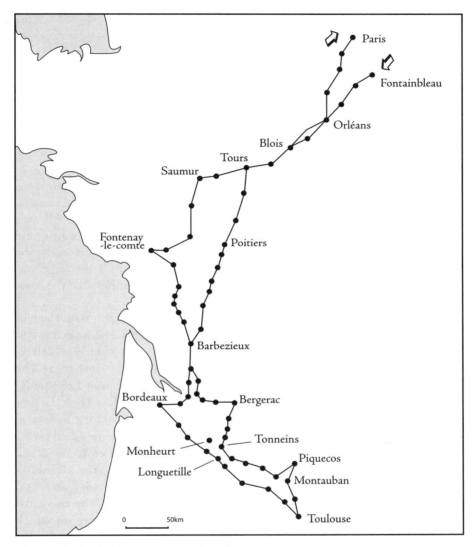

Figure 8 The 1621 Campaign against the Protestants.

opened their gates to the royal army, and the fate of Saint Jean d'Angély was meant as a lesson to those that refused. When the town finally surrendered, it was sacked; its walls were torn down; a Catholic garrison was installed; some of its privileges were revoked; but no one was hanged.[3]

In late June the king and his army continued their march south, stopping at Brisembourg, Cognac, and Pons, which opened their gates, and arriving at Nérac, which briefly resisted and then surrendered to the duc de Mayenne on

9 July. The king and Luynes had gone on 5 July to Barbezieux where an army was being assembled to blockade La Rochelle by land. The blockade was unsuccessful because it did not prevent the city from being supplied by sea, but it did separate the city from its Protestant hinterland. The army continued south, and received the keys to Montguyon, Coutras, Castillon, Bergerac, Sainte Foy, and Tonneins, whose fortifications were torn down and Catholic garrisons installed. Clairac on the river Lot refused to open its gates, so the royal army besieged it from 23 July until it surrendered on 5 August. Four of its inhabitants were hanged; its fortifications were razed; a Catholic garrison was installed; and the town paid 1,000 livres to avoid being sacked.[4]

On 7 August, the duc de Mayenne captured Aubiac only one league from Montauban, hanged twenty-two of its citizens, and sacked the town. Caussade, Negreplisse, Agen, Valence, and Moissac quickly opened their gates. At Agen on 11 August, the king and the council decided to besiege Montauban, and the siege began on 17 August, when the king arrived at his headquarters in the château of Piquecos about five miles away. The decision to lift the siege was made on 2 November; the king left for Toulouse on 6 November; and the royal army began to withdraw on 10 November.

The king and Luynes now decided to besiege the little Protestant town of Monheurt on the Garonne river northwest of Montauban because its Protestant governor had been murdered for declaring his loyalty to the king. With thirty-five or forty houses and a church, Monheurt looks much the same today. The king and Luynes established their headquarters at the château of Longuetille near Condom, and the siege began on 1 December. Two days later, Luynes was stricken with scarlet fever, which was rife in the army, and the town was sacked and burned after it surrendered on 11 December.[5] Luynes died on 15 December, effectively ending the campaign because the king fled to Bordeaux for Christmas, and then returned to Paris in January. During the 10-month campaign, the royal army had marched 4,000 kilometers, occupied about 60 Huguenot cities, towns, and châteaux, and besieged 4 of them. The two most important cities, La Rochelle and Montauban, had escaped capture for which Luynes as constable was blamed.[6]

The first question about Luynes's role in the 1621 campaign is why did he change his mind and agree to go? The king had been talking about a campaign against the Huguenots since early in 1620, and he had become insistent after his success in Béarn, which he wanted to repeat. If Luynes intended to remain the favorite, he had to accompany the king, who had been gone for only two weeks in Béarn, but would be gone for months in the southwest, which was too long for them to be separated. Luynes had to go if he did not want to be replaced as the favorite-in-chief. The office of constable, which gave him a role and a rank in the army, was his price for agreeing to go.

To what extent was Luynes a self-interested sycophant who went with the king to retain favor, and to what extent did he really believe in the campaign's necessity? Luynes can justifiably be accused of sycophancy on many occasions, but not on this one. He genuinely believed that the Huguenots' behavior endangered the monarchy, which he was committed to preserve, as well as the life of the king, whom he was sworn to protect. So, he agreed to go on campaign as much from conviction as from self-interest.

Luynes's piety has been widely accepted by historians as the reason for his change of mind. A staunch Catholic like his father, he was influenced by the Catholic party at court.[7] In particular, he was influenced by Père Arnoux, his Jesuit confessor who was also the king's confessor. The devout Arnoux regarded the campaign as a crusade or a holy war, and advocated it constantly. Eventually, his meddling became too much for Luynes, whom he had begun to contradict and even criticize to the king. Luynes got rid of him. He convinced the king to send him to Toulouse in late November 1621, and to write Cardinal de La Rochefoucauld in Paris to ask for the name of another Jesuit confessor. Gaspard de Séguiran now became the confessor of Luynes and the king, and mindful of his predecessor's fate, he did not interfere in politics.[8]

To attribute Luynes's change of mind solely to Catholic piety, however, is simplistic. The traditional interpretation is flawed because it puts too much emphasis on personalities, and not enough on context.[9] Luynes's change of mind was a pragmatic decision that was also based on the political realities of the day, not just on emotional piety. He had decided that the Protestants were a serious threat to the king and the monarchy as early as October 1619, when the Huguenot Assembly at Loudun had sent deputies to the Queen Mother, and she had formally received them.

The Queen Mother's power base was in the southwest, an important Protestant stronghold, and an alliance between her and the Protestants, however temporary, would endanger the king's throne. Her supporters included leading Huguenot great nobles such as the duc de Rohan, commander of the Huguenot army in 1621; his brother, the duc de Soubise, commander of the garrison at Saint Jean d'Angély; the duc de La Force, former governor of Béarn and commander of the garrison at Montauban; his son, the marquis de Montpouillan, the king's former favorite, who died of a head wound received at Tonneins; and the ducs de Châtillon and de La Trémoille, who fought against the king during the 1621 campaign.[10] Luynes first perceived the Protestants as a threat during the Queen Mother's revolt because of this political reality.

Luynes feared the Queen Mother's enmity as much as he feared being assassinated. Shortly before his death, he wrote in a letter, "I fear neither this woman [the Queen Mother] nor her intrigues because the man [the king] fears me so much that he will do nothing without informing me. After the capture of Monheurt, I shall make peace [with the Protestants], and arrange things so well to suit myself that I shall no longer have anything to fear."[11] Luynes was whistling in the dark because he knew that he was doomed if the Queen Mother regained power. He justifiably feared her vengeance and her influence over the king, which she quickly reasserted after Luynes's death.

Fighting a common Protestant foe unified the Queen Mother's Catholic supporters behind the king, an important political advantage of the campaign. The 19-year-old king personally participated in the marches, sieges, and skirmishes, riding from early in the morning until late at night, supervising the placement of cannons, visiting the trenches, chatting with the officers and men, and staying with them when they were being shelled. For the first time, the army saw in him his father's courage and fortitude.[12] It was a propaganda victory for the king as a soldier in the field, while his mother was a plump middle-aged woman far away in Paris.

Luynes's perception of the Protestants as a threat was reinforced by their intransigence, particularly the Huguenot Assembly meeting at La Rochelle after 25 December 1620. The king had prohibited this assembly, but it met anyway, since it regarded what had happened in Béarn as the fate awaiting them all. On 10 May 1621, the assembly voted to divide France into eight military districts under the command of Protestant great nobles, a clear signal that they intended to fight.[13] The king responded on 13 May by announcing the siege of Saint Jean d'Angély.

Luynes regarded the decision of the La Rochelle assembly to create separate military districts as an act of rebellion similar to the Dutch revolt. He believed that the Huguenots wanted to establish a republic within the kingdom of France. In speaking to Du Plessis-Mornay at Saumur on 12 May 1621, two days after the La Rochelle assembly had made its decision, Luynes denounced "the absurd and intolerable behavior of the assembly which seems to be establishing a form of republic ... under the guise of a just defense ... This could only lead to the ruin of the monarchy as it did in Holland."[14] Jeannin thought the same, and Lesdiguières declared that the seal the assembly was using for its documents was a public declaration of its disobedience and an attempt to "create a new Holland in France."[15]

Luynes also considered the Protestants a threat because he had been unable to use personal diplomacy to convince them to cooperate. He had difficulty in managing the Huguenot Assembly that opened on 26 September 1619 at Loudun in Poitou. The assembly deputies presented a list of demands to the king on 20 December, which they repeated on 25 January 1620, and vowed not to disperse until they had a satisfactory reply. Condé and Luynes represented the king in negotiating with them, and Condé was so annoyed by their attitude that he proposed taking severe measures against them. Luynes temporized, and suggested appointing a commission to discuss their demands, which he promised to try to persuade the king to approve within six months. He simultaneously solicited the support of Lesdiguières, a moderate Protestant whose grandson would marry his niece on 1 June 1620.

The Loudun assembly now voted to reconvene to discuss the situation if their demands had not been met within six months. This was too much for Luynes, who told them that he had not been empowered to make promises on the king's behalf, and he asked the assembly to disperse, which they did on 20 March 1620.[16] Undoubtedly, he knew that the king would refuse their demands. Before dispersing, they chose Jean Favas, comte de Castets, as their representative to the king. Favas arrived in September 1620 at the court in Bordeaux and followed it to Paris. Luynes summoned him to Saint-Germain-en-Laye on 2 March to tell him that the king had refused to agree to the Protestant demands. He talked in private with Favas often during that month, trying to find a compromise, but he was unsuccessful, and Favas left court at the end of March.[17]

On 15 May at Saumur, two days after the king had decided to besiege Saint Jean d'Angély, Luynes had an interview with Benjamin de Rohan, duc de Soubise, who commanded the town's garrison. Luynes asked Soubise to persuade the town to obey the king's orders and open its gates. Soubise replied that he preferred a military solution.[18] Luynes's efforts six months earlier to negotiate a compromise with the duc de La Force had also been unsuccessful, and his failure convinced him that Protestant intransigence was dangerous to the monarchy. So, he decided to try to separate the majority of loyal obedient Huguenots from the militant minority.[19] This was the classic strategy of divide-and-rule that he had learned in court politics, and used so successfully against the Queen Mother. Moderate Protestants had already disassociated themselves from the radical assembly at La Rochelle, and Luynes sought to recruit them to the king's cause, hoping to use the moderate majority's obedience to weaken the radicals' resolve and avert a civil war.

Whose decision was it to besiege Montauban? The royal council met at Agen on 11 August to discuss the king's proposal to besiege the city, and since he was so insistent the council agreed, and the siege began five days later.[20] Richelieu noted that the king had made the decision to besiege Montauban on the advice of the duc de Mayenne.[21] Luynes said that the king himself had made this decision.[22] Most historians, including Louis Batiffol, have agreed that the king and the council together decided to besiege Montauban, and that Luynes participated only to the extent that he did not oppose their decision.[23] Fontenay-Mareuil, however, credited Luynes with the decision, noting that there had been two points of view during the council debate. One view held that Mayenne with an army should take the towns around Montauban, blockading it for the winter rather than besieging it, while the king led an army into Languedoc to seize Montpellier and Nîmes. The other view held that the royal army should besiege Montauban. When it fell, the towns around it would surrender, and then the royal army could march into Languedoc without risking an attack from the rear. Luynes favored the second view, and the council adopted it.[24] Probably, it would be more accurate to say that the king, who was overconfident after two quick successful sieges, favored the second view which Luynes supported, and the council adopted.

During the campaign, the king called frequent Conseils de guerre or councils of war attended by Luynes, the marshals, camp marshals, section commanders, and a few council members and greybeards, most of whom had remained in Paris. Luynes said little at these meetings, although as the king's spokesman he occasionally gave short pep talks. He talked frequently with the king in private, and consulted his own advisers including Chaulnes, Luxembourg, Modène, Ornano, Bassompierre, Schomberg, Arnoux, and Ruccellai.[25] Bassompierre noted that the king and Luynes together, without consulting the council, decided to lift the siege on 2 November.[26] Decision-making, therefore, remained much the same during the 1621 campaign, the major difference being that the greybeards had less influence and the marshals more.

Why did the siege of Montauban fail? Fancan, the pamphleteer, blamed Luynes whose decision he said it was to besiege the city, and he blamed Luynes for starting the war against the Huguenots as well.[27] Fancan was widely read, so the other pamphleteers, the Parisian reading public, and the court also blamed Luynes for the siege and the war, which was ironic considering that Luynes had opposed the war. A pro-Luynes pamphleteer insisted that he had not advised the king to go to war against the Huguenots, and that the king had made this decision himself on the advice of his council, since allowing the continued disobedience of the most heavily fortified cities in France would destroy his authority.[28] The myth of Luynes's responsibility, however, was asserted by seventeenth-century historians François Eudes de Mézeray and Scipion Dupleix, and repeated by eighteenth-century historians Gabriel Daniel, Henri Griffet, and Henri Philippe de Limiers, and so entered the historical literature.[29]

Richelieu did not hold Luynes responsible for besieging Montauban because the king himself had made this decision. Luynes was not responsible for lifting the siege either because he had not been the field commander. Richelieu noted that the reasons for the army's withdrawal included an insufficient number of troops; an epidemic of disease; cold weather; persistent rain; a shortage of money and supplies; and the cost of paying the troops versus their lack of success.[30] In addition, the most popular field commander, the duc de Mayenne, was killed by a bullet in the eye during a skirmish on 17 September, which demoralized the troops even more.[31]

The council members opposing the siege argued against it for similar reasons. The weather would soon be cold with winter approaching. There had been constant rain, and the ground around Montauban was wet and soggy, making military operations difficult. The rain had been so heavy that it had filled the trenches in places, and the river Tarn had overflowed its banks. [32] There was an epidemic of scarlet fever among the troops; reinforcements were needed; supplies were low; and there were insufficient funds to pay for either. Montauban was strongly fortified with thick walls and plenty of munitions and food. Rohan, the commander-in-chief, was known for his stubbornness and would never surrender. In short, they thought that the city would be able to hold out longer than the royal army, and they were right. [33]

The papal nuncio gave additional reasons for the siege's failure. The royal army had begun the siege without enough troops, munitions, or supplies, and had failed to protect the troops in the trenches with covering fire because of these shortages. The result was a high casualty rate and low troop morale. Luynes as constable had been responsible for bringing in reinforcements and supplies, but he had failed to do so because of his incompetence and inexperience. He had also wasted time on futile negotiations. [34]

The nuncio was probably referring to an interview that Luynes had with the duc de Rohan on 8 October. Luynes told the duke that the king would not sign a general peace treaty, only a specific treaty on Montauban. If the city would surrender and accept having its walls torn down and a Catholic garrison installed, nothing else would happen. All the towns around it would be spared, and Rohan's property and offices would not be confiscated. Luynes asked Rohan to accept these terms and order Montauban to open its gates, but he refused. Luynes noted that the king could confiscate everything he owned if he refused. (The king did confiscate his government of Poitou.) Rohan would agree only to a general peace treaty. He said that he knew his own danger, and asked Luynes if he knew his. He said that Luynes was a widely hated favorite whom everyone envied, and if the royal army failed to take Montauban, he would be blamed, which would encourage more conspiracies and intrigues against him. Rohan did not have to add that the army was unlikely to take Montauban, and that Luynes might well share Concini's fate if it did not. He urged Luynes to persuade the king to sign a general peace treaty replacing the Edict of Nantes. Luynes replied that he would ask the king and the council, which he did on 13 October, but they rejected Rohan's terms. [35]

Although his attempt to secure the surrender of Montauban through negotiation had failed, Luynes continued to try. A council meeting on 22 October at Piquecos was attended by the king, Luynes, Cardinal de Retz, Modène, Bassompierre, and the abbé Ruccellai. Afterward, Luynes told Bassompierre that his brother Chaulnes could arrange an interview with the duc de la Force, commander of the Montauban garrison, and he asked if Bassompierre thought such a meeting would be worthwhile, or if another interview with Rohan might be useful. Bassompierre said no to both, but Luynes decided to try, anyway.[36] Richelieu said that Luynes saw Rohan several times, but he may have been including two trips by Desplan to set up their only face-to-face meeting on 8 October.[37] Gabriel Hanotaux observed that Luynes "impeded everything by his eternal negotiations," an observation without foundation.[38] Luynes's efforts to negotiate an end to a costly siege were commendable if unsuccessful.

The siege had to be lifted because of a lack of supplies and munitions, a shortage of money, a dwindling number of troops, and poor planning. The royal army was low on food and munitions when it began the siege of Montauban on 17 August, less than two weeks after Clairac had surrendered. Clairac had been under siege for two weeks from 23 July to 5 August, and the army should have been resupplied before beginning another siege. The king had decided to besiege Montauban immediately without resupplying, and to use massive cannonades against its walls to force a quick surrender. He was overconfident because of the short sieges of Saint Jean d'Angély and Clairac, which had weak crumbling walls in contrast to Montauban's strong walls. The army used more cannon balls in besieging Montauban than it had used in the three other sieges combined, 8,000 at Saint Jean d'Angély, 2,000 at Clairac, 2,000 at Monheurt, and 14,000 at Montauban. On 16 September, 400 cannon balls were fired high over the city for psychological effect to frighten the inhabitants, a waste of ammunition because the city had already been shelled for a month. There was much wasted ammunition during the siege. On 1 September, 10,000 pounds of gunpowder accidentally caught fire and caused 40 deaths. On the same day in another section, 8,000 pounds of gunpowder burned, causing more deaths. Moreover, the royalists lacked good intelligence about the city's defenses after Luynes's spy in Montauban was caught and hanged.[39] The royalists needed a new source of intelligence, but never found it.

Mid-August was too late in the season to begin another siege. The weather quickly became cold and wet and stayed that way, making the men miserable, filling the trenches with water, wetting the gunpowder, and covering everything with mud that bogged down the cannon and made redeployment difficult.[40] The weather made bad roads worse and resupplying by wagon more difficult. In addition, there was a shortage of money with which to supply and pay the troops. The king in April had secured 400,000 livres for the campaign, but he had spent 600,000 livres by December. He sent to Paris for more money, which came in late November in 10 carts of gold coins escorted by 500 horsemen, but too late to be useful.[41] The army's morale was low because of the high fatality rate and a high death rate from an epidemic of scarlet fever. Secretaries of state Sceaux and Pontchartrain, keeper of the seals Du Vair, Cardinal Guise, the archbishop of Sens, the bishops of Marseille and Carcassonne, and royal historian Pierre Matthieu died of scarlet fever that autumn, while Luynes died of it in December, and Bassompierre and Arnauld d'Andilly nearly died of it.[42] Both men participated in the siege, and their memoirs are filled with the names of officers and noble volunteers who were wounded or killed in the repeated assaults on the walls.

There were also high casualty and death rates from mining accidents such as the explosion on 22 September that nearly killed Bassompierre. There were eighteen or twenty men killed in that accident and fifty to sixty wounded, while Ornano was shot in the arm and received a saber wound on the thigh during the skirmish that followed.[43] There were other serious mining accidents on 28 September and 24–25 October.[44] Fontenay-Mareuil, who participated in the siege, reported that the army was full of untrained, inexperienced officers who knew nothing about siege warfare, and there were almost no mining engineers, which resulted in a high accident rate.[45] The captain in charge of constructing the 22 September mine was killed in the explosion. He had only wanted to use 600 or 700 pounds of gunpowder, but Chaulnes, who knew nothing about mining, had insisted on adding another 2,000 pounds, and so caused needless deaths.[46]

The army had not been large enough in August to surround Montauban entirely, and it had become smaller by November.[47] Reinforcements were badly needed, but not forthcoming because of the poor roads and wet weather, which made travel difficult, and because of the shortage of money with which to pay the troops. Fontenay-Mareuil blamed Luynes for the lack of reinforcements. He said that the duc de Vendôme, governor of Brittany, had levied 6,000 to 7,000 Breton replacements whom he intended to send by boat to Bordeaux and then up river to Montauban, but Luynes had said they were not needed.[48] Vendôme had arrived at Montauban two weeks after the siege began.[49] Luynes may have still thought at this time that there would be a quick surrender, so he told Vendôme that his recruits were not be needed because the siege would be over before they arrived, which was a serious mistake. Luynes also told Condé that his replacements levied as governor of Berry were not needed, probably because he did not want Condé back at court. The duc de Montmorency had arrived in October with recruits from his government of Languedoc, but he had promptly caught scarlet fever and gone home, taking them with him.[50] Luynes, therefore, must share some of the blame for failing to secure the troops needed to prevent the reinforcement of Montauban. His poor performance as constable increased his unpopularity.

By the end of October, the royal army was exhausted and discouraged. On 29 October, the day after Rohan's reinforcements had gotten through, Luynes went to the Moustier section as the king's envoy to meet with the marshals and section commanders to decide whether or not to continue the siege. He asked the opinion of each in turn, and they all thought it was hopeless, but no one wanted to say so. Finally, Bassompierre told Luynes that the army was tired after eight months of campaigning and disheartened by the long siege. Autumn had ended; winter was coming; and the fatality rate continued to climb. Bassompierre advised ending the siege immediately, and three days later with the king's approval, Luynes announced the army's withdrawal.[51]

A lack of planning had turned the siege into a shambles. Most of the problems had been apparent during the siege of Saint Jean d'Angély three months earlier, but they had not been addressed. There had been numerous mining accidents.[52] The lack of mining engineers made the use of explosives dangerous, and there was a high fatality rate from the repeated assaults and skirmishes.[53] About 1,500 royalist soldiers and 400 gentlemen were killed at Saint Jean d'Angély compared to only 70 Protestant defenders.[54] It was obvious that a siege strategy of assault-after-assault, and a campaign strategy of siege-after-siege, would be costly in lives, munitions, supplies, and money, but no precautions were taken.

It was also apparent that there were command problems. There were endless councils of war, which in the case of Montauban were held miles behind the front lines at siege headquarters.[55] These meetings were attended by the king, Luynes, the marshals, and the three section (*quartier*) commanders who had to leave the lines, a trip of at least an hour each way. The chain of command was clear in theory but muddled in practice. The king was supreme commander with final authority, and Luynes was commander-in-chief with overall responsibility for the army under the king, while Schomberg was in command of the artillery needed for the siege. The authority of these three men in the field overlapped. The marshals were under Luynes, and normally over the section commanders, but at Montauban the section commanders had final authority, so there were endless quarrels between the marshals and section commanders. Mayenne, who was not a marshal, was a section commander to whom the king listened, and he became so influential that he was acting as commander-in-chief when he was killed in September.[56] Lesdiguières, a marshal and the army's general camp marshal, commanded the Moustiers section at Montauban, and because of his military experience he became acting commander-in-chief after Mayenne's death. If his advice on defending the open section at Montauban with moveable fortifications had been taken, Rohan's reinforcements would not have gotten through. The king listened to Lesdiguières, but did not fully trust him because he was a Protestant. There was no one else of comparable experience or ability.[57]

As constable, Luynes's duties were advisory and administrative. He regularly attended councils of war, made inspection tours, and advised the king on strategy and tactics including the deployment of artillery and personnel. He had overall responsibility for logistics, that is, for the procurement and transportation of supplies and men, and for army discipline in his own judicial court. The office of constable, however, had been vacant since 1614, and its authority and duties had never been well-defined.[58] There was a basic conflict between Luynes's role as constable, and his role as favorite-in-chief. As favorite, he had to remain behind the lines at siege headquarters with the king, but as constable he should have been at the front with the army. Although the king had final authority, Luynes was his second-in-command and spokesman in dealing with the section commanders, in particular Mayenne and Lesdiguières, both of whom, in fact, replaced him as commander-in-chief at the front. The lines of authority were muddled and confused, and Luynes's duties were never clear.

Luynes as constable was held responsible for the shortages of supplies and men, but there were extenuating circumstances. The king, not he, had made the decision to besiege Montauban without resupplying or bringing in reinforcements, and the king, not he, had ordered the heavy shelling that consumed ammunition at an alarming rate. Luynes was not responsible for the bad weather or bad roads, which made the delivery of supplies and new troops more difficult, and the king, not he, was responsible for the lack of money to pay the troops. The king had borrowed money at Bordeaux in August but not enough.[59] Luynes was not the field commander, so he was not responsible for the high fatality rate or the epidemic of scarlet fever. His harshest critic, Richelieu, said that he was not responsible for the siege's failure. Luynes became the scapegoat, however, and the siege's failure was blamed on his inexperience and incompetence.[60]

Luynes and the king made regular trips to the front, visiting the artillery batteries and inspecting the earthwork defenses. On 28 and 29 May, Luynes inspected the trenches at the siege of Saint Jean d'Angély, and reported to the king and the council that the trenches were too shallow because the bedrock was so close to the surface. The king accompanied by Luynes ordered twelve cannon fired to check their emplacements on 29 May. Two days later he visited the trenches accompanied by Luynes, Cardinal Guise, marshal Praslin, the duc de La Rochefoucauld, and the baron de Termes. On 1 June, the king inspected the trenches with Luynes, who had prepared a map of the artillery emplacements. There were three batteries of five cannon each per section for a total of forty-five cannon. Luynes spread out a map for the king to see, and the king ordered the repositioning of some cannon. On 3 June, when Luynes, Schomberg, and Modène checked their repositioning, they were fired upon and had to run for their lives. Luynes made a report to the king who ordered an attack. On 23 June, Luynes, his brothers, and his guard company participated in the final assault on Saint Jean d'Angély through a breach in the city wall by the Aunis gate after it had been shelled for hours. The king came in person at noon to check the progress of the shelling. Soubise sent a messenger to Luynes offering to surrender, and after negotiating terms and discussing them in a council meeting, the king and Luynes took the town's surrender.[61]

On 23 July, the king on horseback visited the siege of Clairac. On 1 August, Luynes and Schomberg inspected the trenches and artillery at Clairac, and on 2 August, the king inspected them again before ordering an attack. On 5 August, after the gates had been opened, Luynes inspected the town on foot accompanied by a large entourage, and made an inventory of its weapons and ammunition. On 22 August, he was fired upon while visiting Bassompierre's section at Montauban, and had to leave in a hurry when the enemy made a sortie.[62] On 12 September, he witnessed an assault on the walls of Montauban. On 22 September, he and the king inspected a defective mine, and on 13 October, Luynes accompanied the king on yet another inspection tour. The king participated in the general assault on 17 October, arising at three o'clock that morning to get ready. He went to mass, ordered his armor taken to the front, mounted his horse, and at four o'clock rode to the front where he breakfasted with Luynes and the abbé Ruccellai. At eleven, he witnessed in turn the assaults in the three different sections, returning to Piquecos at eight that evening. On 21 October, the king and Luynes visited the Picardy section to witness yet another assault, accompanied by Schomberg, Puysieux, Père Arnoux, and Cardinal de Retz. On 29, October Luynes visited the Moustiers section commanded by Lesdiguières, and four days later he announced the army's withdrawal.[63]

Richelieu had been wrong when he said that Luynes had never gotten within cannon range of the city. Luynes had visited the front regularly, been shelled several times, and participated in a general assault. He was not a coward. He was interested in the effective deployment of artillery and men, and he tried to learn more about siege tactics. He was not responsible for the failure of the siege of Montauban, and his attempts to negotiate its end were commendable if unsuccessful. Luynes was militarily inexperienced, however, and his overall performance as constable was poor. What role did he play in making foreign policy?

The Valteline affair

The English ambassador to France, Edward, Lord Herbert of Cherbury, received instructions from James I to offer to mediate a peace between Louis XIII and the Huguenots, and if that proved impossible, to inform Louis that James would not permit the "total ruin and extirpation" of the French Protestants. So, in June 1621, Sir Edward went by coach from Paris to Saint Jean d'Angély, which was under siege, for an audience with the king. Louis did not reply except to tell him to speak to Luynes, who would give him an answer. Luynes often acted the king's spokesman in dealing with foreign ambassadors, and he cordially received Sir Edward, asking what his business was. Sir Edward replied that his master had asked him to negotiate a peace between the French king and his Protestant subjects. Luynes replied, "What has the king your master to do with us? Why does he meddle in our affairs?" Sir Edward replied that his master did not need to give his reasons, and for himself, it was enough that he obeyed him, which was not a diplomatic reply. Luynes answered curtly with one word, "Bien."

Sir Edward said that if he could successfully broker a French peace, James hoped that France would then help his son-in-law, Frederick V, count-elector of the Palatinate, who had recently been deposed by the Austrian Holy Roman Emperor Ferdinand II, to regain his throne. Finding this suggestion presumptuous, Luynes declared abruptly, "We will have none of your advice." He was referring to repeated English admonishments about the Huguenots, and undoubtedly speaking for the king. Sir Edward replied that he regretted the French rejection of his offer, and added obscurely, "We know very well what we have to do," probably meaning to negotiate separately with the Habsburgs. He wisely did not deliver the inflammatory second part of his message. Luynes replied, "We are not afraid of you," and Sir Edward repeated, "We know what we have to do." His repetition of this quasi-threat angered Luynes who said, "By God, if you weren't Monsieur the Ambassador, I would treat you differently." Sir Edward answered that he was the ambassador and a gentleman, and he put his hand on the hilt of his sword, saying that it would answer for him, and rose to go. Luynes did not answer, but rose, too, offering to accompany him to the door. Sir Edward told him there was no need for that after "so rude an enter-tainment," and left the room.[64] He was recalled shortly thereafter, and replaced by James Hay, Viscount Doncaster and Earl of Carlisle, whom Luynes received as extraordinary ambassador in November 1621.[65]

This unpleasant interview tells us something about Luynes's diplomatic role. He frequently received ambassadors because the king found audiences with them tiresome and boring. He was knowledgeable about foreign affairs, and read at least some of the ambassadorial correspondence.[66] He was also influential in making foreign policy, demonstrated by the Valteline affair. Sir Edward had lost his temper, but Luynes had been abrupt. Why was the affable Luynes so rude? Undoubtedly, he shared the king's resentment at the unsatisfac-tory outcome of the French embassy to the English court a few months earlier. Luynes's brother had been sent in January 1621 to discuss a joint Anglo-French military operation in the Valteline and Germany; a marriage alliance between the Prince of Wales and Louis XIII's sister; and an English promise not to aid the Huguenots.[67] The negative English response to these requests had angered

the king, and Luynes as his spokesman was sending a strong message to James I
about meddling in French affairs and failing to cooperate.

Louis XIII's desire to go on campaign in the southwest motivated his
handling of the Valteline affair. The Valteline was the Italian-speaking valley of
the Adda river, which controlled the passes and communication routes between
Lombardy and the Tyrol. Additional routes ran through the valley up into
southern Germany and down to Venice. Until the early sixteenth century, the
Valteline had belonged to Milan, and then it had come under the control of the
Protestant Grisons, the three Grey Leagues of southeastern Switzerland over
which France had a protectorate. In 1603, Henri IV had renewed the French
alliance with the Grisons, who had closed the Valteline passes to Spanish troops.
These passes were an essential link between Milan, now under Spanish control,
and the Austrian Tyrol.[68] Henri IV had been pursuing an anti-Spanish foreign
policy by building up anti-Habsburg alliances with the English, Dutch, and
German Protestant states, and with Savoy, the Grisons, and Venice as neighbors
of Milan, and he had advocated toleration for French Protestants to keep the
support of European Protestants. His foreign policy was still in place in 1617,
although the Queen Mother had been more conciliatory in arranging Spanish
Habsburg marriages for her eldest son and daughter.[69] Louis XIII maintained his
father's alliances by marrying his sister Christine to the duke of Savoy's son in
February 1619, a marriage that Luynes's client Modène helped to arrange.[70]

Spain in this period was an expansionistic empire-builder, and she had
been a French rival and enemy for a century. France was encircled by Habsburg
possessions, and the Spanish had contested territory on three of its borders,
Flanders in the north, Roussillon, Catalonia, and Béarn in the south, and the
Franche-Comté in the east.[71] Spain now sought to add the French sphere of
interest of the Valteline to her empire. In July 1620, the duc de Feria, the
Spanish governor of Milan, had taken advantage of the king's preoccupation with
suppressing the Queen Mother's revolt and sent troops to occupy the Valteline,
ostensibly to protect its Catholic inhabitants from persecution by their Protestant overlords. Using the Valteline passes, the Spanish could now move troops
from Italy through Switzerland to the Rhineland, Low Countries, and Austria,
which frightened neighboring Venice, Savoy, and the Grisons. As allies, they
requested French aid in forcing the Spanish to withdraw their troops.[72]

During all-day council meetings on 10, 11, and 12 December 1620, the
decision was made not to intervene militarily in the Valteline, but to use negotiation to persuade the Spanish to leave voluntarily. On 14 December, the king
left Paris for a month to inspect Luynes's government of Picardy on the border
of the Spanish Netherlands and did not return until 12 January.[73] At the same
time, Bassompierre was named extraordinary ambassador to Spain to negotiate
a treaty settling the Valteline dispute, although he actually left Paris two months

later on 10 February. His instructions stated that he should use "terms which could not be interpreted as menacing."[74] Luynes's brother Cadenet was chosen in mid-December to go as extraordinary ambassador to London with the authority to propose and reply, but not to conclude a treaty. He took ship at Calais on 31 December, and his title was elevated to that of duc de Chaulnes when he returned in late January. The king and Luynes waited to hear his report before sending Bassompierre to Madrid.[75]

During March and April 1621, Bassompierre successfully negotiated the Treaty of Madrid, which stipulated that the Spanish would withdraw their troops from the Valteline, turn over control of the valley to the Grisons, and declare a general amnesty.[76] Bassompierre's original written instructions had allowed him only to hear the Spanish reply, not to negotiate a treaty, but at his leave-taking in February, the king and Luynes had verbally instructed him to conclude a treaty as quickly as possible, and he did so.[77] Bassompierre sent a letter to the king on 17 April reporting that he was making good progress, and on 20 April that an agreement had been reached. On 27 April, he sent letters to the king, Luynes, and Puysieux, who was secretary of state for foreign affairs, announcing that a treaty had been formally signed two days earlier on 25 April.[78]

The critical event in reaching an agreement was the death of Philip III on 31 March. Elizabeth, the wife of the sixteen-year-old Philip IV, was the sister of Louis XIII. The French hoped that the new king would initiate a détente by meeting their terms to show his good will, and he did.[79] In anticipation of this, Luynes was sworn in as constable on 2 April, and the next day the king went to the Parlement of Paris to secure its approval of a subsidy of 400,000 livres, drawn on the salt tax, to levy an army for the campaign against the Huguenots.[80] The council approved his request on 20 April, three days after he had heard from Bassompierre that the negotiations were going well, and the same day that an agreement was reached.[81] A week later on 28 April, the king and Luynes left Fontainebleau for Orléans to begin their campaign against the Huguenots. They had waited until they knew for certain that the treaty would be signed.

The king and Luynes used military intimidation to increase the likelihood of Bassompierre's success in negotiating a treaty. On 5 April, they had gone from Paris to Fontainebleau where they remained for three weeks. From Fontainebleau, the king and his army could go southeast to Lyon and the Valteline, or southwest to Orléans and Poitou. The implied threat was that if a treaty were not signed, the king would change his mind about where to use his army.[82] Chaulnes's mission to England in January 1621 was another subtle form of pressure. The French knew that his discussions with the king, even those that were secret, would be reported by the Spanish ambassador, and they were right.[83] Joint discussions on Anglo-French military operations, therefore, were meant to persuade the Spanish to negotiate. The king's visit of inspection in January 1621 to Luynes's government of Picardy on the border of the Spanish Netherlands was also meant to pressure the Spanish into negotiating a settlement. The king and Luynes visited Abbeville, Montreuil, Boulogne, Calais, and Ardres, and the king put two additional guard companies before Ardres.[84]

It was widely known at court that Louis XIII wanted to go on campaign against the Huguenots, and that he sought to negotiate a quick settlement of the Valteline affair for this reason. In March 1621, Brûlart de Sillery had told the Venetian ambassador, "I want to tell you in confidence, Monsieur, that I don't know what our future is going to be. The problem is in our blood and entrails. These Huguenots are prejudicial to the king's authority, and would take the scepter from his hand. They assembled at La Rochelle without permission ... they are recalcitrant; they don't want to obey, and from day to day they become more insolent. If His Majesty wants to go outside his kingdom, it is certain that the king of Spain would foment their rebellion, and give them money to set fire to our house."[85] The king and Luynes feared Spanish intervention in Béarn if there were a campaign against the Protestants in the southwest. Luynes said to the Venetian ambassador in March 1621, "I am going to tell you, and please keep it to yourself, that we will finish by settling our domestic affairs and dealing with the Huguenots. Then we will forcefully solve our foreign problems."[86]

Luynes and the conservatives on the council convinced the king to negotiate treaties with Spain and Germany that would allow France to settle her domestic problems first. The French responded to the Valteline affair in the same way they had responded to the German crisis a year earlier. Luynes and the conservatives had advised the king then not to intervene militarily but to offer to mediate instead, and he had taken their advice.[87] Charles de Valois, duc d'Angoulême, was sent to Germany as extraordinary ambassador in June 1620 to negotiate a peace between the Catholic and Protestant German states, and the resulting Treaty of Ulm was signed on 3 July. The king had known a few days earlier that an agreement had been reached.[88] Consequently, he knew that it was safe to lead an army into Normandy after news reached Paris on 1 July of the revolt in that province. Council meetings had been held on 2 and 3 July to decide what to do. The conservatives and Luynes had opposed Condé's plan to take an army into Normandy, but the king had agreed with Condé. The king had announced his departure on 4 July, and left for Rouen on 7 July, but only after he knew that the Treaty of Ulm had been signed.[89] Ten months later, the king and Luynes would repeat this maneuver. They would leave Fontainebleau for Orléans only when they knew that the Treaty of Madrid would be signed. Timing was everything.

Luynes belonged to a small group of conservatives on the council who advocated compromise, and who convinced the king to adopt a policy of military non-intervention in the Valteline and negotiate a compromise instead. During the council meetings after the Queen Mother's escape, the king had wanted to march south with an army to confront her, but Brûlart de Sillery and Jeannin had urged sending envoys to negotiate a reconciliation instead, and Luynes had agreed with them. During the council meeting on the Holy Roman Emperor's request for assistance, Condé had proposed invading Germany, but Schomberg, Jeannin, and Puysieux had vetoed this as too risky and urged mediation instead. Luynes had agreed. The king's resolve had weakened during Christmas after a fiery sermon by Père Arnoux on his duty to help the Catholic cause in Europe, and he had announced in January 1621 that he was sending troops to aid the emperor, but these troops had never crossed the border.[90] The conservatives, who were doves, had again persuaded him not to intervene.

On 2 and 3 July 1620, during the council meetings on the Normandy revolt, Condé and the hawks had wanted to send an army, but Brûlart de Sillery, Jeannin, Puysieux, Du Vair, and Luynes had opposed it. During the 9 October council meeting on whether to invade Béarn, Luynes and Mayenne had opposed the campaign, but the conservatives had reversed their usual position and supported it because they belonged to the Catholic party at court. It seems likely, therefore, that during the council meetings on the Valteline affair in December 1620, Luynes would have sided with the doves and voted against military intervention. His brother Chaulnes and his client Bassompierre were chosen at this time as extraordinary ambassadors, indicating that he favored negotiation.[91] Conciliatory by nature, Luynes regarded himself as a peacemaker, and since he had opposed the Normandy, Béarn, and German campaigns, it seems likely that he would have opposed the Valteline campaign, too.

Luynes drew on his experience in negotiating compromises with the Protestants and the Queen Mother when he advised the king to use negotiation in solving the Valteline problem. Victor Tapié believed that Puysieux, Luynes, and the king had made foreign policy in 1620–21.[92] Louis Batiffol, on the other hand, believed that the king, Brûlart de Sillery, Puysieux, Du Vair, and Jeannin had made foreign policy without Luynes.[93] This chapter argues that the conservatives on the council, who included Brûlart de Sillery, Puysieux, Du Vair, Jeannin, Schomberg, Modène, and Chaulnes, had made foreign policy in 1620–21 along with Luynes and the king, another instance of group decision-making. They were all doves on the Valteline affair.

Schomberg, Modène, and Chaulnes sat on both the small and large councils, and were members of Luynes's personal advisory group. Luynes had served as an ordinary gentleman in the household of Schomberg's sister whose husband was the comte Du Lude. Schomberg's family was German in origin, and he had ties to the German Protestant princes. Having served Richelieu as extraordinary ambassador to Germany in 1617, he was regarded as an expert on German affairs. Modène, Luynes's cousin from the Comtat, had served as extraordinary ambassador to Savoy in 1618, and as an envoy to the Queen Mother at Angers. He would later serve as extraordinary ambassador to Rome, and he was regarded as an expert on Italian affairs.[94] Chaulnes, the favorite's brother, was considered knowledgeable about English affairs after his ambassadorial mission in January 1621. So, Luynes had his own foreign-policy advisers on the council, and they voted with the conservatives.

Jeannin was a dove, which he demonstrated in a February 1620 memorandum to the king urging the use of mediation rather than force in solving the German problem. Old and cautious, he was probably the wisest and most experienced of the king's ministers.[95] Du Vair had voted with the hawks in February 1619 because he had quarreled with Epernon, and he had criticized Puysieux's foreign policy to the Venetian ambassador in January 1621, but this does not mean that he supported military intervention in the Valteline. Du Vair was an old friend of Brûlart de Sillery and a neostoic philosopher, a former first president of the Parlement of Aix, and a legal conservative, which he demonstrated in a speech that he gave to the Parlement of Paris on 18 February 1620.[96] Given this background, Du Vair almost certainly did not support military intervention in the Valteline. Du Vair, Jeannin, Brûlart de Sillery, and Puysieux belonged to the Catholic party at court, while Luynes was a devout Catholic. They all supported the king's campaign against the Protestants, and they were in favor of whatever made that possible including the Treaty of Madrid. The leading hawk, Condé, was no longer at court.

Two policy decisions in 1620 and 1621 had significant long-term results. The first was abandoning Henri IV's policy of religious toleration in attacking the Protestants in the southwest, beginning a series of similar military campaigns across the Midi during the next eight years. The second was not to intervene in Habsburg affairs while these campaigns were under way. Both decisions were criticized by the pamphleteers, especially Fancan.[97] Gabriel Hanotaux regarded both decisions as disastrous. The first led to a loss of religious toleration in France, and the second to more than a century of warfare. Blaming Luynes for these decisions, Hanotaux wrote:

> If during the crisis of 1621, seldom mentioned in the history books, France had been governed by a firm, far-sighted leadership, the Thirty Years War could probably have been avoided. At this time, a word said by Louis XIII, an attitude, or strong ministerial language could have changed the course of events. Afterward, it was necessary to have a Richelieu and a Mazarin … a Gustavus-Adolphus, Condé, and Turenne, to repair the harm created by the negligence and incapacity of a Luynes or a Puysieux … The house of Austria, saved by Luynes in 1621, imposed on France more than a century of bloody effort.[98]

Hanotaux considered Luynes's timidity responsible for these disastrous blunders.[99] Victor Tapié agreed that these decisions were mistakes, but he did not hold Luynes responsible.[100] A. Lloyd Moote regarded French foreign policy as a series of fumbling mistakes based on inexperience, but he did not hold Luynes responsible either.[101] Cousin, Zeller, and Lublinskaya believed that Luynes had influenced the Valteline decisions, but they considered this policy prudent because it allowed the resolution of internal problems before dealing with external problems.[102]

The conservatives on the council wanted a strong monarchy and a lasting peace. They believed that Protestant disobedience was a serious obstacle to achieving peace, and had to be dealt with before tackling the problem of Spanish expansionism. The conservatives wanted France to be a first-ranked European power, so they knew that one day Spain would have to be confronted, but they did not think that the Valteline affair was the right time or place. They advocated playing for time, maintaining the anti-Spanish alliances, and dealing with the Habsburgs later, a sensible if cautious foreign policy pursued by Richelieu until 1630.

These policy decisions may seem flawed in the light of later events, but they were a logical response to events at the time. From a short-term perspective of what the king wanted to do, the Treaty of Madrid was a success because it allowed him to go on campaign against the Protestants. From a long-term perspective, the treaty was less successful because it was not enforced. As the international situation tipped in favor of the Spanish, they became reluctant to implement the terms of the treaty, and a series of French diplomatic protests achieved nothing. French ministers grappled unsuccessfully with this problem until Richelieu joined the council and was able to achieve a partially satisfactory solution in 1626.[103] Hanotaux echoed the pamphleteers when he blamed Luynes for the Valteline decision, and unfairly criticized him for not realizing that the Thirty Years War would occur, that the Austrians would become a serious problem, and that Louis XIV would revoke the Edict of Nantes.[104] French foreign policy from 1610 until the mid-1620s may be criticized as erratic, fumbling, and inconsistent, but it was not a calamity, and it was not Luynes's fault.

Luynes had significant influence on the foreign-policy decisions of 1620 and 1621, but he was not solely responsible. He opposed military intervention and favored negotiation, and he helped to convince the king to follow this policy, but he was not alone in this advice, nor the only council member to whom the king listened. He belonged to a small group of influential conservatives who favored compromise, and whose advice the king usually followed. Luynes was not the sole architect of French foreign policy in these years. He was never that powerful.

Notes

1 Charles Bernard, *Histoire des guerres de Louis XIII contre les religionnaires rebelles* (Paris, 1633), pp. 205–30; Louis de Pontis, *Mémoires du sieur de Pontis*, ed. Petitot, 2nd ser., vol. 31 (Paris, 1824), 316; François Du Val, marquis de Fontenay-Mareuil, *Mémoires du Messire Du Val*, ed. Louis Monmerqué, 2 vols. (Paris, 1826), I, 516–8; Claude Malingre, *Histoire de la rebellion excitée en France par les rebelles de la religion prétendue réformée* (Paris, 1626), pp. 500–63, 611–20, 627–35; A.D. Lublinskaya, *French Absolutism. The Crucial Phase 1620–1629* (Cambridge, 1968), pp. 189–94; Auguste de Caumont, duc de La Force, *Le Maréchal de La Force* (Paris, 1950), pp. 237–61; John Lynn, *Giant of the Grand Siècle* (Cambridge, 1977), pp. 547–93; Berthold Zeller, *Le Connêtable de Luynes* (Paris, 1879), p. 96; Hector Joly, *Histoire des choses mémorables au siège de Montauban* (n.p., 1624).

2 François de Bassompierre. *Journal de ma vie. Mémoires du maréchal de Bassompierre*, ed. Edouard de Chanterac. 4 vols. (Paris, 1870–77), II, 290, n. 2, 318–26; Paul Bondois, *Le Maréchal de Bassompierre* (Paris, 1925), pp. 231–3; La Force, *Le Maréchal de La Force*, pp. 240–2.

3 Louis Claude Saudau, *Saint-Jean d'Angély d'après les archives de l'échevinage* (Saint-Jean d'Angély, 1886, Marseille, 1978), pp. 259–86; Malingre, *Histoire de la rebellion*, pp. 297–327.

4 *Mercure françois*, 25 vols. (Paris, 1605–44), VII (1621), 642–6; Bernard, *Histoire des guerres de Louis XIII*, pp. 190–200; Malingre, *Histoire de la rebellion*, pp. 410–25; B.N., imprimés Lb 36, *L'Ordre du siège et réduction de la ville de Clérac avec les articles accordés aux inhabitants par Sa Majesté, le 5 août* (1621).

5 Malingre, *Histoire de la rebellion*, pp. 662–70; B.N., imprimés Lb 36, *La Prise de Monheur par l'armée royale avec le saccagement de la place* (1621); *L'Assassinat du sieur de Boisse Pardaillan, gouverneur de Monheur, avec la prise de la ville rebelle* (Bordeaux, n.d., 1621?).

6 Eugène Halphen, ed. *Journal inédit d'Arnauld d'Andilly 1621* (Paris, 1891), passim; Jean Héroard, *Journal*, ed. Madeleine Foisil, 2 vols. (Paris, 1989), I, 327–9, II, 2732–2820; *Histoire journalière au voyage du Roy depuis son départ de Fontainbleau (avril 1621)*, in *Archives curieuses de l'histoire de France*, eds. F. Danjou and M.L. Cimber, 2nd ser., vol. 2 (Paris, 1838), pp. 241–83; For the siege of Monheurt, see Bernard, *Histoire des guerres de Louis XIII*, pp. 236–42; *Mercure françois*, VII (1621), 926–9. For maps of the four sieges, see ibid., pp. 528–30, 642–3, 822–5, 926–7.

7 Zeller, *Le Connêtable de Luynes*, pp. 27–9, 41, 45, 48–54; Gabriel Hanotaux and the duc de La Force, *Histoire du Cardinal de Richelieu*, 6 vols. (Paris, 1893–1947), II, part 2, 423–9, 440–3; Victor-Lucien Tapié, *France in the Age of Louis XIII and Richelieu*, trans. D. McN. Lockie (Cambridge, 1974), pp. 117–23; Lublinskaya, *French Absolutism*, p. 152; Roland Mousnier, *L'Homme rouge ou la vie du Cardinal de Richelieu* (Paris, 1992), p. 195; Pierre Blet, *Le Clergé de France et la monarchie* (Rome, 1959), pp. 235–6; J.A. Clarke, *Huguenot Warrior: Henri de Rohan* (The Hague, 1966), pp. 76–7; Raoul Patry, *Philippe Du Plessis-Mornay* (Paris, 1933), p. 585; John Viénot, *Histoire de la réforme française de l'Edit de Nantes à sa révocation* (Paris, 1934), pp. 168–93.

8 Bernard, *Histoire des guerres de Louis XIII*, pp. 234–6; Malingre, *Histoire de la rebellion*, p. 236; Robert Bireley, *The Jesuits and the Thirty Years War* (Cambridge, 2003), pp. 46–51; Zeller, *Le Connêtable de Luynes*, pp. 235–61; Hanotaux, *Histoire du Cardinal de Richelieu*, II, part 2, 380–2.

9 Joseph Bergin, *The Making of the French Episcopate* (New Haven, 1996), p. 417.

10 Eusèbe Pavie, *La Guerre entre Louis XIII et Marie de Médicis* (Angers, 1899), pp. 66–8, 92, 124–33, 136–7, 206–7.

11 Louis Batiffol, *Le Roi Louis XIII à vingt ans* (Paris, 1910), pp. 552–3 and n. 1. "Je ne crains ni cette femme [Marie de Médicis], ni ses brigues, car l'homme [le roi] me craint telle-ment qu'il ne sauroit rien faire que je ne sache. Après la prise de Monheurt, je ferai la paix et m'accommoderai si bien que je ne craindrai plus rien." The authenticity of this letter is questionable. It was found among the papers of the abbé Dangeau (1638–1720), neither dated nor signed. Batiffol dated it 1621, and attributed it to Luynes because of his "charac-teristic" handwriting, although Luynes always used secretaries.

12 A. Lloyd Moote, *Louis XIII* (Berkeley, 1989), p. 126; Lublinskaya, *French Absolutism*, p. 154.

13 *Mercure françois*, VII (1621), 311–12; Malingre, *Histoire de la rebellion*, p. 142; Jacques Nompar de Caumont, duc de La Force *Mémoires*, ed. Marquis de la Grange, 4 vols., I, 490–521.

14 Patry, *DuPlessis-Mornay*, p. 588. "… s'estendit lors sur les absurdes et insupportables procedures de l'Assemblée, … sur une forme de Republique establie … sous ombre d'une juste defense … Ce qui ne pouvait tendre qu'à la ruine de la Monarchie, à l'exemple de la Hollande …"

15 David Parker, *La Rochelle and the French Monarchy* (London, 1980), pp. 155–6; Richard Bonney, *The King's Debts* (Oxford, 1981), p. 105.

16 Victor Cousin, "Le Duc et connêtable de Luynes," *Journal des Savants* (July 1861), 441–52.

17 La Force, *Mémoires*, I, 501–4; Zeller, *Le Connêtable de Luynes*, p. 28; Léon Anquez, *Histoire des assemblées politiques des réformées de France* (Paris, 1859), p. 337.

18 Saudau, *Saint-Jean d'Angély*, p. 259; Malingre, *Histoire de la rebellion*, p. 297.

19 Clarke, *Huguenot Warrior*, p. 77.

20 *Mercure françois*, VII (1621), 817–20; Héroard, *Journal*, II, 2773; Bernard, *Histoire des guerres de Louis XIII*, I, 204–5.

21 Charles, comte Horric de Beaucaire, ed., *Mémoires du Cardinal de Richelieu*, 10 vols. (Paris, 1907–13), III, 154.

22 B.N., imprimés Lb 36, *Lettres de Monsieur le Connestable à Monsieur de Modène* (1621); *Lettre de Monsieur le Connestable à Monsieur de Montbazon* (1621).

23 Batiffol, *Le Roi Louis XIII*, pp. 554–5; Pierre Chevallier, *Louis XIII* (Paris, 1979), p. 203; Lublinskaya, *French Absolutism*, p. 190; Mousnier, *L'Homme rouge*, p. 205; Moote, *Louis XIII*, p. 127.

24 Fontenay-Mareuil, *Mémoires*, I, 516; Hanotaux, *Histoire du Cardinal de Richelieu*, II, part 2, 500.

25 Bassompierre, *Mémoires*, II, 290–395, esp. 338–9, 356–7; Héroard, *Journal*, II, 2755–98; Batiffol, *Le Roi Louis XIII*, p. 556.

26 Ibid., II, 363.

27 *Recueil des pièces les plus curieuses qui ont esté faites pendant le règne du Connestable Monsieur de Luynes* (Paris, 1628), pp. 447–50; *La Chronique des Favoris* (1622), p. 378, *L'Ombre de Monseigneur le duc de Mayenne* (1622), p. 340; *Méditations de l'hermite Valérien* (1621).

28 B.N., imprimés Lb 36, *Apologie ou response à La Chronique des Favoris* (1622), pp. 7–14.

29 See chapter 9.

30 Beaucaire, *Mémoires de Richelieu*, III, 164–7.

31 Bassompierre, *Mémoires*, II, 314–5; *Journal d'Arnauld 1621*, pp. 84–5; Fontenay-Mareuil, *Mémoires*, I, 520; Zeller, *Le Connêtable de Luynes*, pp. 101–2; Hanotaux, *Histoire du Cardinal de Richelieu*, II, part 2, 502–3.

32 Bassompierre, *Mémoires*, II, 336.

33 *Mercure françois*, VII (1621), 817–18.

34 Zeller, *Le Connêtable de Luynes*, p. 104.

35 Henri de Rohan, *Mémoires du duc de Rohan*, eds. Michaud and Poujoulat, 2nd ser., vol. 5 (Paris, 1837), p. 527; *Journal d'Arnauld 1621*, p. 97; Fontenay-Mareuil, *Mémoires*, I, 523; Bassompierre, *Mémoires*, II, 345–7.

36 Ibid., II, 355–6; Bernard, *Histoire des guerres de Louis XIII*, p. 226; La Force, *Le Maréchal de La Force*, pp. 250–51.

37 Rohan, *Mémoires*, p. 527 ; Bassompierre, *Mémoires*, II, 362; *Journal d'Arnauld 1621*, pp. 85, 89, 20 and 25 September 1621.

38 Beaucaire, *Mémoires de Richelieu*, III, 176–7; Hanotaux, *Histoire du Cardinal de Richelieu*, II, part 2, 501.

39 Bassompierre, *Mémoires*, II, 299, 301, 316; *Journal d'Arnauld 1621*, pp. 77, 105; Fontenay-Mareuil, *Mémoires*, I, 516, 518; Bernard, *Histoire des guerres de Louis XIII*, pp. 210–11; Malingre, *Histoire de la rebellion*, pp. 529–30; Beaucaire, *Mémoires de Richelieu*, III, 155.

40 Louis Videl, *Histoire de la vie du connêtable de Lesdiguières* (Paris, 1638), p. 369.

41 Ibid., pp. 20, 105; A.A.E., Fonds France 774, fol. 5; Zeller, *Le Connêtable de Luynes*, p. 102.

42 Bernard, *Histoire de guerres de Louis XIII*, p. 230.

43 Ibid., p. 88.

44 Bassompierre, *Mémoires*, II, 335, 357.

45 Fontenay-Mareuil, *Mémoires*, I, 508–10; *Journal d'Arnauld 1621*, p. 38.

46 Bassompierre, *Mémoires*, II, 317–19.

47 The royal army may have numbered as few as 10,000 by September. Bernard, *Histoire des guerres de Louis XIII*, p. 208.

48 Fontenay-Mareuil, *Mémoires*, I, 516–17.

49 Bassompierre, *Mémoires*, II, 313 and n. 4; *Journal d'Arnauld 1621*, p. 82.

50 Bernard, *Histoire des guerres de Louis XIII*, pp. 225–6, 229–30.

51 Ibid., 358–62.

52 Pontis, *Mémoires*, pp. 283–5; Saudau, *Saint-Jean d'Angély*, pp. 268–9.

53 Fontenay-Mareuil, *Mémoires*, I, 508–9.

54 Saudau, *Saint-Jean d'Angély*, p. 281; Malingre, *Histoire de la rébellion*, pp. 332–3.

55 Héroard, *Journal*, II, 2755–98.

56 Bernard, *Histoire des guerres de Louis XIII*, p. 206.

57 Videl, *Histoire de la vie de Lesdiguières*, pp. 368–70; Zeller, *Le Connêtable de Luynes*, pp. 71, 96, 102.

58 Marcel Marion, *Dictionnaire des institutions au XVIIe et XVIIIe siècles* (Paris, 1968), pp. 129–30; Roger Doucet, *Les Institutions au XVIe siècle*, 2 vols. (Paris, 1948), I, 112–13; Lynn, *Giant of the Grand Siècle*, pp. 98–9; David Parrott, *Richelieu's Army* (Cambridge, 2001), pp. 469–70; John Mitchell, *The Court of the Connêtablie* (New Haven, 1947), passim.

59 *Journal d'Arnauld 1621*, p. 69.

60 Bernard, *Histoire des guerres de Louis XIII*, pp. 232–4.

61 *Mercure françois*, VII (1621), 509–10, 518, 527; Jacques de Castenet, sieur de Puységur, *Mémoires*, 2 vols. (Paris, 1888), I, 10; Saudau, *Saint-Jean d'Angély*, pp. 274–5, 278–80; Héroard, *Journal*, II, 2757, 2763; Bernard, *Histoire des guerres de Louis XIII*, p. 211; A.A.E., Fonds France, 75, fol. 56v, 24 August 1621.

62 Héroard, *Journal*, II, 2769; *Mercure françois*, VII (1621), 646; *Journal d'Arnauld 1621*, pp. 69–70; Bassompierre, *Mémoires*, II, 292–3, 298.

63 *Journal d'Arnauld 1621*, pp. 83–4, 101; Héroard, *Journal*, II, 2786, 2797; La Force, *Le Maréchal de La Force*, pp. 252–3; Bassompierre, *Mémoires*, II, 353–4, 358–62; Malingre, *Histoire de la rebellion*, pp. 424–5, 636–7.

64 Sidney Lee, ed., *The Autobiography of Edward, Lord Herbert of Cherbury* (London, 1906), pp. 118–20.

65 Ibid., p. 121, n. 3; Bassompierre, *Mémoires*, II, 385.

66 Victor-Lucien Tapié, *La Politique étrangère de la France et le début de la Guerre de Trente Ans (1617–1621)* (Paris, 1934), pp. 231 and n. 2, 425–9, 453, 534; Louis Battifol, "Le Duc et connêtable de Luynes," *Rev hist* 103 (1910), 32.

67 Charles Howard Carter, *The Secret Diplomacy of the Habsburgs 1598–1625* (New York, 1964), pp. 182–206; Hanotaux, *Histoire du Cardinal de Richelieu*, II, part 2, 433.

68 Lublinskaya, *French Absolutism*, p. 175; Hanotaux, *Histoire du Cardinal de Richelieu*, II, part 2, 397–401; Edouard Rott, *Histoire de la représentation diplomatique de la France auprès des cantons suisses*, 10 vols. (Berne, 1900–35), III, 550–650.

69 Roland Mousnier, *The Assassination of Henri IV*, trans. Joan Spencer (New York, 1964), pp. 116–38; Jean-Pierre Babelon, *Henri IV* (Paris, 1982), pp. 910–41; J. Michael Hayden, "Continuity in the France of Henri IV and Louis XIII: French Foreign Policy, 1598–1615," *Journal of Modern History* 45 (1973), 1–23; Joseph Nouillac, *Villeroy, secrétaire d'état et ministre* (Paris, 1908), pp. 265–515; Edmund Dickerman, *Bellièvre and Villeroy* (Providence, RI, 1971), pp. 85–117; Maurice Lee, *James I and Henri IV* (Urbana, Ill, 1970), pp. 168–85; Edouard Rott, *Henri IV, les Suisses et la haute Italie, la lutte pour les Alpes (1598–1610)* (Paris, 1882).

70 Achille Halphen, ed., *Journal d'Arnauld d'Andilly 1614–1620* (Paris, 1851), pp. 345, 378, 383–5.

71 Mousnier, *The Assassination of Henri IV*, pp. 116–20.

72 Zeller, *Le Connêtable de Luynes*, pp. 143–73.

73 Héroard, *Journal*, II, 2727–37.

74 *Journal d'Arnauld 1621*, p. 8; Bassompierre, *Mémoires*, II, 228; *Ambassade du mareschal de Bassompierre en Espagne l'an 1621* (Cologne, 1668), pp. 5–17.

75 Eugène and Jules Halphen, eds., *Journal inédit d'Arnauld d'Andilly 1620* (Paris, 1888), pp. 59–60; *Mercure françois*, VI (1620), 467–9; Carter, *Secret Diplomacy*, p. 207. See B.N., Ms. fr. 15989 for Chaulnes's instructions, and B.N. Ms. fr. 15989 for his correspondence.

76 *Mercure françois*, VIII (1622), 329–30; *Ambassade*, pp. 128–33; Zeller, *Le Connêtable de Luynes*, pp. 199–201; Hanotaux, *Histoire du Cardinal de Richelieu*, II, part 2, 434–5.

77 B.N., ms. Fr. 3687, fols. 17–19 ; 4149, fols. 150–52 ; Zeller, *Le Connêtable de Luynes*, pp. 177–9; *Ambassade*, pp. 49–50; Carter, *Secret Diplomacy*, p. 210.

78 Bassompierre, *Mémoires*, II, 267, 272, 276; *Ambassade*, pp. 18–20, 124–5. See ibid., pp. 20–48, for his other letters to Puysieux.

79 Tapié, *Politique étrangère*, p. 621.

80 *Journal d'Arnauld 1621*, p. 20.

81 Lee, *Autobiography of Cherbury*, p. 116; Héroard, *Journal*, II, 2752.

82 Lublinskaya, *French Absolutism*, pp. 179–80.

83 Carter, *Secret Diplomacy*, pp. 182–206.

84 *Mercure françois*, VI (1620), 467; B.N., imprimés Lb 36, *Le Voyage du Roi à Calais (24 décembre 1620) et l'ambassade de M. le maréchal de Cadenet en Angleterre (28 décembre 1620)* (1621).

85 Zeller, *Le Connêtable de Luynes*, pp. 39–40. "Je veux vous le dire en confidence, messieurs, je ne sais ce qui va advenir de nous. Le mal est dans notre sang, dans nos entrailles. Ces huguenots ont formé un corps qui préjudicie à l'autorité du roi et qui lui enlève le sceptre de la main. A la Rochelle, ils font leur assemblée sans en demander licence … Mais les huguenots sont récalcitrants, ils ne veulent pas obéir, et de jour en jour ils deviennent plus insolents. Si Sa Majesté se met en marche pour aller hors de son royaume, il est certain que le roi d'Espagne fomentera encore davantage leur rébellion et qu'il leur donnera de l'argent pour mettre le feu à notre maison."

86 Hanotaux, *Histoire du Cardinal de Richelieu*, II, part -2, 435. "… je vais vous le dire, mais je vous en prie, gardez cela pour vous: nous finirons par nous débarrasser des affaires domestiques et de contentir les huguenots; après cela, on se mettra vigoureusement aux affaires du dehors."

87 Tapié, *Politique étrangère*, pp. 425–6.

88 Ibid., pp. 479–516. For brief accounts of European foreign affairs, especially German, see Mousnier, *L'Homme rouge*, pp. 189–202; Pierre Chevallier, *Louis XIII* (Paris, 1979), pp. 237–45; Bireley, *The Jesuits and the Thirty Years War*, pp. 33–62.

89 *Journal d'Arnauld 1620*, pp. 20–1.

90 Tapié, *Politique étrangère*, pp. 430–2.

91 Bassompierre, *Mémoires*, II, 215–28.

92 Tapié, *Politique étrangère*, pp. 231–3.

93 Batiffol, "Le Duc et connêtable de Luynes," *Rev hist* 103 (1910), 32–3.

94 Père Anselme de Sainte Marie, *Histoire généalogique et chronologique de la Maison royale de France*, 9 vols. (Paris, 1726–33, New York, 1967), IV, 333–5; Mousnier, *L'Homme rouge*, pp. 133–4, 154; Hanotaux, *Histoire du Cardinal de Richelieu*, II, part 2, 175–6; Jean-Antoine Pithon-Curt, *Histoire de la noblesse du Comté Venaissin*, 4 vols. (Paris, 1743–50), III, 19.

95 Henri Ballande, *Le Président Jeannin* (Paris, 1981), p. 246; Pierre Jeannin, *Oeuvres mêlées du président Jeannin*, ed. Petitot, 2nd ser., vol. 16 (Paris, 1822), pp. 63–76; Hanotaux, *Histoire du Cardinal de Richelieu*, II, part 2, 384–5.

96 René Radouant, *Guillaume Du Vair* (Paris, 1907, Geneva, 1970), pp. 404, 434–5; Zeller, *Le Connêtable de Luynes*, pp. 176–7.

97 *Recueil*, pp. 375–92, *L'Ombre de Monseigneur le duc de Mayenne* (1622); pp. 426–38, *L'Ombre de Monseigneur le Connestable* (1622); *La Chronique des Favoris* (1622); pp. 489–535, *La France*

mourante (1621); pp. 536–80, *La Voix publique au Roy* (1622).

98 Hanotaux, *Histoire du Cardinal de Richelieu*, II, part 2, 394. "Si, dans cette crise de 1621, qui est à peine mentionnée par nos histoires, la France eût eu à sa tête un gouvernement ferme et prévoyant, les maux de tente ans de guerre eussent probablement été évités. A cette date, une parole dite par le roi Louis XIII, une attitude, un langage ferme tenu par ses ministres, eussent changé le cours des choses. Par la suite, il a fallu la double et étonnante carrière d'un Richelieu et d'un Mazarin, il a fallu un génie militaire des Gustave-Adolphe, des Condé et des Turenne pour réparer le mal que la négligence ou l'incapacité d'un Luynes ou d'un Puysieux … La Maison d'Autriche, sauvée par Luynes en 1621, imposa à la France plus d'un siècle de sanglants efforts."
99 Ibid., II, part 2, 357–405.
100 Tapié, *Politique étrangère*, pp. 474–5.
101 Moote, *Louis XIII*, pp. 104–5, 329–30.
102 Cousin, "Le Duc et connêtable de Luynes" (May 1861), 262; Zeller, *Le Connêtable de Luynes*, p. 175; Lublinskaya, *French Absolutism*, pp. 176–80.
103 David Parrott, *Richelieu's Army* (Cambridge, 2001), pp. 84–8; Rémy Pithon, "Les Débuts difficiles du ministère de Richelieu et la crise de Valteline (1621–1627)," *Revue d'histoire diplomatique* 74 (1960), 298–322.
104 Hanotaux, *Histoire du Cardinal de Richelieu*, II, part 2, 455–65.

9

The anti-Luynes campaign

In his memoirs, Michel de Marolles, abbé de Villeloin, described an incident in which Luynes was ridiculed before the whole court. The incident probably occurred late in 1620 or early in 1621, because the youth who insulted him, François de Paule, duc de Rethélois, the fifteen-year-old son of the duc de Nevers, died of dysentery sometime during 1621. François commanded an army regiment in Champagne, and shared with his father the government of that province. Although he and his father had supported Luynes during the civil war, he felt free to insult the favorite in front of the king and the whole court because he thought his quip would be appreciated.

François was a good-looking young man with a full head of curled, powdered hair. When Luynes saw him, he teasingly joked that he knew François must have a mistress because he was so well coiffed. François replied that this was not the case because his hair was naturally curly. Luynes repeated this exchange to the king who asked François if it were true. He replied, "No, Sire." Luynes asked him, "Then why did you tell me that?" François replied, "I tell the King the truth, and I tell you whatever it pleases me to say." Everyone laughed, and Marolles, a client of the young man's father, noted his retort with approval.[1]

This exchange tells us something about Luynes's position at court. The duc de Rethélois belonged to a great noble family, and he may have regarded Luynes's teasing as insulting to his rank. He disdainfully put Luynes in his place, and expected approval for so doing. As an unpopular royal favorite, Luynes was frequently the target of sarcastic remarks, but these were usually made behind his back, not to his face. Such insults were the price of favor. Luynes did not reply because he wanted to maintain his image of affability and charm. Ridicule was an indoor sport at the court, and he had been playing this game himself when he remarked upon François's hair. The teenager replied in the same spirit. The king played this game when he sniped at Luynes, and he made similar nasty remarks about Richelieu.

Public ridicule was lethal in the small, closed world of the royal court. It could irreparably damage an individual's honor and reputation, thereby threatening his rank and status. Honor was a noble's understanding of who he was and where he belonged within the ranks of society. He lost his honor when public opinion judged him negatively, causing him to lose the esteem and consideration of others. When he lost his honor, he lost his social identity and sense of self-worth. A noble accused of cowardice and duplicity had to refute these accusations or be dishonored and disgraced. So, nobles duelled to defend their honor, although it was illegal.[2] If Luynes was openly ridiculed at court, he could become a laughingstock and so lose the king's favor, the goal of the pamphlet campaign against him in 1620–21. This chapter discusses what the pamphlets said, what Luynes did to counteract them, and what their long-term impact was.

There was a tradition of political pamphleteering in France that had begun in the sixteenth century. During the 1580s and 1590s, printers in Paris and Lyon had published hundreds of pamphlets for and against the Catholic League. There was an outburst of pamphleteering in 1588–89 after the assassinations of the Guise brothers and Henri III, and more outbursts during Henri IV's reign. During the years from 1614 to 1617, there was a steady exchange of pamphlets between the Queen Mother's government and the rebel nobles, followed by a flurry of pamphlets during the meeting of the Estates General in 1614 and 1615. Twenty-two pamphlets defending Concini were published in 1616–17 and twenty-seven attacking him, with seventy-six more after his death justifying his murder.

The pamphlet attack on Luynes began with the Queen Mother's revolt. The *Mercure françois* reported that "at the beginning of this year 1620 one only sees pamphlets against those who possess the king's favor." Arnauld d'Andilly reported that there was much poisonous talk and many printed pamphlets against Luynes circulating in Paris that April.[3] The anti-Luynes attack accelerated with the southwestern campaign against the Protestants, and continued for a year after his death. Of one hundred and four pamphlets on Luynes published from 1617 through 1622, three quarters or seventy-three attacked him, and one quarter or thirty-one defended him. The most damaging pamphlets were sponsored by the Queen Mother and her supporters, and they must have worried the affable Luynes, who justifiably feared the effects of widespread unpopularity. After his death, the pamphleteers attacked Richelieu's opponents on the royal council including the prince de Condé, the Brûlarts father and son, and La Vieuville, the superintendent of finance. The intense political pamphleteering subsided after Richelieu joined the royal council in 1624, but resumed in the 1630s with attacks on the Cardinal himself, and accelerated in the 1640s during the Fronde.[4] Pamphlets functioned as newspapers to inform the reading public, and as propaganda to influence their opinions. The only newspaper at this time, the *Mercure françois*, appeared once a year in book form. The weekly *Gazette de France* did not begin publication until 1631.[5]

Early seventeenth-century pamphlets were half the size of a standard sheet of paper, three to seven pages in length, hastily printed, mediocre in quality, expensive to buy, and passed from hand to hand. Sold in the streets and bookshops, they were reissued in multiple editions, usually about 500 to 600 copies, but sometimes more. They could reach several thousand readers when passed from hand to hand. A large number of political pamphlets were published at this time, 200 to 300 a year from 1620 through 1622. Most of the pamphlets on Luynes were printed and sold in Paris where there was great interest in the royal court. The anti-Luynes pamphlets did not give the author's or publisher's name, often not even the date or place of publication, in order to avoid the harsh punishment for sedition.[6] Many of the authors were members of the Queen Mother's household or her entourage. Richelieu was a member of her household at this time. What role did he play in the campaign against Luynes?

The pamphlet campaign against Luynes

Historians agree that Richelieu participated in this campaign, but they disagree on his role. Some say that he masterminded the campaign, and others that he was only sympathetic to its goals. They agree that he collaborated on some of the pamphlets, especially those written by Morgues and Fancan, but disagree on the nature of his contribution. He may have commissioned or approved some of the pamphlets, supervised the writing of others, provided the ideas for some, and the information about court politics and intrigues for others. He may even have written some parts himself.[7]

Matthieu de Morgues, abbé de Saint Germain, was a preacher in the Queen Mother's household. Richelieu was associated with Morgues's publication of *Véritez Chrestiennes au Roy Très Chrestien* (1620) and *Manifeste de la Royne Mère envoyé au Roy* (1620), which attacked Luynes. Retitled and republished several times, the latter pamphlet was also known as the *Manifeste d'Angers*, and Richelieu may have commissioned it or even written parts of it.[8] He was also associated with the publication of the anti-Luynes *Remonstrance au Roy importante pour son Estat* (1620) and *La Chronique des Favoris* (1622). They were written by François Dorval Langlois, sieur de Fancan, abbé de Beaulieu, a canon in the Paris church of Saint Germain l'Auxerrois, Richelieu's client, secretary, and household member.[9] Richelieu probably supplied Fancan with ideas. Other participants in the anti-Luynes campaign included the Queen Mother's supporter, the

duc de Mayenne, who commissioned pamphlets; her secretary, Jacques Pelle-
tier, who wrote them; and Jacques d'Apchon, sieur de Chanteloube, another
household member who also wrote anti-Luynes pamphlets.[10]

Chanteloube was named the governor of Chinon in 1618 as a reward for
having helped to arrange the Queen Mother's escape from Blois. He was a rival
of Richelieu for her favor. When Richelieu became her household intendant,
he confiscated Chinon and gave it to one of his clients. Despite their rivalry,
Richelieu used Chanteloube's pamphlet, *Le Comtadin Provençal* (1620), extensively in his memoirs. Chanteloube may also have written *La Sibylle françoise
parlant au Roy* (1620), exhorting the second nobility of which he was a member
to support the Queen Mother's revolt, and *L'Advis au Roy sur le Restablissement de
l'office de Connestable* (1620), warning against reviving the office of constable as
politically dangerous. Fancan may also have written these pamphlets. Accompanying the Queen Mother into exile in 1631, Chanteloube and Morgues became
bitter enemies of Richelieu, and wrote virulent pamphlets against him. Because
of their political differences, Richelieu sent Fancan to the Bastille where he
died, probably in 1627.[11]

Circumstantial evidence for Richelieu's participation in the campaign
against Luynes includes the publication of a collection of about sixty anti-
Luynes prose pamphlets and satiric verses in a book entitled, *Recueil des pièces
les plus curieuses qui ont esté faites pendant le règne du Connestable M. de Luynes*. The
first edition appeared in 1622, and subsequent editions were published in 1623,
1624, 1626, 1628, and 1632.[12] The last three editions were probably published
with Richelieu's permission because he attempted to enforce press censorship
after 1626, although without much success. The last two editions contained
pamphlets by Fancan attacking La Vieuville and the Brûlarts, and a one-page
pamphlet praising Richelieu.[13] After 1623, Richelieu maintained a group of
pamphleteers and historians to endorse his policies and attack his enemies.
They included Fancan, Morgues, François Eudes de Mézeray, Scipion Dupleix,
Jean Sirmond, Jean Sillon, Paul Hay du Chastelet, Louis Guron, Jean-Baptiste
Matthieu, the abbé Boisrobert, Père Joseph, and Achille Harlay de Sancy among
others.[14] Richelieu also sought to influence the Parisian elite through his clients
Père Joseph as editor of the *Mercure françois*, and Théophraste Renaudot as editor
of the *Gazette*.[15]

The short-term effects of the anti-Luynes pamphlet campaign are difficult
to determine because of Luynes's sudden death. Richard Bonney has suggested
that the campaign may have changed the king's attitude toward Luynes, but this
was probably not the case because Luynes was still in favor when he died.[16] The
long-term effects, however, were catastrophic because the pamphlet campaign
destroyed Luynes's reputation. Richelieu's damaging comments about him,
taken from the pamphlets and incorporated into his memoirs, became the

basis of a negative historiographical tradition that exists to this day. Which anti-Luynes pamphlets did Richelieu use in his memoirs?

There were two types of anti-Luynes pamphlet, serious well-written prose accounts and nasty personal attacks in verse, and the nastiest were published during the year after Luynes's death. Most were doggerel in which he was described as a footman, stable valet, porter in a brothel, *coquin* (rogue or knave), *poltron* (coward), and *aluyne* (the old French word for absinthe or bitter). He and his brothers were described as charlatans, devils, criminals, beggars, harpies, a three-headed dog, a howling monster with three heads, a three-headed hydra, and ants eating the lily of France. His sword complained that he was an impotent coward who was afraid of his own candlelit shadow on the wall, and his horoscope predicted an early violent death.[17]

Richelieu incorporated eight of the prose pamphlets into his memoirs. Well argued with precise, accurate information, they varied in length from seven to forty-nine pages, and were published anonymously in multiple editions. Richelieu knew their authors and had been associated with their publication. Five of the pamphlets were written by Fancan, two by Morgues, and one by Chanteloube. Gabriel Naudé remarked in a 1639 book that the pamphlets by Chanteloube and Fancan had been "marvelously effective."[18] Richelieu quoted directly from these pamphlets when he remarked upon Luynes's excessive ambition in wanting to become duke of Brittany and king of Austrasia.[19] He quoted directly when he mentioned Luynes's debt to La Varenne for his advancement,[20] and when he held Luynes responsible for Du Travail's execution to conceal his own role in Concini's murder.[21] The first two accusations were invented by Fancan, and the third by Chanteloube. Richelieu included at least another five accusations from the pamphlets in his memoirs, although he paraphrased rather than quoted them. He jeered at Luynes's low birth, foreign origins, and domestic service as a bird keeper.[22] He deplored Luynes's greed, ambition, and advancement of his numerous unworthy dependents.[23] He declared that Luynes had controlled the king by isolating him and surrounding him with his own kin and clients,[24] and he accused Luynes of alienating the Queen Mother from her son and causing their quarrel.[25] He also accused Luynes of cowardice during the Concini conspiracy and the siege of Montauban, which had failed because of his bungling.[26]

The anti-Luynes pamphleteers compared Luynes to Concini, Sejanus, and Biron, favorites who had caused strife and conflict. According to the pamphleteers, Concini had provoked the noble revolt of 1614 through his greed, ambition, and arrogance. A low-born foreigner, he was a tyrant and a usurper who had dominated the royal council and controlled decision-making through his influence over the Queen Mother. Concini had all the flaws of a favorite, and Luynes had all the same flaws.[27]

Richelieu quoted Chanteloube's pamphlet word-for-word when he described Luynes in his memoirs. He declared that Luynes was low-born and uneducated, and that his family was obscure and foreign. Luynes was arrogant, insolent, and rude because he did not know his place in society. He was an ambitious tyrant who wanted to become king and gave the king bad advice. He was incompetent, cowardly, ungrateful, and disloyal, and he had caused the quarrel between the king and his mother. He had angered the nobility by monopolizing the distribution of royal patronage, which he gave to undeserving individuals such as his candidates for the Order of Saint Esprit, and his ingratitude had motivated nobles to join the Queen Mother in revolt. He was insatiably greedy, and after obtaining Concini's fortune, he had doubled it by pillaging the state and draining the royal treasury to benefit himself and his unworthy relatives and friends.[28] Fancan declared that Luynes's ignorance had caused the attack on the French Protestants when the crown should have been attacking the Spanish Habsburgs. Most of the 1620 and 1621 pamphlets criticized the king's foreign policy, which was blamed on Luynes.[29] In fact, he was blamed for all the ills of France, and the pamphleteers declared that he was worse than Concini.

There were, however, some important differences between Concini and Luynes. Concini and his wife were favorites of the Queen Mother, while Luynes was the king's favorite. As the favorite-in-chief, Luynes had a clear ascendancy over other court nobles, while Concini's position was more ambiguous because his power depended on the Queen Mother. Concini had begun his career as a personal favorite and became a political favorite, but unlike Luynes he never became a minister favorite. Luynes had a more extensive power base than Concini because he was a provincial governor who controlled numerous fortress governorships, and he created a large noble clientele that he used politically. He was also named constable and keeper of the seals, offices that Concini never acquired. Luynes was French by birth, and more tactful and discreet than Concini, who was an Italian widely despised for his arrogant bravado. Luynes was charming and affable to everyone, and he endeavored to please, placate, and manipulate the court nobility. He worked hard to create a good public image, which had not interested Concini. Luynes was a better politician than Concini, and so he enjoyed greater power.

Luynes counterattacks

Ten of the thirty-one pamphlets in Luynes's favor were published in 1619 after the Queen Mother had escaped from Blois. She blamed Luynes for the harsh treatment that she said had motivated her escape, and she made these charges public by publishing her letters of explanation to the king and his ministers in the *Mercure françois*, then separately as pamphlets. In response, Luynes published pamphlets defending his conduct. One pamphlet directly refuted her charges by declaring that he was not responsible for exiling her to Blois, persuading the king to take up arms against her, dictating the terms of the Treaty of Angoulême, or obstructing a reconciliation with her son because the king had made these decisions. In fact, Luynes had sent numerous envoys to her urging a reconciliation. The king had not treated his mother harshly, and Luynes's favor, based on their mutual affection, did not depend on her absence from the court.[30]

Most of the other pamphlets took a more general approach. They argued that Luynes was a virtuous man who would never have treated the Queen Mother unfairly. Affable to everyone, he was prudent, temperate, fair, honest, sincere, courageous, loyal, and generous with "an open, frank countenance."[31] He was an esteemed royal adviser who sought to reconcile the quarrelling factions at court and secure a lasting peace for France.[32] Pamphlets on his ducal reception stated that he was awarded this title for his services to the crown.[33] Scipion Gramont's dedication to Luynes of the ballet, in "Tancrède in the Enchanted Forest", praised his services to the king, and the ballet's libretto was published and circulated as a pamphlet in 1619.[34]

Luynes knew that the pamphleteers' accusations had to be refuted or he could lose his reputation, honor, and the king's favor. He knew that the pamphlet campaign of 1616–17 had destroyed Concini's reputation, increased his unpopularity, and convinced the king that his permanent removal would be welcomed by the court and the nobility. So, the king had agreed to his murder. Fearing the effects of widespread unpopularity, Luynes launched a vigorous counterattack by publishing pamphlets that defended his role as a favorite. Pro-Luynes pamphlets declared that royal favorites had existed for centuries because they served a useful purpose. Surrounded by greedy, grasping courtiers, a king needed friends and advisers whom he could trust and who would be loyal. Favorites were faithful servants acting as instruments of the king's will. Unpopular because they were envied, they were often made scapegoats for the mistakes of others, and were victimized by lies and calumnies. Luynes was urged to ignore these personal attacks and continue his useful service to the king.[35]

Pro-Luynes pamphlets published after 1619 answered specific charges. Richard de Romany, a royal attorney from the Comtat town of Villeneuve-lès-Avignon, stated in *Le Tourment de l'envie courtisane* that although Luynes did not come from the old Comtat nobility, his cousin Modène did and noted that being born in Avignon did not make Modène a foreigner. Romany declared that Luynes came from an old Provençal noble family, and that his father had been the royal governor of Beaucaire and Pont-Saint-Esprit.[36] Other pamphlets declared that Luynes had merited the king's gifts because of his services to the crown. He and his brothers were "bons François," modest humble men who wanted what was best for France, not for themselves. They did not seek self-enrichment, and Luynes had frequently declared that he preferred the public good to his own good.[37]

Several pamphlets defended Luynes's appointment as constable by noting that a wise prudent king such as Louis XIII would never have named an unworthy man to such a high office. Luynes was appointed because of his merit. The office of constable dated back to the Gauls and Romans because of its utility. The king needed a captain general to command his army, suppress rebellions, and stop foreign invasions. Luynes had been named constable to keep France peaceful and well governed, and because of his efforts France was now prosperous and allied to powerful princes. The charges against him were untrue. He and his brothers had been forced to endure the slander, calumnies, and lies of jealous courtiers notorious for maligning those whom they envied. The court, in fact, was a hotbed of gossip and rumor encouraging strife and sedition.[38]

Pamphlets defended Luynes's role in the Huguenot campaign by declaring that the king himself had made the decision to go to war against the Protestants, not Luynes. Punishing arrogant rebels and seditious inhabitants of fortified Protestant cities was a just cause intended to restore peace to France. Luynes had supported the king's decision, following him to the southwest as a soldier, a faithful servant, and a trusted adviser. To blame Luynes for the campaign was to blame the king. To attack the war against the Huguenots was to attack the king, who had made the decision to besiege Montauban because it was the gateway to Languedoc and its capture was necessary for victory. Luynes was not reponsible for having to lift the siege of Montauban, which was lifted because an epidemic of disease had caused a high fatality rate in the army.[39]

Luynes used royal ballets, court receptions, and literary patronage as propaganda to improve his public image. He danced the lead role as Apollo in two royal ballets staged in February and March 1621, followed in April by a lavish court reception as constable, and he had earlier been received as a duke and a knight of Saint Esprit in elaborate court ceremonies. He became a patron to writers whom he encouraged to praise him in print. Théophile de Viau, a poet in the service of Epernon's son, was banished from court in June 1619 for writing verses satirizing Luynes, but was allowed to return ten months later after publishing verses praising him. Viau wrote a widely read ode glorifying Luynes, and the verse libretto for the *Ballet of Apollo*. He became Luynes's client and went with him on campaign in 1621.[40] Charles Bernard was a client of royal minister Pierre Jeannin, who had secured him the post as a reader in the king's household, but Luynes had approved his appointment as a royal historian. So, Bernard was always careful in what he had to say about

Luynes, whom he described as skillful, obliging, persuasive, and capable, and never accused of incompetence, inexperience, or cowardice. In fact, he did not often mention Luynes in his history of Louis XIII's wars. Bernard enjoyed his patronage but was not a client, although Luynes may have hoped that he would become one.[41]

It was customary to dedicate literary work to patrons in the hope of receiving financial support, and favorites were often the subjects of such dedications. In 1620, the royal historian Gilbert de Golefer published *Les Epistres d'Héros*, which he dedicated to Luynes's brother Chaulnes. A 1621 pamphlet attacking the Protestants by Dardenne, prior of Domerat, was dedicated to Luynes, and Scipion Gramont dedicated a ballet to him.[42] The poet François de Malherbe, having received support from several of Luynes's friends including the duc de Bellegarde, sought Luynes's patronage with a six-page dedication to him of his translation of the thirty-third book of the Roman historian Titus Livius, but he received nothing because Luynes died soon afterward. Still seeking patronage, Malherbe wrote an ode to La Vieuville in 1623, and one to Richelieu in 1624.[43] La Vieuville's suppression of Luynes's pensions to men of letters after his death caused a scandal at court.[44]

Luynes's literary clients included pamphleteers such as Richard de Romany (Dromani) who dedicated his pamphlet, *Le Tourment de l'envie courtisane*, to the favorite and his brothers. The pamphlet embellished Luynes's background by declaring that his father had successfully fought a duel to defend his honor, which was reported in the *Mercure françois* in 1619. The pamphlet itself was excerpted in this newspaper in 1620 with the libretti of Luynes's ballets. Louis Tronson, a royal secretary and a Concini conspirator, probably wrote the pro-Luynes pamphlet, *Lettre de Cléophon à Polémandre*, published in 1618. Gabriel Naudé published a pamphlet in 1620 entitled, *Le Marfore ou discours contre les libelles*, which dismissed the anti-Luynes pamphlets as full of "calumnies, lies, and blasphemies." He declared that the king and his government were the only bulwarks against chaos. Because favorites were necessary to the happiness and well being of kings, they were necessary to good government and should be accepted for this reason. Naudé had been seeking patronage by publishing this pamphlet, and was rewarded with the post of librarian to the 8,000-volume library of Henri de Mesmes, the Parlement of Paris president who had been a civil lieutenant of the *prévoté* court during the Concini conspiracy. Most of Luynes's pamphleteers belonged to his own or to the king's household, and their work was mediocre.[45]

Hélène Duccini has noted that public political discourse thrived during the great nobles' revolt of 1614 to 1617 without the constraints suggested by Jürgen Habermas, who differentiated between a traditional public sphere controlled by the monarchy, and a new bourgeois public sphere that began to flourish outside royal control during the late eighteenth century. Duccini has observed that "the public voice of the [early seventeenth-century] pamphlet-eers was the expression of an active exchange in no way restricted by sovereign power." In other words, public political discourse as defined by Habermas appeared a century earlier than he recognized.[46]

The exchanges between pro-Luynes and anti-Luynes pamphleteers support Duccini's observations. The pro-Luynes verse pamphlets by Théophile de Viau, published in 1620, were answered in the same year by an anonymous, anti-Luynes pamphlet entitled, *Remonstrance à Théophile*.[47] The anti-Luynes pamphlet, *La Chronique des Favoris*, published by Fancan in 1622, was answered in the same year by an anonymous, pro-Luynes pamphlet entitled, *Apologie ou Response à La Chronique des Favoris*.[48] The pamphlet, *Lettre de Monseigneur le Cardinal de La Rochefoucauld à Monsieur de Luynes sur la Reformation de l'Estat* (1620), was published with a reply entitled, *La Response de M. de Luynes* (1620).[49] The 1620 protest against the office of constable, entitled *Advis au Roy sur le Restablissement de l'office de Connestable*, was answered in the same year by a pamphlet entitled *Response à l'Advis intitulé Advis au Roy sur le Restablissement de la charge du Connes-table*, and in the next year by one entitled *Le Bon françois à Messieurs du Parlement sur le nouveau connestable*, advocating that the office be reestablished and given to Luynes. The pro-Luynes pamphlet, *Le Reveil de maître Guillaume* (1619) was answered in the same year by *Response au séditieux auteur du Reveil de maître Guillaume*. The original pamphlet was then republished in 1622.[50] This lively political exchange was not controlled by the crown or stifled by press censorship.

Historians have largely ignored Luynes's multi-media counterattack, but its vigor deserves recognition, especially his pamphlet campaign.[51] Pro-Luynes pamphlets appealed to the cult of royalty, that is, the popularity of the young king and the respect for royal authority. They advocated the king's policies, praised his military victories, celebrated his virtues, and defended his favorite. Royalist propaganda, however, tended to be self-laudatory, repetitious, and dull when compared with the inventive vituperation of the anti-Luynes pamphlets, which were better written, more colorful, and more interesting to read. Unfortunately, Luynes did not have a Fancan, Morgues, or Chanteloube among his pamphleteers. The tidal wave of anti-Luynes pamphlets after 1620 outnumbered the pro-Luynes pamphlets three to one, and the pro-Luynes pamphlets, not so widely read, had less influence. They were not incorporated into Richelieu's memoirs, and their arguments have been ignored by historians.

Luynes's historical reputation

Richelieu's memoirs were probably intended to be a history of Louis XIII's reign, and so are not autobiographical in content. Their authenticity has been debated for years. Opinions have ranged from the memoirs being written entirely by Richelieu to their being entirely written by someone else. Most historians agree that the memoirs were based on a compilation of authentic documents including Richelieu's own papers, the papers of contemporary political figures, articles from the *Mercure françois*, political pamphlets, and contemporary histories of the reign. They also agree that some of these documents were written by historians and pamphleteers in Richelieu's pay at his direction. The disagreement has been over the extent to which Richelieu himself wrote the memoirs, the extent to which he supervised their production by secretaries such as Charpentier, and the extent to which the memoirs were written after his death by clients such as Achille Harlay de Sancy, bishop of Saint Malo.

Richelieu strongly believed in the need for an official history of France reflecting his own view of issues and events. Most historians agree that the memoirs represented his ideas and opinions whoever wrote them. For our purpose, their authorship is unimportant because they were widely attributed to Richelieu during the seventeenth century and accepted as his work representing his thinking. The memoirs are not always accurate or reliable as an historical source because they were written years later to express his views, and they sometimes concealed or changed the truth. For example, Richelieu found all his predecessors sadly lacking in ability and criticized them severely, while his comments on Luynes reflected an intense personal dislike. For these reasons, his memoirs do not provide an accurate portrayal of Luynes or his years in power, and they had a devastating effect on his posthumous reputation.[52]

Seventeenth-century historians adopted Richelieu's views with few if any changes. The most influential historian in this respect was François Eudes de Mézeray, who had attracted Richelieu's attention with a defense of his policies in a 1631 pamphlet. A few years later, Mézeray began a three-volume history of France to which Richelieu contributed financially.[53] The standard edition of Richelieu's memoirs, published during the early decades of the twentieth century, was based on two manuscript copies, one found among his own papers and the other belonging to Mézeray. The first part of Mézeray's copy covered the years 1600 to 1619, and was published separately in 1730 as a history of mother and son (Marie de Médicis and Louis XIII). It repeated verbatim the Cardinal's memoirs.[54] It was then republished without changes as the Queen Mother's memoirs, and as a history of her regency.[55] Richelieu's version of events became widely known through these histories of Mézeray.[56]

Richelieu's description of Luynes's origins, for example, was repeated by a historian of the next generation, Gédéon Tallemant des Réaux, who knew Mézeray's work. The wealthy son of a bourgeois Protestant banker, Tallemant des Réaux was the author of the *Historiettes* (1655–57). As a non-noble Protestant, he had little hope of securing ministerial patronage, so he was less influenced by the views of Richelieu and Mazarin than some of his contemporaries, and he was less critical of Luynes as a result. His history was first published in the nineteenth century, and remained in manuscript form until then, so it was not widely known or used by his contemporaries.[57]

A more influential seventeenth-century historian, Scipion Dupleix, was the ablest and most prolific of Richelieu's historians. A royal historian who enjoyed an annual pension, Dupleix wrote a three-volume history of France in the 1620s, and then at Richelieu's request during the 1630s, he wrote histories of the reigns of Henri III, Henri IV, and Louis XIII.[58] His hero was Richelieu whom he depicted as a divinely chosen and inspired royal minister. He regularly submitted his work to Richelieu for approval and scrupulously made any suggested changes. Basing his comments on Richelieu's memoirs and the anti-Luynes pamphlets, Dupleix charged the greedy, low-born, and ambitious Luynes with Concini's murder, and insisted that he had mistreated the Queen Mother and shown himself a coward before the walls of Montauban. Dupleix was criticized by his contemporaries, especially by Bassompierre and Matthieu de Morgues, for acting as Richelieu's mouthpiece and distorting historical facts to fit his views.[59]

Charles Bernard published a history of Louis XIII's war against the Protestants in 1633, which he revised and republished in 1635 as a history of the king's war against the Spanish. He arranged for his post of royal historian to go to his nephew Charles Sorel, who posthumously republished the same book as a history of Louis XIII's reign. Bernard praised the king's prowess, minimized Luynes's role, and sought to satisfy Richelieu, not an easy task which he accomplished by omission and indirection. For example, he summarized a speech that deputies from the Parlement of Toulouse had made to the king criticizing Luynes whom they blamed for the failure of the siege of Montauban. Bernard noted that provincial judges living far from the royal court were able to speak more freely than courtiers, the implication being that he agreed with them but did not dare say so. He never directly accused Luynes of incompetence or cowardice, and he did not often mention him.[60] Criticism of a royal favorite was impolitic if it implied criticism of the king who favored him.

Antoine Aubery was an historian dependent on ministerial patronage. He achieved prominence through a five-volume history of cardinals of the Church. The first volume, published in 1642, was dedicated to Richelieu, and the other four volumes, published from 1643 to 1649, were dedicated to Mazarin who gave him a royal pension. In 1660, he published a history of Cardinal Richelieu dedicated to Cardinal Mazarin as Richelieu's successor. Aubery declared in the first sentence that Richelieu was known for his judgment and zeal, and that Mazarin was known for sharing his predecessor's attitudes toward government and affairs of state. There were only three brief references to Luynes in the entire work. In 1667, Aubery published a collection of documents on Richelieu's ministry in which there was not a single reference to Luynes. In fact, his work contained almost nothing on the royal favorite.[61] Luynes was in power for only four years, and as a historian writing a generation later, Aubery may have considered this period too brief to be important. More significantly, if he wanted to continue receiving Mazarin's patronage, it was unwise to praise or defend Luynes, who was often ignored by contemporary historians for this reason. The animosity of the Cardinals toward Luynes was well known.

The career of Vittorio Siri, an Italian-born Benedictine monk, demonstrates the profitability of writing history to please the Cardinals. In 1640, Siri published a history in which he praised French diplomacy earning him Richelieu's patronage. A two-volume synopsis of Siri's history of Richelieu's ministry, translated from the Italian and published in Amsterdam in 1717, extravagantly praised Richelieu, and contained only one brief derogatory reference to Luynes. Siri's fifteen-volume history of European foreign affairs praised French diplomacy to earn him Mazarin's patronage, and he was rewarded with a pension, a benefice, an office in the abbey of Saint Michel, and employment on several diplomatic missions.[62]

Contemporary biographers often attacked Luynes. Louis Videl, secretary of the duc de Lesdiguières, published a biography of the duke in 1638 dedicated to Richelieu. Videl based his book on the duke's voluminous correspondence, and portrayed Luynes as an envious, self-interested rival of the duke. Videl insisted that Luynes had engineered Déagent's disgrace from jealousy and ambition, and that Luynes always acted in his own interests in contrast to Déagent, a statesman who always acted in the crown's interests. Déagent was a client of Lesdiguières, who had arranged his appointment as first president of the *Chambre des Comptes* or financial high court of Grenoble. Since Déagent considered Luynes responsible for his exile from court, he slandered him to the duke and so influenced Videl. For instance, Videl insisted that Luynes had persuaded the king to demand Lesdiguières's conversion to Catholicism before his appointment as constable because he wanted the office for himself, and had gotten it when the duke refused to convert. Videl's devotion to his patron resulted in a highly colored, negative account of Luynes's motives and actions.[63]

A contemporary biography of the duc d'Epernon, written by his long-time secretary Guillaume Girard, also attacked Luynes, and like Videl's biography, it became a standard historical source. Girard described Luynes as ambitious, deceitful, jealous, and suspicious, all accusations made by Richelieu, and noted that Luynes's avarice surpassed even that of Concini. He declared that Luynes had abused the Queen Mother, separated her from her son, and caused their quarrel. Girard acknowledged Epernon's enmity toward the favorite, but refused to admit that the duke's hostility was the reason for his own antagonism toward Luynes.[64] Contemporary memoirists also tended to be highly critical of Luynes as we have seen.

Eighteenth-century historians repeated the polemics of earlier historians. In 1729, the Jesuit Gabriel Daniel published a history of France in which he listed his sources in the margins. These included Mézeray's histories; the memoirs of Bassompierre and Fontenay-Mareuil; Girard's biography of Epernon; and the histories of Bernard and Aubery, all unfavorable to Luynes. Daniel repeated both the dubious anecdote about servants playing cards on Luynes's coffin, and the Richelieu-Mézeray portrayal of him as ambitious, greedy, deceitful, cowardly, and incompetent. Daniel declared that Luynes had mistreated the Queen Mother, and was responsible for the failure of the siege of Montauban. He repeated Richelieu's assertions that Luynes controlled the king by surrounding him with his own kin and clients, alienated the king from his mother, and persuaded him to murder Concini.[65]

Henri Griffet, another Jesuit, published a history of Louis XIII's reign in 1758 that repeated Daniel's history word-for-word. His sources included Richelieu's memoirs; the histories of Mézeray and Dupleix; the memoirs of Bassompierre and Fontenay-Mareuil; Girard's biography; the collection of documents by Aubery; and Bernard's history, all hostile to Luynes.[66] Griffet made the usual disparaging remarks about Luynes's low birth, foreign origins, domestic service, cowardice, greed, ambition, and responsibility for the king's treatment of his mother, Concini's murder, and the failed siege of Montauban. Daniel and Griffet both relied upon a history of Louis XIII's reign by Michel LeVassor published a half-century earlier.

Michel LeVassor was an Oratorian who had left the order to devote himself to the study of letters. In 1700, he published a history of the reign of Louis XIII that covered the years from 1610 to 1617, listing his sources in the margins. His portrayal of Luynes relied heavily upon Mézeray's histories; the memoirs of Déagent and Bassompierre; and Girard's biography of Epernon. LeVassor insisted that Luynes was responsible for what had happened to Concini and the Queen Mother, and that he was avaricious, ambitious, deceitful, and cowardly. He insisted that Luynes was responsible for the execution of Du Travail, which came from Richelieu's memoirs and Chanteloube's pamphlet. LeVassor's history was used extensively by Daniel, Griffet, Limiers, and Madame d'Arconville.[67]

In 1718, Henri Philippe de Limiers published a history of seventeenth-century France that added a fourth volume to Mézeray's history, which had ended with the death of Henri IV. This additional volume covered the reigns of Louis

XIII and Louis XIV, and portrayed Luynes as an evil adviser to the king whom he controlled by isolating him. Limiers was strongly influenced by Mézeray and Richelieu. He insisted that Luynes had murdered Concini, separated the king from his mother, and caused the failure of the siege of Montauban.[68] Voltaire's history of the age of Louis XIV, published in 1751, also held Luynes responsible for the siege's failure. The assertion of Luynes's responsibility for this failure had originated in two pamphlets by Fancan, *La Chronique des Favoris* and *L'Ombre du Monseigneur le duc de Mayenne*, published in 1622.[69]

Madame Thiroux d'Arconville published in 1778 a biography of the Queen Mother in which Luynes was portrayed as greedy, ambitious, deceitful, and disloyal. She held him responsible for Concini's murder and for the Queen Mother's quarrel with her son. Her sources included the histories of Mézeray, LeVassor, and Griffet; the memoirs of Bassompierre, Déagent, and the maréchal d'Estrées; and Girard's biography of Epernon. Considering the bias in her sources and her obvious sympathy for the Queen Mother, Madame d'Arconville's hostility to Luynes is understandable.[70]

Around the mid-eighteenth century, regional genealogical histories of the nobility began to appear. These histories listed noble families alphabetically, described their origins, traced family branches, and listed their members' achievements. Several histories of the Provençal nobility contained new information about the Albert de Luynes family based on documents that have since disappeared.[71] Noble genealogical histories continued to be published during the nineteenth century along with biographical dictionaries of eminent men, and these works were heavily influenced by earlier histories.[72] The entry for Luynes in the *Grand dictionnaire universel du XIXe siècle* of Pierre Larousse, for instance, included a long quotation from Richelieu's memoirs.[73]

A series of articles was now published that would revolutionize the way in which historians regarded Luynes. Victor Cousin endeavored to rehabilitate Luynes's reputation in thirteen articles published in the *Journal des Savants* between May 1861 and January 1863.[74] The availability of new documentation prompted his effort, specifically the letters of the papal nuncios at the French court and the diplomatic correspondence of the Venetian ambassadors, which had recently been published for the first time.[75] Cousin used this correspondence and the Parisian newspaper the *Mercure françois* to take another look at Luynes. He began by stating that Richelieu's memoirs as published by Mézeray had done Luynes's reputation irreparable harm. He observed that Richelieu had an implacable hatred of Luynes and noted his vindictiveness. Richelieu never forgot or forgave what he considered a slight or a wrong, and when he decided to retaliate against an enemy he annihilated him, which he did to Luynes if posthumously. Cousin insisted that historians needed to take another look at Luynes using documents untainted by the malice of Richelieu.

Cousin argued that Luynes was a successful minister-favorite whose innovations were significant enough to be adopted by Richelieu. He noted that Luynes had restored Henri IV's anti-Habsburg, anti-Spanish foreign policy, and had returned to office Henri IV's ministers removed by Concini and the Queen Mother, whose unpopular policies Luynes had reversed to pacify the rebellious nobility, and he had sought unsuccessfully to be reconciled with the Queen Mother and with the Protestant great nobles. Luynes was a peacemaker who urged moderation and reconciliation at a time of civil war, and for this reason he was unjustly accused of timidity and cowardice.

There are problems with Cousin's interpretation, however. He used as his evidence the Italian diplomatic correspondence, especially the letters of the papal nuncios and Venetian ambassadors. The ambassadors were well connected with excellent sources of information, but as Cousin himself admitted, being anti-Spanish and anti-Habsburg did not make them pro-Luynes. The papal nuncios were critical of Luynes, whom they regarded as a Protestant sympathizer and an enemy of the devoutly Catholic Queen Mother. The Venetian ambassadors were more sympathetic to Luynes, especially after the Valteline affair in July 1620, but they had their own agenda. Although Cousin quoted extensively from the newly published ambassadorial correspondence, he was accused of making interpretative suppositions for which he did not have the evidence. His non-historical background lent weight to criticisms that he had overgeneralized, and his interpretation published in thirteen articles over a year and a half should have been presented in a book. Cousin ended his account in 1620, and did not discuss the 1621 campaign, the Valteline affair, or Luynes's death. Briefer and more ephemeral than his earlier articles, his last articles just faded away and stopped abruptly without an explanation. Cousin was seventy-one at the time, so he may have lost interest or been unable to finish. The flaws in his interpretation limited its acceptance and made it controversial.[76] Nonetheless, Cousin had established beyond a doubt that Richelieu's posthumous attack on Luynes had damaged the favorite's reputation so seriously that much of what had been written about him was questionable.

Berthold Zeller began where Cousin had ended. Zeller stated in the preface to his 1879 book, Le Connêtable de Luynes, that he had investigated the last year of Luynes's life in order to validate Cousin's interpretation. He insisted that Luynes had been the ministerial precursor of Richelieu, not an inept bungler.[77] Zeller paid particular attention to the Valteline affair and the siege of Montauban, insisting that these events demonstrated Luynes's innovative policies adopted by Richelieu, and argued that Luynes was not responsible for the Montauban failure. Zeller used as evidence if uncritically the correspondence of the Florentine ambassadors, papal nuncios, and Venetian ambassadors, and he published a number of their letters in an eighty-two-page appendix.[78]

His book supplied the substantive evidence for Cousin's argument, and since he was a historian by profession, his well-written analytical study based on extensive archival evidence did much to validate Cousin's thesis. His interpretation influenced the work of Eusèbe Pavie, Léon Geley, A.D. Lublinskaya, and A. Lloyd Moote, who remarked that Zeller had written "the most sympathetic portrait of the much maligned Luynes." Moote regarded Luynes as an able if opportunistic politician.[79]

The Cousin/Zeller interpretation did not convince everyone, however. Gabriel Hanotaux, a sympathetic biographer of Richelieu, uncritically used the Cardinal's memoirs with Griffet's history based on them, and ignored the revisionism of Cousin and Zeller. Hanotaux contrasted Richelieu's strong rule based on *raison d'état* with the vacillating, indecisive government of Luynes, whom he characterized as weak, unstable, and cowardly. Hanotaux wrote that Luynes was " without depth of soul, shallow, timid, and fearful … his mind (was) always troubled without pleasure or joy, and his sugary sweetness turned quickly to bitterness and hate. Like all great favorites, he had an insatiable ambition …" Hanotaux cited Richelieu's memoirs as the source of this description. His work was based largely on Richelieu's memoirs, and on ambassadorial dispatches hostile to Luynes, and he offered no new evidence for his criticisms of the favorite. His six-volume biography contributed significantly to the negative view of Luynes that became widespread among twentieth-century historians.[80]

The second volume of Hanotaux's biography covering Luynes's years in power was published in 1896, and influenced the work of Louis Batiffol, who also rejected the Cousin/Zeller revisionism. Batiffol declared that "although Monsieur de Luynes was a sweet and charming man, he had a naive and pitifully weak character … he does not merit the praise given him by V. Cousin and B. Zeller. An attentive study of the documents shows that everything clear and firm in government policy during his ministry was due to the personal intervention of Louis XIII."[81] Batiffol wrote a point-by-point refutation of the Cousin/Zeller interpretation in an article published in the *Revue historique* in 1909 and 1910, which he incorporated as a chapter in his 1910 biography of the young Louis XIII.[82] Trained as an archivist at the École des Chartes, Batiffol was a superb archival researcher, and his study was based on new archival evidence including the anti-Luynes pamphlets, unpublished Italian ambassadorial correspondence in the Bibliothèque Nationale, Spanish ambassadorial correspondence, and letters of Louis XIII, Marie de Médicis, and Luynes. Batiffol wrote, "If the reputation of Luynes was destroyed, Richelieu was largely responsible, but it is also necessary to say that Luynes contributed significantly by his character and conduct."[83] Batiffol published the only archival study of Luynes during the twentieth century, and his interpretation influenced numerous contemporary

historians including the study of Luynes by Jean Claude Pascal, and the histories of Michel Carmona, Pierre Chevallier, Roland Mousnier, François Bluche,
Françoise Hildesheimer, and Philippe Erlanger.[84]

Batiffol agreed with Richelieu that Luynes was cowardly, weak, unstable,
indecisive, ambitious, and greedy, and regarded him as an opportunistic
blunderer. He believed that Déagent and Louis XIII had provided the direction and decisiveness in royal government. Batiffol published his study just
before the First World War, an intensely jingoistic period, so he may have
found Luynes's conciliatory attempts at peacemaking distasteful and an indication of his cowardice, vacillation, and weakness. Batiffol also depended heavily
on anti-Luynes sources and uncritically accepted as valid evidence defama-
tory pamphlets, hostile ambassadorial dispatches, and biased contemporary
memoirs, histories, and biographies. He used the accusations in the anti-Luynes
pamphlets as the source for his character analysis of the favorite, and although
he cited these pamphlets, he did not indicate their bias.[85]

Batiffol's study had other problems besides a lack of objectivity. Briefer
than the studies of Cousin or Zeller, his account tended to be sketchy, super-
ficial, and unclear. His research was excellent and his facts sound, but his
interpretation was weak, more descriptive than analytical. Although Batiffol
acknowledged that Richelieu despised Luynes, he adopted word-for-word the
Cardinal's views on him as his own. Aware that the pamphlets he used selectively
had been written by Luynes's enemies, he still considered them valid evidence,
and he relied upon the Spanish ambassadorial correspondence, which he knew
was anti-Luynes. In short, Batiffol's account contained enough problems to
fail in its goal of refuting the Cousin/Zeller interpretation. The outbreak of
the First World War abruptly ended the debate about Luynes's character and
actions, and it was not resumed at the war's end.

Richelieu sponsored some of the most effective anti-Luynes pamphlets,
which were included in his memoirs, and were extensively used by contemporary
historians, many of whom were his clients. Richelieu's memoirs became a
major historical source, and his negative comments on Luynes significantly
influenced later historiography. Twentieth-century historians have tended to
accept the Batiffol-Hanotaux interpretation challenged by this book, and ignore
the Cousin/Zeller revisionism.

Richelieu and Luynes

Why did Richelieu despise Luynes? Richelieu blamed Luynes for the loss of
his office of secretary of state in 1617, and for his subsequent exile to Coussay,
Luçon, and Avignon, a major setback to his career. When he finally returned

to the Queen Mother's household in March 1619, he had to be obsequious to Luynes, which he abhorred, and he was forced to marry his niece to Luynes's nephew, which he resented. His comment on the marriage was that "Monsieur de Luynes wanted only the appearance of friendship, not the result."[86] The Queen Mother loathed Luynes, so Richelieu as a member of her household had to loathe him, too. Having convinced her to be more cooperative, Richelieu expected a reward from Luynes, which he did not receive. The king nominated him for a cardinal's hat in August 1620, but the hat went to Epernon's son. Richelieu may have felt cheated and betrayed, although historians have probably overemphasized his disappointment as the reason for his loathing of Luynes.[87] It was symptomatic of a deeper, more serious problem.

Richelieu was ambitious, and Luynes stood in the way of his advancement. As long as Luynes was the king's favorite, the Queen Mother would play a secondary political role, and so would Richelieu as her client. Her loss of status and power was his loss. It was unlikely that Luynes would advance Richelieu because he did not like or trust him, and he did not tolerate ambitious rivals. Richelieu wanted Luynes's place, and he feared political obscurity or even worse oblivion as long as Luynes was in power. He could not know that Luynes would die in December 1621. He feared that Luynes would stand in his way for years, and bitterly resented him for that.

Besides, they had very different personalities. Luynes was warm, affable, and charming, while Richlieu was cold, arrogant, ruthless, and unforgiving. Richelieu was a political not a personal favorite. He did not have the same type of personal relationship with the king that Luynes had, and he probably felt threatened by their affectionate family relationship because he could not reproduce it. Richelieu feared negative comparisons in the king's mind, and so he criticized Luynes whenever he had the chance during his lifetime and afterward.

Richelieu's political style was harsher than that of Luynes. He preferred to use the stick in governing, and he had a well-deserved reputation for being implacable and vindictive toward his enemies. He imprisoned Déagent (1624), Ornano and his brothers (1626), Modène (1626), the Vendôme brothers (1626), Fancan (1627), Bassompierre (1631), the Marillac brothers (1631), and Vitry (1637). He exiled La Vieuville (1625), Marie de Rohan (1626), Modène (1626), Marie de Médicis (1631), Guise (1631), and the duc de Rohan (1639). He executed Chalais (1626), Bouteville (1627), Marillac (1632), and Montmorency (1632), and he removed from office a large number of provincial governors.[88] Richelieu regarded Luynes as a dangerous enemy, and unable to retaliate against him in life, he destroyed his reputation after death.

Luynes in contrast used the carrot in governing, preferring to manipulate rather than intimidate, and used his charm, influence, and control over patronage to get what he wanted. He was more conciliatory than Richelieu. He showed sympathy to the Queen Mother in 1617, and sent a number of personal envoys to her in 1619. He went down on his knees to her at Couzières, and agreed to favorable terms for her in the Treaties of Angoulême and Ponts-de-Cé. He rescued Richelieu from disgrace after Concini's murder, and from exile in Avignon a year and a half later. When Luynes sent his rivals and enemies from court, he sometimes allowed them to return as he did Vitry, Bassompierre, and Viau, but Richelieu never did.

Luynes was the forerunner of Richelieu as a minister favorite. Louis XIII had initially disliked Richelieu because of his arrogance, but Richelieu learned from Luynes how to manage the king by making him feel appreciated and understood. Richelieu saw the king often, and together they discussed the council's agenda just as Luynes had done with the king. They worked together as a team in governing, and the king more readily accepted a political partnership with Richelieu because he had previously had one with Luynes. Richelieu was the king's openly acknowledged principal adviser, however, and he acted in public as the king's first minister, which Luynes had never done. Richelieu openly dominated the royal council after 1631, which Luynes had never done either. Luynes had a consultative political style that sharply contrasted with Richelieu's own absolutist style. Richelieu enjoyed considerably more decision-making power than Luynes.

Richelieu joined the Paris government when the pamphlet campaign against Concini was under way. He participated in the Queen Mother's pamphlet campaign against Luynes, and used this political tactic against his enemies for the rest of his life, maintaining a large group of pamphleteers, historians, and journalists whom he paid to praise him and attack his enemies. He adopted other propaganda tactics that Luynes had used including the staging of court ballets and the induction of new members into the Order of Saint Esprit. Richelieu benefited from Luynes's experience as a self-publicist.

Richelieu continued the foreign policy decisions of 1620 and 1621 for nearly a decade. He agreed that the threat to royal authority posed by Protestant disobedience had to be dealt with before tackling the problem of Spanish expansionism, so he maintained the anti-Habsburg alliances and played for time. The prince of Wales married the king's sister Henriette Marie in 1625. The Venetian and Savoyard alliances were renewed, and a new treaty was signed with the Dutch. After Protestant disobedience was suppressed, Richelieu began an undeclared war against the Spanish Habsburgs that became open in 1635. He was able to convince the king to exile his intransigent mother from France because Luynes's experience in exiling her from court had led to a civil war. At the same time, he got rid of her most important allies and supporters including Guise, Epernon, Soissons, Vendôme, Montmorency, and the Marillac brothers, and he initiated a rapprochement with Condé, having learned from Luynes that Condé was easier to manage as a friend than as an enemy.[89]

Luynes was the bridge between Concini, a personal favorite who briefly became a political favorite, and Richelieu, a first minister favorite who created a national administrative clientele.[90] Luynes was a transitional minister favorite who created a large noble clientele that he used for political purposes. His historical importance has been overlooked because Richelieu's dislike of him has dominated the historical literature. Richelieu ignored his debt to his predecessors whom he severely criticized, particularly Luynes whom he despised. Richelieu was in power for eighteen years (1624–1642) in contrast to Luynes's five years (1617–1621). Because Richelieu came to power after Luynes's death and outlived him by twenty-one years, his version of events became the accepted version and the standard historical interpretation. Richelieu had the last word. This book has challenged the traditional interpretation by demonstrating that Luynes was not the timid, bungling opportunist described by Richelieu.

Notes

1 Michel de Marolles, *Mémoires*, 3 vols. (Paris, 1656), I, 46–7; Emile Baudson, *Charles de Gonzague, duc de Nevers* (Paris, 1947), pp. 159–61, 203.

2 Roland Mousnier, *The Institutions of France*, 2 vols., *Society and State*, trans. Brian Pearce (Chicago, 1979), I, 139–46; idem, *L'Homme rouge ou la vie du Cardinal de Richelieu* (Paris, 1992), pp. 152–3; Julian Pitt-Rivers, "Honor and Social Status," in *Honor and Shame*, ed. Jean Péristiany (Chicago, 1966), pp. 21–77; idem, "Honor," in *International Encyclopedia of the Social Sciences*, ed. David Sills, 14 vols. (New York, 1968), VI, 503–11; François Billaçois, *Le Duel dans la société française* (Paris, 1986).

3 *Mercure françois*, 25 vols. (Paris, 1605–44), VI (1620), 263; Eugène and Jules Halphen, eds., *Journal inédit d'Arnauld d'Andilly 1620* (Paris, 1888–1909), p. 16.

4 Christian Jouhaud, *Mazarinades: La Fronde des mots* (Paris, 1985); Hubert Carrier, *La Presse de la Fronde 1648–1653: Les Mazarinades*, 2 vols. (Geneva, 1989–91).

5 Hélène Duccini, *FaireVoir, Faire Croire* (Paris, 2003), pp. 375–407; idem, *Concini* (Paris, 1991), pp. 347–61; idem, "Regard sur la littérature pamphletaire," *Rev hist* 260 (1978), 313–39; idem, "Une campagne de presse sous Louis XIII," in *Histoire sociale. Mélanges Robert Mandrou*, ed. Philippe Joutard (Paris, 1985), pp. 291–301; idem, "L'Etat sur la place publique. Pamphlets et libelles," in *L'Etat baroque*, ed. Henry Méchoulan (Paris, 1985), pp. 290–9; Jeffrey Sawyer, *Printed Poison* (Berkeley, 1990); J. Michael Hayden, "The Uses of Political Pamphlets," *Canadian Journal of History*, 21 (1986), 143–65; idem, *France and the Estates General of 1614* (Cambridge, 1974), pp. 68–9, 147–8, 164–6; Claude Belland et al., *Histoire générale de la presse française*, 5 vols. (Paris, 1969–76), I, 63–81; Henri-Jean Martin and Roger Chartier, eds., *Histoire de l'édition française*, 4 vols. (Paris, 1983–9), I, 405–25; Henri-Jean Martin, *Livre, pouvoirs et société à Paris au XVIIe siècle*, 2 vols. (Geneva, 1969), I, passim; idem, *Le Livre français sous l'Ancien Régime* (Paris, 1987), pp. 133–43; Howard Solomon, *Public Welfare, Science, and Propaganda* (Princeton, 1972).

6 Duccini, "Regard sur la littérature pamphletaire," 313, 332–3; idem, "L'Etat sur la place publique," pp. 293–6; Sawyer, *Printed Poison*, p. 27; Hayden, "The Uses of Political Pamphlets," 144, n. 3; Emile Bourgeois and Louis André, *Les Sources de l'histoire de France XVIIe siècle*, 8 vols. (Paris, 1924), IV, 176–83, 194–6.

7 Léon Geley, *Fancan et la politique de Richelieu* (Paris, 1884), pp. 1–134; Maximin Deloche, *Autour de la plume de Richelieu* (Paris, 1920), pp. 190–241; Eusèbe Pavie, *La Guerre entre Louis XIII et Marie de Médicis* (Angers, 1899), pp. 621–2; Gabriel Hanotaux and the duc de La

Force, *Histoire du Cardinal de Richelieu*, 6 vols. (Paris, 1893–1947), II, part 2, 464–5; William Church, *Richelieu and Reason of State* (Princeton, 1972), pp. 96–101; Etienne Thuau, *Raison d'état et la pensée politique à l'époque de Richelieu* (Paris, 1966), pp. 174–7; Mousnier, *L'Homme rouge*, pp. 203–4.

8 *Recueil des pièces les plus curieuses qui ont esté faites pendant le règne du Connestable M. de Luynes* (Paris, 1628), *Veritez Chrestiennes au Roy* (1620), pp. 126–48; *Manifeste de la Royne Mère* (1620), pp. 261–8; Duccini, *FaireVoir*, pp. 382–4; Maximin Deloche, *La Maison du Cardinal de Richelieu* (Paris, 1912), pp. 33–4; idem, *Autour de la plume*, pp. 190–213; Donald Bailey, "Writers against the Cardinal, 1630–1640" (Ph.D. dissertation, University of Minnesota, 1972), pp. 91–100; idem, "Les Pamphlets de Mathieu Morgues," *Revue française d'histoire du livre* 18 (1978), 3–48; Joseph Bergin, *The Rise of Richelieu* (New Haven, 1991), pp. 182, 207–8.

9 *Recueil*, *Remonstrance au Roy importante* (1620), pp. 16–28; *La Chronique des Favoris* (1622), pp. 440–89; Geley, *Fancan et la politique de Richelieu*, pp. 407–34; Deloche, *Autour de la plume*, pp. 214–41; Gustave Fagniez, "L'Opinion publique et la presse politique sous Louis XIII, 1624–1626," *Revue d'histoire diplomatique* 96 (1900), 352–401; idem, "Fancan et Richelieu," *Rev hist* 107 (1911), 59–75, 108 (1911), 75–87; Theodor Kuelkaus, "Zur Geschichte Richelieus. Unbekannte Papiere Fancans," *Historische vierteljahrschrift* 2 (1899), 18–39; Thuau, *Raison d'état*, p. 177, n. 2; Bailey, "Writers against the Cardinal," pp. 100–4.

10 Victor Cousin, "Le Duc et connêtable de Luynes," *Journal des Savants* (September 1861), 532; Fagniez, "L'Opinion publique," 365.

11 Duccini, *Faire Voir*, pp. 386–8; Bailey, "Writers against the Cardinal," pp. 89–91; idem, "Les Pamphlets des associés polémistes de Mathieu de Morgues," *Revue française d'histoire du livre* 27 (1980), 232–3; Geley, *Fancan et la politique de Richelieu*, p. 8; Pavie, *La Guerre*, pp. 11, n. 1, 98–9, 652–65; Bergin, *Rise of Richelieu*, pp. 179, 202, and n. 190; Denis Avenel, ed., *Lettres, instructions diplomatiques et papiers d'état du Cardinal de Richelieu*, 8 vols. (Paris, 1853–7), I, 645–6, 627, n. 1; Charles, comte Horric de Beaucaire, *Mémoires du Cardinal de Richelieu*, 10 vols. (Paris, 1907–13), II, 390–1.

12 Geley, *Fancan et la politique de Richelieu*, pp. v–vi. My special thanks to Orest Ranum for lending me his copy of the *Recueil*.

13 Sawyer, *Poison Pen*, pp. 137–43; Georges Minos, *Censure et Culture sous l'Ancien Régime* (Paris, 1995), pp. 77–82; *Recueil*, *La France mourante* (1622, Fancan), pp. 489–535; *LaVoix Publique au Roy* (1622, Fancan), pp. 536–81; *Le Mot à l'Oreille* (1624, Fancan), pp. 581–99; *Lux orta à M. de Luçon*, p. 440.

14 Duccini, *Faire Voir*, pp. 397–410; Church, *Richelieu and Reason of State*, pp. 461–504; Deloche, *Autour de la plume*, pp. 245–511; Minos, *Censure et Culture*, pp. 92–101; Françoise Hildesheimer, *Relectures de Richelieu* (Paris, 2000), pp. 209–19; Thuau, *Raison d'état*, pp. 177–8; Orest Ranum, *Artisans of Glory* (Chapel Hill, 1980), pp. 148–68; Bailey, "Writers against the Cardinal," pp. 84–146; Louis Dedouvres, *Le Père Joseph, polémiste, ses premiers écrits* (Paris, 1895).

15 Victor-Lucien Tapié, *France in the Age of Louis XIII and Richelieu*, trans. D. McN. Lockie (Cambridge, 1974), p. 275; Michèle Fogel, *Les Cérémonies de l'information* (Paris, 1989), p. 225.

16 Richard Bonney, *The King's Debts* (Oxford, 1981), p. 91.

17 *Recueil*, *Le Qu'as-tu-veu de la Cour* (1620), pp. 43–7; *Les Contre-veritez de la Cour* (1620), pp. 63–7; *Le Monstre à Trois Testes* (1620), pp. 67–8; *La Sybille françoise* (1620), p. 281; *Le Tout en Tout de la Cour* (1620), pp. 70–1; *Le Chien à Trois Testes* (1622), pp. 392–3; *Les Soupirs de la Fleur de Lys* (1622), pp. 406–8; *Plaintes de l'espée de M. le Connestable* (1621), pp. 149–50; *L'Horoscope du Connestable* (1621, Fancan), pp. 151–4; *Les Admirables Propriétés de l'Aluyne* (1620, Fancan), pp. 49–55; *Le Passe Par-Tout des Favoris* (1622, Fancan), pp. 154–65; *Cancellus* (1622), pp. 152–4.

18 *Recueil*, *Le Comtadin Provençal* (1620, Chanteloube), pp. 79–111; *Veritez Chrestiennes au Roy très Chrestien* (1620, Morgues), pp. 126–48; *Manifeste de la Royne Mère envoyé au Roy* (1618, 1620, Morgues), pp. 261–8; *Remonstrance au Roy importante pour son Estat* (1620, Fancan), pp. 16–28; *Méditations de l'hermite Valérien* (1621, Fancan), pp. 303–42; *L'Ombre de Monseigneur le duc de*

Mayenne (1622, Fancan), pp. 375–92; *L'Ombre de Monsieur le Connestable* (1622, Fancan), pp. 426–38; *La Chronique des Favoris* (1622, Fancan), pp. 440–89; Carrier, *La Presse de la Fronde*, I, 439–40. The pamphlets cited by Naudé were *Le Comtadin* and *Méditations*.

19 Beaucaire, *Mémoires de Richelieu*, III, 183 and n. 1; *Recueil, Méditations de l'hermite Valérien*, p. 317.

20 Ibid., p. 322; Beaucaire, *Mémoires de Richelieu*, I, 307.

21 Ibid., II, 201–7; *Recueil, Le Contadin Provençal*, pp. 92–3.

22 Ibid., pp. 83–5; Beaucaire, *Mémoires de Richelieu*, I, 304–7, II, 188.

23 Ibid., III, 190–1; *Recueil, Remonstrance au Roy importante pour son Estat*, pp. 16–28; *Le Contadin Provençal*, pp. 95–104; *L'Ombre de Monseigneur le duc de Mayenne*, pp. 376–7, 380–2.

24 Ibid., *Manifeste de la Royne Mère envoyé au Roy*, p. 267; Beaucaire, *Mémoires de Richelieu*, III, 185–6.

25 Ibid., II, 171–8, 200–1, 276–7; *Recueil, Veritez Chrestiennes au Roy*, pp. 133–46; *La Chronique des Favoris*, p. 475; *L'Ombre de Monsieur le Connestable*, p. 435; *Le Contadin Provençal*, pp. 87–9.

26 Ibid., *La Chronique des Favoris*, pp. 465, 477; *Le Contadin Provençal*, pp. 88–9; *L'Ombre de Monseigneur le duc de Mayenne*, pp. 378–9; *Méditations de l'hermite Valérien*, pp. 331–2; *Plaintes de l'espée de M. le Connestable*, pp. 149–50; *Le Passe Par-Tout des Favoris*, pp. 151–4; *L'Horoscope du Connestable*, p. 156; Beaucaire, *Mémoires de Richelieu*, II, 175–6, 178–9, III, 166.

27 Duccini, *Concini*, pp. 325–57.

28 Beaucaire, *Mémoires de Richelieu*, III, 164–97; *Recueil, Le Noel* and *Le Pasquil des Chevaliers* (1620), pp. 34–8; *Les Admirables Propriétés de l'Aluyne* (1620), pp. 49–55; *Le Contadin Provençal* (1620), pp 84–111, esp. 106; *Le Tout en Tout de la Cour* (1620), pp. 70–1; *Le Qu'as-tu-veu de la Cour* (1620), p. 44; *Les Psaumes des Courtisans* (1620), pp. 393–406; *Requeste presentée au Roy par Conchino Conchini* (1620), pp. 72–7.

29 Ibid., *L'Ombre de Monseigneur le duc de Mayenne*, pp. 375–92; *L'Ombre de Monsieur le Connestable*, pp. 426–38; *La Chronique des Favoris*, pp. 440–89; *Discours et salutaire avis à la France mourante* (1621), pp. 343–74; B.N., imprimés Lb 36, *Discours politique sur les occurrences et mouvements de ce temps* (1621); Geley, *Fancan et la politique de Richelieu*, pp. 100–35; Hanotaux, *Histoire du Cardinal de Richelieu*, II, part 2, 463–5.

30 *Mercure françois*, V (1619), pp. 137–77; B.N., imprimés Lb 36, *Requête présentée au Roy par M. de Luynes* (1619).

31 Ibid., *Apologie pour M. de Luynes* (1619); *Lettre de Cléophon à Polémandre* (1619); *Plaidoyé pour M. de Luynes* (1619); *La Fulminante contre les Calomniateurs* (1620).

32 Ibid., *Discours fait à M. de Luynes par le sieur Dryon* (1617); *Advis ou discours à M. de Luynes par M. de Ryom* (1617?); *Advis donné à M. de Luynes par un fidèle serviteur du Roy* (1618); *Apologie ou Response à la Chronique des Favoris* (1622).

33 Ibid., *Cérémonies observées à la réception de M. de Luynes en la qualité de duc* (1619); *Le Manifeste de Picardie au Roy* (1620).

34 B.N., imprimés Lb 36, *Relation du grand ballet du roi, dansé dans la salle du Louvre, le 12 février, sur l'aventure de Tancrède en la forêt enchantée* (1619), published by Scipion Gramont.

35 *Recueil, Eloges du duc de Luynes* (1620), pp. 111–20; B.N., imprimés Lb 36, *Apologie pour M. de Luynes*; *Le Tourment de l'envie courtisane* (1619); *Plaidoyé pour M. de Luynes*; *Le Favory du Roi* (1620); *Seconde partie et responce à La Chronique des Favoris* (1622).

36 Ibid., *Le Tourment de l'envie courtisane*, pp. 7–10.

37 Ibid., *Plaidoyé pour M. de Luynes*, pp. 13–14; *Apologie ou response à La Chronique de Favoris*, p. 14; *Requeste présentée au Roy par M. de Luynes*; *Lettre de Monsieur le Connestable à Monsieur Modène* (1621), p. 5; *Apologie pour M. de Luynes*, p. 16; *Lettre de Monseigneur le Cardinal de La Rochefoucauld à M. de Luynes et response* (1620); *Lettre consolatoire du Roy à Madame la Connestable* (1622).

38 Ibid., *Apologie pour M. de Luynes*; *Apologie ou response à La Chronique des Favoris*, pp. 24, 26–7; *Les Cérémonies royales faictes en baillant par les mains du Roy l'espée de connestable à M. de Luynes* (1621); *Déclaration sur la Réception de M. de Luynes Connestable* (1621); *Plaidoyé pour M. de Luynes*; *Le Tourment de l'envie courtisane*.

39 Ibid., *Apologie ou response à La Chronique des Favoris*, pp. 7–9, 11–13, 26; *Lettre de M. le Connestable à M. de Modène*; *Lettre de M. le Connestable à M. de Montbazon* (1621).
40 *Recueil, Eloges du duc de Luyne* (1620) with *L'Advis au Roy par Théophile* (1620) and *Conseil de Théophile au Roy* (1620), pp. 111–26; Antoine Adam, *Théophile de Viau et la libre pensée française en 1620* (Paris, 1954), pp. 154–63; Christian Jouhaud, *Les Pouvoirs de la littérature* (Paris, 2000), pp. 45–6.
41 Charles Bernard, *Histoire des guerres de Louis XIII contre les religionnaires rebelles* (Paris, 1633), pp. 242–3; Orest Ranum, *Artisans of Glory* (Chapel Hill, 1980), pp. 103–47, esp. 110.
42 Orest Ranum, "L'Honneur, l'argent. Gilbert Golefer," *L'Age d'or du mécénat*, eds. Roland Mousnier and Jean Mesnard (Paris, 1985), p. 394; Raoul Patry, *Philippe Du Plessis-Mornay* (Paris, 1933), p. 578.
43 François Malherbe, *Oeuvres*, ed. Ludovic Lalanne, 5 vols (Paris, 1862–9), I, 250, 391–6; René Fromilhague, *La Vie de Malherbe* (Paris, 1954), pp. 133, 185–6, 209; Gilles Henry, *François de Malherbe* (Caen, 1984), pp. 55, 64, 69–81, 89–90; Raymond Lebègue, *Malherbe et Du Perier* (Paris, 1957), p. 70.
44 Urbain-Victor Chatelain, *Le Surintendant Nicolas Foucquet* (Paris, 1905, Geneva, 1971), p. 140.
45 Eugène Griselle, *Etat de la maison du Roy Louis XIII* (Paris, 1912), p. 28; Orest and Patricia Ranum, eds., *Mémoires de Guillaume de Tronson* (Paris, 2003), pp. 16–18; Bourgeois and André, *Les Sources de l'histoire de France*, IV, 145, 182–3, 194; Joseph-François Michaud, ed., *Biographie universelle*, 45 vols. (Paris, 1854, Graz, 1968), XXX, 239–41; James Rice, *Gabriel Naudé* (Baltimore, 1973 [1939]); J.A. Clarke, *Gabriel Naudé* (Hamden, Conn., 1970), pp. 4–5, 8–9; *Mercure françois*, VI (1619), 191; B.N., imprimés Lb 36, *Tourment de l'envie courtisane* (1619), p. 11; Billaçois, *Le Duel*, p. 380, n. 46; Carrier, *La Presse de la Fronde*, I, 447 and n. 305.
46 Duccini, *Faire Voir*, p. 60.
47 *Recueil*, pp. 122–6.
48 B.N., imprimés Lb 36, *Apologie ou response à La Chronique des Favoris*, pp. 7, 13–14, 30.
49 B.N., imprimés Lb 36. See *Catalogue de l'histoire de France*, 16 vols. (Paris, 1968–9), vol. 1, for pamphlets published in this period.
50 B.N., imprimés Lb 36; *Recueil*, pp. 5–10.
51 Duccini, *Faire Voir*, pp. 375–97; Gustave Fagniez, "L'Opinion publique et la polémique au temps de Richelieu," *Revue des questions historiques* 60 (1896), 456–61.
52 Beaucaire, *Mémoires de Richelieu*, I, ii–iii; Françoise Hildesheimer, *Richelieu* (Paris, 2004), pp. 508–18; Louis Delavaud, *Quelques collaborateurs de Richelieu* (Paris, 1915), pp. 40–1; Berthold Zeller, *Richelieu et les ministres de 1621 à 1624* (Paris, 1880), pp. v, 4–5; Bergin, *Rise of Richelieu*, pp. 6–7; Jouhaud, *Les Pouvoirs*, pp. 217–33; Mousnier, *L'Homme rouge*, pp. 463–84.
53 François Eudes de Mézeray, *Histoire de France depuis Paramond jusqu'au règne de Louis le Juste* (Paris, 1685); Ranum, *Artisans of Glory*, pp. 200–9; Wilfrid Evans, *L'Historien Mézeray* (Paris, 1930), pp. 40–3; Phyllis Leffler, "From Humanist to Enlightenment Historiography," *Fr Hist Stud* 10 (1978), 416–38.
54 Beaucaire, *Mémoires de Richelieu*, I, 1–2, n. 1, 304; François Eudes de Mézeray, *Histoire de la Mère et du Fils*, 2 vols. (Amsterdam, 1731), I, 282, II, 169–219; Hildesheimer, *Richelieu*, p. 509.
55 Evans, *L'historien Mézeray*, p. 43, n. 2; *Les Mémoires de la Reyne Marie de Médicis* (Paris, 1666); *Histoire de la régence de la reine Marie de Médicis* (The Hague, 1743).
56 Ranum, *Artisans of Glory*, pp. 217–32; Cousin, "Le Duc et connêtable de Luynes," (May 1861), 261.
57 Gédéon Tallemant des Réaux, *Historiettes*, ed. Antoine Adam, 2 vols. (Paris, 1960–61), I, vii–xxvi, 157–9; Emile Magne, *La Joyeuse jeunesse de Tallemant des Réaux* (Paris, 1921); idem, *La Fin troublée de Tallemant des Réaux* (Paris, 1922).
58 Scipion Dupleix, *Histoire générale de la France*, 3 vols. (Paris, 1621–28); idem, *Histoire de Henri III* (Paris, 1630); idem, *Histoire de Henri le Grand* (Paris, 1632); idem, *Histoire de Louis le Juste, XIII du Nom* (Paris, 1637).

59 Ibid., pp. 97–8, 108–9, 198–9; Church, *Richelieu and Reason of State*, pp. 464–70; Jouhaud, *Les Pouvoirs*, pp. 191–217; DBF, XIII, 389; Duccini, *Concini*, pp. 391–4; Robert Knecht, *Richelieu* (London, 1990), p. 177; idem, "Cardinal Richelieu," *History Today* (March 2003), 11; Jean Charay, ed., *Vie du maréchal Alphonse d'Ornano* (Aubenas-en-Vivarais, 1975), p. 189, n. 153; *Remarques de Monsieur le Mareschal de Bassompierre* (Paris, 1665), pp. 181–544; Matthieu de Morgues, *Lumières pour l'histoire de France* (Condom, 1645).

60 Bernard, *Histoire des guerres de Louis XIII*, pp. 69, 116–21, 232–4; Charles Bernard, *Histoire de Louis XIII jusqu'à la guerre déclarée contre les Espagnols* (Paris, 1635); idem, *Histoire du Roi Louis XIII* (Paris, 1646); Ranum, *Artisans of Glory*, pp. 103–47; DBF, VI, 50; Jouhaud, *Les Pouvoirs*, pp. 161–91.

61 Antoine Aubery, *Histoire générale des cardinaux*, 5 vols. (Paris, 1642–9); idem, *L'Histoire du Cardinal Duc de Richelieu* (Paris, 1660), pp. 13, 17, 18; idem, *Mémoires pour l'histoire du Cardinal Duc de Richelieu*, 5 vols. (Cologne, 1667); DBF, IV, 98–9.

62 Vittorio Siri, *Anecdotes du ministère du cardinal de Richelieu et du règne de Louis XIII*, trans.Valdory, 2 vols. (Amsterdam, 1717), I; Joseph-François Michaud, ed., *Biographie universelle*, 45 vols. (Paris, 1854, Graz, 1968), XXXIX, 412–13.

63 Louis Videl, *Histoire de la vie du connestable de Lesdiguières* (Paris, 1638), pp. 331, 338, 355–7, 361, 371, 382–3; Mousnier, *L'Homme rouge*, p. 155.

64 Guillaume Girard, *The History of the Life of the Duke of Espernon*, trans. Charles Cotton (London, 1670), pp. 308–14; DBF, XVI, 150.

65 Gabriel Daniel, *Histoire de France depuis l'établissement de la monarchie française*, 10 vols. (Paris, 1729); ibid., 17 vols. (Paris, 1756), XIII, 175–331; DBF, X, 111; Beaucaire, *Mémoires de Richelieu*, II, 171–82.

66 Griffet, *Histoire du règne de Louis XIII*, vol. 1, 1610–30; DBF, XVI, 1214; Duccini, *Concini*, pp. 398–9.

67 Michel LeVassor, *The History of the Reign of Lewis XIII, King of France and Navarre*, 3 vols. (London, 1700–02), III, 375–533; Michaud, *Biographie universelle*, XXIV, 392; F.E. Sutcliffe, *Guez de Balzac* (Paris, 1959), pp. 23–4.

68 Henri Philippe de Limiers, *Abrégé chronologique de l'histoire de France. Tome quatrième contenant les règnes de Louis XIII et Louis XIV pour servir à celui de Mézeray* (Amsterdam, 1740), pp. 50–132.

69 François Marie Arouet de Voltaire, *Le Siècle de Louis XIV*, 2 vols. (Berlin, 1751), II, 230–1; *Recueil, La Chronique des Favoris*, pp. 440–89; *L'Ombre de Monseigneur le duc de Mayenne*, pp. 375–92.

70 Geneviève-Charlotte d'Artus, Madame Thiroux d'Arconville, *Vie de Marie de Médicis*, 3 vols. (Paris, 1778), II, 208–332; III, 93–5; DBF, III, 416–17.

71 Jean-Antoine Pithon-Curt, *Histoire de la noblesse du Comté Venaissin*, 4 vols. (Paris, 1743–50); Charles Achard, *Dictionnaire de la Provence et du Comtat Venaissin*, 4 vols. (Marseille, 1786–7); Louis Ventre de la Touloubre d'Artefeuil, *Histoire héroique et universelle de la noblesse de Provence*, 3 vols. (Avignon, 1757); Père Anselme de Sainte Marie, *Histoire généalogique et chronologique de la Maison Royale de France*, 9 vols. (Paris, 1726–33); Louis Moréri, *Grand dictionnaire historique*, 6 vols. (Paris, 1759).

72 François-Alexandre Aubert de La Chesnaye-Desbois, *Dictionnaire de la noblesse*, 19 vols. (Paris, 1863–76); Casimir-François-Henri Barjavel, *Dictionnaire historique du département de Vaucluse*, 2 vols. (Carpentras, 1841); Michaud, *Biographie universelle*; Auguste Aubert, *Les Vauclusiens*, 2 vols. (Avignon, 1890–2); Auguste Jal, *Dictionnaire critique et biographique*, 2nd edn (Paris, 1872).

73 Pierre Larousse, *Grand dictionnaire universel du XIXe siècle*, 17 vols. (Paris, 1866–79), X–1, 813.

74 Victor Cousin, "Le Duc et connêtable de Luynes," *Journal des Savants* (May 1861–January 1863); DBF, IX, 1070–4.

75 *Lettere diplomatische de Guido Bentivoglio*, 4 vols. (Turin, 1852); Luigi Steffani, ed., *La Nunziatura de Francia de Guido di Bentivoglio*, 4 vols. (Florence, 1863–70); Nicolo Barozzi and Guglielmo

Berchet, *Relazioni degli stati europei. Lettere et Senato degli ambasciatori Veneti nel secolo XVII*, 10 vols. (Venice, 1856–78).

76 Duccini, *Concini*, p. 405.

77 Berthold Zeller, *Le Connêtable de Luynes. Montauban et la Valteline d'après les Archives d'Italie* (Paris, 1879), pp. i–ii.

78 Ibid., pp. iv–xv, 277–363; Duccini, *Concini*, p. 405.

79 Pavie, *La Guerre*, p. 638; Geley, *Fancan et la politique de Richelieu*, p. 26; A.D. Lublinskaya, *French Absolutism: The Crucial Phase, 1620–1629*, trans. Brian Pearce (Cambridge, 1968), pp. 146–96; A. Lloyd Moote, "Richelieu's Chief Minister," *Richelieu and His Age*, eds. Joseph Bergin and Laurence Brockliss (Oxford, 1992), p. 17, n. 14; idem, *Louis XIII*, pp. 148, 104.

80 Hanotaux, *Histoire du Cardinal de Richelieu*, II, part 2, 209 and notes. "[Luynes] ... sans fond, sans âme et sans suite, léger, timide et craintif ... l'âme toujours en peine, sans plaisir et sans joie; et, dans sa douceur sucrée, un levain tournant vite à l'aigreur et à la haine. Comme tous les grands favoris, d'une ambition inassouvissable ...", DBF, XVII, 591; Duccini, *Concini*, p. 404; Lublinskaya, *French Absolutism*, pp. 149–53.

81 Louis Batiffol, "Le Coup d'état du 24 avril 1617," *Rev hist* 97 (108), 64, n. 1. "M. de Luynes était un homme doux et charmant, mais un caractère d'une faiblesse pitoyable, et un naïf ... il ne mérite pas les éloges qui lui ont donnés V. Cousin et B. Zeller. L'étude attentive des documents montre que tout ce qu'il y a eu de netteté et de fermeté dans la politique du gouvernment durant sa prépondérance est dû à l'intervention personelle de Louis XIII."

82 Idem, "Louis XIII et le duc de Luynes," ibid., 102 (1909), 241–64; 103 (1910), 32–62, 248–79; idem, *Le Roi Louis XIII à vingt ans* (Paris, 1910), pp. 478–573.

83 Idem, "Louis XIII et le duc de Luynes," *Rev hist* 103 (1910), 62; idem, *Le Roi Louis XIII*, p. 540. "Si la réputation de M. de Luynes a été perdue, Richelieu y est pour beaucoup; mais, il faut le dire aussi, M. de Luynes y a, de son côté, notablement contribué par son caractère et son conduit."

84 Mousnier, *L'Homme rouge*, p. 155; Hildesheimer, *Richelieu*, pp. 75–107; Pierre Chevallier, *Louis XIII* (Paris, 1979), pp. 173–208; Michel Carmona, *Marie de Médicis* (Paris, 1984), pp. 345–68; François Bluche, *Richelieu* (Paris, 2003), pp. 115–16; Jean-Claude Pascal, *L'Amant du Roi* (Monaco, 1991), pp. 10–11, 109–202, 417–18; Philippe Erlanger, *Louis XIII* (Paris, 1972), pp. 111–224.

85 Batiffol, "Louis XIII et le duc de Luynes," *Rev hist*, 102 (1909), 250 and n. 2.

86 Armand Jean du Plessis de Richelieu, *Mémoires de Richelieu*, eds. Michaud and Poujoulat, 2nd ser., vol. 7 (Paris, 1837), 229. Richelieu's letters to Luynes are in A.A.E., Fonds France 771, 772, 775; Avenel, *Lettres du Cardinal de Richelieu*, vols. 1 and 8.

87 Bergin, *Rise of Richelieu*, pp. 161–236; Batiffol, "Louis XIII et le duc de Luynes," *Rev hist*, 103 (1910), 49–62; Zeller, *Le Connêtable de Luynes*, pp. 129–32.

88 Richard Bonney, *Political Change in France under Richelieu and Mazarin* (Oxford, 1978), pp. 284–92; Arlette Jouanna, *Le Devoir de révolte. La Noblesse française et l'etat moderne* (Paris, 1989), pp. 232–3.

89 Henri d'Orléans, duc d'Aumale, *Histoire des princes de Condé pendant les XVIe XVIIe siècles*, 7 vols. (Paris, 1863–96), II, 169–183.

90 A. Lloyd Moote, "Richelieu as Chief Minister," *Richelieu and His Age*, eds. Joseph Bergin and Laurence Brockliss (Oxford, 1992), pp. 13–43; Klaus Malettke, "The Crown, Ministériat and Nobility at the Court of Louis XIII," *Princes, Patronage and the Nobility*, eds. Ronald Ash and Adolf Birke (London, 1991), pp. 415–39; Jean-François Dubost, "Between Mignons and Principal Ministers: Concini, 1610–1617," *The World of the Favourite*, eds. J.H. Elliott and L.W.B. Brockliss (New Haven, 1999), pp. 71–8; Jean-Marie Constant, "Luynes," *Dictionnaire du Grand Siècle*, ed. François Bluche (Paris, 1990), pp. 922–3.

Conclusion:
death of a favorite

Luynes became ill with a high fever and a runny nose during the early morning hours of 3 December 1621.[1] Four days later, a bright red rash appeared all over his body, and eight days later on 15 December he died of scarlet fever.[2] He had probably caught this highly contagious disease, spread by hand contact, while visiting the troops in the trenches before Monheurt. Scarlet fever is a strep infection that occurs during the cold months of the year, peaking in December and January, and disappears during the summer months when the bacteria is destroyed by heat. So, as the weather got colder during the autumn of 1621, the disease reached epidemic proportions in the army. The rash lasts ten to twenty days and is accompanied by a high fever, rapid pulse, discharge from the mouth, nose, and throat, and peeling, scaly skin. During the final stages of the disease, there may be difficulty in breathing, delirium, vomiting, and convulsions.[3]

When Luynes became ill, the duc de Montmorency, governor of Languedoc, sent a famous physician from the Montpellier medical faculty, François Rauchin, to his bedside. Rauchin decided not to bleed Luynes, although he had a high fever. Fontenay-Mareuil considered this decision unwise because "he [Luynes] had become fat from eating too much, and would assuredly have had a great abundance of blood."[4] Too much blood was thought to cause a high fever. Now in his forties, Luynes was no longer riding as much as he had in his youth. During the last two days of his life, he suffered frequent convulsions, and he died at about three o'clock on the afternoon of Wednesday 15 December. Only the abbé Ruccellai was with him when he died. Luynes had already confessed to a Jesuit priest from Agen, and he had written a letter to the king asking him to look after his family. The king had not been allowed to visit him after he became seriously ill, and was not allowed to touch the letter, which was read to him.[5]

Both Fontenay-Mareuil and Bassompierre believed that by the time of his death, Luynes was out of favor because the king showed no grief in public.[6] Héroard, the king's doctor, however, wrote in his journal that in private Louis was greatly distressed, while royal historian Charles Bernard noted that Luynes was still in "full favor" when he died.[7] The king told Condé that he was much saddened at losing Luynes, and he wrote a letter of condolence to Luynes's wife, published as a pamphlet, in which he declared that "he [Luynes] was very dear to me … I regarded him as good and strong." The king promised to take care of her and her children in Luynes's memory.[8] After the 1622 Huguenot campaign, the king returned to Paris through the Comtat Venaissin, stopping at Mornas to see where Luynes had spent his childhood.[9] Esprit d'Alart, sieur d'Esplan, briefly became a royal favorite after Luynes's death because he, too, was a charming Provençal, and the king missed Luynes.[10] Luynes's brothers and his infant son, Louis-Charles, for whom his uncle Chaulnes became the guardian, were allowed to keep their wealth, property, and titles. Only Luynes's politically important offices such as constable, keeper of the seals, and governor of Picardy were given to others. His fortress governorships were given to his friends, and his wife's new husband got his offices of first gentleman of the king's bedchamber and grand falconer.[11] This would suggest that Luynes was still in favor when he died. His death went unlamented at court where everyone was scrambling to take his place.[12] Malherbe wrote a witty, nasty epigram about his death: "Cet aluyne au nez de barbet, En ce tombeau fait sa demeure, Chacun en rit et moi j'en pleure, Je le voulais voir au gibet."[13] A spate of nasty verses circulated about Luynes after his death.[14] Brienne published one in his memoirs.[15]

This book has tried to refute the biased accounts of Luynes's career by Richelieu, the pamphleteers, and contemporary historians that have dominated the historical literature. Luynes's silence has made him an enigma, and he remains a shadowy figure behind his affability and charm. His elusiveness is partly a result of his political style, and partly a result of the limited available documentation.

Luynes was a model courtier, suave, elegant, and full of bonhomie with a sleek, sophisticated façade that hid a darker, more complicated reality. Courtiers were known for their duplicity and deceit in this period.[16] Richelieu grudgingly admitted that Luynes was a kind, caring man who was deeply concerned about his family.[17] He had been tall, dark, and handsome in his youth, and he was gregarious with a good sense of humor. He was also a shrewd psychologist who knew how to use his charm to manipulate others. As a royal falconer, he saw the young king often and gained his favor as an amusing companion who could make him laugh and enjoy himself. Luynes's years as a falconer, spent in catching and taming wild birds of prey, demonstrated a calm patient temperament, while the skill with which he reassured and guided an insecure teenager demonstrated his intelligence. Luynes was twenty-three years older than the king, whom he treated as a son, and for whom he provided a surrogate family more supportive than his own family.

Favorites were always portrayed as greedy, ambitious nobodies who were social climbers, but Luynes came from a respected family of the *noblesse seconde* of the Rhône river valley. He became an early modern success story when he acquired royal favor, using it to accumulate a large fortune, although not as large as the pamphleteers claimed, and to provide generously for his family, although not for the horde of penniless relatives that his enemies claimed. He acquired lands, wealth, the titles of duke and peer, a large noble clientele, a provincial government, numerous fortress governorships, and the offices of constable, keeper of the seals, first gentleman of the king's bedchamber, and grand falconer. His success caused much envy and resentment among his contemporaries, which was also true of Concini and Richelieu. Favorites were never popular. Luynes worried about the effects of his unpopularity because he knew that royal favor could be fleeting and possibly fatal. He feared being assassinated like Concini. So, he became a dedicated self-publicist who worked hard at creating a good public image. He knew that acceptance by the court nobility was necessary for his survival as a favorite.

Luynes had a near monopoly on the distribution of royal patronage, but he found that using it to secure the cooperation of the court nobility was a double-edged sword making him as many enemies as friends. He worked hard to placate his enemies and turn them into friends, using his personal charm, influence, control over patronage, and access to the king. He sought a reconciliation with the Queen Mother, Epernon, Mayenne, and Richelieu, and ties to the high-ranking and powerful including the young queen, the king's brother, the prince de Condé, the Lorraine and Rohan families. Luynes used his patronage power to create a party of court nobles who helped him to suppress the Queen Mother's revolt, and he created a provincial power base around the court and city of Paris that helped him to stay in power. Concini and Richelieu created similar power bases. An experienced courtier and a political sophisticate, Luynes hid his thoughts behind an affable, genial facade that allowed others to underestimate him. He remained in the shadows, acting behind the scenes as favorites tended to do, which gave him the reputation for being ignorant and incompetent, although he was neither.

Luynes worked hard at performing the traditional functions of a favorite, and he made significant contributions to the early years of Louis XIII's government. He guided and advised the young king, acting as a channel of communication and a buffer between him and the court nobility, Protestant great nobles, foreign ambassadors, army commanders, and high government officials. He acted as a lightning rod to deflect criticism from the king, and as a scapegoat to cover his mistakes. He was the king's spokesman, messenger, go-between, and troubleshooter, and he became skilled at negotiating compromises and solving problems. He did what the king did not want to do.

After helping to eliminate Concini, Luynes began to attend council meetings and offer the king political advice, and he quickly developed from a personal into a political favorite, becoming a minister favorite when he acquired the offices of constable and keeper of the seals. Although he was the ministerial precursor of Richelieu, Luynes was not a typical minister favorite. He was never the king's only adviser, and he did not dominate the council or the decision-making process as Richelieu did. Luynes had a consultative political style that emphasized group decision-making, and he used his clients as political advisers to help him present ideas and options to the king, who made the final decisions with the help of his councils. Luynes had to defer to the king's strongly held opinions in order to retain favor, which gave him a reputation for being indecisive, and his initial opposition to the campaign against the Protestants gave him a reputation for cowardice. However, he was never the timid, vacillating bungler described by Richelieu. The continuing influence of Richelieu's animosity on the historical literature needs to be recognized.

Louis XIII was not a weak, disinterested, or lazy king in need of a minister favorite to govern for him. He wanted to rule by himself, and he developed a political partnership with Luynes that Richelieu would imitate. The king and Luynes worked together to govern France with the advice and help of a small group of conservative council members. Luynes was by nature a conciliator and a peacemaker who had a moderating influence on the king. He preferred to negotiate compromises rather than use military force, and he sided with the conservatives on the council in advising the king against undertaking the Normandy and Béarn campaigns, and against military intervention in Germany and the Valteline. He opposed the Protestant campaign in the southwest for more than a year before finally agreeing to go.

Luynes gave Louis XIII the chance to rule alone by removing the Queen Mother's favorite Concini and ending her political dominance, and by thwarting her attempt to reestablish herself in power two years later. He secured the court nobility's support for the new regime and for himself as the new favorite. He guided and supported the young king, developed an effective political partnership with him, and encouraged him to seek the royal councils' advice in governing. He nullified the influence of the rash, impulsive Condé, sought to curb the king's own tendency toward belligerence, and advocated a policy of non-intervention in European affairs until domestic problems could be solved, a policy that Richelieu pursued. Historians have insufficiently appreciated Luynes's contributions to the early years of Louis XIII's government. He helped an inexperienced young king learn how to govern, and provided the model for his later relationship with Richelieu.

Notes

1 Jean Héroard, *Journal*, ed. Madeleine Foisil, 2 vols. (Paris, 1989), II, 2795.

2 Ibid., II, 2797–8; Eugène Halphen, ed., *Journal inédit d'Arnaud d'Andilly 1621* (Paris, 1891), p. 102; Louis Batiffol, *Le Roi Louis XIII à vingt ans* (Paris, 1910), pp. 564–5.

3 J.W. Schereschewsky, *Scarlet Fever: Its Prevention and Control* (Washington, D.C., 1915), pp. 3–9.

4 François Du Val, marquis de Fontenay-Mareuil, *Mémoires du Messire Du Val*, ed. Louis Monmerqué, 2 vols. (Paris, 1826), I, 525.

5 Claude Malingre, *Histoire de la rebellion excitée en France par les rebelles de la religion prétendue réformée* (Paris, 1626), p. 673; *Journal d'Arnauld 1621*, p. 104; Batiffol, *Le Roi Louis XIII*, pp. 564–73; Berthold Zeller, *Le Connêtable de Luynes* (Paris, 1879), p. 265.

6 Fontenay-Mareuil, *Mémoires*, p. 526; François de Bassompierre. *Journal de ma vie. Mémoires du maréchal de Bassompierre*, ed. Edouard de Chanterac. 4 vols. (Paris, 1870–77), II, 395.

7 Héroard, *Journal*, II, 2797–8; Charles Bernard, *Histoire des guerres de Louis XIII contre les religionnaires rebelles* (Paris, 1633), p. 242.

8 Eugène Griselle, ed., *Lettres à la main de Louis XIII*, 2 vols. (Paris, 1914), I, 259; Malingre, *Histoire de la rebellion*, p. 674; B.N., imprimés Lb 36, *Lettre consolatoire du Roy à Madame la Connestable* (Paris, 1622).

9 Bernard, *Histoire des guerres de Louis XIII*, pp. 242–3.

10 Batiffol, *Le Roi Louis XIII*, p. 496; Gédéon Tallemant des Réaux, *Historiettes*, ed. Antoine Adam, 2 vols. (Paris, 1960–61), I, 159, 844–5, ns. 1 and 2.

11 Scipion Dupleix, *Histoire de Louis le Juste, XIII du Nom* (Paris, 1635), p. 294; Père Anselme de Sainte Marie, *Histoire généalogique et chronologique de la Maison Royale de France*, 9 vols. (Paris, 1726–33, New York 1967), III, 493, IV, 272, 274, VIII, 733; Berthold Zeller, *Richelieu et les ministres de Louis XIII de 1621 à 1624* (Paris, 1880), pp. 5–6.

12 Ibid., pp. 3–4.

13 François Malherbe, *Oeuvres*, ed. Ludovic Lalanne, 5 vols. (Paris, 1862–9), I, 250. "This bitter absinthe with the nose of a spaniel now makes his home in a tomb. Everyone is laughing about it, but I am crying because I wanted to see him on the gallows."

14 *Recueil des pièces les plus curieuses qui ont esté faites pendant le règne du Connestable Monsieur de Luynes* (Paris, 1628), *Le De Profundis sur la mort de Luynes* (1622), pp. 411–19; *Le Confiteor de Monsieur le Connestable qu'il a fait devant mourir* (1622), pp. 419–22; *Le Tombeau des deux frères* (1622), pp. 422–3; *Le Te Deum chanté sur la mort de Monsieur le Connestable* (1622), pp. 423–4.

15 Henri de Loménie de Brienne, *Mémoires du comte de Brienne*, eds. Michaud and Poujoulat, 3rd ser., vol. 3 (Paris, 1838), p. 21 and n. 1.

16 Xavier Le Person, *"Practiques"et"Practiqueurs."La vie politique à la fin du règne de Henri III* (Geneva, 2002).

17 Charles, comte Horric de Beaucaire, ed., *Mémoires du Cardinal de Richelieu*, 10 vols. (Paris, 1907–13), II, 26–7, III, 185, 188, 190.

Select bibliography

Primary sources

Archival

Archives du Ministère des Affaires Etrangères, Paris, Fonds France, 772–5.

Archives Nationales, Paris, MC (Minutier central) VII, 9, 11; VIII, 896; XXXVI, 109; XXXIX, 55; XLIV, 87; LI, 723; LXXV, 408; CVIII, 115; KK145.

Archives départementales, Maine-et-Loire, E 2189, fols. 1–69.

Archives départementales, Vaucluse, Avignon, E 22, 26–7.

Archives communales, Beaucaire, BB 12, 13, 14, 16; EE 26.

Archives communales, Mornas, GG 1.

Archives communales, Pont-Saint-Esprit, BB 1; CC 3, 7, 46, 57–8; FF 4; GG 1, 2.

Bibliothèque de l'Arsenal, Paris, Manuscrits 5260, 5424.

Bibliothèque Inguimbertine, Carpentras, Manuscrits 1789, 1800, 1805, 1826–7, 1847, 1864.

Bibliothèque de l'Institut de France, Paris, Collection Godefroy, Manuscrits 15, 215–16, 268–9, 271, 461, 519, 548.

Bibliothèque municipale d'Avignon, Manuscrits 1786, 2082, 2098, 3245, 3421, 3424–5.

Bibliothèque municipale de Nancy, Manuscrit 1401.

Bibliothèque nationale de France, Paris

Baluze 214, 323.

Cabinet des Titres, Dossiers bleus 8.

Cinq Cents de Colbert 9, 46, 86–9, 91, 94, 96–8, 221, 324, 325.

Clairambault 374–7, 737, 837, 1132, 1135, 1148.

Duchesne 58.

Dupuy 62, 92–3, 487, 511, 631, 662, 850, 853, 937.

Manuscrits français 2748, 2758, 3420, 3687, 3722, 3795, 3802, 4112, 4149, 4330, 4587, 4876, 7854, 7856, 15617, 15989, 16802, 17341, 17345, 17363, 18470, 19187, 20614, 20631, 20742, 22061, 25196–99.

Mélanges de Colbert 16, 46, 82, 324–5.

Nouveau d'Hozier 5.

Nouvelles acquisitions françaises 1278, 3145, 4334, 5131.
Pièces originales 21, 1780.
Bibliothèque Sainte-Geneviève, Paris, Manuscrit 833.

Published

Claude Bernard Petitot edited a collection of printed primary sources entitled *Mémoires relatifs à l'histoire de France*. Joseph François Michaud and Jean-Joseph-François Poujoulat edited a collection of printed primary sources entitled *Nouvelle collection des mémoires pour servir à l'histoire de France*. Both collections are identified here only by the editors' last names. The abbreviation SHF refers to printed primary sources published by the *Société de l'histoire de France*. Titles have been shortened. The following is a selected list of primary published sources used in this study.

Achard, Charles. *Dictionnaire de la Provence et du Comtat Venaissin*. 4 vols. Marseille, 1786–7. Geneva, 1971.
Agrippa, d'Aubigné, Théodore. *Histoire universelle*, ed. A. de Ruble. 10 vols. Paris, 1886–1909. Geneva, 1987.
Ambassade du mareschal de Bassompierre en Espagne l'an 1621. Cologne, 1668.
Anselme de Sainte Marie, Père. *Histoire généalogique et chronologique de la Maison Royale de France*. 9 vols. Paris, 1726–33. New York, 1967.
Archives curieuses de l'histoire de France depuis Louis XI jusqu'à Louis XVIII, eds. F. Danjou and M.L. Cimber, 1 ser. vol. 14, 2nd ser. vol. 2. Paris, 1837–38.
Arconville, Geneviève-Charlotte d'Artus, Madame Thiroux d'. *Vie de Marie de Médicis, princesse de Toscane, reine de France et de Navarre*. 3 vols. Paris, 1778.
Arcussia, Charles d'. *La Fauconnerie de Charles d'Arcussia de Capre, seigneur d'Esparron, de Pallières et du Revest*. Rouen, 1643.
Arnauld d'Andilly, Robert. *Journal inédit 1614–1620*, ed. Achille Halphen. Paris, 1857.
Arnauld d'Andilly, Robert. *Journal inédit 1620–1632*, ed. Eugène and Jules Halphen, 9 vols. Paris, 1888–1909. Vols. 1620 and 1621–22.
Arnauld d'Andilly, Robert. *Mémoires de Messire Robert Arnauld d'Andilly*, ed. Petitot. 2nd ser. vols. 33–4. 2 vols. Paris, 1824.
Artefeuil, Louis Ventre de la Touloubre d'. *Histoire héroique et universelle de la noblesse de Provence*. 3 vols. Avignon, 1757.
Articles concluded and agreed upon by the Lords, the Cardinal de La Rochefoucauld and de Béthune in the name of the King of France to the Queen Mother. London, 1619.
Aubery, Antoine. *Mémoires pour l'histoire du cardinal duc de Richelieu*. 5 vols. Cologne, 1667.
Bassompierre, François de. *Journal de ma vie. Mémoires du maréchal de Bassompierre*, ed. Edouard de Chanterac. 4 vols. Paris, 1870–77.
Bassompierre, François de. *Remarques de Monsieur le mareschal de Bassompierre sur les vies des Roys Henry IV et Louis XIII de Dupleix*. Paris, 1665.
Beauvais-Nangis, Nicolas de Brichanteau, marquis de. *Histoire des favoris françois depuis Henri II jusqu'à Louis XIII*. Paris, 1665. p. 3.

Beauvais-Nangis, Nicolas de Brichanteau, marquis de. *Mémoires*, eds. Louis Monmerqué and A.H. Taillandier. Paris, 1862.

Bernard, Charles. *Histoire des guerres de Louis XIII contre les religionnaires rebelles*. Paris, 1633.

Bernard, Charles. *Histoire de Louis XIII jusqu'à la guerre déclarée contre les Espagnols*. Paris, 1635.

Bernard, Charles. *Histoire du roi Louis XIII*. Paris, 1646.

Boitel de Gaubertin, Pierre. *Histoire des guerres et choses mémorables arrivés sous le règne de Louis le Juste*. Rouen, 1623.

Boitel de Gaubertin, Pierre. *Relation historique ... la réception des chevaliers de l'Ordre du Saint Esprit 1620*. Paris, 1620.

Bouges, Père. *Histoire des commandeurs, chevaliers, et officiers de l'Ordre du Saint Esprit*. Paris, 1737.

Brienne, Henri-Auguste de Loménie, comte de. *Mémoires*, ed. Petitot, 2nd ser. vol. 36. Paris, 1824. eds. Michaud and Poujoulat, 3rd ser. vol. 3, Paris 1838.

Canault, Jean. *Vie du maréchal Alphonse d'Ornano (1548–1610)*, ed. Jean Charay. Aubenas-en-Vivarais, 1975.

Canault, Jean. *Vie du maréchal Jean-Baptiste d'Ornano (1581–1626)*, ed. Jean Charay. Grenoble, 1971.

Catalogue of the collection of autograph letters and historical documents formed by Alfred Morrison, ed. Alphonse Thibaudeau, ser. 1 vols. 1–6. London 1883–97.

Chorier, Nicolas. *Histoire de la vie de Charles de Créquy de Blanchefort, duc de Lesdiguières*. Grenoble, 1683.

Crèvecoeur, R. *Un document nouveau sur la succession des Concini*. Paris, 1891.

Daniel, Gabriel. *Histoire de France depuis l'établissement de la monarchie française*. 10 vols. Paris, 1729. 17 vols. Paris, 1756.

Déagent de Saint Martin (Marcellin), Guichard Claude. *Mémoires de Monsieur Déagent envoyez à Monsieur le Cardinal de Richelieu*. Grenoble, 1668. London, 1690.

Douglas, comte de, and Roman, J., eds. *Actes et correspondance du connêtable de Lesdiguières*. 3 vols. Grenoble, 1878. volume 2.

Dupleix, Scipion. *Histoire de Louis le Juste, XIII du nom*. Paris, 1637.

Duplessis-Mornay, Philippe. *Mémoires et correspondance de Duplessis-Mornay, depuis l'an 1571 jusqu'en 1623*, eds. A.D. La Fontenelle de Vaudoré and P.R. Auguis. 12 vols. Paris, 1824–5.

Dupuy, Pierre. *Histoire des plus illustres favoris anciens et modernes*. Paris, 1660.

Estrées, François Annibal d', duc d', maréchal d'. *Mémoires*, ed. Petitot, 2nd ser. vol. 16. Paris, 1822. ed. Paul Bonnefon. SHF. Paris, 1910.

Fleury, Claude. *Le Devoir des maîtres et des domestiques*. Paris, 1688.

Fontenay-Mareuil, François Du Val, marquis de. *Mémoires du Messire Du Val*, ed. Louis Monmerqué, 2 vols. Paris, 1826. ed. Michaud and Poujoulat, 2nd ser. vol. 5, Paris, 1837.

Fournier, Edouard, *Variétés historiques et littéraires*, 10 vols. Paris, 1855–63. vol. 3.

Girard, Guillaume. *Histoire de la vie du duc d'Epernon*. Paris, 1655. English tr. London, 1670.

Gonzague, Louis de, duc de Nevers. *Mémoires*, ed. Marin Le Roy, sieur de Gomberville. 2 vols. Paris, 1665.

Goulas, Nicolas. *Mémoires*, ed. Charles Constant. SHF. 3 vols. Paris, 1879–82.

Griffet, Henri. *Histoire du règne de Louis XIII*. 3 vols. Paris, 1758.

Griselle, Eugène. *Documents d'histoire (XVIIe, XVIIIe et XIXe siècles)*. Paris, 1910.

Griselle, Eugène. *Ecurie, vénerie, fauconnerie et louveterie du Roi Louis XIII*. Paris, 1912.

Griselle, Eugène. *Etat de la maison du Roi Louis XIII*. Paris, 1912.

Griselle, Eugène. *Lettres à la main de Louis XIII*. 2 vols. Paris, 1914.

Griselle, Eugène. *Louis XIII et Richelieu. Lettres et pièces diplomatiques*. Paris, 1911.

Griselle, Eugène. "Louis XIII et sa mère." (letters) *Revue historique* 105 (1910): 302–31; 106 (1911): 83–100, 295–308.

Griselle, Eugène. *Maisons de la Grande Mademoiselle et de Gaston d'Orléans*. Paris, 1912.

Griselle, Eugène. *Supplément à la maison du Roi Louis XIII*. Paris, 1912.

Héroard, Jean. *Journal*, ed. Madeleine Foisil. 2 vols. Paris, 1989.

Jeannin, Pierre. *Oeuvres mélées du Président Jeannin*, ed. Petitot. Paris, 1822.

Joly, Hector. *Histoire particulière des choses mémorables qui se sont passés au siège de Montauban*. n.p., 1624.

LaCroix, Paul. *Ballets et mascarades de cour de Henri III à Louis XIV (1581–1652)*. 6 vols. Geneva, 1868, vol. 2.

La Force, Jacques Nompar de Caumont, duc de. *Mémoires authentiques de Jacques Nompar de Caumont, duc de La Force, maréchal de France, et de deux fils, les marquis de Montpouillan et de Castelnaut*, ed. Marquis de La Grange. 4 vols. Paris, 1843.

La Rochefoucauld, François VI, duc de. *Mémoires*, ed. Petitot, 2nd ser. vols. 51–52. Paris, 1826.

Lee, Sidney, ed. *The Autobiography of Edward, Lord Herbert of Cherbury*. London, 1906.

Legrain, Baptiste. *Décade commençant l'histoire du Roy Louis XIII du nom*. Paris, 1618.

Lettres de Henri III, roi de France. ed. Michel François. 4 vols. Paris, 1959–84.

Lettres de Nicolas Pasquier, fils d'Estienne. Paris, 1623.

LeVassor, Michel. *The History of the Reign of Lewis XIII, King of France and Navarre*. 3 vols. London. 1700–1702. English tr. of French original. vols. 1, 10.

Limiers, Henri Philippe de. *Abrégé chronologique de l'histoire de France*. Amsterdam, 1740.

Loyseau, Charles. *Cinq livres du droict des offices*, 2nd edn, Paris, 1613.

Malherbe, François. *Oeuvres*, ed. Ludovic Lalanne, 5 vols. Paris, 1862–9. ed. Antoine Adam. Paris, 1971.

Malingre, Claude. *Histoire de la rébellion excitée en France par les rebelles de la religion prétendue réformée (1620–1622)*. Paris, 1626.

Malingre, Claude. *Histoire du règne de Louis XIII, Roy de France et de Navarre (1610–1643)*. Paris, 1646.

Marolles, Michel de, abbé de Villeloin. *Mémoires*. 3 vols. Paris, 1656.

Martignac, Etienne Algay de. *Mémoires du Gaston, duc d'Orléans*, ed. Petitot. 2nd ser. vol. 31. Paris, 1824. Jean Lasseré may also be the author.

Matthieu, Jean-Baptiste. *Histoire de Louis XIII, roy de France et de Navarre*. End of vol. 2 in Pierre Matthieu, *Histoire de France du règne du roy Henry IV*. 2 vols. Paris, 1631.

Matthieu, Pierre. *Histoire d'Aelius Séjanus*. 1617.

Matthieu, Pierre. *La Magicienne étrangère*. 1617.

Médicis, Catherine. *Lettres*, eds. Hector de La Ferrière and Gustave Baguenault de Puchesse. 11 vols. Paris, 1880–95.

Mercure françois. 25 vols. Paris, 1605–44. vols. 4–7, 1617–21.

Mézeray, François Eudes de. *Histoire de France depuis Paramond jusqu'au règne de Louis le Juste*. Paris, 1685.

Mézeray, François Eudes de. *Histoire de la mère et du fils*. 2 vols. Amsterdam, 1731.

Mézeray, François Eudes de. *Histoire de la régence de la reine Marie de Médicis*. The Hague, 1743.

Mézeray, François Eudes de. *Les Mémoires de la Reyne Marie de Médicis*. Paris, 1666.

Molé, Mathieu. *Mémoires*, ed. Aimé Champollion-Figeac. SHF. 4 vols. Paris, 1855–7.

Montglat, François de Paule de Clermont, marquis de. *Mémoires*, ed. Petitot, 2nd ser. vol. 49. Paris, 1825. eds. Michaud and Poujoulat, 3rd ser. vol. 5. Paris, 1838.

Morgues, Matthieu de. *Diverses pièces pour la défense de la Royne Mère du Roy très-chrestien Louys XIII*. 2 vols. Paris, 1643.

Morgues, Matthieu de. *Lumières pour l'histoire de France et pour faire voir les calomnies, flatteries et autres défauts de Scipion Dupleix*. Condom, 1645.

Motteville, Françoise Bertaut de. *Mémoires pour servir à l'histoire d'Anne d'Autriche*, ed. Petitot. 2nd ser. vol. 36. Paris, 1824. ed. Michaud and Poujoulat. 2nd ser. vol. 10. Paris, 1838.

Négociation commencée au mois de mars 1619 avec la reine mère Marie de Médicis par Monsieur le comte de Béthune. Paris, 1672.

Négociations du président Jeannin, ed. Bouchon. Paris, 1838.

Pithon-Curt, Jean-Antoine. *Histoire de la noblesse du Comté Venaissin*. 4 vols. Paris, 1743–50.

Pontchartrain, Paul Phélypeaux de. *Mémoires concernant les affaires de France sous la régence de Marie de Médicis*, ed. Michaud and Poujoulat, 2nd ser. vol. 5. Paris, 1837. ed. Petitot, 2nd ser. vols. 16–17. Paris, 1822.

Pontis, Louis de. *Mémoires du sieur de Pontis, qui a servi dans les armées cinquante-six ans, sous les rois Henri IV, Louis XIII, Louis XIV*, ed. Petitot, 2nd ser. vols. 31–32. Paris, 1824.

Puységur, Jacques de Castenet de. *Mémoires. Les guerres du règne de Louis XIII et la minorité de Louis XIV*, ed. Tamizey de Laorroque. 2 vols. Paris, 1883. vol. 1.

Rabutin, Roger de, comte de Bussy. *Mémoires*, ed. Ludovic Lalanne. 2 vols. Paris, 1857.

Rapports et notices sur l'édition des Mémoires du Cardinal de Richelieu, ed. Jules Lair et al. 3 vols. Paris, 1907–14.

Récit et véritable discours de l'entrée de la reine mère dans la ville d'Angers faite le 16 octobre 1619. Angers, 1619.

Recueil des lettres missives de Henri IV, eds. Berger de Xivrey and Joseph Gaudet. 9 vols. Paris, 1843–76.

Recueil des pièces les plus curieuses qui ont esté faites pendant le règne du Contestable M. de Luynes, Paris, 1628.

Relation exacte de tout de qui s'est passé à la mort du mareschal d'Ancre, ed. Michaud and Poujoulat, 2nd ser. vol. 5. Paris, 1837.

Retz, Henri de Gondi, Cardinal de. *Mémoires*, ed. Michaud and Poujoulat, 3rd ser. vol. 1. Paris, 1837.

Richelieu, Armand Jean du Plessis, Cardinal de. *Lettres, instructions et papiers d'état du Cardinal de Richelieu*, ed. Denis-Louis-Martial Avenel. 8 vols. Paris, 1853–7.

Richelieu, Armand Jean du Plessis, Cardinal de. *Mémoires du Cardinal de Richelieu* (to 1630), ed. Charles comte Horric de Beaucaire, 10 vols. SHF. Paris, 1907–13. (for 1630–1643), ed. Michaud and Poujoulat, 2nd ser. vols. 7–9. Paris, 1837. ed. Petitot. 2nd ser. vols. 21bis-30. Paris, 1819–1829.

Rohan, Henri de, duc de. *Mémoires du duc de Rohan*, ed. Michaud and Poujoulat, 2nd ser. vol. 5. Paris, 1837.

Saudau, Louis Claude. *Saint-Jean d'Angély d'après les archives de l'échevinage et les sources directes de son histoire*. Saint-Jean d'Angély, 1886. Marseille, 1978.

Sauval, Henry. *Histoire et recherches des antiquités de la ville de Paris*. 3 vols. Paris, 1733. volume 2.

Siri, Vittorio. *Anecdotes du ministère du cardinal de Richelieu et du règne de Louis XIII*. trans. Valdory. 2 vols. Amsterdam, 1717.

Souvigny, Jean Grangières, comte de. *Mémoires*, ed. baron Ludovic de Contenson, 3 vols. SHF. Paris, 1906–9.

Tallemant des Réaux, Gédéon. *Historiettes*, ed. Antoine Adam, 2 vols. Paris, 1960–61.

Vanel, Gabriel, ed. *Journal de Simon Le Marchand bourgeois de Caen*. Caen, 1903.

Videl, Louis. *Histoire de la vie du Connestable de Lesdiguières*. Paris, 1638.

Willems, Hubert and Conan, Jean-Yves. *Liste alphabétique des pages de la Grande Ecurie du Roi*. Dison-Verviers, 1962.

Willems, Hubert and Conan, Jean-Yves. *Liste alphabétique des pages de la Petite Ecurie du Roi*. Dison-Verviers, 1966.

Pamphlets

The following pamphlets for and against Luynes are short-titled and listed chronologically, although some of the dates are approximate. The place of publication has been included only if different from Paris. For another descriptive listing, see Emile Bourgeois and Louis André, *Les Sources de l'histoire de France XVIIe siècle (1610–1715)*, 8 vols., Paris 1924, vol. 4, *Journaux et pamphlets*, pp. 176–96. With a few exceptions, all the pamphlets listed are available in either the 1628 edition of *Recueil des pièces les plus curieuses qui ont esté faites pendant le règne du Connestable M. de Luynes*, at the Library of Congress and the Bibliothèque nationale de France, or in the Lb 36 series of the département des imprimés of the Bibliothèque nationale de France, listed with call numbers in the *Catalogue de l'histoire de France*, 16 vols., Paris, 1855–95, 1968–9, I, 477–530, or in the manuscript collection of the Bibliothèque nationale de France, Manuscrits français 19187, fols. 245–346, "Recueil des pièces sur Concini et Luynes." These pamphlets are also available in the microfilm series, *French Political Pamphlets, 1547–1648*, 62 vols., Woodbridge, CT, 1977–80, and in the Newberry Library, Chicago, the Folger Library and Library of Congress in Washington, D.C., and the library of the Univer-

sity of Wisconsin in Madison. The pamphlets in American collections are listed by
Doris Varner Welsh, *A Checklist of French Political Pamphlets, 1560–1644, in the Newberry
Library*, 2 vols., Chicago, 1950, 1955, and Robert Lindsay and John Neu, *French Political
Pamphlets 1547–1648. A Catalog of Major Collections in American Libraries and Supplement*,
Madison, WI, 1969, 1981.

Pamphlets for Luynes

1617

Advis ou discours à Monsieur de Luyne à son arrivé à la faveur par M. de Ryom (1617?); also
   published as *Advertissement à Monsieur de Luynes à son avènement en faveur auprès du
   Roy après la mort du Mareschal d'Ancre par M. de Ryom*.
Discours à M. de Luynes par le sieur Dryon, gentilhomme, serviteur du Roi.

1619

Apologie pour Monseigneur de Luynes; also published same year as *Discours en forme d'apologie
   envoyée à Monseigneur le duc Despernon*.
Cérémonies observées à la réception de Monsieur de Luynes en la qualité de duc et pair.
La Concorde politique.
Harangue faite au Roi par un des principaux habitants de Saint-Germain-en-Laye.
Lettre de Cléophon à Polémandre sur les affaires de ce temps (1618, 1619).
Le Manifeste de Picardie au Roi.
Plaidoyé pour Monsieur de Luynes.
Requête présentée au Roy par Monsieur de Luynes.
Le Reveil de maître Guillaume avec sa remonstrance aux séditieux (1619, 1622); also published
   1620 as *La Rencontre de maître Guillaume et un message de fortune parlant des affaires
   du temps*.
Le Tourment de l'envie courtisane by Richard de Romany.

1620

Advis sur l'Etat et les affaires de ce temps.
Conseil de Théophile au Roy ensemble la Replique by Théophile de Viau.
Eloges du duc de Luyne ensemble les Repliques avec L'Advis au Roy par Théophile by Théophile
   de Viau.
Le Favory du Roi.
La Fulminante contre les calomniateurs; same year republished as *Contre les calomniateurs*
   and *La Bienveillance royale contre les envieux*.
*Lettre de Monseigneur le Cardinal de Rochefoucauld à Monsieur de Luynes, sur la Reformation de
   l'Estat, ensemble de la response de Monsieur de Luynes*.
Lettre de la ville de Tours à celle de Paris.
Le Marfore ou discours contre les libelles by Gabriel Naudé.
Response à l'Avis intitulé Avis au Roy sur le Restablissement de la charge du connestable (also
   1622).

1621

Le Bon françois à Messieurs du Parlement sur le nouveau connestable.

Les Cérémonies royales faictes en baillant par les mains du Roy l'espée de Connestable à Monseigneur le duc de Luynes le 2 avril.
Déclaration sur la réception de Monseigneur le duc de Luynes connestable.
La Défaite des envieux.
Lettre de M. le Connestable à M. de Modène.
Lettre de M. le Connestable à M. de Montbazon.

1622
Apologie en faveur du Roi addressée à la France.
Apologie ou response à La Chronique des Favoris.
Lettre consolatoire du Roy à Mme la Connestable.
Remonstrance aux malcontents.

Pamphlets against Luynes

1617
La Disgrace du Favory de la Fortune.

1619
Extrait des Raisons et Plaintes que la Royne Mère fait au Roy son fils (also 1620).
Lettres et advis sur les affaires de ce temps envoyé à Monsieur de Luynes.
La Magie des favoris.
Response au séditieux auteur du Reveil de maître Guillaume.

1620
A Monseigneur le Prince de Condé.
Les Admirables Propriétés de l'Aluyne.
L'Adoration du veau d'or; same year also published as *La Tête de boeuf couronnée.*
Advis à Monsieur de Luynes sur les libelles diffamatoires qui courent.
Advis au Roy sur le restablissment de l'office de Connestable par un bon françois, et Response à l'Advis sur le Restablissement.
L'Avant-courrier du guidon françois.
Les Bigarures de maistre Guillaume envoyées à Madame Mathurine.
Le Comtadin Provençal; republished 1622 as *Seconde partie et response à La Chronique des Favoris.*
Les Contre-veritez de la Cour.
Le Diable étonné sur l'ombre du Marquis d'Ancre et sa femme adressées à Messieurs de Luynes.
Discours au Sujet des Favoris.
Le Dragon / Monstre à Trois Testes; republished 1622 as *Le Chien à Trois Testes.*
Elogie d'un vieil cavalier françois.
Le Guidon françois; ensemble Radamante, armée de vengeance.
Harangue faite au Roy par Messire Louis Servin; also published as *Remonstrance faite au Roy par Messire Louis Servin.*
Les Jeux de la Cour.
Le Jugement de Minos contre les trois Géryons qui pillent la France; also published as *L'Enfer étonné à l'arrivée des trois Géryons.*

Lettre de Monseigneur le Cardinal de Guise à Monsieur le Duc de Guise sur l'alliance que Luynes
    prétendait faire de sa fille avec le dernier fils dudit sieur duc.
Manifeste de la Royne Mère envoyé au Roy.
Noel.
L'Ombre du Marquis d'Ancre à la France.
Le Pasquil des Chevaliers.
Plainte de Monsieur de Luynes.
La Pourmenade des bons hommes ou jugement de nostre siècle.
Prière pour le Roy.
Les Psaumes des Courtisans (also 1622).
Le Qu'as-tu-veu de la Cour.
Raisons de la Royne Mère.
Remonstrance au Roy importante pour son Estat (also 1622).
Remonstrance à Théophile et stances.
Requeste presentée au Roy Pluton par Conchino Conchini contre Monsieur de Luynes.
Les Reveries de la Royne.
La Sybille françoise parlant au Roy.
Le Syndicq du Peuple au Roy.
Le Tout en Tout de La Cour.
Véritez Chrestiennes au Roy Très Chrestien.

1621
Discours politique sur les occurrences et mouvements de ce temps.
Discours salutaire et avis de la France mourante au Roi.
L'Horoscope du Connestable.
Méditations de l'hermite Valérien.
Le Passe Par-Tout des Favoris.
Plaintes de l'espée de M. le Connestable.
Seconde remonstrance faite à Sa Majesté sur les affaires importantes au Royaume.

1622
Cancellus.
Changement sur la faveur de Luynes.
La Chronique des Favoris.
Le Confiteor de Monsieur le Connestable qu'il a fait devant mourir.
Le De Profundis sur la mort de Luynes.
L'Echo dauphinois sur le congé donné au Connestable de Luynes.
Factum sur la mort de Monsieur le Connestable.
La Fatalité du nombre quatorze sur le décès de M. le Connestable.
Le Géant françois au Roy.
Les Matines de la cour faites par un bon françois.
Le Mercure et fidèle messager de la cour.
Noel nouveau sur la mort de Monsieur le Connestable.
L'Ombre de Monseigneur le Duc de Mayenne.
L'Ombre de Monsieur le Connestable apparue à Monsieurs ses frères.

Pasquil satyrique du duc de Luynes.

Le Pasquin des affaires de ce temps et le pourquoy.

Prosopopée du Connestable Luynes.

Rejouissance de toute la France sur la mort du connestable.

Sizain.

Les Soupirs de la Fleur de Lys et Quatrain.

Sur la mort de Luynes.

Sur la vanité du secretaire du Connestable qui pensoit estre secretaire d'estat.

Sur le mesme temps des Luynes.

Le Te Deum chanté sur la mort de Monsieur le Connestable.

Le Tombeau des deux Frères.

La Voix publique au Roy.

Other pamphlets

1617
La Vie et mort misérable de Séjanus.

1618
La Conjuration de Conchine.

1619
Accord et réconciliation du Roy avec la Reine sa mère.

Articles accordés par MM. le Cardinal de La Rochefoucauld et de Béthune au nom du Roi à la Reine mère le 20 mai.

Discours du ballet de la reine, tiré de la fable de Psyché.

La Justification de Monseigneur le prince de Condé.

La Liberté donné par le Roi a Monseigneur le prince de Condé.

Le Manifeste de Monseigneur le prince de Condé, envoyé aux bons Français.

La Réception véritable faite par le Roi à Monseigneur le prince de Condé au château de Chantilly.

Récit et véritable discours de l'entrée de la Reine mère dans la ville d'Angers le 16 octobre.

Relation du grand ballet du Roi, dansé en la salle du Louvre, le 12 février sur l'aventure de Tancrède en la forêt enchantée.

Les Triomphes et magnificences faits à l'entrée de la Reine mère en la ville de Tours le 6 septembre.

1620
Ballet dansé en la présence du roi, princes et seigneurs de la cour, en la ville de Bordeaux, au Chasteau-Trompette, le 27 septembre.

L'Entrevue du Roi et de la Reine sa mère au château de Brissac.

Récit véritable de ce qui s'est passé au Palais à la séance du Roi samedi le 4 juillet; ensemble la volonté de Sa Majesté déclarée a son parlement.

Traité de la paix par l'amiable accord du Roi avec la Reine mère le 10 août.

1621

L'Arrivée de l'armée du Roi avant la ville de Montauban le 20 août.

L'Assassinat du sieur de Boisse Pardaillan, gouverneur de Monheur, avec la prise de la ville rebelle
(Bordeaux, n.d.,?1621).

Lettre de M le duc de Nevers pour supplier Sa Majesté de permettre le combat audit sieur duc avec
le Cardinal de Guise ou le prince de Joinville son frère le 24 avril.

L'Ordre du siège et reduction de la ville de Clérac avec les articles accordés aux inhabitants par
Sa Majesté, le 5 août.

La Prise de Monheur par l'armée royale avec le saccagement de la place le 13 décembre.

Le Voyage du Roi à Calais le 24 décembre 1620 et l'ambassade de M. le maréchal de Cadenet en
Angleterre le 28 décembre 1620.

1622

Accord de la querelle de MM les duc de Nevers et prince de Joinville fait par le Roi, le 19 mars.

Secondary sources

The secondary sources are cited in the Notes.

Index